Legal Aspects of the Cyprus Problem

Nijhoff Law Specials

Volume 67

The titles published in this series are listed at the end of this volume.

Legal Aspects of the Cyprus Problem

Annan Plan and EU Accession

Frank Hoffmeister

Martinus Nijhoff Publishers
Leiden • Boston

A C.I.P. Catalogue record for this book is available from the Library of Congress.

Printed on acid-free paper.

ISBN 90 04 15223 7

Koninklijke Brill NV incorporates the imprints Brill Academic Publishers, Martinus Nijhoff Publishers and VSP.

http://www.brill.nl

Printed and bound in The Netherlands.

Contents

Part VI – EU Accession Negotiations and Annan Plan I–III

Chapter VII – EU Accession and Annan Plan IV–V

Chapter VIII – Cyprus as EU Member State

Acknowledgements

From 1999–2001 I worked as academic assistant at the Chair for Public Law, European Law and International Law from 1999–2001 for Prof. Dr. *Ingolf Pernice* at the Humboldt University of Berlin. Participating in the activities of the *Walter Hallstein* Insititute for European Constitutional Law, and learning how to conceive the European public order as *Verfassungsverbund* deepened my interest for the fascinating topic of comparative public law. He also stimulated me to combine my theoretical interest with practical experience. Following his friendly advice, I accepted a post at the European Commission, while being reassured that the door is kept open for academic research at any given time. I cannot but thank him wholeheartedly for this flexibility and his encouragement to write this book.

Expressing my thanks to Prof. Dr. *Christian Tomuschat* for valuable comments on the draft only would be greatly understating my sincere attachment to him. During these years at *Humboldt*, I used every opportunity to take part in the courses and seminars of this eminent scholar of international law. With his distinguished support, I was accepted as the German participant in the International Law Seminar of the International Law Commission in Geneva in summer 2000. This touchdown with inner circle of international law-making proved to be very fruitful for my following responsibilities in the European Commission. Facing from time to time urgent, but not-easy-to-resolve international law questions in practice there after I could always count on receiving valuable and timely advice from him.

Certainly, this book is not the outcome of my academic years. Rather, I could dwell on my theoretical formation when being confronted with the Cyprus problem in practice. Much of the material presented here was relevant during my time as official at the Cyprus desk at DG Enlargement of the European Commission

(March 2001–October 2002) and as EU expert seconded to the United Nations for the preparation of the latest version of the Annan plan (February–March 2004). Working in the external relations team of the Commission Legal Service since November 2002 also added some insights as regards specific details of the Cyprus problem. The book may hence offer some details, which some observers would find difficult to find from other publications. Nevertheless, this study is in no way an offical or even semi-official account of my own limited role in dealing with legal aspects of the Cyprus problem from an EU or an UN perspective. It does not represent the official views of the European Commission. I present conclusions, which reflect my own legal assessment of the situation only.

Finally, it is impossible to present here a fair list of persons connected with the Cyprus file to which I owe a great degree of thanks. *In lieu* of many, I would express my deep gratitude to *Leopold Maurer*, Head of the Cyprus team under Enlargement Commissioner Verheugen, *Adriaan van der Meer*, Head of the Commission Delegation in Cyprus, *Pieter Jan Kuijper*, Principal Legal Advisor and *Jörn Sack*, Legal Advisor in the European Commission responsible for enlargement issues. I also would like to thank *Robert Dann* and *Didier Pfirter*, the Political and Legal Advisors to Alvaro de Soto, Special Advisor to UN Secretary-General Annan on Cyprus. I would like to mention, but cannot name the many Cypriots, be they Greek Cypriot or Turkish Cypriot, with whom I have also collaborated in the most cordial manner.

Benefiting from their experience, advice and friendship made working on the Cyprus issue worthwhile. The book is dedicated to my wife Sornitza and the greater part of the Cypriot people, who are committed to a comprehensive settlement of the Cyprus problem and share a common vision of peaceful existence on the island as member of the European Union, based on democracy, the rule of law and human rights.

Introduction

On 24 April 2004, two thirds of the Turkish Cypriots voted in favour of the "Comprehensive settlement of the Cyprus Problem", as proposed by the UN-General Secretary, Kofi Annan (the Annan Plan), while slightly more than three quarters of the Greek Cypriots rejected it. A week later, on 1 May 2004, the Republic of Cyprus joined the European Union under the condition that the application of European law is suspended in the areas that are not under control of the Cyprus Government pending a political settlement.[1] Those who did not follow the Cyprus problem closely in the last years are usually surprised by this sequence of events. How could the European Union accept membership of the Republic of Cyprus without a prior settlement of the political problem? Or even more intriguing: why can those who voted against the Annan Plan (Greek Cypriots) benefit from EU membership, whereas those who supported the Plan (Turkish Cypriots) are excluded from the realm of EU law? In order to give an answer to these questions one may recall the international political framework in which Cyprus' accession to the EU occurred. In particular, the relations between Cyprus, the EU, the Guarantor powers (United Kingdom, Greece and Turkey) and the UN between 1990 and 2004 need to be taken into account. This exercise leads to related questions on the practice of international organizations. When the Cyprus government of President Vassiliou applied for EU membership in 1990, the European institutions were from the beginning faced with the question how to deal with the *de facto* division on the island. In this regard, the European Union's role with respect to the UN needed to be defined. Should it openly or silently concur with the UN's

[1] Article 1 of Protocol 10 on Cyprus, annexed to the Act of Accession (OJ 2003, L 236, pp. 33, 955) – Appendix 1.

efforts for a comprehensive settlement of the Cyprus problem or should it play a more active role itself?

Responding to these questions focused on international relations leads to further inquiries, more of an international and European law character. It is crucial to understand the legal value of the UN efforts for a comprehensive settlement and the basic legal parameter of the European Union. The relationship between international law prerogatives and the requirements of EU membership arises. Can the EU take over the international law standards for the resolution of the Cyprus problem as coined in practice by the UN? Or must it insist, as a matter of law, on its own standards in view of the fact that a unified Cyprus should become an EU Member State? Can the EU accept derogations from its own body of law, and how far could such derogations reach?

This study touches upon the first set of questions since it offers a detailed account of the relevant facts. However, it does not describe the political motivations and moves of the various actors involved.[2] It neither portrays the UN good offices mission on Cyprus as perceived by a participant.[3] Rather, the facts are presented to allow for meaningful analytical parts highlighting the second set of legal questions. This study hereby focuses on those international, European or constitutional law arguments of the two parties in Cyprus, of Turkey, of the EU and of the UN that shaped their practice. The analytical parts of the book try to identify the significance of international law and European law in the most recent efforts for a settlement of the Cyprus problem. The book is thus designed as a contribution to the political and legal discussion surrounding the Cyprus problem, the Annan plan, and Cyprus' EU membership.

The study is structured in ten chapters. The first chapter concerns the independence of Cyprus, because many arguments relating to the status of the two sides point back to the legal significance of the Zurich/London agreements of 1959. The second chapter will assess the breakdown of the bi-communal Republic in 1963/1964 and its legal consequences under constitutional and international law. Turkey's intervention in 1974 and its continued presence in the northern part of Cyprus is the subject of the third chapter. In the fourth chapter, we will have a look at the UN efforts to foster a settlement until 1995. The Turkish Cypriot objections against Cyprus' application for EU membership will be dealt with thereafter (Chapter Five). The legal questions surrounding the comprehensive plan

[2] For an account of the most recent negotiations (1997–2004), see D. Hannay, The Search for a Solution. Hannay sets as objective of his book to "describe the anatomy of a negotiation" (p. ix).

[3] For a critical account of the UN good offices mission as perceived by the constitutional advisor to the Greek Cypriot side from 1979–2004, see C. Palley, An International Relations Debacle – The UN Secretary's Mission of Good Offices in Cyprus 1994–2004. Her intention is to "portray events as they were perceived by one close to Greek Cypriot participants in the process set up by the Secretary-General", aiming at "presenting the actions of the parties concerned more accurately and correcting errors and misrepresentations in the [UN] Secretariat's Report" [of 28 May 2004] (p. 1).

of UN-Secretary General Annan, submitted to the parties in The Hague in March 2003 (Annan III) constitute Chapter Six, followed by another chapter focusing on the respective modifications of the plan arising out of the Bürgenstock negotiations a year later and its accommodation in EU law (Annan V). Chapter Eight is dedicated to specific questions of EU law pertaining to Cyprus' current EU membership. The book closes with Chapter Nine on the current relations between Cyprus and Turkey, before concluding.

Each chapter contains two sections. The first sections present the facts that are needed to carry out a legal assessment. Material, which might be politically important like e.g. the geostrategic interests of the actors involved, their negotiation tactics or the political interaction of their steps, is omitted. Other publications are better suited to shed light on the political side of the Cyprus problem. I dwelled on them in order to look at both accounts of history and to accept only those facts, which are not disputed. If there is disagreement about what actually happened, this is indicated. In the second sections, the legal arguments put forward by the two Cypriot sides, States, International Organisations and academic authorities are reviewed.

As regards the use of titles, denominations of institutions and other politically sensitive issues, I opted to refrain from any value judgement. Hence, the institutions of the Turkish Cypriot Community will be referred to in this book by the name that the Turkish Cypriots themselves have given to them without quotation marks. No legal, political or other conclusion can be inferred from that.

Chapter I

The Independence of Cyprus

A. THE FACTS

In ancient times, Cyprus was ruled by different powers. A Roman province from 58 BC to 395 AD, it became part of the Byzantine Empire (395–1184), and after periods of Lusignan (1192–1489) and Venetian (1489–1571) reign, the Ottoman Empire took over (1571–1878). Finally, Great Britain administered Cyprus on lease from the Sultan from 1878–1914 and thereafter, upon annexation in view of the outbreak of the First World War, as a colony until 1960. At that date, the population on the island consisted of 80% Greek Cypriots and 18% Turkish Cypriots. They lived inter-mingled, sometimes in mixed villages or towns, and scattered all over the island.

1. The UN General Assembly resolutions on independence

In 1950, the Greek Cypriot Orthodox Church, under the leadership of the newly elected Archbishop Makarios III, initiated a petition. Any inhabitant of Cyprus could sign into large books in which the phrase "We demand the unification of Cyprus with Greece" was printed on each page. Reportedly 215,000 out of the 224,000 Greek Cypriots (and an insignificant number of Turkish Cypriots) expressed their support for union with Greece. The result was transmitted to the UN Secretary-

Legal Aspects of the Cyprus Problem, pp. 1–11.

General. The latter remained inactive. Neither was there a reaction from Great Britain and Greece, who did not want to disturb their bilateral relations.[1]

A change in Greek foreign policy occurred after a statement of the then British Minister for the Colonies, Hopkinson, on 28 July 1954. Asked whether some day Cyprus could enjoy self-determination he said in Parliament "it has always been recognised and agreed that there are certain territories in the Commonwealth, which, owing to their particular circumstances, can never expect to be fully independent."[2]

This "never" prompted the Greek Foreign Minister Papagos, on 16 August 1954, to send a letter to the UN General Assembly calling for the application of the principle of self-determination in the case of the population of Cyprus under the auspices of the United Nations.[3] However, considering the predominantly Greek character of the island, the request was regarded more as a British-Greek conflict on sovereignty over Cyprus than as a case for self-determination of the Cypriot people. Hence, the General Assembly unanimously decided on 17 December 1954 that a resolution on Cyprus would not be opportune "for the time being".[4]

The military resistance of the underground organisation "EOKA", under the command of the Cyprus born Greek General Grivas, against the British colonial system since 1955 did not change this international perception. In spring 1957, the British government proposed a resolution to condemn the Greek support of a "terrorist group" in form of arms, munitions and money as a forbidden interference in its domestic affairs. In its competing proposal, the Greek government asked the General Assembly to express its wish that the people of Cyprus should have the opportunity to determine their future by applying the principle of self-determination.[5] The Assembly, in its plenary sessions of 11 February 1957[6] and 5 December 1958,[7] declared that a peaceful, democratic and just solution should be found in accordance with the principles and purposes of the UN through negotiations. In this diplomatic tone, it made it clear that neither the violent methods nor the aim of the "EOKA" fighters that Cyprus should join Greece found sympathy in the international community at large.

---

[1] P. Tzermias, Geschichte der Republik Zypern, p. 53.

[2] House of Commons debates, vol. 531, cols. 504–506.

[3] Tzermias, loc. cit. (note 1), p. 93.

[4] UNGA Res 814 (IX) of 17 December 1954 (50 votes in favour with 8 abstentions), reprinted in P. Varvaroussis, Deutschland und die Zypernfrage, p. 135.

[5] Both proposals are cited in Archiv der Gegenwart of 27.02.1957, p. 6286 A.

[6] UNGA Resolution 1013 (XI) of 26 February 1957, reprinted in Varvaroussis, loc. cit. (note 4), p. 136.

[7] UNGA Resolution 1287 (XIII) of 5 December 1958, reprinted Varvaroussis, loc. cit. (note 4), pp. 136–137.

2. The proposals of Lord Radcliffe 1956

Meanwhile, the British Governor in Cyprus, Harding, and Archbishop Makarios engaged in negotiations about the future status of the island. That process was halted when the British Government deported the latter in March 1956 because of his intimate co-operation with EOKA leader Grivas. The British Government presented in November 1956 constitutional proposals to the British Parliament. The author, Lord Radcliffe, envisaged a single-chamber legislature with six representatives for the Turkish Cypriot community and 24 for the Greek Cypriot community and others. There were carefully designed safeguards for the Turkish community, and there was to be a Ministry for Turkish affairs, which would include education. A Tribunal of Guarantees should be empowered to deal with allegations of administrative discrimination. The Governor would be responsible for defence, foreign affairs and internal security, but there would be a joint Council of elected ministers and officials to discuss matters of common concern.[8]

During the session in the House of 19 December 1956, Colonial Secretary Lennox-Boyd declared the following:

> *When the international and strategic situation permits, and provided self-government is working satisfactorily, Her Majesty's Government will be ready to review the question of application of self-determination. When the time comes for this review, (. . .) it will be the purpose of Her Majesty's Government to ensure that any exercise of self-determination should be effected in such a manner that the Turkish Cypriot community, no less than the Greek Cypriot community, shall, in the special circumstances of Cyprus, be given freedom to decide for themselves their future status. In other words, Her Majesty's Government recognise that the exercise of self-determination in such a mixed population must include partition among the eventual options.*[9]

The purpose of the Statement may have been "both to assuage any misgivings Turkey may have had about the Radcliffe proposals (and to ensure Turkey's acceptance of them) and also to warn Greece and the Greek Cypriots of the consequences if they rejected it".[10]

3. The MacMillan Plan 1958

In spring 1958, Governor Sir Hugh Foot (who had replaced Sir John Harding at the end of 1957) failed to agree with Makarios on a system of self-government. The British Government decided to proceed unilaterally. On 19 June 1958, Prime Minister MacMillan presented a Cyprus plan to the House of Commons. The United Kingdom, Greece and Turkey should jointly administer Cyprus. Each

---

[8] Constitutional Proposals for Cyprus, Report submitted to the Secretary of State for the Colonies by the Rt. Hon. Lord Radcliffe, GBE, Presented by the Secretary for State for the Colonies to Parliament by Command of Her Majesty, London, December 1956 (Cmnd. 42).

[9] House of Commons debates, vo. 562, col. 1268.

[10] J. Reddaway, Burdened with Cyprus, pp. 49–50.

community should be endowed with its own Parliament to rule their own affairs. There should be a twofold citizenship, enabling Cypriots to receive Greek or Turkish nationality, while retaining British nationality. During the House of Commons debate on 26 June 1958, MacMillan re-emphasised that in case of a failure, the British position not to rule out partition was still valid.

The Tridominium plan was subsequently discussed in Athens and in Ankara. MacMillan explained to the Greek Prime Minister Karamanlis that it was necessary to take account of the interests of both Greece and Turkey. Karamanlis rejected the plan, but indicated a readiness to accept self-government under British rule and the shelving of the question of sovereignty until a more appropriate time. The initial reaction from the Turkish government was unfavourable since it excluded partition; it indicated, however, that the plan might nevertheless be reconcilable with Turkey's objectives. Following these discussions, the British government announced on 15 August 1958 the implementation of the slightly amended plan before 1 October 1958.[11]

This clear road map resulted in a shift in Makarios' policy. In an interview on 22 September 1958, he declared that the independence of Cyprus under a UN guarantee should be envisaged and wrote a letter to MacMillan accordingly. In parallel, the Greek President informed NATO General-Secretary, Spaak, that the membership of Greece in NATO was at stake, if Britain continued its project. A diplomatic mission of Spaak to convene a multilateral Cyprus conference failed, due to Greek resistance.

4. The Zurich and London Agreements 1959

Instead, the Greek and Turkish Foreign Ministers Averoff and Zorlu agreed in December 1958 to enter into bilateral negotiations. Following secret sessions with consultation of both leaders of the two Cypriot communities they came up with three documents that were initialled by their respective Prime Ministers on 11 February 1959 in Zurich: (a) the basic structure of the Republic of Cyprus, (b) a Draft Treaty of Guarantee and, (c) a Draft Treaty of Alliance.

A conference was then held in London. On 19 February 1959, the Prime Ministers of the three powers signed a "Memorandum setting out the agreed foundation of the final settlement of the problem of Cyprus" which repeated the results of the Zurich negotiations while inserting an additional article into the Treaty of Guarantee. This memorandum was accompanied by four declarations. Most importantly, Archbishop Makarios (after some hesitation), on behalf of the Greek Cypriot community, and Dr. Küçük, on behalf of the Turkish Cypriot community, declared that they "accept the documents and declarations as an agreed foundation for the final settlement".[12]

---

[11] The MacMillan plan and the Statement of 15 August 1958 are reproduced by Reddaway, loc. cit. (note 10), pp. 108–113.

[12] Conference on Cyprus, Documents signed and initialled at Lancaster House on 19 February 1959, London, Her Majesty's Stationary Office, Cmnd. 679, Annexes G and H.

4.1. *The Constitution*

The agreed basic structure of the Republic constituted the outline for the future Constitution.[13] A mixed commission developed out of the 27 Basic Articles a fully-fledged constitution consisting of 199 articles. The Constitution, signed on 6 April 1960 by representatives of Greece, Turkey, the Greek Cypriots and the Turkish Cypriots and the Swiss Legal Advisor Prof. Bridel,[14] came into force on 16 August 1960, the day of independence. It was agreed that the 27 Basic Articles could not be amended by way of constitutional change.[15] This arrangement made the Cypriot Constitution one of the most rigid one in the world.[16]

The basic features of the Constitution have been aptly summarised as follows:

> *The Republic was to have a presidential regime under a Greek president and a Turkish vice-president. Executive authority was vested in them, except for communal affairs, and they would have important powers of veto, reference back and recourse to a Constitutional Court. Some of these powers would be exercised jointly, some either jointly or separately. The president and vice-president would also appoint the heads of certain key offices and the heads of security forces, with deputies in each case drawn from the other community from that to which the head belonged. The president and vice-president would have ministerial council of Greeks and Turks in the ratio of 7:3. A Turk would hold one of the key ministries of foreign affairs, defence and finance. The legislature would be similarly composed on a 7:3 basis and would decide by simple majority; but in three important fields (including taxation), separate majorities of both Greeks and Turks would be required. There would be separate communal chambers dealing with religion, education, other communal affairs and questions of personal status. The public services would be composed on the 7:3 basis, but for an initial period the percentage might be 6:4 in the security forces. One of the heads of the three security forces would be a Turk. A public service commission of 7 Greeks and 3 Turks would administer the service, but if two of the Turkish members objected to the choice of a Greek rather than a Turk to fill a vacancy, then the matter would go to the Constitutional Court. That court would be composed of one Greek, one Turk and one neutral, presiding judge. It would have power of final decision on questions of discrimination and constitutionality and would adjudicate on disputes between other organs of the republic. In other respects, the judiciary would consist of a high court, subordinate courts and one neutral judge, who would preside and have two votes. There would be separate Turkish municipalities in the five main towns. Union with any other State and separatist independence were outlawed.*[17]

[13] For a summary of the significance of the Basic Articles of February 1959 for the future Constitution of August 1960, see P. Tzermias, Der neue Status Cypern, AöR 1959, p. 459, 478 et seq.

[14] P. Tzermias, Die Verfassung der Republik Zypern, JöR 1961, p. 485 (487).

[15] See Article 182(1) of the 1960 Constitution.

[16] A. Filos, Die Entwicklung der Zypern-Frage unter besonderer Berücksichtigung der geplanten EU-Mitgliedschaft der Republik Zypern, ZaöRV 1999, p. 185 (190) with further reference.

[17] Reddaway, loc. cit. (note 10), pp. 121–122.

4.2. *The three Treaties*

4.2.1. The Treaty of Guarantee

Implementing the London Agreement, the Treaty of Guarantee was concluded on 16 August 1960 between the independent state of Cyprus, Greece, Britain and Turkey. Cyprus undertook not to participate in "union with any other State" or to proceed to partition (Article I). The three powers guaranteed the "independence, territorial integrity and security" of the Republic as well as the basic articles of its Constitution (Article II). Most importantly, Article IV gave each Guarantor Power a right to take action in the event of a breach of the treaty.[18]

4.2.2. The Treaty of Alliance

The Treaty of Alliance between Cyprus, Greece and Turkey provided for tripartite headquarters and for the stationing of 950 Greek and 650 Turkish troops on the island. Their mandate was to assist in the training of the Cypriot army. However, there can be no doubt that they were also intended as an assurance for the two communities in regard to their future security and as a deterrent against attempts to renew the conflict.

4.2.3. The Treaty of Establishment

Finally, Cyprus, Greece, the United Kingdom and Turkey concluded the Treaty of Establishment. According to the preamble, its purpose was to give effect to the Declarations made at the London Conference. In its operative part, the treaty defined the territory of the Republic of Cyprus as the Island of Cyprus with the exception of the two British Military Bases, "which areas remain under the sovereignty of the United Kingdom" (Article I). Its annexes further spell out rules for the transfer of sovereignty from the former colonial power to the newly founded Republic.

B. LEGAL EVALUATION

1. Self-determination

Both sides claimed the right to self-determination for their purposes. The Greek Cypriot leaders (and the Greek Government) used the concept extensively in the 1950ies to justify union with Greece (*Enosis*), whereas the Turkish Cypriots relied on it for the purpose of partition (*Taksim*).[19] Both reasonings find no support in international law.

---

[18] See in detail Chapter III B 1.

[19] N.M. Ertekün, In search of a negotiated Cyprus settlement, p. 2: "In fact, as no Cypriot nation existed and as the peoples of Cyprus comprised two entirely different ethnic communities, the principle of self-determination could not be applied to the peoples of

1.1. *No "dual" right to self-determination of Greek Cypriots and Turkish Cypriots*

In so far as the Turkish Cypriot contention is concerned, one cannot deny that the British government defended the existence of two parallel rights of self-determination. However, it is wrong to assert that this statement properly reflected the legal situation.[20] Former colonial officer Reddaway describes the British attitude as follows:

> *The thesis was acceptance in principle of unitary self-determination (meaning Enosis). The antithesis was contingent acceptance of dual self-determination (meaning partition). The synthesis was the rejection of both unitary and dual self-determination (excluding both Enosis and partition) and the adoption of a different method for the realisation of Cypriot national aspirations (namely, self-government within a framework or partnership, and eventually shared sovereignty between Greece, Turkey and Britain). The British had found they could not untie the Gordian knot. They were not prepared to cut it. In the end they simply decided to side-step it in favour of tripartite partnership and shared sovereignty.*[21]

The British considerations on the "dual" right to self-determination were purely political in order to pressure the Greek Cypriots into accepting the need for a compromise. However, in the process of decolonisation in the 1960's – 1970's, the right to self-determination as laid down in Article 1(2) of the UN Charter was never applied to any sort of ethnic, religious or linguistic group. Rather, only the population living in the colonised territory as a whole, regardless of whether this population is ethnically homogeneous or consists of two or several peoples, was able to claim rights under that provision.[22] UN practice was clear at the time.[23] Following the General Assembly's Resolution 1514 (XV) of 14 December 1960

Cyprus as a whole. This principle and right of self-determination could only be applied to, and be exercised by, the two Communities separately". Later on, the right of self-determination was called upon to justify the proclamation of the TRNC – see below Chapter III B.2.

[20] E. Lauterpacht, The Right of Self-determination of the Turkish Cypriots, Opinion of 9 March 1990, in: Ertekün (ed.), The Status of the Two Peoples in Cyprus – Legal Opinions, p. 11, §§ 9–10 who defends his thesis that the emergence of Cyprus was based on the self-determination of both the Greek Cypriots and the Turkish Cypriots mainly by citing the British statement.

[21] Reddaway, loc. cit. (note 10), p. 89.

[22] M. Akehurst/P. Malanczuk, Modern Introduction into International Law, p. 335. See also T. Franck, Postmodern Tribalism and the Right to Secession, in: Brölmann/Lefeber/Zieck (eds.), Peoples and Minorities in International Law, 1993, 3–27 at 9: "Peoples entitled to self-determination were defined as the inhabitants of a colony". Dissenting, without any reference to international practice, P. Pernthaler, Some critical aspects regarding the UN Secretary-General's proposal for a comprehensive settlement of the Cyprus problem, in: Yeditepe Üniversitesi Hukuk Fakültesi Dergisi I/1, 2004, p. 119 (119), arguing that Turkish Cypriots and Greek Cypriots are holders of the right to self-determination because there was no "homogenous nation" that could have exercised that right.

[23] UN practice may have evolved over time, given that Eritrea (which seceded from

on the granting of independence to "colonial countries and peoples", only the population of an integral former colony could invoke Article 1(2) of the UN-Charter to justify their claim for independence. Henceforth, the UN supported the independence of former African and Asian colonies in the course of the 1960's and 1970's only when the former borders were kept ("*uti possidetis*"). It was immaterial how many peoples and ethnic groups lived, for example in Nigeria or Indonesia, to become independent from the United Kingdom or the Netherlands as long as independence was granted to the former colony as such. Even when an ethnic people, like the Ewes split between British and French Togoland, expressly asked the UN to hold a referendum on independence whereby existing borders would be changed, this was denied. Hence, there was never a right to "dual" self-determination of the Greek Cypriots and the Turkish Cypriots alike. Rather, only the Cypriot people as a whole could have exercised the right to self-determination in the 1950's.[24]

1.2. *Self-determination of the Cypriot people*

As regards the Greek Cypriot contention on unitary self-determination, it is true that a colonial people can exercise its right to self-determination also by joining another State.[25] Therefore, in principle, self-determination could amount to unification with Greece. However, the decisive question is what can be deemed as an act of self-determination of this people.

1.2.1. Enosis petition of 1950 not an act of self-determination of the people's majority

A Greek author argues that the outcome of the 1950 Greek Cypriot petition (on ENOSIS) could be considered as an act of Cypriot self-determination since it was supported by 80 % of the people.[26] A Greek Cypriot writer also points to the will of the "majority" that had gained independence for the people as a whole.[27] These contentions raise the question whether a numerical majority can shape the will of a colonial people to exercise self-determination. Principle XI of General Assembly Resolution 1541 (XV) of 15 December 1960 recalls that the decision about self-determination

Ethiopia) and the Successor States of dissolved Yugoslavia were admitted to the United Nations in the 1990s.

[24] K. Chrysostomides, The Republic of Cyprus, A Study in International Law, p. 57; C. Rumpf, Die Staats- und völkerrechtliche Lage Zyperns, EuGRZ 1997, p. 533, 545.

[25] According to UNGA Res 1514 (XV) of 14 December 1960, there are three forms of exercising the right to self-determination: Foundation of an independent State, association or integration into an existing State or emergence into another political status. In 1961, the former Trusteeship area Northern Cameroon chose to freely integrate into Nigeria, whereas Southern Cameroon joined Cameroon. In 1963, Sabali and Sarawak joined Malaya, which became Malaysia (see A. Verdross/B. Simma, Universelles Völkerrecht, p. 318, note 9).

[26] Tzermias, loc. cit. (note 1), p. 53 ff (54, 77).

[27] Chrysostomides, loc. cit. (note 24), p. 57.

> *should be the result of the freely expressed wishes of the territory's peoples acting with full knowledge in their status, their wishes having been expressed through informed and democratic processes, impartially conducted and based on universal adult suffrage.*

The French version of the expression "wishes of the territory's *peoples*" speaks of "la volonte *des populations* du territoire". Referring to this resolution, the International Court of Justice advocated the principle of self-determination through the free and genuine expression of the will of the *peoples/populations*[28] in Western Sahara. These formulations indicate that a simple numerical majority of the predominant ethnic group in the territory is not sufficient. Rather, there must be at least a majority within each substantial ethnic group ("people/population") of the territory. The resolution does not require that such groups live territorially apart from the majority. Rather, it seems to be decisive that the collective will of such a group may be democratically expressed. If so, it is important for the formation of the overall will of the people as whole.

Since the overwhelming majority of the Turkish Cypriots did not support the 1950 petition (which was open to their participation), one may well conclude that the collective will of the Turkish Cypriots was opposed to ENOSIS. Accordingly, the will of the Greek Cypriot majority of 80% of the Cypriot people as a whole, was not sufficient for joining Greece under the right to self-determination as it stood in 1950.

1.2.2. Independence of Cyprus as an act of self-determination of the people's majority

In contrast to the ENOSIS petition of 1950, the declarations made by Makarios on behalf of the Greek Cypriot community and Küçük on behalf of the Turkish Cypriot community at the 1959 London Conference, can be considered as an act of self-determination of the Cypriot people. This form of self-determination had gained at least a majority in both constituent groups. At the stage of implementation, the Cypriot people accepted in 1960 the transfer of sovereignty from the United Kingdom to the Republic of Cyprus[29] (and not to the two communities first, passing it on to the Republic)[30] by the Cyprus Act of 29 July 1960.[31] Therefore, the parallel will of both constituents of the Cypriot people resulted in the

[28] ICJ, Western Sahara, Advisory Opinion, ICJ Reports 1975, p. 12 (39), § 57 and p. 68, § 162.

[29] Chrysostomides, loc. cit. (note 24), p. 54 with further references.

[30] E. Lauterpacht/M. Leigh, On sovereignty in Cyprus and its relationship to proposals for a solution of the Cyprus problem along federal lines, Opinion of 31 May 1991, in: Ertekün (ed.), The Status of the Two Peoples in Cyprus – Legal Opinions, p. 69, 71, § 7. In contradiction to this assessment, Leigh, in his previous opinion of 20 July 1990, The Legal Status in International Law of the Turkish Cypriot and the Greek Cypriot communities in Cyprus, ibid., p. 54 (55, note 1), held the view that sovereignty was passed from Britain to the Republic of Cyprus by the Cyprus Act.

[31] The Cyprus Act of 29 July 1960, Statutory instrument No. 1368 of 1960. Section 1 is

creation of one sovereign Republic that was endowed with a single international legal personality. This Republic, again, accepted limits to its newly gained sovereignty as defined in the Treaties of Establishment, Guarantee and Alliance, since Article 195 of the Constitution empowered both leaders to have done so.

However, politically, the international legal approach that the Cypriot people as a whole had exercised its right to self-determination through a common will of both constituents was not rooted in everyday life at the time.[32] There had been no nation-building process in Cyprus, since secondary education provided in the Greek gymnasia and the Turkish lycées followed the same curricula as in Greece and Turkey,[33] and a good many of the teachers were Greek and Turkish nationals. Hence, it is not surprising that the Cypriots at the time believed themselves to be Greeks and Turks, not Cypriots.[34] The legal analysis that self-determination was to be and had indeed been commonly exercised did not correspond to reality.

2. Bi-communalism

A number of elements point to the dualist system of governance as agreed between the two constituents. Both leaders were signatories in London and were authorised in Article 195 of the Constitution to conclude the founding treaties. Both constituents were granted the autonomous power that respective "Communal Chambers" adopt rules in certain specific areas. Parallel administration in the five biggest cities was foreseen. In the common State institutions, the smaller constituent was protected against majorisation by the right of veto of the Vice-President and the Turkish Cypriot Members of Parliament in certain areas. The Republic's High Justices had to be Greek Cypriots and Turkish Cypriots. The Treaty of Alliance gave the respective "motherlands" a certain right to protect their respective constituents.

Throughout the 1959 Zurich/London agreements and the 1960 Constitution, the term "communities" is used. In an attempt to characterise the power-sharing arrangements between the two constituent groups of a common State, combined

sufficiently clear in the respect: "Her Majesty may, by Order in Council (to be laid before Parliament after being made) declare that the Constitution designated in the Order as the Constitution of the Republic shall come into force on such day as may be specified in the Order; and on that day there shall be established in the Island of Cyprus and independent sovereign Republic of Cyprus, and Her Majesty shall have no sovereignty or jurisdiction over the Republic of Cyprus."

[32] J.S. Joseph, Ethnic Conflict and International Politics, p. 18, concludes that church dominance, millet system, fragmented ethnic education, antagonistic national loyalties, political polarization and the British policy of "divide and rule" had contributed to the generation of a political schism between the two Cypriot communities.

[33] Y. Papadakis, Echoes from the Dead Zone – Across the Cyprus Divide, p. 65, speaks of the "poisonous messages of the two educational systems".

[34] Ö.A. Özgür, Cyprus in My Life, p. 34.

with certain elements of autonomy and special relationship to their motherlands, the description "bi-communalism" was coined. For the legal analysis this meant that the two communities were political equals in the sense that each existed as political entity.[35]

3. Summary

Externally, the right to self-determination of the Cypriot people under Article 1 (2) of the UN Charter was exercised against the former colonial power by the signature of the representatives of the constituent groups, Makarios and Küçük, to the London agreement. There is no separate right of self-determination neither of the Greek Cypriots nor of the Turkish Cypriots. Internally, both constituents accepted a sophisticated system of power sharing and a certain degree of autonomy of both. This system was labelled as bi-communalism.

[35] Z. Necatigil, The Cyprus question and the Turkish position in international law, pp. 15–16; P. Tzermias, Die Entstehung der Republik Zypern, JöR 1960, p. 245 (279 et seq.); Filos, loc. cit. (note 16), pp. 189–190.

Chapter II

The breakdown of the bi-communal Republic

A. THE FACTS

1. The political confrontation

The Republic of Cyprus was admitted to the United Nations on 21 September 1960 and to the Council of Europe in May 1961. It did not accede to NATO since President Makarios preferred a policy of non-alignment.

Cyprus's internal stability was soon at stake. According to Article 173 (1) of the Constitution "separate municipalities should be created by the Turkish inhabitants" of Nicosia, Limassol, Famagusta, Larnaca and Paphos. This provision pointed to a long-standing conflict on the issue. Since 1930 the Turkish Cypriots demanded self-administration for the Turkish quarters in these towns because the Greek Cypriot mayors, especially in Nicosia, neglected their development.[1] In addition, in the late years of the EOKA conflict, the Turkish quarters had become "no-go areas" for Greek Cypriots, and the existing municipalities could no longer provide services for Turkish Cypriots.

[1] Reddaway, loc. cit. (page 3, note 10), p. 92, describes the then mayor of Nicosia, Dr. Themistocles Dervis, as "notorious for his contempt for the Turkish Cypriots".

Legal Aspects of the Cyprus Problem, pp. 12–33.

Against this background, in 1958, the Turkish Cypriots set up their proper councils, and Britain granted them the power to collect revenue and provide public service by law 33/1959.[2] According to Article 188 (2) of the Constitution, this British law remained in force for six months and was prolonged by the House of Representatives until the end of 1962. However, although Article 177 of the Constitution called upon the President and Vice-President to compromise on the delimitation of the geographical areas concerned, Makarios and Küçük could not reach an agreement. Makarios objected to the very principle of geographical separation although it had been a Greek Cypriot position in the negotiations in Zurich that the Turkish Cypriot themselves should bear the burden of bringing their quarters to the same standards as the Greek quarters.[3]

In the light of this failure, the Turkish Cypriot Communal Chamber declared, on 29 December 1962, that the existence of separate Turkish Cypriot municipalities would conform to the Constitution and established them by law. In return, the Greek-Cypriot-dominated central government decided to put the administration of the five municipalities under the control of joint "improvement boards". The Constitutional Court (with the decisive vote of its President) decided on 25 April 1963 that both decisions were illegal.[4] However, already in February that year, President Makarios had announced not to follow any ruling on the matter. As a result of this affront, the German President of the Court, Prof. Forsthoff, resigned from the office thereafter, with effect as from 31 July 1963.[5]

A second disagreement about implementing the Constitution emerged in connection with the army. The Greek Cypriots proposed to amalgamate the police and the gendarmerie, which would then have the effect of nullifying the provision that one of the three commands (army, police, gendarmerie) should be held by a Turkish Cypriot.[6] The Turkish Cypriots wanted separate Greek and Turkish units and the Vice-President vetoed legislation for mixed units. They were also concerned about slow progress to reach the 70:30 ratio for civil service posts and about the fact that "far too many" EOKA men were given such posts.[7]

Another serious dispute arose about taxation. Under Article 188(2) of the Constitution, the British law on income taxes was to stay in force until the end of 1960. A new Cypriot law needed the consensus of both communities in Parliament (Article 78(2)). After a provisional prolongation until April 1961, Makarios ordered by decree to continue collecting taxes – without statutory basis. Any attempt to vote a new law was blocked by the Turkish Cypriot members of Parliament in December 1961 who insisted on a fair solution of the dispute on local self-administration. Later on, both community chambers adopted their own tax rules.[8]

---

[2] Tzermias, loc. cit. (page 2, note 1) p. 172.

[3] Reddaway, loc. cit. (page 3, note 10), p. 122.

[4] Turkish Communal Chamber vs. Council of Ministers, 5 CLR (1963), pp. 59, 77–78.

[5] Necatigil, loc. cit. (page 11, note 35) p. 23.

[6] Reddaway, loc. cit. (page 3, note 10), p. 145.

[7] Necatigil, loc. cit. (page 11, note 35), p. 20.

[8] Tzermias, loc. cit. (page 2, note 1), p. 256.

The tension rose even higher, when, in November 1963, President Makarios proposed a revision of the Constitution. In his 13 points, submitted to Vice-President Küçük,[9] he suggested

1. The abolition of a veto power of the President and the Vice-President;
2. The Vice President's right to act as President in cases of the latter's absence or temporary incapacity to perform his duty;
3. The election of both Presidents by the House of Representatives;
4. The right of the Parliament's Vice-President to act as President of the Parliament in cases of the latter's absence or temporary incapacity to perform his duty;
5. The abolition of the special voting procedure in Parliament on laws relating to the municipalities or imposing duties or taxes;
6. The founding of unitary municipalities;
7. The unification of the judiciary;
8. The unification of the police and the gendarmerie;
9. The determination of the amount of security forces and military troops by law;
10. The participation of Greek and Turkish Cypriots in the public and the military service in proportion to the strength of the population;
11. The reduction of the Commission for the Public Service from 10 to five members;
12. The voting in this Commission with simple majority;
13. The abolition of the Greek Cypriot Communal Chambers, while the Turkish Cypriots could maintain their Communal Chamber if they wished to do so.

Turkey vigorously opposed the proposals on 16 December 1963 threatening with an intervention if they were to be unilaterally implemented.

2. The military confrontation

2.1. *The Nicosia incident*

On 21 December 1963, as a few Turkish Cypriots refused to show their identity papers to Greek Cypriot police in Nicosia, two Turkish Cypriots were killed and one of the Greek Cypriot policemen was injured. Subsequently, members of the 7,000 men strong Turkish secret para-military organization TMT[10] attacked the mixed-population village of Omorfita, a suburb of Nicosia, where the families of the Greek Cypriot policemen were living. On 24 December, Greek Cypriot paramilitary troops under the command of Nicos Sampson attacked Turkish Cypriot

---

[9] Suggested Measures to Facilitate the Smooth Functioning of the State and Remove Certain Causes of Inter-Communal Frictions, Memorandum of President Makarios of 30 November 1963. Reprinted in Joseph, loc. cit. (page 10, note 32), Appendix 4, p. 146.

[10] TMT is the abbreviation for Türk Mukavemet Teşkilati = Turkish Defence Organization.

quarters.[11] The Turkish contingent on the island moved from its barracks to a new camp on the Nicosia-Kyrenia road, while Turkish jet fighters flew a "warning flight" on Christmas Day.[12] Whereas the estimates on the total number of deaths vary,[13] it is undisputed that more Turkish Cypriots than Greek Cypriots were killed and that Sampson earned the unholy nickname of "Turk killer"[14] during the strife. As a result of the fighting, 109 villages, most of them Turkish or mixed villages were partially or completely destroyed or damaged.[15] 25,000–30,000 Turkish Cypriots[16] (about a quarter of the Turkish Cypriot population) were uprooted from their homes and became internally displaced.

2.2. *The attempts of the Guarantor powers to restore peace and order*

In late December 1963, the three Guarantor powers consulted each other. With the consent of Makarios and Küçük they agreed to station a joint truce force under the British commander Young. The 2,700 British and the Turkish and Greek contingents on the island were to maintain public peace and order. A "green line" was drawn between the quarters of Nicosia, including a neutral zone. On 1 January 1964, Makarios denounced the Treaties of Guarantee and Alliance, but withdrew this declaration upon British pressure.[17] An international conference from 15 January – 10 February 1964 ended without success. Whereas the Greek Cypriots asked for a revision of the Zurich/London agreement, the Turkish Cypriots insisted on separate regions. Also the proposal of the British Minister for the Commonwealth, Sandy, to send NATO troops was not accepted.[18]

2.3. *The deployment of UNFICYP*

After the failure of the international conference the British and Cypriot governments brought the case before the UN Security Council on 14 February 1964. Meanwhile, the fighting continued, and there was evidence of arms imports from

[11] This paramilitary group was also known as the "Green barets". See U. Berner, Das vergessene Volk, p. 17.

[12] Necatigil, loc. cit. (page 11, note 35) p. 34.

[13] Tzermias, loc. cit. (page 2, note 1), p. 301, speaks of 1000 Turkish Cypriot victims and 200 Greek Cypriots. J.-F. Drevet, Chypre en Europe, p. 135, accounts 134 death, 108 of them Turkish Cypriots. According to Palley, loc. cit. (page xii, note 3), p. C.17, approximately 350 Turkish Cypriots and 200 Greek Cypriots and mainland Greeks were killed between 21 December 1963 and 10 August 1964.

[14] Tzermias, loc. cit. (page 2, note 1), p. 301.

[15] Report of the UN Secretary-General of 10 September 1964, UN Doc S/5950, § 160.

[16] Reddaway, loc. cit. (page 3, note 10), p. 146, refers to 25.000 Turkish Cypriot refugees. Ertekün, loc. cit. (page 6, note 19), pp. 9 and 13, mentions nearly 30.000 Turkish Cypriots that had to be evacuated from 103 villages.

[17] Reddaway, loc. cit. (page 3, note 10), p. 157.

[18] Tzermias, loc. cit. (page 2, note 1), p. 324 et seq.

Greece, against which Britain protested.[19] On 4 March 1964, the Security Council adopted an important resolution.[20] It called upon all Member States to refrain from any action or threat of action to worsen the situation in Cyprus or to endanger international peace (§ 1) – a clear warning to Turkey not to intervene. The Government of Cyprus should take all additional measures necessary to stop violence and bloodshed (§ 2) and the communities and their leaders should act with the utmost restraint (§ 3). The Security Council recommended the creation of a United Nations Peacekeeping Force in Cyprus (UNFICYP), with the consent of the Government of Cyprus (§ 4) for an initial period of three months. UNFICYP's main function was to prevent a recurrence of the fighting and to contribute to the maintenance and restoration of law and order and a return to normal conditions. It had to ensure that there was no alteration of the *status quo* along the two ceasefire lines. Neither side was to exercise authority or jurisdiction or to make any military moves beyond its own military lines.

The adoption of the resolution did not prevent further fighting. Following a riot in Paphos, Turkey threatened to intervene on 13 March 1964, which prompted the Security Council to issue another resolution.[21] At the end of March, approximately 6,000 UN soldiers from Western countries were deployed on the island.

On 2 April 1964, President Makarios denounced the Treaty of Alliance. This action was accepted by Greece, but not by Turkey and the United Kingdom.[22] In parallel, despite the presence of UN troops, a Greek Cypriot combat unit led by the Minister of Interior Georghadjis tried to conquer St. Hilarion in April 1964. The Turkish air force flew over some Cypriot cities. In May 1964, another incident in Famagusta caused 3 Greek Cypriot and about 30 Turkish Cypriot deaths (also the British investigator, Major Masey, is said to have been killed by Greek Cypriot fighters).[23] However, in the context of the cold war, the US was striving to avoid a military conflict between the two NATO allies Greece and Turkey. It did not back a Turkish military intervention, and later on, in June 1964, the American President, Johnson, explicitly warned the Turkish Prime Minister to refrain from any unilateral action in order not to cause a conflict with the Soviet Union.

Against this background, Athens deployed well-equipped volunteers – about 8,000–20,000[24] to Cyprus, since the middle of 1964, to reinforce the Cyprus forces. In addition, General Grivas was allowed to return to Cyprus in July 1964 and was entrusted with the High Command of all Cypriot forces in case of bel-

---

[19] Reddaway, loc. cit. (page 3, note 10), p. 158.

[20] UNSC Resolution 186 (1964) of 4 March 1964.

[21] UNSC Resolution 187 (1964) of 13 March 1964, § 1.

[22] Tzermias, loc. cit. (page 2, note 1), pp. 334–335.

[23] Drevet, loc. cit. (note 13), p. 141.

[24] There is a dispute about the amount of the Greek volunteers. See Tzermias, loc. cit. (page 2, note 1), pp. 338–339. Drevet, loc. cit. (note 13), reports that Athens should have received an "authorisation" from the USA to ship in 5.000 soldiers. In any case, the Treaty of Alliance only allowed for 650 Greek officers.

ligerence.[25] Soon after his arrival, Grivas instigated a military attack against Turkish Cypriots living in Kokkina in early August 1964. The Turkish air force bombed Greek Cypriot towns in retaliation. Only when the UN Security Council, in its resolution of 9 August 1964,[26] called on both sides for an immediate ending of the (Turkish) bombing and the (Greek Cypriot) attacks on the ground, did the military confrontation stop.

3. The hellenisation of the Republic and the Turkish Cypriot enclaves

3.1. *The hellenisation of the Republic*

3.1.1. The Turkish Cypriot absence in the State institutions

Ever since the last week in December 1963, neither the Turkish Cypriot Vice-President nor the Turkish Cypriot Ministers or Members of the House of Representatives participated in the affairs of the government. In early January 1964 the Turkish Cypriot leadership issued several statements that the Cyprus government had lost its legality and that they would not recognise it as the lawful government any longer.[27] The Turkish Cypriot Vice-President and his Ministers chaired a "General Committee" administering life in Turkish Cypriot controlled areas,[28] and the Turkish Cypriot members of the House met separately.[29] Many Turkish Cypriots serving as civil servants in the Ministries did not show up in office anymore, reportedly upon instructions from the Turkish Cypriot leadership to quit office.[30]

Since the resignation of Professor Forsthoff as President of the Constitutional Court, with effect from 31 July 1963, the Constitutional Court did not sit anymore. Whereas, on 16 December 1963, the appointment of an Australian judge as his successor had been announced, the latter did not take up his appointment due to the outbreak of the fighting. The neutral judge in the High Court, the Canadian justice Wilson, quit his post with effect from 31 May 1964. At District Court level, with one or two exceptions, no Turkish or mixed cases were tried by

---

[25] Tzermias, loc. cit. (page 2, note 1), p. 342.

[26] UNSC Resolution 193 (1964) of 9 August 1964.

[27] See several quotes of Vice-President Küçük of 31.12.1963 and 05.01.1964, reproduced in Press and Information Office, The Cyprus problem, p. 10.

[28] This Committee was headed by the Vice-President Küçük and the three Turkish Cypriot ministers of the Republic of Cyprus. See M. Soysal, Inequality of status: impediment to a solution in Cyprus, in: R. Arim, Cyprus and International Law, Ankara 2002, p. 121 (122), note 1.

[29] Necatigil, loc. cit. (page 11, note 35), p. 66.

[30] Özgür, loc. cit. (page 10, note 34), p. 104, a Turkish Cypriot who worked in the Cyprus diplomatic service, reports that most Turkish Cypriot civil servants did not follow a broadcast call from the Government to return to their work because "the Turkish Cypriot leadership did not allow this to happen".

Turkish Judges of the District Courts in all towns, except Nicosia, between 21 December 1963 and June 1964. Nevertheless, Turkish Cypriot judges served in the lower courts until June 1966,[31] when the Cyprus police enforced a blockade of the Turkish quarter of Nicosia. These restrictions also prevented Turkish Cypriot judges from going to their offices and one judge of the Nicosia District court, already on the court premises, had been ordered to go back to the Turkish quarter under humiliating circumstances.[32]

3.1.2. The Greek Cypriot revisions of the constitutional system

In 1964 the Makarios government took a series of measures to change the constitutional system. On 28 May, the police and the gendarmerie were merged under a central command. As of 1 June, recruitment to the National Guard became compulsory. Law 33/1964 of 9 July created a new Supreme Court. It took over the functions of the Constitutional Court and the High Court, while abolishing the system of proportional representation of Greek and Turkish Cypriot judges and the existence of neutral Presidents. It also mandated the District Courts to adjudicate all civil and criminal cases regardless of the ethnic origin of the plaintiffs, defendants or accused.

In November, the House of Parliament empowered the government to appoint representatives in the local councils. The Greek Cypriot Communal Chamber was dissolved by a law of 31 March 1965, transferring its legislative competencies to the House of Representatives and judicial competencies to the ordinary Courts. Finally, in July 1965, the separate lists for the election of the Turkish Cypriot Members of Parliament and the Turkish Cypriot Vice-President were abolished. The purely Greek Cypriot House of Representatives also prolonged the mandate of President Makarios (not the one of Vice-President Küçük) and its own mandate by a decision of 27 July 1965. Greek Cypriots took over the ministerial posts that were reserved for Turkish Cypriots.[33]

In relation to the relevant debates, the Turkish Cypriot members of the House of Representatives approached the UN Special Representative and asked him to inquire with the Greek Cypriot side whether they could attend such meetings in safety. The President of the House, Clerides replied positively, provided that agreement was reached beforehand on the following points:

(a) The Turkish Cypriot members would resume their seats permanently rather than only for the purpose of the present debate;
(b) The Turkish Cypriot members would accept that the laws enacted by the House of Representatives would be applied to the whole of Cyprus, including the Turkish areas, by the Government using the normal authorized administrative organs;

[31] Necatigil, loc. cit. (note 38), pp. 62–63; C. Heinze, The position of the Greek and Turkish Communities under the Cyprus Constitution of 1960, in: C. Heinze (ed.), Cyprus 2000, p. 22 (28).

[32] Report of the UN-Secretary-General of 10 June 1966, S/7350, § 154.

[33] Rumpf, loc. cit. (note 27), EuGRZ 1997, p. 533 (542).

(c) While the Greek Cypriot members would regard attendance at the House by the Turkish Cypriot members as implying recognition by them of the present Cyprus Government, the Turkish Cypriot members would not be called upon to make a statement to that effect, and the Greek Cypriot members would likewise refrain from making any such statement on the record of the House;
(d) It must be understood that the provision in Article 78 of the Constitution concerning separate majorities had been abolished and every member of the House would have one vote for all decisions.[34]

On 22 July 1965, the Turkish Cypriot Members of the House met with Clerides to discuss these conditions. Since they regarded them as eliminating their constitutional rights, no agreement was reached and they continued not to attend the House.

3.2. *The Turkish Cypriot enclaves*

In 1960, 296 mixed villages had existed on the island. Following the riots in late 1963, the Turkish Cypriot leaders started to organise a resettlement of their community. Whereas the Turkish Cypriots from the cities were in general willing to do so, due to their violent experiences in Nicosia, the farmers were more or less forced by the TMT to leave their land and to live in the Turkish Cypriot enclaves. In 1964, these represented only 2% of the island's territory, but were inhabited by 59,000 Turkish Cypriots, including 25–30,000 refugees from 103 villages. Another 79,000 Turkish Cypriots continued to live outside the enclaves.[35]

Daily life in the enclaves was difficult since certain economic goods and public services were not made available by the Greek Cypriot authorities.[36] Until 1968, President Makarios led a policy of isolation forcing the Turkish Cypriots to rely on Turkish aid. On the other hand, the Turkish Cypriot administration did not allow Turkish Cypriots to leave the enclaves without permission, and using force to implement this rule.[37] Already at the end of 1964, the average income of a Turkish Cypriot in the enclaves amounted to only 24% of the average income of a Greek Cypriot (as compared to 86% in the year before).[38]

During the 1960's, the Turkish Cypriots established provisional administrative bodies. The former Members of Parliament, voting for the law 1/65, prolonged their mandate and the mandate of the Vice-President. The latter was the chief of

---

[34] Report of the UN Secretary-General of 29 July 1965, S/6569, § 8.

[35] Chrysostomides, loc. cit. (page 8, note 24), p. 92.

[36] Report of the UN-Secretary-General of 10 September 1964, S/5950, § 223: "The policy of economic pressures has definitely caused much hardship to the Turkish population: it has nourished bitterness on the Turkish side; it has hardened the Turkish position, it has greatly increased the tensions . . .". Further examples from UN-Secretary-General reports are cited by Ertekün, loc. cit. (page 6, note 19), Appendix 8, pp. 179–183.

[37] Tzermias, loc. cit. (page 2, note 1), p. 305.

[38] Drevet, loc. cit. (note 13), p. 153.

the Turkish Cypriot police and gendarmerie (all TC forces including TMT fighters were estimated at about 10,000).[39] On 28 December 1967 – as a reaction to the Greek Cypriot armed attack on Kofinu of 15 November 1967 – the Turkish Cypriot members of Parliament and of the Communal Chamber took the decision to unify the legislature. Six new colleagues, forming together the Council of Ministers complemented the three former Ministers of the Republic. The former Republic's Vice-President remained the Head of the Executive, with the President of the Communal Chamber as his aid. Under the basic law, the judiciary should be independent. These provisions were deemed to be valid as long as the Republic's Constitution did not fully apply.[40]

3.3. *Parallel elections in 1968, 1970 and 1973*

The strange situation that both communities kept on relying on the 1960 Constitution in principle, while at the same time changing some institutional parts in practice, led to parallel elections in 1968 and 1970 and 1973.

At the presidential elections of 25 February 1968, the Greek Cypriots again elected Makarios with 95% of the votes. He marginalised his competitor Evdokas who had promised immediate ENOSIS in the campaign. The Turkish Cypriots in the enclaves voted for Küçük as their President. The parliamentary elections of 5 July 1970 presented a similar picture. The Greek Cypriots voted for their 35 Members of Parliament, with the United Party gaining the lead (15), followed by AKEL (9). The leader of the strongest formation, Clerides, assumed the office of Speaker of the House. At the same time, the Turkish Cypriots elected their 15 Members of Parliament as well as their Communal Chamber. Necdet Ünel became Vice-President of the House, Rauf Denktaş President of the Communal Chamber. After Denktaş's visit to Ankara, the 15 Turkish Cypriot MPs declared that they would not take their seats in the common House of Representatives.[41]

Finally, in February 1973, Makarios was declared President for another period of five years since no other candidate challenged him. On the side of the Turkish Cypriots, Denktaş replaced Küçük in rather dubious circumstances. There are allegations that his competitor, Berberoğlu, was forced to withdraw his candidacy. Greek Cypriot press reports that he was held in arrest;[42] the critical Turkish Cypriot press alleges that he was threatened with a pistol in the Turkish embassy in the north.[43] In any case, Berberoğlu was sentenced to 10 years imprisonment because of a critical article soon after the elections, and later on released on bail.

[39] Drevet, loc. cit. (note 13), p. 43.

[40] For a detailed account see Necatigil, loc. cit (page 11, note 35), pp. 65–68. Similar to the Greek Cypriot doctrine of necessity, the Turkish Cypriots justified those unconstitutional measures with a reference to the "anomalous situation" (p. 66, note 85).

[41] Tzermias, loc. cit. (page 2, note 1), p. 312.

[42] Tzermias, loc. cit. (page 2, note 1), p. 313.

[43] Africa, 5 April 2002, commenting on the deceased Berberoğlu.

4. Hidden agendas

With the benefit of hindsight, the political and military confrontation between both communities as well as the following separation does not seem to be pure coincidence.

On the Greek Cypriot side, the so-called Akritas plan of 1963,[44] written by the then Interior Minister Georghadjis, explained how the right to self-determination of the Greek Cypriots could be implemented in four stages. In stage one, the "negative elements" of the Constitution should be abolished, followed by a denunciation of the Treaties of Guarantee and Alliance in stage two. Third, self-determination should be exercised and any foreign intervention was to be opposed in stage four. Although it is debated whether President Makarios in fact subscribed to that plan,[45] the compliance of his 13 points with the first stage of the Akritas-plan and the resemblance of political and military steps in the plan and in reality is striking.[46]

On the Turkish Cypriot side, there were plans for partition. The secret organisation TMT worked to that aim; some connections of TMT members to the Turkish-Cypriot-dominated Auxiliary Police of the Colonial Power cannot be excluded.[47] A Greek Cypriot search of the Vice-President's office in December 1963 is reported to have found two documents: one of TMT origin, one from Küçük/Denktaş. The first one, dated 23 April 1962, accepts the Zurich agreements as interim stage for partition.[48] The second one, of September 1963,[49] mentions that the Turkish Cypriots would be forced to found their own Republic on the island, if necessary with the help of Turkey. Therefore, Turkish Cypriots should

[44] The Akritas plan is reproduced in Reddaway, loc. cit. (page 3, note 10), Appendix III, p. 199, and was circulated as an UN document to the GA and the SC on 30 May 1978 (A/33/115; S/12722).

[45] See Tzermias, loc. cit. (page 2, note 1), pp. 287–288 (Makarios not part of the Akritas-plan authors); Reddaway, loc. cit. (page 3, note 10), p. 33 (Makarios approved the plan); Ertekün, loc. cit. (page 6, note 19), p. 153 (Makarios appointed the then Interior Minister Gheorgadijis to be "Chief Akritas").

[46] See Reddaway, loc. cit. (page 3, note 10), p. 134: "In this context (Akritas plan) the Archbishop's action in bringing forward his proposals for amending the constitution at the end of 1963 assumes a much more sinister character".

[47] According to Reddaway, loc. cit. (page 3, note 10), pp. 90–91, the Auxiliary Police counted 1.700 Turkish Cypriots and only 70 Greek Cypriots in 1958. He observes that "Turkish Cypriots serving in the Police forces may have collaborated with the T.M.T. organisation – just as on the other side, there were undoubtedly Greek Cypriot policemen who collaborated with EOKA".

[48] The document is reprinted in Chrysostomides, loc. cit. (page 8, note 24), Annex II. According to Özgür, loc. cit. (page 10, note 34), p. 40, it was found in the safety box of the Turkish Cypriot Minister for Agriculture, Fazil Plumer.

[49] According to Tzermias, loc. cit. (page 2, note 1), p. 297, the documents are dated 14 September, according to Reddaway, loc. cit. (page 3, note 10), p. 135, they were signed on 2 September.

defend themselves together in a certain region of the island.[50] Here, again, it is striking that the Turkish Cypriot leadership opted towards a partitionist policy rather than trying to maintain their constitutionally entrenched rights with the help of the Guarantor powers in a time of severe fighting.

B. LEGAL EVALUATION

The events of 1963/1964 raise at least three crucial legal questions. 1. Could the Greek Cypriot measures of hellenisation be justified under the rigid bi-communal Constitution? 2. Did the Republic of Cyprus, as a State, continue to exist under international law? 3. Could President Makarios still be considered as representing the legitimate government after the hellenisation of the Republic? Albeit closely linked to the same events, these questions have to be treated separately, since the applicable body of law varies.

1. Partial illegality of the Republic's hellenisation under Constitutional law

1.1. *The contravention of the Constitution*

Certain of Makarios' 13 points of November 1963 suggested changes to "unamendable" provisions of the 1960 Constitution.[51] Hence, they would have entailed a revision of the basic articles. Such a revision could have only brought about with the consent of the Guarantor powers. Whereas, politically, this move can be seen as a provocation of the latter since it would be surprising that they would change their political will so soon after the agreements of 1959, it nevertheless was not illegal to make such proposals.[52]

Therefore, the decisive question concerns the legality of those Greek Cypriot measures that were actually implemented in the years 1964–1965. It should be recalled that

- Merging the police and gendarmerie infringes Article 130 according to which these institutions should be separate;
- Introducing compulsory recruitment to the National Guard needs the consensus of the Vice-President under Article 129(2);

[50] Tzermias, loc. cit. (page 2, note 1), pp. 297–298.

[51] Proposal No. 1= abolition of Article 50; Proposal No. 5 = abolition of Art. 78 II; Proposal No. 6 = abolition of Art. 173(1); Proposal No. 10 = abolition of Art. 123, 129; Proposal No. 13 = abolition of Art. 86.

[52] Chrysostomides, loc. cit. (page 8, note 24), p. 34. Unconvincing Heinze, loc. cit. (note 31), p. 22 (27), identifying Makarios' proposals as the "abrogation" of the Basic Articles, "as subsequent action proves".

- Appointing local councils by government runs contrary to the idea of separate local self-administration in the five big cities as laid down in Art. 173 et seq.;
- Merging the Constitutional Court and the High Court into a Supreme Court eliminates the necessity to appoint Turkish Cypriot judges and neutral Judges as Presidents and thus contravenes Articles 133 and 153;
- Allowing District Courts to try Turkish Cypriots, accused of committing a crime against a Greek Cypriot, by Greek Cypriot judges only, violated the guarantee of mixed benches as enshrined in Article 159(3);
- Publishing laws needs the consensus of the Vice-President according to Article 52;
- Publishing laws in Greek only, violates Article 3(2) according to which legislation shall be published in both Greek and Turkish, the official languages of the Republic.

Thus, a whole range of Greek Cypriot revisions contravened the letter of the Constitution.

1.2. *The doctrine of necessity*

Already in October 1964, the newly established Supreme Court handed down a fundamental decision.[53] An appeal had been filed by the Attorney General against a decision of a District Judge to grant bail to Turkish Cypriots who were accused of having committed offences of preparing war or warlike activities. The defendant had raised the preliminary objection that the Supreme Court had no jurisdiction over the appeal since its establishment under law 33/1964 of 9 July 1964 was unconstitutional. Justices Vassiliades, Triantafyllides and Josephides rejected that objection. They interpreted the Constitution to include the doctrine of necessity as an implied exception to particular provisions of the Constitution in exceptional circumstances so as to ensure the very existence of the State. Facing the systematic absence of Turkish Cypriots in the State institutions and a situation of civil strife, it was necessary for the Cyprus legislature to adopt laws without following the letter of the constitution in order to preserve the constitutional order.

The Court's approach met different sorts of criticism:[54]

- The Court was partial when deciding about the lawfulness of its own existence;
- The legal foundation of an unwritten doctrine of necessity is doubtful;
- A written Constitution cannot be supplemented by an unwritten doctrine.

With regard to the first argument, it is a common feature of modern judicial systems that Courts have the power to interpret whether or not they have jurisdiction. This can even go the extent of scrutinising the legality of the act of establishment. The ICJ accepted such a power for international tribunals holding that

[53] Supreme Court of Cyprus, The Attorney-General of the Republic v. Mustafa Ibrahim and others, 6 CLR (1964), p. 195 et seq.

[54] Necatigil, loc. cit. (page 11, note 35), pp. 60–65.

> *Since the Alabama case it has been generally recognised that, following the earlier precedents, and in the absence of any agreements to the contrary, the international tribunal has the power to interpret for this purpose the instruments which govern that jurisdiction.*[55]

The same rationale can be found in many national court systems. There is simply no other body than the Court itself that is suited to decide about the actual scope and meaning of its jurisdiction. Finally, the European Court of Human Rights did not doubt that the Supreme Court of Cyprus could declare valid and constitutional the law on which it was established. The Court expressly referred to the Ibrahim case when concluding that the Supreme Cout of Cyprus constitutes a tribunal established by law within the meaning of Article 6 (1) ECHR.[56]

As to the second objection, there is no clear-cut legal foundation of the doctrine of necessity in comparative constitutional law. Certainly, the idea that a contravention of a written rule can be justified to preserve a higher good can be found in the criminal systems of many countries, including Cyprus. But it only relieves an individual from criminal responsibility. It does not offer guidance on the powers and limitations of public authority under a constitutional system.[57] When looking at pertinent public law cases of different countries, the situation appears to be mixed. The Greek Council of State accepted the doctrine in 1945,[58] and it has found judicial support in France.[59] On the other hand, it can hardly be said that the doctrine is known in contemporary Germany.[60] The doctrine of necessity was even rejected by the Privy Council in a case relating to Southern Rhodesia.[61] Thus, comparative constitutional law neither makes it necessary to apply it in Cyprus, nor does it exclude it.

The relevance of the doctrine of necessity for Cyprus must therefore be assessed in the domestic context, leading to the third objection. The Cypriot Constitution allows for the suspension of its own rules. Article 183 empowers the Council of

---

[55] ICJ, Nottebohm case (Preliminary Objection), Judgment of November 18th, 1953, ICJ reports 1953, p. 111 (119).

[56] ECtHR, Aziz v. Cyprus, Greece, Turkey and the U.K., Application No. 69959/01, Partial Decision as to the Admissibility of 23 April 2002, para. 3.

[57] Therefore the reasoning of Justice Vassiliades, Ibrahim case, loc. cit. (note 53), pp. 210, 214 referring to section 17 of the Cypriot Penal Code is beside the point.

[58] Council of State Decision 2/45: "it could be accepted, in case this was indispensably and imperatively necessary and unavoidable, that such governments were entitled to regulate, even in deviation from the Constitution, matters related to the primary purposes for which they were called to govern, namely the restoration of law and order and public security" (Ibrahim case, loc. cit., note 53, p. 231).

[59] Conseil d'Etat, Heyries, 28 June 1918, Rec. 651 (Ibrahim case, loc. cit., note 53, p. 258).

[60] In contrast, Art. 79 (1) GG makes it a mandatory requirement that all parts of constitutional law must be included in the written text of the Grundgesetz. Thus, no unwritten exceptions are allowed. Justice Josephides, Ibrahim case, loc. cit. (note 53), p. 260, overlooked this fact when referring to one German writer of the 19th century.

[61] Madzimbamuto v. Lardner – Burke, (1968) 3 All ER, p. 561 et seq. (Privy Council).

Ministers to issue a Proclamation of Emergency "in case of war or other public danger threatening the life of the Republic or any part thereof". This Proclamation is subject to the veto of either the President or the Vice-President and has to be confirmed by the House of Representatives (par. 5). The Proclamation shall specify which Articles of the Constitution shall be suspended, allowing only derogations to those human rights that are listed in Article 183 par. 2. The decisive question is whether the procedure and limitations of suspending only certain human rights, as laid down in Article 183, is exhaustive. The answer must be negative. The workability of the Cypriot Constitution depended on the good will of both communities to share sovereignty.[62] Even the provision on emergency presumes that the State institutions perform their functions properly. A procedure, let alone substantial framework, covering the absence of the Turkish Cypriot members of government and parliament, does not exist in the Constitution. It has to be found outside the written text of the Constitution itself. Thus, there is indeed room to apply the doctrine of necessity in the case of Cyprus, in order to meet the unforeseen extra-ordinary challenge. The Supreme Court of Cyprus was therefore right in stating that for the preservation of social order,[63] the doctrine of necessity is implied in the bi-communal Constitution of the Republic of Cyprus.

1.3. *The application of the doctrine of necessity*

Affirming the general applicability of the doctrine in Cyprus[64] is not enough to justify the measures of hellenisation. Rather, as the Cypriot Supreme Court held, four prerequisites must be satisfied before the suspension of some constitutional provisions may be based on this doctrine:

(1) There is an imperative and inevitable necessity or exceptional circumstance;
(2) There is no other remedy;
(3) The measure taken must be proportionate to the necessity;
(4) The measure must be of a temporary character limited to the duration of the exceptional circumstances.[65]

Exceptional circumstances exist in a bi-communal constitutional system when representatives of one community systematically do not assume their offices. In such a case, suspending the relevant rights seems to be the only proportionate reaction, provided that it is of a temporary character. However, before concluding so, it must also be assessed whether the other community bears legal responsibility for the absence. Such would certainly be the case if Turkish Cypriot representatives had been physically or legally prevented to exercise their constitutional functions.

---

[62] Reddaway, loc. cit. (page 13, note 10), p. 130, also citing the First President of the Constitutional Court, Forsthoff, in an interview of January 1964; Tzermias, loc. cit. (page 2, note 1), p. 143.

[63] Supreme Court, Ibrahim case, loc. cit. (note 53), p. 197.

[64] Chrysostomides, loc. cit. (page 8, note 24), p. 110.

[65] Supreme Court, Ibrahim case, loc. cit. (note 53), p. 265.

This analysis shall now be carried out as regards the Turkish Cypriot absences in all the three branches of government.

1.3.1. The absence of Turkish Cypriots in the executive

As regards the absence of the Turkish Cypriot Vice-President and the three Turkish Cypriot Ministers from their respective offices since the last week of December 1963, there are no reports that they had been legally or physically barred from office.[66] According to the Greek Cypriot version, the Turkish Cypriot members of government were continuously invited to attend meetings of the Council of Ministers. Descriptions that the Turkish Cypriots were "prevented"[67] from holding office or "expelled from the legislature and government"[68] do not specify whether this is meant in a physical sense. The most accurate description seems to be that the "Turkish Cypriot Vice-President and the ministers *found it impossible to attend* their ministries or the meetings of the Council of Ministers which were being held on the Greek side".[69] Another official Turkish Cypriot version suggests as well that the orchestrated absence was a political reaction to the events in the streets.[70]

In that regard, the first question is whether force against members of the group in the streets are attributable to (Greek Cypriot led) State institutions. International customary law on State responsibility, as reflected in UN General Assembly Resolution 56/83 of 12 December 2001, offers the relevant criteria.[71] Conduct can be attributed to a State because its own organs or entities exercising governmental authority have acted or because conduct was instructed, directed or controlled by the State.

As a starting point, it has to be noted that the Greek Cypriot attacks on Turkish Cypriot quarters in Nicosia or an Turkish Cypriot villages were conducted by paramilitary troops under the leadership of Nicos Sampson. Since these were neither organs of the State nor exercising elements of governmental authority, their

---

[66] Leigh, loc. cit. (page 9, note 30), Opinion of 20 July 1990, p. 54 (59) with further references.

[67] Reddaway, loc. cit. (page 3, note 10), p. 151.

[68] A. Pearce, Is a settlement in Cyprus still possible, in: Yeditepe Üniversitesi Hukuk Fakültesi Dergisi I/1, 2004, p. 149 (160).

[69] Necatigil, loc. cit. (page 11, note 35), p. 54.

[70] See Turkish Cypriot Memorandum of 12 July 1990, reprinted in: Ertekün (ed.), The Status of the Two Peoples in Cyprus – Legal Opinions, p. 39 (43): "Since December 1963, the Turkish Cypriot community, faced by discrimination, threats and physical attacks was, for its self-preservation, compelled gradually to withdraw into self-administering enclaves (. . .).

[71] UNGA Resolution 59/83 of 12 December 2001 on State responsibility for an internationally wrongful act. The GA took note of the relevant draft of the International Law Commission (Report of the International Law Commission on the work of its Fifty-third session, Official Records of the General Assembly, Fifty-sixth session, Supplement No. 10 (A/56/10), p. 43 et seq., November 2001). The ILC's parts on attribution of conduct embodies to a large extent customary international law as it already stood in the 1960s.

acts cannot be directly attributed to the government. According to Article 8 of the ILC articles, however, the conduct of a group of persons shall be considered an act of State under international law if the group is in fact acting on the instructions of, or under the direction or control of that State in carrying out the conduct. There are allegations that the commander of the paramilitary troops, Sampson, was instructed by the Ministry of Interior, Georghadjis, to carry out the attacks. It is also reported that Interior Minister and author of the aggressive Akritas plan had disarmed the Turkish police force the day before the fighting started.[72] If this were true, the responsibility of the State would be clearly established under Article 8, first alternative ("under the instructions of"). Given the factual uncertainties, the third alternative of Article 8 should also be considered, namely that private conduct was carried out under the "control" of the State.[73] In the Cypriot case, there are several relevant factors. First, the State Police under the command of Georghadjis deliberately did not defend the Turkish Cypriot citizens, although they would have had the power to do so. It is also reported that Major Ionnidis, the leader of the Greek contingent on the island,[74] was involved. Tolerating the attacks shows that the Minister of Interior[75] and perhaps the President of the Republic[76] used Sampson's troops for their goals. It is also revealing that Sampson was never punished for his grave crimes, which again points to an official political backing of the action. Finally, the attack on the Kyrenia pass end of March 1964 by Georghadjis himself was qualified by the UN-Secretary-General as "planned and organized military effort".[77] In the light of this evidence, the aggression against the Turkish Cypriots in late 1963 has to be attributed to the State under customary international law.[78]

It must now be inquired whether these internationally wrongful acts can be understood as indirect force against Turkish Cypriot representatives. One author argues that violence against the group is sufficient proof that the absence of the Turkish Cypriot officials was not voluntary.[79] Another author inquires into the contribution of the State to the occurrence of the state of necessity pointing to an

---

[72] Reddaway, loc. cit. (page 3, note 10), p. 146.

[73] For the traditional test (effective control of each military and paramilitary operation) compare ICJ, Military and Paramilitary Activities in and against Nicaragua (Nicaragua v. United States of America), Merits, Judgment, I.C.J. Reports 1986, p. 14 (64–65), § 115. The Appeals Chamber of the ICTY, Case IT-94–1 Prosecutor v. Tadic (1999), ILM, Vol. 38, p. 1518 and p. 1541, § 117 required a lesser degree of control. However, that test only arose in the 1990s and is therefore not relevant to assess facts from the 1960s.

[74] Tzermias, loc. cit. (page 2, note 1), p. 290.

[75] Drevet, loc. cit. (note 13), p. 136.

[76] Reddaway, loc. cit. (page 3, note 10), pp. 146–147.

[77] Report of the UN-Secretary-General of 29 April 1964, S/5671.

[78] In a Report of 1987, the Foreign Affairs Committee of the British House of Commons comes to a similar result, finding that "violence was either directly inspired by, or certainly connived at, by the Greek Cypriot leadership". Report No. 23, para. 27 (cited from Necatigil, loc. cit. (note 38), p. 134).

[79] Rumpf, loc. cit. (page 8, note 24), EuGRZ 1997, p. 533 (542).

analogy in the general law of State responsibility.[80] Indeed, under Article 25 (2) (b) of the ILC articles necessity may not be invoked by a State against another State as a ground for precluding wrongfulness if "the State has contributed to the situtation of necessity". Such would have been the correct yardstick when evaluating if Cyprus had invoked "necessity" vis-à-vis Turkey, Greece or the United Kingdom in order to justify the violation of the basic articles of the Cyprus constitution, being protected by the Treaty of Guarantee as well. However, in the domestic context of a constitutional deadlock in bi-communal Cyprus, the relevant yardstick is stricter. In contrast to sovereign states, the relationship between the two communities is governed by a common constitution, creating certain loyalties to the constitutional order. Since the constitution was only workable on the basis of mutual co-operation, complete withdrawal of one community in the political affairs of the Republic could therefore only be acceptable as an *ultima ratio.* Only if efforts of the group's representatives in the government fail to restore peace and security for their compatriots they might have had no other option than to stay away from office.

Makarios and Küçük had been able to agree in late 1963 to ask for international help. The stationing of the British led truce force bore their corresponding consent.[81] It is hardly understandable why the Turkish Cypriot Vice-President became unable to exercise his functions during the implementation of that operation. The continuing international involvement of first the Guarantor powers and later on the UN, suggests that the Turkish Cypriot representatives could have ensured, *in their official capacities*, to do their utmost to end the fights quickly. The aggression of the nationalist parts of the Greek Cypriots did not necessitate the same nationalist response. The Turkish Cypriot conduct was itself partitionist in nature. The systematic absence of Turkish Cypriots in the government as well as instructions of the Turkish Cypriot leadership to Turkish Cypriot civil servants to quit office from State institutions hinted at an obstructionist policy as a political reaction to the events in the streets. In sum, the Greek Cypriot violent attacks against the group of Turkish Cypriots did not force their representatives to abstain *immediately* from office without exhausting normal remedies in cases of unrest.

1.3.2. The absence of Turkish Cypriots in the legislature

The 30% elected Turkish Cypriot Members of Parliament did not attend the House anymore since the latest week of 1963. Again, formulations that they were "not

[80] K. Özersay, The Excuse of State Necessity and its implication on the Cyprus Conflict, Perceptions – Journal of international affairs, Winter 2004/2005, Vol. IX (4), p. 33 (54 et seq.).

[81] See the telegram of the British Foreign Office to the Head of the UK Mission to the UN, dated 2 March 1964: "Regarding the constitutional procedures, you should draw attention to the fact that our own peacekeeping force was properly established with the agreement of both the President and the Vice-President of Cyprus". Cited from A. Karaosmanoğlu, UNFICYP and the problem of consent, in: R. Arim (ed.), Cyprus and International Law, p. 104.

able to attend any more the House of Representatives",[82] implying physcial or legal barriers, seem to be inaccurate. There was no parliamentary decision barring Turkish MPs from attending the House. Rather, as a leading Turkish Cypriot author put it, the Turkish Cypriot members of the House of Representatives "*found it impossible* to attend the deliberations of the House".[83]

Whereas a necessity to deliberate without them can therefore clearly be affirmed, it must also be shown that they had the possibility to re-assume office under constitutional terms. In this regard, the condition for return by the then President of the House of Representatives Clerides in July 1965[84] creates some controversy. Some of Clerides' conditions were of political nature and did not curtail any other parliamentary rights for the Turkish Cypriots in future. When taking up their duties again, Turkish Cypriot MPs would have had the possibility to vote like any other Member of Parliament. The most sensitive issue is, however, the denial of special majority rights under Article 78(2) of the Constitution. Not to apply separate majorities anymore seems to have been still justified under the doctrine of necessity given the experience with the veto of Turkish Cypriot MPs on the taxation law in 1962. Otherwise, the Republic would have faced the risk to run short of financial means if Turkish Cypriots were again to block the adoption of the tax law.

However, the condition not to apply separate majority voting in the Parliament was not limited in time. It did not only avoid a "financial impasse" in the near future, but also abolished completely a special safeguard for the Turkish Cypriot community in the long run, not only relating to tax matters. Therefore, it is doubtful whether the Clerides' requirement to accept the hellenisation measures of 1964 was proportional and temporary, thereby impeding the return of Turkish Cypriot MPs to the House of Representatives in 1965.

1.3.3. The absence of a neutral judge and Turkish Cypriots in the judiciary

As regards the abolition of the Constitutional Court and of the High Court (and the necessity to appoint neutral judges as their Presidents), the situation is even more complicated. In the *Ibrahim* case, the Supreme Court simply referred to the fact that both high jurisdictions (as from August 1963 and from June 1964) had ceased to function because of the vacancy of the posts. While it is certainly relevant that both Courts did not work anymore, it is disturbing that the Supreme Court refrained from examining the reasons for that.[85] In the case of the Constitutional

---

[82] Bouony, The status of the Turkish Republic of Northern Cyprus and its adherence to the Organisation of the Islamic Conference, Opinion of 6 June 1991, in: Ertekün (ed.), The Status of the Two Peoples in Cyprus – Legal Opinions, p. 112 (116).

[83] Necatigil, loc. cit. (page 11, note 35), p. 54.

[84] See above note 34.

[85] Judge Vassiliades states, that the reasons for the non-functioning of these two courts do not matter, and could in any way be traced in the Constitution itself (Ibrahim case, loc. cit. (note 53), p. 207). For Judge Triantafyllides, it would have been impossible in the

Court, President Makarios' openly declared unwillingness to implement the Court's decision in the important bi-communal case of the five municipalities had prompted the resignation of its President in summer 1963. A governmental contempt of court cannot justify the abolition of the entire Court. To ensure proper administration of justice, it would have been sufficient to appoint another non-Cypriot President.

On the other hand, unsafe living conditions in Cyprus during 1964 must be taken account of. An already selected Australian judge did not take up office in early 1964 as agreed. The decisive question is therefore whether the Constitutional and the High Court temporarily could have continued working without a neutral President. In July 1964, when both Courts had been abolished, it was not foreseeable whether public order would have been restored to such extent that willing candidates for the presidential posts could have been found quickly thereafter. Therefore, from an *ex ante perspective*, the full hellenisation of the highest judiciary seems to have been reasonable. Thus, the doctrine of necessity could also justify the abolition of the Constitutional and the High Court in 1964. It remains, however, an open question whether the restoration of both jurisdictions, or at least the creation of the post of a neutral President of the Supreme Court would not have been necessary in the more peaceful times thereafter, when non-Cypriot candidates for this post would have been available again. But apparently, these considerations were not made in the second half of the 1960's.

The Greek Cypriot measures as regards Turkish Cypriot judges were neither satisfactory. Although there is evidence that some Turkish Cypriot judges who still wanted to co-operate with the Greek Cypriots to uphold the bi-communal system, were prevented by their own leaders from doing so,[86] others resumed office in July 1964. But even these Turkish Cypriot judges loyal to the Republic were stopped at the checkpoints near the law courts on 2 June 1966 and prevented from further attending.[87] Here, already the first requirement of the doctrine of necessity was not met. Therefore, the hellenisation of the District Courts could not be justified and remained unconstitutional until 1974. Only when the access of Turkish Cypriots (including Turkish Cypriot judges) to the south was blocked by Turkish Cypriot authorities north rather than by authorities of the Republic, became the hellenisation of the District Courts justified under the doctrine of necessity.

The final question refers to the publication of laws and other legal acts in both Greek and Turkish. In the *Ibrahim* case, two judges argue that the publication in Turkish was unnecessary since the Turkish Officers in the Government did not

circumstances to secure the services of, and appoint, suitable persons to serve as neutral Presidents (ibid., p. 224). Similarly, Judge Josephides felt that it was the imperative duty of the Government to provide for the undelayed administration of justice (ibid., p. 267).

[86] Justice Josephides gives account of the case of a Turkish Cypriot District Court Judge who was, in March 1964, prevented by members of his community from holding a session in Famagusta, even after the President of the High Court had intervened and cared for adequate security arrangements (Ibrahim case, loc. cit., note 91, p. 251).

[87] See above Chapter II A 3.1.1.

attend their offices any more. Justice Vassiliades had greatest difficulties to accept that argument.[88] He is right in stressing that the Government could certainly find suitable persons to draft and print the Turkish text of legislative enactments at a time when many thousands of Turkish Cypriots were still to be found in areas controlled by the Government. Even later on, the Cypriot government can only seriously back its claim to represent the whole population if it enacts laws that are accessible to the Turkish Cypriot citizens. Thus, not to publish laws in Turkish anymore was not dictated by circumstances. The doctrine of necessity could therefore not justify the continuing violation of Article 3(2) of the Constitution.

1.4. *Conclusion*

Since the Constitution only functions when both communities co-operate, the doctrine of necessity could apply to remedy the absence of the Turkish Cypriots in the common State institutions. Although the Republic of Cyprus bears responsibility for organised crimes against Turkish Cypriot citizens in December 1963 under international law, the oppression against some of the citizens did not give rise to a legal right for Turkish Cypriot representatives to withdraw from their offices. The elected Turkish Cypriots could have stayed on in a representative government and in Parliament until law and order would have been restored with international help. Their choice to leave the common State institutions in early 1964 was premature. Therefore, it was constitutional not to apply institutional safeguards given to Turkish Cypriot members of Parliament or the Executive. Although more delicate, it was also acceptable in the circumstances of the year 1964 to abolish the Constitutional and the High Court because it was uncertain whether a neutral President could be found in the near future. On the other hand, it is more doubtful whether it was justified not to re-apply special majority voting for Turkish Cypriot members of Parliament, when they asked for return in 1965. The prevention of Turkish Cypriot judges to hold office after July 1966 as well as the continuous non-publication of legal acts in Turkish, as one of the two official languages, was not justified under the doctrine of necessity. The government could have made an effort to find Turkish Cypriots or Turkish speaking persons to assist in the drafting of these texts. There was no need to exclude the Turkish Cypriot judges at District Court level. These measures of hellenisation were unconstitutional.

2. The continuity of the Republic of Cyprus under international law

It is a well-established principle of international law that a State exists if at least three objective criteria are met: a permanent population, a defined territory, and an independent government. The existence of a State is not affected by changes

[88] Justice Vassiliades, Ibrahim case, loc. cit. (note 53), p. 216.

in its system of governance, even in most drastic events like internal revolutions.[89] Statehood was not called into question in West-European countries when they changed from authoritarian to democratic regimes or vice-versa. Comparably, in the case of Cyprus, the measures of hellenisation destroyed the bi-communal character, but not the State of Cyprus. The UN Security Council resolution 186 on the mandate of UNFICYP maintained the view that the Republic of Cyprus continuously existed in its entirety. The General Assembly of 18 December 1965 was even more explicit in this regard,[90] revealing the large support Makarios had in the Group of non-allied States. Even Turkey only questioned the legitimacy of the Makarios government, but not the existence of the Republic of Cyprus.

Therefore, any contention that the abrogation of the 1960 Constitution had led to the transformation of the Republic to a Greek State of Southern Cyprus in 1964[91] is devoid of substance.

3. The international legitimacy of the Cyprus government

Under customary international law, each State may freely decide whether to recognise a certain foreign government as representing another State. There are no strict rules that direct the State's discretion in that respect. Hence, political considerations play a large role, e.g. whether a government exercises effective control over a territory.[92]

As regards the international legitimacy of the Cyprus government under President Makarios as representing the Republic of Cyprus, resolution 186 of the UN Security Council of 4 March 1964 plays a crucial role. Despite a letter from Küçük to the Secretary-General, stating that the Greek Cypriot representation to the Council was unlawful without his consent,[93] the Council preferred not enter into the details of constitutional legitimacy. For the sake of stability of Cyprus – a newly independent State –, it opted to deal with an effective government. Hence, it implicitly recognised the government under President Makarios as the legitimate government of Cyprus when referring to the "Government of Cyprus" (§ 2) as distinct from "the communities and their leaders" (§ 3).[94]

---

89 Akehurst/Malanczuk, loc. cit. (page 7, note 22), p. 82. J. Crawford, The Creation of States in International Law, p. 405 with further references.

90 UNGA Resolution 2077 (XX) of 18 December 1965, § 1: "Takes cognisance of the fact that the Republic of Cyprus, as an equal member of the United Nations, is, in accordance with the Charter of the United Nations, entitled to enjoy, and should enjoy, full sovereignty and complete independence without any foreign intervention or interference."

91 Necatigil, loc. cit. (page 11, note 35), p. 70.

92 M. Shaw, International Law, p. 377.

93 UN Doc S/5491. Telegram from the Vice-President of Cyprus to the UN Secretary-General.

94 Tzermias, loc. cit. (page 2, note 1), p. 329; Joseph, loc. cit. (page 10, note 32), p. 100.

In short, the international community, with the exception of Turkey, treated the Makarios government as the legitimate Government of Cyprus. Any Turkish Cypriot claim that there were indeed two governments did therefore not find any international support from the very beginning.

4. Summary

Although the Greek Cypriot members of Government bore some responsibility for the illegal attacks against Turkish Cypriots in late 1963 and early 1964, the Turkish Cypriot members of Government and Parliament could have exercised their official functions until public security was restored with international help. In refraining from doing so, they allowed a large hellenisation of the Republic. Not all measures were justified under the law of necessity. In particular, an unconstitutional situation arose out of the fact that the return of Turkish Cypriot Members of Parliament to the House was unduly impeded and that legislation was not published in the Turkish language, as it should have been, even in difficult circumstances. This partially illegal hellenisation of the Republic did, however, not call into question its statehood. Under international law the Member States of the United Nations were free to regard the Makarios government as the legitimate government of the Republic of Cyprus although the Vice-President had left office and no Turkish Cypriot ministers were present in the Council of Ministers anymore.

Chapter III

The Turkish Intervention and Turkey's Continued Presence in the Northern Part of Cyprus

A. THE FACTS

1. The Turkish Intervention

1.1. *The Coup d'Etat against President Makarios*

In 1967, a military junta took power in Athens. The leader of the original EOKA, Grivas, returned to the island in 1971 and his newly founded "EOKA B" openly undermined Makarios' authority.[1] After his death in early 1974, the command of his EOKA B came into the hands of the "Athens Cyprus Office", i.e. the General Staff of the Greek military junta and its collaborators on the island. In April 1974, Makarios issued a decree declaring the EOKA B illegal. He started to build a "reserve corps" fearing the Greek influence over his own National Guard. In a letter of 2 July 1974 to the Greek President, Gizikes, he demanded from Greece to withdraw the Greek officers from the Cyprus National Guard from the island.

---

[1] Tzermias, loc. cit. (page 2, note 1), p. 416.

Legal Aspects of the Cyprus Problem, pp. 34–59.

The Greek dictator, Ioannidis, ordered the coup against Makarios on 15 July 1974. The Cyprus National Guard, led by Greek officers, occupied the Presidential Palace. Makarios escaped, and was flown out of Cyprus by the British. The former Bishop from Paphos, Gennadios, appointed Nicos Sampson as the new President. His newly chosen ministers were well known for their *enosis* sympathies.[2] However, they did not declare union with Greece. It appears that the primary goal of the Greek Junta was to eliminate Makarios who had severely attacked their regime.[3] Nevertheless, bringing about *enosis* had become an option for the new government at a later stage. According to Sampson's own confession, he was about to proclaim *enosis* when he had to quit as a result of the Turkish intervention.[4]

The coup resulted in several deaths, the exact figures of which are debated.[5] The junta eliminated or detained some Greek Cypriots that were known to support Makarios.[6] It is disputed whether Turkish Cypriots immediately suffered after the coup.[7] It seems that Sampson was cautious not to provoke a Turkish intervention at an early stage by concerted action. In any case, he was not trustworthy in the eyes of the Turkish Cypriot population and Turkey given the brutal role he had played during the 1963/1964 clashes.[8]

1.2. *The Turkish reaction*

1.2.1. The first phase (20–22 July 1974)

In Turkey, the Social Democrat Prime Minister Eçevit, governing in coalition with the National Salvation Party, ordered the landing of the Turkish army on 20 July 1974. The National Guard was not able to defend the island due to its involvement in the coup. On the same day, the UN Security Council adopted a resolution[9] that was primarily prepared to address the coup. Having learnt of the Turkish intervention, the Council added a new § 3 in which it demanded the immediate end to foreign military intervention that did not respect the sovereignty, independence and territorial integrity of Cyprus. Nevertheless, Turkish troops seized Kyrenia on 21 July. The next day, Athens and Ankara agreed a cease-fire upon a

---

[2] Tzermias, loc. cit. (page 2, note 1), pp. 449–450.

[3] L. Rühl, Der Zypernkonflikt von 1974 und der griechisch-türkische Interessenkonflikt, Europaarchiv 1975, p. 699 (701).

[4] Cyprus Mail, 17 July 1975.

[5] The figures vary from 100–200 up to approximately 1000 deaths.

[6] Necatigil, loc. cit. (page 11, note 35), p. 91.

[7] Ertekün, loc. cit. (page 6, note 19), p. 30 states that "16.000 more Turks had to abandon 38 villages". Official Greek Cypriot sources do not refer such massive movements; but see Papadakis, loc. cit. (page 10, note 33), pp. 73 et seq., collecting reports from eyewitnesses about persecution and the degradation of living conditions in Limassol for Turkish Cypriots after the coup, causing their leaving to the north.

[8] W. Hale/J.D. Norton, Die Türkei und die Zypern-Krise, EA 1974, p. 639 (641).

[9] UNSC Resolution 353 of 20 July 1974. For an account of the discussions in the Security Council prior to adoption see Özgür, loc. cit. (page 10, note 34), pp. 89–93.

proposal of US Foreign Minister Kissinger. On the ground, the Turkish troops continued their operation, which earned them another warning from the Security Council.[10] The Greek Junta broke down on 23 July, and Karamanlis returned from exile. At the same time, Sampson resigned as President of Cyprus, and the Speaker of the House of Representatives, Clerides, assumed office. He did not reshuffle Sampsons' cabinet of Ministers until 8 August.[11] At the end of the first phase, Turkey was in control of about 5%[12] of Cypriot territory.

1.2.2. The second phase (14–16 August 1974)

In § 5 of its resolution of 20 July, the Security Council had called on Turkey, Greece and the United Kingdom to enter into consultations. Meeting from 25–30 July 1974 in Geneva, Foreign Ministers Callaghan, Mavros and Güneş consented on a communiqué in which a timely and phased reduction of the number of armed forces on the island was demanded. Furthermore, negotiations over the re-establishment of a constitutional government in Cyprus should be held. In this respect, the three ministers "noted the existence in practice in the Republic of Cyprus of two autonomous administrations, that of the Greek Cypriot Community and that of the Turkish Cypriot Community", affirming that they agreed to consider at the next meeting the problems raised by their existence. The Vice President should consider re-assuming his functions under the 1960 Constitution.

The inter-communal talks started on 8 August 1974. Denktaş demanded a bi-communal and bi-zonal State; the territory of the Turkish Federated State should amount to 34%. Güneş asked for the creation of two Greek Cypriot and six Turkish Cypriot cantons (which together would account for 34% of the territory).[13] Clerides called for a break of 36 to 48 hours in order to hold consultations in Athens and London (where Makarios was). In the night of 13/14 August, the conference broke down. In the eyes of a German commentator, Eçevit felt that the Greek delegation was trying to buy time to mobilise an international coalition against Turkey whereas his General Staff advised him to stabilise their military advantages on the island by a quick second operation.[14] From 14–16 August, the Turkish troops that had meanwhile been re-enforced to 35,000–40,000 soldiers, 250–300 tanks and more than 1000 automobiles, advanced to the "Attila-line". They brought 36,4% of the territory, with about 60% of the island's industry, 65% of its agriculture and 80% of its tourism, under their control.

1.3. *The international reaction*

The UN Security Council adopted four successive resolutions during the second phase of the Turkish intervention. Whereas the first three resolutions merely

[10] UNSC Resolution 354 of 23 July 1974.
[11] Tzermias, loc. cit. (page 2, note 1), p. 457.
[12] Drevet, loc. cit. (page 15, note 13), p. 193.
[13] Tzermias, loc. cit. (page 2, note 1), pp. 461–462.
[14] Rühl, loc. cit. (note 3), Europaarchiv 1975, pp. 699 (704–705).

repeated the call on both sides not to violate the cease-fire agreement,[15] and not to kill members of UNFICYP,[16] the final one of 16 August "records its formal disapproval of the unilateral military action undertaken against the Republic of Cyprus".[17] It also urges the parties to comply immediately with its demand concerning the withdrawal without delay from the Republic of Cyprus of foreign military personnel present otherwise than under the authority of international agreements. The other guarantor powers did not react. It became clear that Greece was not capable of defending Cyprus militarily.[18] Comparably, Britain did not risk a military conflict with Turkey. Finally, the UN Secretary-General brokered intercommunal talks for 6 September 1974, which the Security Council noted with satisfaction.[19] In parallel, the prolongation of UNFICYP was agreed upon in December 1974[20] after Makarios had resumed the President's office on 7 December 1974.

2. Turkey's continued presence in the northern part of Cyprus

2.1. *The demographic changes*

According to Greek Cypriot estimates, the intervention caused 6,000 deaths.[21] The European Commission of Human Rights, in its report of 10 July 1976,[22] pointed to severe violations of human rights committed by the Turkish army against Greek Cypriot civilian population. Also Greek Cypriot troops are said to have attacked civilians, e.g. in three Turkish Cypriot villages (Aloa, Sandallaris and Martha). Official figures point to 1,619 missing Greek Cypriots and some Turkish Cypriots.

Most Greek Cypriots fled from the territories under the control of the Turkish army. The numbers vary between 105,000[23] and 200,000.[24] In any case, about 95% of the Greek Cypriots living in the northern parts of the island left their towns and villages for the south. On the other hand, about 40,000–45,000 Turkish

[15] UNSC Resolution 357 of 14 August 1974; UNSC Resolution 358 of 15 August 1974.

[16] UNSC Resolution 359 of 15 August 1974.

[17] UNSC Resolution 360 of 16 August 1974, § 1.

[18] Joseph, loc. cit. (page 10, note 32), p. 55.

[19] UNSC Resolution 361 of 30 August 1974.

[20] UNSC Resolution 364 of 13 December 1974.

[21] Chrysostomides, loc. cit. (page 8, note 24), p. 176.

[22] European Commission of Human Rights, Applications No. 6780/74 und 6950/75 – Cyprus ./. Turkey, Report of 10.07.1976, Vol. I und II (Annex I–XIV). This report was only published on 31 August 1979 after Resolution DH (79) I of the Committee of Ministers of 20 January 1979. A third State application was filed by Cyprus on 6 September 1977. The Commission's Report of 4 October 1983 was only published after the Committee of Ministers' Decision of 2 April 1992, Resolution DH 92 (12).

[23] Ertekün, loc. cit (page 6, note 19), p. 102.

[24] Press and Information Office, loc. cit. (page 17, note 27), p. 112; Tzermias, loc. cit. (page 2, note 1), p. 468.

Cypriots were still living in the south before the intervention. According to the Vienna III agreement reached in 1975 and the high-level agreement of 1977 between the leaders of the two communities, the Republic, reluctantly, allowed them to settle in the north, reducing the number of Turkish Cypriots in the south to less than 1,000. After the Greek Cypriot exodus had been completed, Turkey started to give incentives to Turkish citizens (mainly from Anatolia) to settle in northern Cyprus, the number of which is disputed between the parties.

2.2. *The Proclamation of the Turkish Republic of Northern Cyprus*

On 13 February 1975, apparently without prior consultation of the Turkish cabinet,[25] the Turkish Cypriot Council of Ministers and the Legislative Assembly declared the foundation of the Turkish Federated State of Cyprus. This entity saw itself as a federated State in an as yet not existing federation. The declaration resolves

> *that the autonomous Turkish Cypriot administration should be restructured and organized on the basis of a secular and federal state, until such time as the 1960 Constitution of the Republic, the basic articles of which were determined by international agreements in compliance with international law, is amended in a similar manner to become the Constitution of the Federal Republic of Cyprus, and until the said Federal Republic is established.*[26]

A constitutional assembly of 50 representatives elaborated a Constitution that was later on adopted, on 8 June 1975, per referendum.[27] In 1975 and 1981, Rauf Denktaş was re-elected as President. The UN Security Council regretted the establishment of the Turkish Federated State of Cyprus as compromising the intercommunal talks.[28]

On 15 November 1983 the Legislative Assembly unanimously adopted a resolution according to which the Turkish Republic of Northern Cyprus (TRNC) was declared an independent State. Whereas the Turkish government recognised the new entity as a State and maintained that Turkey stood as a Guarantor power for its existence, the United Kingdom and Greece sharply condemned the move. On 18 November 1983, the UN Security Council declared that the proclamation of the TRNC should be considered "null and void".[29] The Council called upon all States not to recognise the TRNC. Although sympathetic to the Turkish Cypriot cause, also Muslim States like Pakistan (which had voted against the Security

[25] L. Ruehl, Der Zypernkonflikt, die Weltmächte und die europäische Sicherheit, EA 1976, p. 19 (30).

[26] The declaration is contained in UN-Secretary-General Report S/11624 of 18 February 1975 and reprinted in Ertekün, loc. cit. (page 6, note 19), pp. 259–260.

[27] Reprinted in A.P. Blaustein/G.H. Flanz, Constitutions of the countries of the World. Supplement Cyprus (Ö.A. Özgür). New York 1978, Doc. 6.

[28] UNSC Resolution 367 of 12 March 1975, § 2.

[29] UNSC Resolution 541 of 18 November 1983. For a detailed account of the relevant discussions in the Security Council see Necatigil, loc. cit. (page 11, note 35), pp. 234–235.

Council Resolution), Bangladesh and other Arab States abstained from recognising the TRNC. Rather, a press communiqué of the Commonwealth Heads of Government, meeting in New Delhi from 23 to 29 November 1983, fully endorsed the UN line. In 1991, the Organisation of Islamic Conference refused to admit the TRNC as a full member. The "Muslim Turkish Cypriot Community" was treated as an observer since 1974.[30]

2.3. *The internal set-up of the TRNC*

After the proclamation of independence, a constitutional assembly worked out the TRNC Constitution. 70% of the voters in the northern part of Cyprus accepted the basic law on 5 May 1985. The Constitution resembles the Turkish Constitution of 1982, but some elements of the 1960 Cypriot Constitution can also be traced back.[31]

According to Article 1, the Republic is based on the principles of democracy, social justice, rule of law and secularism. A catalogue of human rights (except the right to assembly) is modelled along the European Convention on Human Rights. There is separation of powers between the Parliament, the executive (President and Council of Ministers) and the judiciary (Supreme Court and District Courts). Like in Turkey, the Constitution provides for the establishment of a Republican Security Council (Art. 111), which was, however, never established.[32]

The status of the Turkish army, with its approximately 35,000 soldiers, is not regulated. The Turkish commander for northern Cyprus also controls the Turkish Cypriot police forces and secret services.[33] The TRNC budget is largely financed by yearly direct payments from Turkey. The currency in the northern part of Cyprus is the Turkish lira.

B. LEGAL EVALUATION

1. The illegality of the Turkish intervention

The Turkish army used force, as prohibited in Article 2(4) UN-Charter, when entering Cyprus and establishing control over 37% of its territory. The UN Security

[30] On the attitude of the OIC see in more detail Bouony, loc. cit. (page 29, note 82), p. 122 et seq.

[31] C. Rumpf, Comments on the Legal Status of Cyprus: Issues of Conflict and their Courses, in T. Giegerich (ed.) The EU Accession of Cyprus, p. 37 (46–50) with details on the TRNC constitution.

[32] Necatigil, loc. cit. (page 11, note 35), p. 303.

[33] This fact is acknowledged by members of the Turkish Cypriot opposition, like Alpay Durduran (see G. Gülistan, Zypern: Hoffnung auf eine baldige Konfliktlösung, in: Südosteuropa-Mitteilungen 1997, pp. 301, 305, note 14) or Mustafa Akinci (see C. Dodd, The Annan Plan and the Cyprus Conflict, in: Yeditepe Üniversitesi Hukuk Fakültesi Dergisi I/1, 2004, pp. 99 and 105).

Council labelled the first phase of the Turkish operation as "foreign military intervention"[34] and found that the second phase constituted a "unilateral military action undertaken against the Republic of Cyprus".[35] The decisive question is therefore whether the action can be justified under international law.

A discussion about humanitarian intervention as a possible customary law justification to intervene is unnecessary in this respect, since the factual requirements were not met in any case.[36] The deplorable living situation in the enclaves cannot be equated with any situation possibly triggering a right to military intervention (such as genozide or crimes against humanity), and there are no reports about systematic and widespread violations of the basic rights of Turkish Cypriots after the coup. As an anticipatory action, the intervention was premature and of a nature and duration in excess of what might have been necessary to achieve a humanitarian objective.[37]

However, more seriously, Turkey claims that Article IV (2) of the Treaty of Guarantee contains a relevant authorisation for its action. It reads:

> *In the event of a breach of the provisions of the present Treaty, Greece, Turkey and the United Kingdom undertake to consult together with respect to the representations or measures necessary to ensure observance of those provisions. In so far as common or concerted action may not prove possible, each of the three guaranteeing Powers reserves the right to take action with the sole aim of re-establishing the State of affairs created by the present Treaty.*

1.1. *The validity of the Treaty of Guarantee*

Before scrutinising the requirements of Article IV, it must be shown that the Treaty of Guarantee of 1960 was still applicable in 1974. Whereas it is impossible to apply the Vienna Convention on the Law of Treaties of 1969 retroactivly (Article 4), recourse must be taken to customary international law. As most of the relevant rules are, however, codified in the Vienna Convention,[38] the latter may serve as an indirect yardstick. Greek Cypriot publications often complain that the Zurich-London Agreements were not freely negotiated, but imposed on the inhabitants of Cyprus, concluding that the Treaty of Guarantee was therefore invalid.[39]

According to Article 51 of the Vienna Convention, force exercised against representatives of the State in order to coerce the signing of a treaty is a ground of

---

[34] UNSC Resolution 353 of 20 July 1974, § 2.

[35] UNSC Resolution 360 of 16 August 1974, § 1.

[36] Chrysostomides, loc. cit. (page 8, note 24), p. 131 et seq.

[37] R. St. MacDonald, International Law and the Conflict in Cyprus, in: The Canadian Yearbook of International Law 1981, 1, p. 28.

[38] ICJ, Legal Consequences for States of the Continued Presence of South Africa in Namibia (South West Africa) Notwithstanding Security Council Resolution 276 (1970), Advisory Opinion, ICJ Reports 1971, p. 16 (45), § 94.

[39] Press and Information Office, loc. cit. (page 17, note 27), pp. 6–8; Joseph, loc. cit. (page 10, note 32), p. 97.

invalidity. Coercion comprises acts affecting the representative as an individual, e.g. by threatening to harm his professional or private life. In the London conference, Makarios was confronted with the "serious consequence" in case he would not sign the Cyprus treaties. However, such threats were of a political nature, referring to the possible implementation of the McMillan plan by the United Kingdom. Such a political "take it or leave it" situation does not constitute coercion against a representative.[40]

Similarly, Article 52 of the Vienna Convention on "coercion against a State" does neither provide for a ground for invalidation. As is well known, this provision relates to the use of military force only, whereas political or economic pressure is not comprised. A proposal of several delegations at the Vienna Conference in 1969 pointing in that direction was firmly rejected by the Western powers. The Conference finally condemned political or economic pressure (which may in extreme cases amount to illegal intervention into domestic affairs), but such pressure does not constitute a reason to invalidate a treaty. Accordingly, the British political threat to opt for another Cyprus plan, did not amount to prohibited coercion against the (not yet existing)[41] State of Cyprus.[42]

Finally, there is no support in international law for the allegation that the Cyprus treaties were invalid because of inequality between the signatories. The negotiation power of Makarios and Küçük was certainly inferior to the one of the United Kingdom and the two interested States, Greece and Turkey. However, mere inequality of bargaining powers does not constitute coercion.[43] Neither is there in customary law or in the Vienna Convention a separate ground for invalidity of "unequal treaties".

1.2. *The requirements of Article IV (2) of the Treaty of Guarantee*

1.2.1. Breach of the Treaty

Article IV applies "in the event of a breach of the provisions of the present Treaty". In Article II, Greece, Turkey and the United Kingdom "recognise and guarantee the independence, territorial integrity and security of the Republic of Cyprus, and also the State of affairs established by the Basic Articles of its Constitution".

With its direct involvement in the coup d'Etat of 15 July 1974, Greece bluntly violated its obligation under Article II. The military overthrow of the government

[40] K. Özersay, The validity and scope of the 1959–1960 Cyprus Treaties, in: Resat Arim (ed.) Cyprus and international law, p. 11 (25).

[41] According to Article 195 of the Constitution, Makarios and Küçük, as the first elected President and Vice-President, were deemed to have had the power to sign and conclude on behalf of Cyprus the founding Treaties.

[42] Özersay, loc. cit. (note 40), p. 28.

[43] Insofar correct Mendelson, The application of "The Republic of Cyprus" to join the European Union, UN Doc A/51/951 and S/1997/585, reprinted in: Ertekün (ed.), The Status of the Two Peoples in Cyprus – Legal Opinions, pp. 137–179, § 83.

put into question the territorial integrity and security of the Republic. Furthermore, the instalment of a pro-*enosis* government ran contrary to the independence of Cyprus and violated the Basic Articles on the election of the President. Hence, a breach of the Treaty by Greece was evident on 20 July 1974, when the first phase of the intervention began.[44]

Slightly more complicated was the situation on the eve of the second phase, 13 August 1974. Meanwhile, Clerides, as the Speaker of the House, had assumed the office of President during Makarios' absence. One author believes that therefore, the constitutional order had been restored so that a breach of the treaty did no longer exist at that date.[45] This argument overlooks that the reasons for a vacancy in the office of the President as outlined in Article 44 (1) of the Constitution, do not include a violent removal of the President. Hence, the stepping in of Clerides was more pragmatic than according to the letters of Article 44 (2) of the Constitution. Makarios' absence in the office of President was therefore still a direct consequence of Greece's breach of the Treaty. For that reason, also on 13 August 1974, the breach of the Treaty of Guarantee remained real.

1.2.2. Consultations between the Guarantor powers

Under Article IV (1), Greece, Turkey and the United Kingdom undertake to consult together with respect to measures necessary to ensure observance of the breached treaty provisions. The Turkish government consulted with the British government in London, but not with Greece prior to 20 July. However, due to Greece's breach and the absence of the Greek government at the consultations in London despite a formal British invitation, Turkey did not have to do so.[46] Therefore, Turkey met this procedural condition.

1.2.3. Right to take action

Article IV (2) reserves each of the three guarantor powers "the right to take action with the sole aim of re-establishing the State of affairs created by the present Treaty". In accordance with Articles 31 and 32 of the Vienna Convention the wording, context and object and purpose of this phrase shall be analysed, before having recourse to additional means, e.g. travaux préparatoires.

The meaning of "action" is not clear. Upon request of the Greek government, the UN Legal Department issued an opinion on 12 May 1959, concluding that the Treaty of Guarantee does not include military action. If military action were allowed, it would have been restricted by the condition to the prior use of peaceful means of dispute settlement.[47] This opinion suggests on the one hand that the wording "action" should be construed narrowly. On the other hand it also admits that use of military force is not out of the normal meaning of the notion

[44] MacDonald, loc. cit. (note 37), CYIL 1981, p. 5.

[45] Tzermias, loc. cit. (page 2, note 1), p. 457.

[46] MacDonald, loc. cit. (note 37), CYIL 1981, p. 5.

[47] Cited by Tzermias, loc. cit. (page 2, note 1), p. 227.

"action".[48] The wording of Article IV of the Treaty of Guarantee is thus rather neutral in this respect.

The context of the phrase is neither conclusive. For sure, the right to action is construed as the *ultima ratio* when consultations under Article IV (1) fail to achieve a satisfactory result. However, this context does not support any interpretation which sort of "action" was deemed to be necessary.

Therefore, the object and purpose of Article IV (2) is decisive. Action is allowed in order to restore the constitutional order of Cyprus. The Treaty of Alliance provided for the stationing of Greek and Turkish contingents on the island. Restoration of the constitutional order was thus thought to include the use of police or military powers.[49] Also prevention of "Enosis", another explicit purpose of the Treaty of Guarantee, could hardly be achieved without military means.[50] If the term "action" excluded military action, Article IV (2) would be ineffective.[51] Hence, "action" in the sense of Article IV (2) covers a military intervention as the measure of last resort.[52] Such was also the opinion of the British government, as stated in the UN Security Council back in 1964.[53]

The travaux préparatoires of that norm do not contradict this result. In the Zurich deliberations, Turkey had asked to use the wording "military action". Later on, it accepted the omission of the adjective.[54] However, that does not mean that the negotiators had excluded military action as a possible option. Rather, the Greek Foreign Minister Averoff stated on 18 February:

> *(. . .) so I want to make myself an official declaration that my Government sees this right of intervention which will be used only if there is a Turkish attempt at partition, or a Turkish attempt to throw out the Government. We will never make an intervention by our own armed forces or by other means, if some Turkish school boys shout about partition or if there is an article in the newspapers on that subject.*[55]

E contrario, the Greek Government saw a right to military intervention under Article IV (2) of the Treaty of Guarantee in cases of partition or of overthrow of the Cypriot government.[56]

Some writers contend that this interpretation would violate the supremacy of UN law, as laid down in Article 103 of the UN-Charter. According to their view, the Treaty of Guarantee could never allow for a military intervention otherwise

[48] Compare Article 42 of the UN Charter speaking of "military action".

[49] M. L. Evriades, The Legal Dimension of the Cyprus Conflict, (1975) 10 Texas International Law Journal, p. 227 (250).

[50] Necatigil, loc. cit. (page 11, note 35), pp. 130–131.

[51] Rumpf, loc. cit. (page 8, note 24), EuGRZ 1997, p. 543.

[52] MacDonald, loc. cit. (note 37), p. 7.

[53] 19 UN SCOR, 1098th meeting, para. 12.

[54] Tzermias, loc. cit. (page 2, note 1), p. 227.

[55] Public Record Office, FO 371/14–4–641–163661 (18 February 1959), pp. 12–13, cited by Özersay, loc. cit. (note 40), note 98.

[56] Özersay, loc. cit. (note 40), p. 36.

forbidden by Article 2 (4) of the Charter, because UN law precedes bilateral treaty law.[57] In the alternative Article 53 of the Vienna Convention is invoked, arguing that the Treaty Guarantee violates a peremptory norm of international law (*jus cogens*), namely the prohibition of the use of force.[58]

Both assertions are correct, in as far as a bilateral treaty allows the use of force against a third State, which has not consented to the intervention. However, if a State has allowed other States to intervene in order to uphold its own sovereignty and constitutional order, there is no violation of Article 2 (4) UN-Charter or any other peremptory norm of international law. Such use of force is consistent with one purpose of the UN, namely the protection of the territorial integrity of Member States by third States in accordance with their will.[59]

The signature of the Cypriot government under Article IV of the Treaty of Guarantee in 1960 constituted an *ex ante* invitation to the Guarantor powers to intervene. There is no principle under international law that restricts the freedom of State to consent *in abstracto ex ante* to intervention. The contention that only consent of the contemporaneous government may legalize a foreign intervention because otherwise the right to self-determination would be violated[60] is hard to reconcile with the sovereignty of the same people, organized in a state, to enter into treaty commitments to that effect. Only if a treaty would give "carte blanche" for foreign intervention the question of its validity may arise; that is not the case when a treaty carefully defines the conditions and limits of intervention.[61]

In that regard, the view of the guarantor power United Kingdom is of interest. As early as 1964, the UK representative in the Security Council rebutted allegations brought forward by Cyprus against the Treaty of Guarantee on the basis of Article 2 (4) of the Charter. He stated that

> *the question whether or not the use of force was permissible under the existing rules of international law and, in particular, under the United Nations Charter, must always depend on the circumstances and the purposes for which it was used. (. . .) In the case of the Treaty of Guarantee concerning Cyprus, its purposes were entirely in accordance with the obligations contained in Article 2 para. 4 of the Charter. The right to*

[57] MacDonald, loc. cit. (note 37), CYIL 1981, pp. 11–15; Tzermias, loc. cit. (page 2, note 1), p. 465; Chryostomides, loc. cit (page 8, note 24), p. 125 et seq; Melakopides, EU enlargement in the mediterranean: Human Rights and the resolution of the Cyprus-Turkey legal and political conundrum, CJES 2001, p. 1 (12).

[58] See Abi-Saab/Blumenwitz/Cassesse/Cot/Crawford/Dugard/Dupuy/Fisler-Damrosch/Flintermans/Franck/Greenwood/Hafner/Lowe/McRae/Pellet/Rideau/Schermers/Simma/Tomuschat, The Treaty of Guarantee and the Legality of the Use of Force in Cyprus, Nicosia 14.12.2000, cited in Palley, loc. cit. (page xii, note 3), p. 149. Unlike other opinions commissioned by the Cyprus Government, this document is not publicly available.

[59] Necatigil, loc. cit. (page 11, note 35), p. 118.

[60] L. Doswald-Beck, The Legal Validity of Military Intervention by Invitation of the Government, BYIL 1985, p. 189 (245).

[61] Özersay, loc. cit. (note 40), pp. 41–42.

> *take action reserved to the guaranteeing Powers as provided in Article IV (2) of the Treaty could only be resorted to in the event of a breach of the provisions of the Treaty, i.e. in circumstances in which there was a threat to the independence, territorial integrity or security of the Republic of Cyprus as established by the Basic Articles of its Constitution. The intervention, however, must be limited to such action as would be necessary for re-establishing the state of affairs created by the Treaty.*[62]

It follows there from that both Turkey and the UK considered the conditions defined in Article IV of the Treaty of Guarantee to be sufficiently precise for justifying a right of intervention based on *ex ante* consent. This consent had been given in 1960 by a Cyprus government to render the external guarantees for both communities effective. If, to the contrary, the Treaty of Guarantee would have asked for actual and contemporaneous consent of the (Greek Cypriot dominated) Government to intervention of a Guarantor power (in particular Turkey) in a given case, this would have minimised the prohibition of *enosis* and the constitutional guarantees for the Turkish Cypriots in Article I of the Treaty of Guarantee to rather theoretical provisions, because every (Greek Cypriot dominated) Government could then refuse to consent to foreign intervention and proceed unimpededly with union with Greece or with an abrogation of the Constitution.

Finally, and significantly, also the Cyprus Government sought additional procedureal guarantees from the Security Council in April 2005, fearing that the Annan Plan had not clarified the uncertain situation whether a right of Turkey for unilateral military intervention under Article IV of the Treaty of Guarantee continued to exist or not,[63] instead of claiming outright that such intervention would be in any event unlawful as a violation of *jus cogens*.

Therefore, Article IV (2) of the Treaty of Guarantee, by providing *ex ante* consent for certain prescribed situations does not contravene Articles 2 (4) and 103 of the UN-Charter. It does not have to be interpreted as excluding the use of force. It can justify a military intervention of a Guarantor power if its procedural and substantial conditions are met even if the Government then in power would not give its actual consent to that intervention. It follows therefrom that Turkey had the right to intervene in Cyprus with military means although the Sampson government did not actually declare its consent for this operation.

1.2.4. Re-establishment of the State of affairs

The relevant action must serve the "sole aim of re-establishing the State of affairs created by the present Treaty". One difficulty of applying this requirement lies in the fact that the "state of affairs" refers to the bi-communal structure of the Republic of Cyprus. This was already broken down for nearly 10 years. The "revised" state of affairs consisted of a Greek-Cypriot-dominated Republic of Cyprus that tolerates, albeit not formally, the *de-facto* self-administration of the

[62] Repertoire of the Practice of the UN Security Council, Supplement 1964–1965, p. 201.

[63] Palley, loc. cit. (page xii, note 3), p. 151.

Turkish Cypriots outside the procedures and institutions as laid down in the 1960 Constitution in certain areas of the island. Any military intervention would thus have to serve at least the purpose of preventing a further deterioration of the position of Turkish Cypriots in Cyprus.

Turkey was never very explicit about the aim of the *first phase*. One goal was certainly to prevent *enosis*, which was perfectly legitimate under the Treaty of Guarantee. Also the UN Security Council, in its resolution of 20 July 1974, spoke about the "necessity to restore the constitutional structure of the Republic of Cyprus established and guaranteed by international agreement".[64] It demanded an end to foreign intervention "that is in contravention of paragraph 1 above" only. Since Paragraph 1 cites the sovereignty, independence and territorial integrity of Cyprus, any intervention that respects these principles would receive the blessing of the Security Council. Comparably, the Consultative Assembly of the Council of Europe, in a resolution of 29 July 1974, believed that the Turkish Government had exercised its "right of intervention in accordance with Article IV of the Guarantee Treaty of 1960".[65] Allegedly, the Greek Supreme Court of Appeals, in an individual case concerning public liability for wrongful acts of Greek military in Cyprus, also found that Turkey intervened on 20 July 1974 "due to reasonable ground according to the Treaty of Guarantee".[66] In conclusion, Turkey's first phase can be judged as still compatible with the international *jus ad bellum*.[67]

However, as regards the *second phase*, the analysis is different. The Turkish government officially declared that the Turkish troops should restore law and order according to the Treaty of Guarantee.[68] That statement is rather vague. Even a Turkish Cypriot author concedes that the second phase did not serve the purpose of re-establishing the previous state of affairs. He tries to justify that deviation as being impracticable after the breakdown of the 1960 Republic and in a situation where UN led negotiations about a new status quo had already begun.[69] That argument is not convincing. Under Article IV (2) of the Treaty of Guarantee Turkey's intervention could have been limited to assist in the restoration of the elected (Greek Cypriot) President. Furthermore, it could have also – as observed by the three Ministers in the Geneva declaration of 30 July 1974 – put his weight in favor of the return of the Turkish Cypriot Vice-President into office and worked for the re-integration of the 1960 bi-communal system. However, the establish-

[64] UNSC Resolution 353 of 20 July 1974, Preamble, 6th indent.

[65] Consultative Assembly of the Council of Europe, Resolution 573 of 29 July 1974 (Council of Europe Doc. 3464).

[66] Supreme Court of Appeals, Case 2658/79 of 31 March 1979, cited by Necatigil, loc. cit. (page 11, note 35), p. 112, note 15.

[67] Another question is whether the Turkish army equally respected the *jus in bello* during the first phase. Serious doubts have been raised to that effect, pointing in particular to the massacre of Kyrenia on 21 July 1974.

[68] Declaration of the Turkish Government of 27 August 1974, reprinted in: EA 1974, D 456.

[69] Necatigil, loc. cit. (page 11, note 35), p. 132, note 64.

ment of a distinct geographical area of control through forcing the departure of the Greek Cypriot population does not serve any legitimate purpose under the Treaty of Guarantee. Rather than protecting the independence and territorial integrity of Cyprus against the Greek Coup, Turkey engaged into a territorial division of Cyprus, which constituted itself a violation of Turkey's undertaking under Article I (2) of the Treaty not to engage in any activity likely to promote partition of the island.[70]

3.1. *Conclusion*

Turkey could reasonably claim that its initial intervention was a legitimate exercise of its right under the Article IV (2) of the Treaty of Guarantee. But the second phase of the Turkish military intervention could not be justified under the Treaty since it did not serve the aim of re-establishing the previous state of affairs.

2. The partial irrelevance of the TRNC under international law

The reorganisation of the Turkish Cypriot administration on 13 February 1975 as a "Turkish Federated State of Cyprus" was peculiar. That entity saw itself as a federated state within the Republic although Cyprus was not organized as a federation. Nevertheless, from an international law point of view such changes did not affect any other States, but remained internal. Accordingly, they could only be assessed against the yardstick of the 1960 constitution. The internal administration of the Turkish Cypriots became, however, a matter of international law with the declaration of the TRNC in 1983, since this entity defines itself as an independent State.

2.1. *No international justification of the TRNC under the right to self-determination*

As a preliminary issue, one has to verify whether the foundation of the TRNC can be justified as an act of self-determination of Turkish Cypriots. Such has been the official position of the Turkish Cypriot leadership.[71]

---

[70] Reddaway, loc. cit. (page 3, note 10), p. 166; Filos, loc. cit. (page 5, note 16), p. 195. Chrysostomides, loc. cit. (page 8, note 24), p. 127; Third Report from the Foreign Affairs Committee – Session 1986–87, H.c.23, § 99. Dissenting Lauterpacht, loc. cit. (note 23), p. 9 (13, § 15) pointing to the Council of Europe resolution of 29 July 1974. However, this resolution does not assess the second phase of the intervention.

[71] See e.g. the position by Mr. Denktaş during the inter-communal talks in 1990, when he referred to Lauterpacht's Opinion of 10 July 1990, entitled "Turkish Republic of Northern Cyprus – The status of the two communities in Cyprus, reprinted in N.M. Ertekün (ed.), The status of the two peoples in Cyprus – Legal Opinions, pp. 15–38.

As has been seen above, Turkish Cypriots did not hold such right in 1960 when the Republic of Cyprus was created – that right belonged to the Cypriot people as a whole in the process of decolonization. Accordingly, any argument along the line that the "old" Turkish Cypriot right to self-determination of 1960 was just "exercised again" in 1983,[72] is without merit. In addition such conceptual link with the pre-1960 situation must fail, because in 1983 there was no situation of "colonisation" against which the Turkish Cypriots could have had the right to act.

Rather, another aspect of the right to self-determination may be of relevance. If one accepts that this right may also apply to a people not yet organized in a sovereign state but being part of a pluri-ethnic state,[73] the question of secession arises. Whereas secession is generally regarded as illegal because it infringes the territorial integrity of a state, contemporary international law acknowledges nevertheless certain narrow cases of lawful secession. In particular, there is a right to secession of a people living in a multi-ethnic state against a non-representative oppressive regime.[74] This *cas de figure* was mentioned in the Friendly-Relations Declaration of 1970. The General Assembly reaffirmed the need to preserve the territorial integrity of sovereign and independent states, provided that they are

> *possessed of a government representing the whole people belonging to the territory without distinction to race, creed or colour.*[75]

Along the same lines as the UN General Assembly, the Arbitration Commission, established in the context of the Yugoslavia Conference held that the Serbian population in Croatia and Bosnia-Hercegovina could enjoy the full range of minority rights in the new Republics but not the right to self-determination,[76] since there was a government fulfilling the above-mentioned criteria. Only if such representativeness is flatly denied by an oppressive regime, may a people suffering from such oppresion inside its own state claim a right to secession. Such could be the measure of last resort, if the government of the country has committed grave crimes to the detriment of the group concerned.[77]

---

[72] Necatigil, loc. cit. (page 11, note 35), p. 228.

[73] Heinze questions that self-determination applies to the Turkish Cypriots, arguing that self-determination can only refer to existing states and not to peoples (C. Heinze, The present stage of the Cyprus conflicts with special reference to the principle of self-determination, in: Heinze (ed.), Cyprus 2000, p. 30 (44 et seq.). His considerations remain purely theoretical and do not have recourse to any relevant contemporary international practice.

[74] Insofar correct Necatigil, loc. cit. (page 11, note 35), pp. 211 and 218.

[75] Resolution 2625 (XXV), 24 October 1970, Section on the principle of equal rights and self-determination of peoples, para. 7.

[76] Conference on Yugoslavia, Arbitration Commission, Opinion No. 2 of 11 January 1992, reprinted in 31 ILM (1992), p. 1497 (1498).

[77] See D. Murswieck, The Issue of a Right of Secession – Reconsidered", in: C. Tomuschat (ed.) Modern Law of Self-Determination, p. 21 (27).

Applied to the Turkish Cypriots such a right of secession did not materialize for them in the period of 1963–1974.[78] Albeit being confronted with a situation of civil strife and attempts of domination as from 1964, the Turkish Cypriots did not take up the possibility to return to constitutional government. Hence, it cannot be argued that secession is an act of "self-defence" against forceful oppression by a non-representative government.

The territorial changes brought about by the Turkish intervention in 1974 and the exchange of population in 1975 do not alter this analysis. The call of the three Foreign Ministers at the Geneva conference of 30 July 1974 that the Turkish Cypriot Vice-President may re-assume its office did, once again, not bear fruit. Rather, the second phase of the Turkish intervention created a territory in northern Cyprus under *de facto* Turkish administration. Such territorial base for the Turkish Cypriot community may have improved Turkish Cypriot chances to organise a successful secession, which, like in the case of Bangladesh's secession from Pakistan in 1971 may then later on also be regarded by the international community as legitimate.[79] But these territorial changes in Cyprus do not fulfill the criteria of a rightful secession against a non-representative oppresive regime. Finally, Article 1 of the Treaty of Guarantee outlawed partition of Cyprus, rendering the foundation of the TRNC unlawful. The UN Security Council expressly subscribed to this analysis.[80]

2.2. *No independent Statehood*

Irrespective of the question of whether the TRNC may claim to have been founded in accordance with international law (*quod non est*), it may nevertheless carry the attributes of effective statehood. It is therefore necessary to assess this claim by applying the customary law principles on Statehood and recognition.

The prevailing view,[81] shaping today's international law practice,[82] is that recognition is declaratory and does not create a State. Other States cannot determine

---

[78] See above Chapter II B 1.2. Dissenting E. Olgun, Confederation: The Last Chance for establishing a New Partnership in Cyprus, Perceptions – Journal of international Affairs, March-May 2001, 1 (13), arguing that after the destruction of the 1960 partnership "through force of arms", the Turkish Cypriots enjoy a right to self-determination and statehood.

[79] Insofar correct Necatigil, loc. cit. (p. 11, note 35), pp. 212–213.

[80] UNSC Resolution 541 of 18 November 1983, 3rd recital: "Considering that this declaration is incompatible with the 1960 Treaty concerning the establishment of the Republic of Cyprus and the 1960 Treaty of Guarantee".

[81] Akehurst/Malanczuk, loc. cit. (p. 7, note 22), p. 84 with further references.

[82] See for example Opinions Nos. 1, 4–7 of the Arbitration Committee of the Conference on Yugoslavia concerning the recognition of Bosnia and Hercegovina, Croatia, the former Yugoslav Republic of Macedonia and Slovenia by the Member States of the European Community. Opinion No. 1 clearly sets out the framework, noting that the effects of recognition by other States are "purely declaratory" (31 ILM (1992), p. 1488 (1495).

whether the TRNC exists as an independent State under international law or not. Therefore, Resolution 541 of the UN Security Council, which considers the establishment of the TRNC as null and void, has not settled the question.[83] Neither is it of interest whether States might be under an international obligation not to recognise the TRNC because it owes its existence to the illegal use of force by Turkey.[84]

For independent Statehood it is only decisive whether certain objective criteria are met. Article 1 of the Montevideo Convention of 26 December 1933 about the rights and obligations of States lists a permanent population, a defined territory, a government and the capacity to enter into relations with other States. However, practice has shown that there is no consensus on the fourth requirement, as the recognition of Guinea-Bissau as an independent State in 1974 has demonstrated. Whereas the US-American government asked for an international capacity to act,[85] the German and Swiss governments only referred to the first three criteria.[86]

There is a permanent population in northern Cyprus. Its small size (of less than approximately 100,000 Turkish Cypriots in 1983) does not change the picture. Many mini-States like Nauru, Palau, Sao Tomé or East-Timor are members of the UN. The Turkish Cypriot population can therefore constitute the basis for a State.[87] The question whether the Turkish settlers can be regarded as a legal part of the population in northern Cyprus is therefore irrelevant in this respect.[88] 37% of the Cypriot territory north of the UN buffer zone with approximately 3250 km^2 constitutes a sufficiently defined territory. For the analysis of effective statehood, it is irrelevant that the Republic of Cyprus regards the very same territory as belonging to it.[89] However, the third criterion, which is the existence of a gov-

---

[83] Pernthaler, loc. cit. (p. 7, note 22), p. 122.

[84] The General Assembly's Friendly Relations Declaration 2625 (XXV) states: "No territorial acquisition resulting from the threat or use of force shall be recognised as legal". Therefore the legality of an acquisition of northern Cyprus (by Turkey through annexation) would certainly be affected by illegal use of force. A different question is, however, how to assess the Statehood of an entity that was established on the territory. In the cases of Manchukuo it was not Japan's use of force with respect to the territory that led to non-recognition of Statehood, but the lack of independent government from Japan (see Crawford, loc. cit., p. 32, note 89, pp. 59–60).

[85] AJIL 68 (1974), p. 309.

[86] See the respective declarations reprinted in ZaöRV 1975, 777 and Müller-Wildhaber, Praxis des Völkerrechts, p. 156.

[87] Necatigil, loc. cit. (page 11, note 35), p. 314; D.K. Nanopoulos, L'adhésion de la République de Chypre et de la Turquie à l'Union européenne et les perspectives de résolution du conflit, p. 18.

[88] For that reason inconclusive Filos, loc. cit. (page 5, note 16), p. 198; Chrysostomides, loc. cit. (p. 8, note 24), pp. 263–264. Even if the settlers outnumbered the Turkish Cypriots that would not change the fact that the latter, as small as their size might be, could constitute a people for Statehood.

[89] Necatigil, loc. cit. (page 11, note 35), p. 320.

ernment with a capacity to establish and maintain legal order in the sense of constitutional autonomy,[90] has to be carefully scrutinised.

In the case of the TRNC, there is a civil government, a legislature and a functioning judiciary under a self-given Constitution. However, at least two aspects may compromise the independence of Turkish Cypriot self-governance: the position of the Turkish army and the large financial influence of Turkey on the TRNC budget.

First, the presence of the Turkish army encroaches on Turkish Cypriot self-governance due to its very broad powers. It is true that Statehood is not put into question if a government invites a foreign army to be deployed on its territory for mutual defence purposes. This has been the practice of many States. Especially parts of the US army and the Soviet army were largely deployed throughout the world on an invitation by the host government. It is therefore arguable that the Turkish army is on TRNC soil with the consent of the latter like any other friendly army.[91] In the case of the Turkish army in northern Cyprus, there are, however, several differences. Amounting to 35,000–40,000 soldiers, the army constitutes a very large segment of the overall population as compared to approximately 100,000 Turkish Cypriot citizens. The Turkish army does not confine itself to narrow tasks of defence against hypothetical Greek Cypriot aggression. The command over the TRNC police and the secret services[92] allows Turkey to regulate aspects of internal security and border control, which would normally be a matter of Turkish Cypriot self-government. The Turkish military is also said to exercise direct influence on internal politics and the policy of various ministries.

Second, it is not uncommon for some States to depend on external financial contributions. Some least developed States only survive because they receive development aid. In the case of the TRNC, however, there is again one important difference. Donations are granted *exclusively* by Turkey, whereas other poor countries' income is at least somewhat diversified. Even if no direct conditionality can be proven, it appears likely that the yearly and extraordinary Turkish contributions to the TRNC budget (which make up to about 60% of it) can be used to influence TRNC policy directly.[93] Hence, the economic dependence also compromises the political independence of the TRNC.[94]

---

[90] Akehurst/Malanczuk, loc. cit. (page 7, note 22), p. 77.

[91] Leigh, loc. cit. (p. 9, note 30), p. 65, note 22; D. Blumenwitz, The legal status of Greek Cypriots and Turkish Cypriots as parties of a future agreement for Cyprus, Opinion of 19 June 1991, in: Ertekün (ed.), The Status of the Two Peoples in Cyprus – Legal Opinions, p. 85 (89).

[92] The official Turkish Cypriot line simply claims that Turkish forces do not exercise governmental authority or control over the territory; Necatigil, loc. cit. (page 11, note 35), p. 327.

[93] The Presidential elections in 2000 may serve as an example in this regard. Whereas 43, 7% of the votes in the first round of 15 April 2000 supported Denktaş, there were 30, 1% of the votes in favour of his competitor Eroğlu. On 19 April, after a meeting of the leaders of the political parties, Eroğlu suddenly declared that he will not contest the second round, with the effect that Denktaş stayed in office for another mandate. The same day,

In sum, the European Court of Human Rights was quite correct when it assumed that Turkey exercises jurisdiction over northern Cyprus,[95] stating:

> *having effective overall control over northern Cyprus, Turkey's responsibility cannot be confined to the acts of its own soldiers or officials in northern Cyprus but must also be engaged by virtue of the acts of the local administration which survives by virtue of Turkish military and other support.*[96]

In a strictly doctrinal sense, this remark only refers to the question whether human rights violations in northern Cyprus can be imputed to Turkey, and does not scrutinise the statehood of the TRNC. However, the Court's ruling avoids implied recognition of the TRNC[97] and confirms the overall international impression that, in view of the Turkish military control on the ground and the need for substantial yearly financial transfers from Turkey to northern Cyprus, the TRNC is far from being independent.[98]

2.3. *The validity of TRNC legal acts*

A related question concerns the validity of TRNC legal acts. Can it be concluded that legal acts of the TRNC are devoid of any value because the latter is not an independent State under international law?

Turkey announced a credit worth 100 million $ to the TRNC. An observer, who does not support any Greek Cypriot view, has qualified this as "manipulation et épisode scandaleuse" (S. Suvarierol, La question de l'adhésion de Chypre à l'Union Européenne et le Problème de la République Turque de Chypre-Nord, www.ceri-sciences-po.org, Septembre 2001, p. 15.).

[94] For more details see e.g. the interviews with Turkish Cypriot politicians recorded by Papadakis (loc. cit., page 10, note 33), pp. 106 et seq.

[95] The case law under the Convention started with several decision of the European Commission on Human Rights. It admitted first the two inter-state applications No. 6780/1974 and 6950/1975 (reported in DR 2, 125) and also the third application No. 8007/77 (reported in DR 13, 85), all directed against Turkey by establishing the Turkey bears responsibility for the alleged acts in northern Cyprus. Later on, the European Court of Human Rights followed a similar line, starting with the case Loizidou v. Turkey, Preliminary Objections, 310 Eur. Ct. H.R. (ser. A) (1995), para. 62, *discussed in* J. Kokott & B. Rudolf, Case note: Loizidou v. Turkey, 90 AJIL 98 (1996). For a description of these findings see also D. Chrysostomides, Les requêtes chypriotes contre la Turquie devant la Commission et la Cour européenne des droits de l'homme et leur importance, pp. 45–56.

[96] ECtHR, Cyprus v. Turkey, Application No. 25781/94, Judgement of 10 May 2001, § 77, discussed in F. Hoffmeister, Case note: Cyprus v. Turkey, 96 AJIL (2002), pp. 445–452.

[97] G. Bertrand/I. Rigoni, Turcs, Kurdes et Chypriotes devant la Cour européenne des droits de l'homme: une contestation judiciaire de questions politiques, in: Revue Etudes internationales 2000, p. 413 (433).

[98] C. Brewin, The G8 Initiative and the status of northern Cyprus in Europe, Marmara Journal of European Studies 9 (2001), pp. 137, 149: "recognition of sovereign independence of a State that is economically and militarily so dependent is close to a contradiction in terms".

The International Court of Justice, when faced with a similar question in the Namibia case, adopted a flexible approach. While acknowledging the illegality of South Africa's presence in Namibia at the time, it held that certain legal arrangements and transactions should be deemed as valid, "the effects of which can be ignored only to the detriment of the inhabitants of the Territory" (*Namibia-principle*).[99] As regards northern Cyprus, Lord Denning in the English Court of Appeal observed "an effective administration in northern Cyprus, which has made laws governing the day-to-day lives of the people".[100] Furthermore, the European Court of Human Rights acknowledged that local remedies in northern Cyprus must be exhausted for the purpose of bringing a claim before it (Article 35 ECHR) provided that such remedies are effective.[101] Following that logic, it may be asserted that decisions of TRNC courts meeting the test of constituting an effective legal remedy may produce international legal effects. Therefore, it has to be scrutinized which TRNC legal acts might be regarded as internationally valid.

2.3.1. Documents relating to personal status

International validity can be assumed for documents, which relate to the personal status of the TRNC population. These concern, i.a., the registration of births, deaths and marriages.[102] In contrast, documents like TRNC passports or identity cards are directly linked with the unrecognised political entity and can therefore not be regarded as internationally valid. An unclear category is technical documents, like driving licences for cars or lorries. Whereas they certify a certain capability of its holder, TRNC law defines the relevant standard. Since TRNC requirements may or may not fall below international standards, the question of international validity must therefore be examined on a case-to-case basis.

2.3.2. Export certificates

Since 1983 export certificates are issued by TRNC-authorities. Some EU Member States accepted them as proving Cypriot origin. Therefore, Turkish Cypriot exports could benefit from privileged access to the European market under the EU-Cyprus Association Agreement of 1972. Upon informal complaints from the Cypriot government, Greece considered to introduce an infringement procedure agains those Member States (under Article 226 EC), but refrained from doing so in order not to irritate the Community.[103] However, in 1994, the European Court of Justice, on reference by the British High Court of Justice, ruled that this practice contravened

---

[99] ICJ, Legal Consequences for States of the Continued Presence of South Africa in Namibia (South West Africa) Notwithstanding Security Council Resolution 276 (1970), Advisory Opinion, ICJ Reports 1971, p. 16 (56), § 125.

[100] Court of Appeal, Hesperides Hotels and another v. Aegean Turkish Holidays and another, (1977) 3 WLR 656; (1978) 1 All ER 277.

[101] ECtHR, Cyprus v. Turkey, loc. cit. (note 96), §§ 101–102.

[102] ICJ, Namibia opinion, loc. cit. (note 99), p. 16 (56), § 125.

[103] C. Lycourgos, L'Association de Chypre à la CEE, p. 21.

the rules of origin.[104] It did not accept the Commission's argument that TRNC export certificates should be recognised in the interest of Turkish Cypriots in light of the *Namibia-principle* and Article 5 of the Association Agreement.[105] The ECJ rather stressed the need to have proper procedures for administrative co-operation to ensure that the rules of origin are complied with.[106] In the absence of any possibility of checks or co-operation with TRNC authorities, the notion "customs authorities of the exporting State" used in the Protocol of origin could only refer to the authorities of the Republic of Cyprus.[107] Moreover, northern exporters might apply for a stamp issued by the Government of the Republic. Since there were – apparently – no such applications, it could not be maintained that the Republic was discriminating against Turkish Cypriot exporters established in the northern part of Cyprus.[108] The Association Agreement therefore precludes acceptance by the competent authorities of a Member State, upon importation of goods from Cyprus, of movement certificates issued by authorities other than the competent authorities of the Republic of Cyprus. The same is true for phytosanitary certificates, which are needed to import citrus fruits into the Community under Directive 77/93.[109]

Turkish Cypriots[110] often complain about this situation as an unjustified "embargo". As can be seen from the context, the term "embargo" is both technically and politically incorrect. Technically, the political organs of the EU have never taken a decision prohibiting the Turkish Cypriots from exporting to the EU. Exports from the northern part of Cyprus to the EU are perfectly legal.[111] They are

[104] ECJ, Case C-432/92, The Queen v. Minister of Agriculture, Fisheries and Food, ex parte S. P. Anastasiou (Pissouri) Ltd and Others, ECJ Reports 1994–I, 3087 (Anastasiou I). In a later case, the Court applied the principles developed for direct exports from the TRNC to an EU Member State, *mutatis mutandis*, to indirect exports *via* Turkey (see ECJ, Case C-219/98, Anastasiou II, ECR I-2000, p. 5241). For a critical review of these cases see S. Talmon, The Cyprus Question before the European Court of Justice, EJIL 2001, p. 727 et seq. Finally, in Anastasiou III, ECR I-2003, p. 10635, the Court decided that Turkish phytosanitary documents cannot be validly issued for products of Turkish Cypriot origin.

[105] Article 5 of the Association Agreement reads: "The rules governing trade between the Contracting Parties may not give rise to any discrimination between the Member States, or between nationals or companies of these States, *nor nationals or companies of Cyprus*" (emphasis added).

[106] ECJ, Anastasiou I, loc. cit (note 104), § 40.

[107] ECJ, Anastasiou I, loc. cit. (note 104), § 54.

[108] ECJ, Anastasiou I, loc. cit. (note 104), § 48.

[109] ECJ, Anastasiou I, loc. cit. (note 104), § 64.

[110] Sometimes, these wrong contentions also stem from Greek Cypriot sources, e.g. the Press and Information Office, loc. cit. (page 17, note 27), p. 39: "the EEC Council of Ministers decided to suspend trade concessions for Turkish Cypriot goods and ruled that products exported from the island must be accompanied by a certificate of origin issued by the Government Authorities of Cyprus".

[111] Incorrect C. Dodd, Storm Clouds over Cyprus, p. 3, and E. Olgun/S. Karabacak,

subject to the general tariff rates like third country products. The European Court has only clarified the rules of origin for *privileged* access to the EU. Politically, the present restrictions are a direct consequence of the 1983 declaration of independence: hence, the Turkish Cypriot leadership has created this sort of "self-isolation" by forcing its exporters to use "TRNC" seals which are not recognised internationally. Whereas non-recognition as such does not necessarily exclude accepting export certificates from a non-recognised entity,[112] in the case of Cyprus it must be understood that exactly the non-cooperative attitude of the TRNC authorities vis-à-vis the Republic of Cyprus has presumably led to the ECJ's conclusion that cooperation with northern authorities would not reach the required level as to allow for privileged access to the European market.

2.3.3. *Judicial protection*

In the case Djavit An, the European Court of Human Rights had to assess the relevance of legal protection before administrative courts in the TRNC as regards decisions on crossing the green line before the opening in summer 2003. The applicant, a doctor, had applied to cross the green line into the south 147 times, but was denied to cross in 122 times. The Court found that he did not have to exhaust remedies before TRNC administrative courts, since it was not clear whether these courts were entitled to make a finding on the issuance of permits for crossing the green line.[113] On general level, decisions of TRNC courts might be internationally valid or invalid, depending on their suitability to protect human rights in the given case.[114]

2.3.4. *Property issues*

In the aftermath of the Turkish intervention in 1974, many Greek Cypriot properties in the north were expropriated. Article 159 (1) (b) of the TRNC constitution of 1985 contains an explicit legal basis for such action.[115] In December 1996, in the Loizidou case (merits), the European Court of Human Rights assessed

---

Cyprus: An opportunity or a threat, p. 12, maintaining that the European Court of Justice did not allow Turkish Cypriots to export to any State in the European Union.

[112] Talmon, loc. cit. (note 104), p. 742 et seq.

[113] ECtHR, Djavit An v. Turkey, no. 20652/92, §§ 31 et seq., ECHR 2003–III.

[114] ECtHR, Cyprus v. Turkey, loc. cit. (note 101), § 98. Since TRNC court decisions might be beneficial to the individual, the local remedies rule under the Convention applies on a case-by-case basis.

[115] The provision reads: All immovable properties, buildings and installations which were found abandoned on 13 February 1975 when the Turkish Federated State of Cyprus was proclaimed or which were considered by law as abandoned or ownerless after abovementioned date, or which should have been in the possession or control of the public even though their ownership had not yet been determined . . . and . . . situated within the boundaries of the TRNC on 15 November 1983, shall be the property of the TRNC notwithstanding the fact that they are not so registered in the books of the Land Registry Office; and the Land Registry Office shall be amended accordingly.

the international validity of this provision. It held that Article 1, 1st Additional Protocol ECHR still protects dispossessed Greek Cypriot owners and dismissed the argument of. the Turkish Government that they had lost their property by virtue of Article 159 (1) (b) of the TRNC Constitution. For the purpose of the Convention (which is to secure human rights) there is no legal validity of this particular provision of the TRNC Constitution[116] (which restricts the right to property). This holding has been confirmed in the Cyprus v. Turkey case.[117] Thus, it can be considered as established case law under the Convention that the acquisition of abandoned property without compensation has no international validity.

A more diffcult matter are decisions taken under TRNC Law No. 49/2003 on "compensation to be paid on immovable properties within the borders of the Turkish Republic of Northern Cyprus that fall within the jurisdiction of Article 159, paragraph 4, of the Constitution". They may be generally regarded as being in the interest of affected owners, and therefore be valid under international law. On the other hand, a certain political bias against Greek Cypriots as well as a risk that such compensation would not be appropriate in financial terms cannot be excluded. The European Court of Human Rights carefully scrutinized the features and limits of the law and concluded that it fell short of providing an effective remedy that Greek Cypriots must exhaust before bringing a claim to Strasbourg. The Court critizised that no provision existed for movable property or non-pecuniary damages. Neither do the terms of compensation allow for the possibility for restitution of the property withheld, lacking an important element in a system of redress. Finally, the composition of the property commission raised concerns since the majority of its members are living in houses owned or built on property owned by Greek Cypriots.[118] In sum, decisions of this Turkish Cypriot property commission cannot be regarded as valid. Nevertheless, it is not impossible under international law that the TRNC could introduce a valid remedy, which secures genuinely effective redress for Greek Cypriot owners by removing the shortcomings of the Law No. 49/2003 as identified by the European Court of Human Rights. It remains to be seen whether the Turkish Cypriot authorities will promptly react to the respective call from the Court to establish such a remedy within the first half of 2006.[119]

2.3.5. Naturalization of Turkish immigrants

The 1975 Constitution only referred to Turkish citizens. Therefore, no distinction was made between Turkish Cypriots and Turks. According to Article 67 of the

[116] ECtHR, Loizidou v. Turkey (merits), 1996–IV Eur. Ct. H. R. 2216, *discussed in* B. Rudolf, Case Report: Loizidou v. Turkey (Merits), 91 AJIL 532 (1997), § 44.

[117] ECtHR, Cyprus v. Turkey, loc. cit. (note 101), paras. 188, 189.

[118] ECtHR, Xenides-Arestis v. Turkey, no. 46347/99, Decision as to the Admissibility, 14 March 2005, pp. 44–45.

[119] ECtHR, Xenides-Arestis v. Turkey, no. 46347/99, Judgment, 22 December 2005, p. 10, para. 40.

1985 TRNC Constitution, the system changed slightly by introducing a TRNC citizenship. Those persons, who had their permanent residence in northern Cyprus on 15 November 1983, are considered TRNC citizens. This provision enabled present Turkish settlers to receive TRNC citizenship. However, immigrants had to apply for TRNC citizenship according to TRNC legislation, which allows for naturalisation of foreigners after five years of permanent residence after that date or after marriage with a Turkish Cypriot.[120]

From a point of view of international law, the deliberate transfer of own population to an occupied territory violates Article 49(6) of the Fourth Geneva Convention,[121] which is (still)[122] applicable to the international conflict between Cyprus and Turkey.[123] Therefore, Turkey is under an obligation not to induce its citizens to settle in northern Cyprus. The UN General Assembly, recalled this in 1975[124] when it

> *urges all parties to refrain from unilateral action in contravention of its resolution 3212 (XXIX), including changes in the demographic structure of Cyprus.*

Whereas a breach of this obligation entailed Turkey's international responsibility, this does, however, not settle the question whether the naturalisation of Turkish settlers by the TRNC is deprived of any legal relevance for the Republic of Cyprus. Decisions to give TRNC citizenship to Turkish citizens might constitute another unwelcome result of a Turkish international wrongful act, having promoted settlements in northern Cyprus. Nevertheless, on humanitarian grounds, one can ask whether the *Namibia-principle* does not apply also in favour of naturalised Turks in the north. Non-recognition of their TRNC citizenship by the Republic would certainly work to the detriment of an affected immigrant since he would also loose the right to stay on the island. However, would non-recognition also be to the detriment of the Turkish Cypriots as a whole?

---

[120] Drevet, loc. cit. (page 15, note 13), p. 15.

[121] Article 49 (6) of the Fourth Geneva Convention reads: "The occupying power shall not deport or transfer parts of its own civilian population into the territories it occupies."

[122] See Article 6 (3) of the Fourth Geneva Convention.

[123] Chrysostomides, loc. cit. (p. 8, note 24), p. 202 et seq. In addition, under Article 85 (4) of the First Additional Protocol, the transfer of the Occupying Power of parts of its own civilian population into the territory it occupies shall be a grave breach of the Convention, amounting to a War Crime. However, whereas Cyprus has ratified the Protocol in 1979, Turkey did not. Similarly, it might be noted that Article 7 (2) (viii) of the Rome Statute of the International Criminal Court qualifies the direct or indirect transfer by the Occupying Power of parts of ist own civilian population into the territory it occupies as a war crime; but since the Statute does not apply retro-actively this is of no relevance for the current study.

[124] UNGA, Resolution 3395 (XXX) of 20 November 1975. See also preamble of UNGA resolution 34/30 of 20 November 1979, "deploring also unilateral actions that change the demographic structure of Cyprus".

One the one hand, it may be noted that the German Constitutional Court[125] derived from the principle of unitary German citizenship and the constitutional goal of re-unification that naturalisations effected by the former German Democratic Republic were valid for the Federal Republic within the limits of the "ordre public". Therefore, many citizens of former socialist "brother countries" who had been naturalised in the GDR could benefit from their "East German" citizenship in the united Germany, since the GDR decision was regarded as having conferred German citizenship. On the other hand, in contrast to the law of the former GDR, the TRNC conditions for naturalisation are discretionary and not tied to certain objective criteria.[126] A blind acceptance of every TRNC naturalisation decision would hence entail the risk of awarding Cypriot citizenship even in very doubtful cases.

Balancing the competing interests at stake, the *Namibia-principle* suggests, however, that the Republic's interest not to accept unlawful settlement at large does not completely outweigh the personal interests of every single immigrant and a possible interest of the Turkish Cypriot population in the north to keep well-integrated Turkish settlers within their society. Whereas the Republic can certainly start from the premise that a settler's presence on Cypriot territory is illegal, naturalisations effected by TRNC authorities are internationally valid, where the settler in question had, at the time of his naturalisation, (also) a legal right to be naturalised under Section 9 of the Republic's citizenship law of 1967. So, for example, a settler who had married a Turkish Cypriot citizen who is a citizen of the Republic,[127] can rely on the TRNC naturalisation decision and be regarded as Cypriot citizen. In addition, all States have an interest to avoid statelessness, for example in cases where the relevant settler could not claim Turkish nationality instead of TRNC nationality. International law considerations would therefore waive the need to re-apply for Cypriot citizenship unter the procedures of the Republic's citizenship law.

3. Summary

The second phase of the Turkish intervention in 1974 breached the international law prohibition against the use of force. It cannot be justified under Article IV (2) of the Treaty of Guarantee because it did not pursue the sole legitimate aim to restore the *status quo ante* that existed before the Coup d'Etat. Turkey's continued

[125] Federal Constitutional Court, Decision of 21.10.1987, BVerfGE 77, p. 137 (149 et seq.).

[126] Section 9 of the TRNC law on citizenship empowers the Council of Ministers to grant TRNC citizenship by a discretionary decision.

[127] According to the *ius sanguinis* principle, Cypriot citizenship will be accorded to the children of a Cypriot mother or father. This allows Turkish Cypriots who were citizens of the Republic in 1960, to transmit Cypriot citizenship to their children even if living in the north.

presence in the northern part of Cyprus has the effect that the TRNC does not meet the objective criteria of independent Statehood. However, legal acts of the TRNC can be regarded as valid under international law if their non-recognition would work to the detriment of the population in the north. This does not include the *ex lege* expropriation without compensation of Greek Cypriot refugees that left their premises during the Turkish intervention and necessitates a case-to-case examination of TRNC decisions to naturalise Turkish immigrants.

Chapter IV

UN Efforts to Foster a Settlement 1975–1995

A. THE FACTS

1. The good offices mission of the UN Secretary-Generals U Thant, Waldheim and Perez de Cuèllar

UN involvement dates back to 1964 when the Security Council, in its resolution establishing UNFICYP, also recommended that Secretary-General U Thant should appoint a mediator in agreement with the three Guarantor powers.[1] Early efforts culminated in the report of mediator Plaza of 1965.[2] Turkey rejected it as being imbalanced. Following another UN Security Council resolution,[3] several inter-communal talks were held between 1968 and 1974. When the two sides had been close to finalise technical details of an agreement on the central powers (abolishment of separated majorities, re-establishment of courts, presidential regime) and on local government (catalogue of powers) the coup d'Etat against President Makarios

[1] UNSC Resolution 186 of 4 March 1964, § 7.

[2] Report of the United Nations Mediator on Cyprus to the Secretary-General, Note by the Secretary-General, S/6253, 26 March 1965.

[3] UNSC Resolution 244 of 22 December 1967, § 3.

Legal Aspects of the Cyprus Problem, pp. 60–82.

occurred on 15 July 1974. Faced with a large Turkish presence on the island from then on, the subsequent UN efforts shall now be reviewed in more detail.

1.1. *The UN efforts 1975–1983*

1.1.1. The Vienna negotiations

After the proclamation, on 13 February 1975, of the Turkish Federated State of Cyprus and the critical reaction of the UN Security Council,[4] the then UN Secretary-General Waldheim appointed Perez de Cuèllar as a new mediator (1975–1977).

Whereas no progress was made in the first two rounds held in Vienna (28 April–3 May 1975 and 5–7 June 1975),[5] Denktaş and Clerides reached an agreement in the third round (31 July–2 August 1975). Under the so-called Vienna III agreement[6] Turkish Cypriots living in the south could settle in the north if they wished to do so (§ 1).[7] Greek Cypriots at present in the north should receive "every help to lead a normal live, including facilities for education and for the practice of their religion, as well as medical care by their own doctors and freedom of movement in the north" (§ 2).[8] If they opted to move to the south, they would be permitted to do so (§ 3). The fourth round (8–10 September 1975) did not produce any result, prompting the UN General Assembly to show its disappointment.[9] After intense lobbying of Waldheim, the fifth round held in Vienna (17–21 February 1976) resulted in an agreement of the parties to exchange written proposals in the next round in May that year. The Greek Cypriot proposals were modelled along the lines of a federation. The Turkish Cypriot proposal followed the principle that equality of status and non-discrimination between the two federated States should be ensured whereas the territorial question was not dealt with. Again, the two positions proved to be irreconcilable, and the proposed meeting to discuss these proposals never took place.

---

[4] UNSC Resolution 367 of 12 March 1975.

[5] UNSC Resolution 370 of 13 June 1975, § 6.

[6] UN Press Communiqué issued after the third round 31 July–2 August 1975; reprinted in Ertekün, loc. cit. (page 6, note 19), p. 264.

[7] Over 8.000 Turkish Cypriots moved to the northern parts of Cyprus due to this agreement. Tzermias, loc. cit. (page 2, note 1), p. 485.

[8] Apparently, this part of the Vienna III agreeement was not properly implemented. In the case Cyprus v. Turkey (loc. cit. page 52, note 96), the European Court of Human Rights reviewed the situation of Greek Cypriots that remained living in the north. It found that the TRNC had violated their freedom of religion and the freedom of expression by imposing restrictions on the attendance on religious ceremonies and by exercising censorship. Furthermore, the Court found that the discriminatory conditions under which the Greek Cypriot population hade to live because of their ethnic origin, race, and religion "violated the very notion of respect for the human dignity of its members" (judgment, para. 309) and thus constitutes degrading treatment forbidden under Article 3 of the European Convention on Human Rights.

[9] UNGA Resolution 3395 (XXX) of 20 November 1975, § 7.

1.1.2. The Makarios-Denktaş High Level Agreement of 1977

Upon another Cyprus resolution of the General Assembly of 12 November 1976,[10] Makarios and Denktaş met on 27 January 1977 – the first encounter after the outbreak of the hostilities in 1963. They agreed on 12 February 1977 the so-called four guidelines.[11] First, Cyprus should be an independent, non-aligned and bi-communal federated Republic. Second, questions relating to the territory under the administration of each community should be discussed in the light of the economic viability or productivity and land-ownership. Third, fundamental questions like the freedom of movement, the right of establishment, the right of property and other special matters should be openly discussed while taking into account the bi-communal federated system and the practical difficulties of the Turkish Cypriot Community. Fourth, the powers and functions of the federal government should acknowledge the unity of the country and its bi-communal character.

However, the following rounds between negotiators Papadopoulos and Onan (31 March–7 April/26 May–3 June 1977) did not succeed, due to the territorial question (the Turkish Cypriot side did not accept the Greek Cypriot proposal to administer only 20% of the territory). The talks finally were brought to an end when, on 3 August 1977, Makarios died and his successor, Kyprianou, rejected the comprehensive Turkish Cypriot proposals of 13 April 1978[12] out of hand. Those were based on the principle of equality of both entities to build a "federation by evolution",[13] small territorial adjustments and the return of Varosha. On 9 November 1978,[14] the General Assembly again supported a continuation of the intercommunal talks and called upon the Security Council to consider a timetable for the withdrawal of foreign troops from the island, whereas the latter, in a much more cautious way, only announced to review the situation in June 1979 in order to continue to promote a just solution to the Cyprus problem.[15]

In November 1978, the United States, the United Kingdom and Canada presented a "framework for a Cyprus settlement". Cyprus was to form an independent, sovereign Republic whose territorial integrity had to be respected. The two federated entities would be equally represented in the Upper House of the federal parliament whereas the Lower House would be constituted in proportion to the population. For the settlement of the territorial question, factors like economic viability, property, security, population and history would be taken into account; the Turkish Cypriot side would make significant concessions on this part. All foreign troops would be withdrawn, with the exception of those mentioned in the Treaty

[10] UNGA Resolution 31/12 of 12 November 1976.

[11] High-Level Agreement of 12 February 1977, reprinted in Press and Information Office, loc. cit. (page 17, note 27), p. 151.

[12] Reprinted in UN Doc S/12723 of 31 May 1978.

[13] For an extensive discussion of the Turkish Cypriot proposal of 13 April 1978 see Ertekün, loc. cit. (page 6, note 19), pp. 57–62 and N. Crawshaw, Zypern in der Sackgasse, EA 1979, p. 82 (84–87).

[14] UNGA Resolution 33/15 of 9 November 1978.

[15] UNSC Resolution 440 of 27 November 1978, § 5.

of Alliance. Refugees would return home provided that this would be compatible with the bi-zonal character of the Republic. The return of Greek Cypriots to Famagusta would be organised by the United Nations. However, the Greek Cypriot side did not accept the plan as a basis for negotiations,[16] and the Turkish Cypriots were unenthusiastic about it.[17]

1.1.3. The Kyprianou-Denktaş High Level Agreement of 1979

The new special UN envoy for Cyprus, Reynaldo Galindo-Pohl (1978–1980), brokered a meeting between Kyprianou and Denktaş. On 18/19 May 1979 they concluded the so-called "10-point agreement".[18] Intercommunal talks should restart (§ 1) on the basis of the guidelines of 12 June 1979 and UN resolutions (§ 2). Human rights of all Cypriot citizens should be respected (§ 3). The talks should include the territorial and procedural issues (§ 4). The return of refugees to Famagusta, the constitutional and territorial questions should have priority; if a settlement for Famagusta under the auspices of the UN were to be agreed, this should be implemented even if a solution to the other two matters was still pending (§ 5). Any action to endanger the talks should be abstained from (§ 6). Questions relating to a demilitarisation of Cyprus could be discussed (§ 7). Independence, sovereignty, territorial integrity and non-alignment should be adequately guaranteed against any form of union with another State or against partition or secession (§ 8). Intercommunal talks were to be conducted on a continuing basis (§ 9) and take place in Nicosia (§ 10).

The good will to conduct the intercommunal talks according to the 10 points did not last long. Already on 22 June 1979 the negotiators agreed not to fix a further meeting.[19] Although the new UN Special Envoy for Cyprus, Hugo Juan Gobbi (1980–1984), arranged for new talks from August 1980 on, the following sessions until April 1983 failed in the end. Kyprianou adopted since December 1981 the position of the then newly elected Greek Prime Minister, Andreas Papandreou that international negotiations in which pressure on Turkey could be exerted were to be preferred to bi-communal talks.[20] The only noteworthy details from that period are twofold: the Greek Cypriots accepted for the first time (in the SG's opening statement of 9 August 1980)[21] the principle of "bi-zonal solution for the territorial aspect" and that security may be discussed having regard to particular Turkish Cypriot needs; the comprehensive Turkish Cypriot position paper of

[16] Tzermias, loc. cit (page 2, note 1), p. 507. J. Christou, Obituary: Spyros Kyprianou, defiant to the last, Cyprus Mail, 13 March 2002, observed that Kyprianou rejected the Western plan because his political ally, AKEL, was opposed to it. Christou alleges that, under the influence of Moscow, AKEL could have never accepted a Western plan during the Cold War.

[17] Necatigil, loc. cit. (page 11, note 35), p. 162.

[18] The 10-Points Agreement of 19 May 1979, reprinted in Press and Information Office, loc. cit. (page 17, note 27), p. 152.

[19] UNGA Resolution 34/30 of 20 November 1979.

[20] R. Meinardus, Eine neue Phase im Zypern-Konflikt, Europaarchiv 1984, p. 297 (301).

[21] Report of the UN Secretary-General, A/35/385–S/14100.

5 August 1981[22] showed, also for the first time, some flexibility on the territorial question. It is reported that Denktaş had proposed to hand over 6 districts and 19 villages to the Greek Cypriot entity. The Greek Cypriots claimed that the proposal referred to only 2, 6% of the under Turkish territory control[23] and considered it inadequate.

1.1.4. The 1983 Aide Memoire of Pèrez de Cuèllar

On 17 June 1983, the Legislative Assembly of the Turkish Federated State of Cyprus adopted a resolution on the self-determination of the Turkish Cypriot population of Cyprus. In the light of this development, the newly elected UN Secretary-General de Cuèllar started a new initiative on 8 August 1983. According to his Aide-Mémoire, three indicators had to be distinguished: the executive, the legislature, and the territorial question. He presented two options.[24]

The first – pro Greek – option divided the territory on a 77% to 23% basis between the south and the north. The Federal executive should be composed of 60% Greek and 40% Turkish Cypriots. The elected President of the south should serve as the central President, assisted by the elected President of the north as Vice-President of the Federation. The legislature should consist of two houses. Whereas the Lower House should follow the principle of proportional representation, the Upper House should represent the two provinces on an equal basis. The second – pro Turkish – option gave 70% of the territory to the south whereas the northern province governed 30% of the territory. 70:30% would also be the ratio of representation in the federal executive. The elected Presidents of the Provinces should rotate; the Upper House of the Parliament should consist of 50% of both Provinces. It was apparently the purpose of this Aide-Mémoire to extract territorial concessions from the Turkish Cypriots in return to constitutional concessions from the Greek Cypriots.[25]

Kyprianou did not react until 15 September 1983 to these proposals. Denktaş requested a face-to-face meeting with him, while the latter asked in vain to negotiate with the Turkish President Evren. The Turkish Cypriot Republic of Northern Cyprus was declared an independent State in November 1983.

1.2. *The efforts 1984–1990*

Already in January 1984 Kyprianou presented new proposals to de Cuèllar.[26] On the procedural level, Kyprianou demanded that the Turkish Cypriot side should first comply with Security Council Resolution 541 before the talks could begin. Since the Turkish Cypriot leader, henceforth "President of the TRNC", did not accept this condition, it was again for the UN Secretary-General to overcome the

---

[22] Ertekün, loc. cit. (page 6, note 19), p. 123.
[23] Press and Information Office, loc. cit. (page 17, note 27), p. 33.
[24] Tzermias, loc. cit. (page 2, note 1), p. 555.
[25] Meinardus, loc. cit. (note 20), p. 303.
[26] A. Hottinger, Das ungelöste Zypern-Problem, EA 1986, p. 51 (54–56).

obstacles. In March 1984, he presented a 5-point "scenario". First, the Turkish Cypriot side would not pursue any follow-up to the 15 November 1983 declaration. Second, no side would strengthen its military forces on the island. Third, the UN would administer Varosha, pending a solution and handed over to the Greek Cypriot side once a settlement would be reached. Fifth, high-level intercommunal talks should start.

The Turkish Cypriot side did not agree with the plan, arguing that there was no compensation for giving up the Varosha region.[27] Rather than "freezing" the 1983 declaration of independence, in April 1984, Denktaş announced constitutional referendum and elections for August and November that year. Turkey and the TRNC exchanged ambassadors. Following a letter from Denktaş to Pèrez de Cuèllar, stating that he would continue the establishment of the TRNC, the UN Security Council, on 11 May 1984, adopted another resolution[28] in which it condemned "all secessionist actions". Denktaş also demanded that the Varosha region should come under the administration of the UN. The Secretary-General was asked to continue his efforts to settle the Cyprus question.

On 10 September 1984, both leaders held separate meetings with the Secretary-General in New York and agreed on the agenda. In the third round (26–30 November/7–12 December 1984) Pèrez de Cuèllar presented a provisional draft of a settlement that seemed to be acceptable to both sides. On territory, upon pressure from the US President Reagan and the Turkish Prime Minister Özal, Denktaş consented to ceding 7% (from 36% to 29%) whereas the constitutional model followed closely the 1960 Constitution. The executive was to be led by a Greek Cypriot President; the Turkish Cypriot Vice-President would have veto powers on vital questions. The Council of Ministers should be composed of 7 Greek Cypriots and 3 Turkish Cypriots. The Lower House of the bi-cameral parliament should consist of 70% Greek Cypriot MPs and 30% Turkish Cypriot MPs whereas the Upper House should be built on parity.[29] On the "three freedoms", a working group should lay down a time frame and practical rules including possible compensation. The Secretary-General announced that Kyprianou and Denktaş were to meet on 17 January 1985 and expressed his hope that they would conclude the prepared draft agreement.[30]

The Cyprus summit, however, ended with a big disappointment. Whereas the Turkish Cypriot leader wanted to sign the draft as final, the Greek Cypriot leader insisted that the framework needed to be specified in some aspects. Especially a time frame for the withdrawal of the Turkish army should be laid down, the right of free movement throughout the island should be guaranteed and a new form of international guarantee for the island should be agreed upon. Last but not least, Kyprianou did not want to form a transitory government immediately, but only

[27] Tzermias, loc. cit. (page 2, note 1), p. 573.

[28] UNSC Resolution 550 of 11 May 1984.

[29] Tzermias, loc. cit. (page 2, note 1), p. 581.

[30] Report of the Secretary-General of 12 December 1984, S/16585, para. 50.

after the final settlement.[31] He did not sign the framework agreement – with great internal repercussions in the Republic. The Foreign Minister, Rolandis, resigned accusing Kyprianou of not really wanting a federal solution and not accepting a political compromise.[32] Parliament was dissolved and early elections were held in December 1985 because the two big Greek Cypriot opposition parties claimed that Kyprianou followed a misguided recommendation from the Greek PM Papandreou and had done harm to the Cypriot cause by his inflexibility.[33]

After another two unsuccessful attempts in 1985 and 1986, Pèrez de Cuèllar did not engage in any more initiatives, but appointed Oscar Camilion on 1 December 1987 as Special representative (1988–1993). The international circumstances improved. In Cyprus, the moderate George Vassiliou won the presidential elections in February 1988. Greece and Turkey were in a phase of rapprochement, building on the "spirit of Davos" between the Prime Ministers Papandreou and Özal since January 1988. In February 1988, Turkey agreed to annul a government decree that had prohibited Turks of Greek origin, and living in Turkey, the right to sell or rent real-estate property. Reciprocally, the Greek government consented to signing the 1988 protocol to the Association Agreement between the EC and Turkey of 1963. On 24 August, the two leaders and the UN Secretary-General agreed in Geneva that substantial talks should begin on 15 September 1988 in Nicosia and be finalised by June 1989. Whereas the first round (15–27 September 1988) served the purpose of defining the positions, the second one (19 December 1988–28 March 1989) worked on written proposals.[34] In a meeting held in New York on 29 June 1989, de Cuèllar presented another proposal:[35]

Cyprus should be a federation of two politically equal federated States. It should have one single personality, and enjoy its independence, security and territorial integrity. All human rights should be guaranteed. The community that has the majority on the respective territory should administer each federated State. The federation should only have the powers detailed in the Constitution (foreign policy, defence policy, monetary policy). The Council of Ministers would be divided on a 7:3 basis. All Cypriots would elect the President. That Community of whose origin the President is not should elect the Vice-President. Both Presidents should jointly appoint the Council of Ministers and have a veto power in certain cases. The bi-cameral Parliament would consist of a Lower House (70:30% MPs) and an Upper House (50:50). The Members of the Supreme Court would be Greek and Turkish Cypriots (50:50) to be jointly appointed by both Presidents. The Supreme Court would act as a Constitutional Court, reviewing both federal and federated

[31] Tzermias, loc. cit. (page 2, note 1) pp. 583–584; Necatigil, loc. cit. (page 11, note 35), p. 290.

[32] Cyprus Mail, 15 March 1985.

[33] Hottinger, loc. cit. (note 26), p. 51.

[34] For a description of the Greek Cypriot and Turkish Cypriot proposals of January and February 1989 see Chrysostomides, loc. cit. (page 8, note 24), pp. 375–385.

[35] The opening Statement of the Secretary-General of 29 June 1989 is reproduced in Necatigil, loc. cit. (page 11, note 35), Appendix 10.

law. Concerning the three freedoms (right to move, right to establishment, right to property), many points were left unresolved. The right to move throughout the island could be restricted by non-discriminatory policy controls. On the right to purchase land and the right to establishment, "territorial provisions" could be foreseen. On security, the paper set out that the ultimate goal should be the demilitarisation of the island according to a time schedule. The Treaties of Guarantee and Alliance should be modernised along the lines of the UN Charter.

Vassiliou accepted the paper as a basis for negotiation. However, on 23 August 1989, the TRNC Parliament adopted a resolution in which it noted that no one except the two sides could make proposals.[36] That amounted effectively to demanding the withdrawal of the Secretary-General's paper. No further changes could be brokered during the next talks between Vassiliou and Denktaş from 26 February 1990–2 March 1990 in New York. In his report of 8 March 1990,[37] the SG observed that in the course of the discussions Mr Denktaş had stated that the term "communities" was to be used in a manner that is synonymous with the term "peoples", each having a right to self-determination. That had posed more than a semantic problem. He also stated that the Turkish Cypriots were not a minority and that the 1960 agreements were still valid. The Security Council endorsed the Secretary-General's approach and outlined the principles for a settlement.[38] It called upon

> *the leaders of the two communities to pursue their efforts to reach freely a mutually acceptable solution providing for the establishment of a federation that will be bi-communal as regards the constitutional aspects and bi-zonal as regards the territorial aspects in line with the present resolutions and their 1977 and 1979 high-level agreements, and to cooperate, on an equal footing, with the Secretary-General in completing in the first instance and on an urgent basis, an outline of an overall agreement, as agreed in June 1989.*

However, after the EC application of Cyprus on 4 July 1990, no more relevant UN initiatives took place. De Cuèllar sounded out whether an international conference including the two parties in Cyprus, and Greece and Turkey, could be held at the end of that year considering both the Greek Prime Minister Mitsotsakis and the Turkish Prime Minister Özal as more flexible as their predecessors. Upon Cuèllar's report to the Security Council in October that year,[39] the latter endorsed this proposal.[40] The Council also added

> *that its position on the solution to the Cyprus problem is based on one State of Cyprus comprising two politically equal communities as defined by the Secretary General in the eleventh paragraph of Annex I to his report dated 8 March 1990.*[41]

[36] Necatigil, loc. cit. (page 11, note 35), p. 362.

[37] Report of UN Secretary-General de Cuellar of 8 March 1990, S/21183.

[38] UNSC Resolution 649 of 12 March 1990, § 3.

[39] Report of UN Secretary-General de Cuellar of 8 October 1991, S/23121.

[40] UNSC Resolution 716 of 11 October 1991, §§ 7–9.

[41] Ibid., § 4.

Although subsequent attempts to convene the above-mentioned conference failed, Pèrez de Cuèllar was quite optimistic when he reported for the last time during his term of office to the Security Council in December 1991. He felt that a set of ideas had evolved from the talks, which should make it possible for the two sides to reach agreement on a significant number of issues.[42]

2. The good offices of Boutros-Ghali

The new Secretary-General, Boutros Boutros-Ghali, used the material inherited from de Cuèllar. After meeting with both sides in spring 1992, he presented a first outline of his ideas to the Security Council in April and expressed hope that an overall solution would be in reach.[43] With the backing of the Security Council,[44] a long series of proximity talks took place in summer 1992 (18–23 June; 15 July–11 August). These culminated in joint meetings between Boutros-Ghali and the leaders of the two communities on 12–14 August, in which Ghali – unlike his predecessors – virtually became a party to the dispute by engaging in arm twisting and not so subtly hinting that he might turn the case over to the Security Council if the parties did not go along with his suggestions.[45] On 21 August 1992, Boutros-Ghali then published his ideas along with a map of the territorial adjustments.[46]

The Ghali Set of Ideas reiterated that there would be one Cyprus consisting of two politically equal communities. The two federated states in the federal Republic would have identical powers and each would administer its own territory. The federal government would only have those powers specifically listed in the settlement. There would be two Houses of Parliament. On some matters, separate majorities of Turkish Cypriot or Greek Cypriot representatives could be requested. Boutros-Ghali also proposed a deblocking mechanism. The executive resembled the 1960 Constitution (President and Vice-President, Council of Minister with a 7:3 ratio). The Judiciary should be composed of an equal number of judges from both communities. Boutros-Ghali proposed to establish the free movement of persons, but allowed restrictions to the right to property. On Security and Guarantee, a numerical balance of Greek and Greek Cypriot troops and equipment on the one hand and of Turkish and Turkish Cypriot troops and equipment on the other should be achieved in several months. UNFICYP, together with the Guarantor Powers and the two Communities, would receive the mandate to monitor the

[42] Report of UN Secretary-General de Cuellar to the Security Council of 19 December 1991, S/23300, § 5.

[43] Report of the UN Secretary-General to the Security Council of 3 April 1992, S/23780, §§ 17–25.

[44] UNSC Resolution 750 of 10 April 1992, § 8.

[45] S. Bolukbasi, Boutros-Ghali's Cyprus Initiative in 1992: Why did it fail?, in: Middle Eastern Studies, 1995, p. 460 (471).

[46] Report of the UN Secretary-General to the Security Council of 21 August 1992, S/24472.

achievement of the agreed numerical balance and further reduction to the agreed level. Transitional arrangements should last 18 months.

The Security Council, meeting on 26 August 1992, fully supported Boutros-Ghali's approach. It called on the parties to manifest the necessary political will and to pursue uninterrupted negotiations at the United Nations Headquarters until an overall framework agreement were reached, when resuming their face-to-face talks with the Secretary-General on 26 October 1992.[47]

These face-to-face talks failed to produce an immediate result. Denktaş agreed to 91 of the 100 paragraphs, while outlining fundamental differences to the remaining ones. *Inter alia*, he objected to EU membership of Cyprus as long as Turkey is not EU member.[48] Vassiliou accepted the Set of Ideas as a basis for reaching an overall framework agreement, subject to subsequent negotiations to ensure compliance with international law, human rights and the functionality of the state. Boutros-Ghali recorded the position of both sides in a so-called "Codification". He clearly stated that some positions of the Turkish Cypriots, in particular on the constitution and on refugees, as well as the rejection of the map, exceeded the terms of his Set of Ideas.[49] Hence, for the first time in the history of the inter-communal talks, a UN Secretary-General openly criticized one of the protagonists.[50] The Security Council took note of Ghali's report, and called upon the Turkish Cypriot side to adopt positions consistent with the Set of Ideas.[51] It furthermore urged both sides to commit themselves to certain listed confidence-building measures before the finalisation of the framework agreement in March 1993.[52]

In 1993, Boutros-Ghali shifted the focus from the framework agreement to confidence-building measures. However, the New York talks (25 May–1 June 1993) between the newly elected Clerides and Denktaş did not even succeed on that subject since the latter did not agree to the measures as proposed by the UN Security Council.[53] Denktaş claims that Clerides won the elections because he had opposed the Set of Ideas in the election campaign, thereby losing all credibility to

[47] UNSC Resolution 774 of 26 August 1992, §§ 5–6.

[48] Necatigil, loc. cit. (note 38), p. 396. This objection is contained in the rejection of the clause that Cyprus may join international organizations in which Turkey and Greece are not both members.

[49] Report of the UN Secretary-General to the Security Council of 11 November 1992, S/24830, § 8.

[50] Bolukbasi, loc. cit. (note 45), p. 460 and p. 474.

[51] UNSC Resolution 789 of 25 November 1992, §§ 5–6.

[52] Ibid., §§ 7–8.

[53] See the Letter dated 7 July 1993 from the President of the Security Council addressed to the Secretary-General (. . . "The Members of the Security Council share your disappointment that Mr. Denktaş has not yet adhered to the agreement of 1 June in which he undertook to promote the acceptance of the package on Varosha and Nicosia International Airport and that he failed to return to New York which prevented the resumption of the joint meetings on 14 June . . ."). Reprinted in: Resolutions Adopted by the United Nations on the Cyprus Problem, 1964–199, Nicosia, 1999, p. 142.

negotiate seriously about confidence building. Indeed, after having assumed office in February 1993 Clerides was never explicit whether he could accept the Ghali Set of Ideas as basis for negotiations.[54] In any case, after the publication of the EU Commission's report on the eligibility of Cyprus for Membership to the EU on 30 June 1993, the talks were discontinued during that year, due to Turkish Cypriot resistance.

In February 1994, Special Envoy Joe Clark led talks in Nicosia with both sides, *inter alia* in order to achieve the reopening of the airport in Nicosia and the return of Varosha. However, the "Draft Ideas for implementing the package of confidence-building measures" submitted by Boutros-Ghali on 21 March 1994,[55] were not accepted. On 29 July 1994, the Security Council noted with concern that neither leader was yet prepared to proceed with the implementation of the agreed measures.[56] Five informal meetings between Clerides and Denktaş in October 1994[57] did not result in action, and there were no relevant UN activities anymore in 1995 due to the fact that the EU had announced in January 1995 that it would start accession negotiations with Cyprus – which will be the subject of the next part.

B. LEGAL EVALUATION

1. The legal status of the various settlement documents

Before assessing the substance of the numerous proposals concerning a settlement, one should first recall their legal value. In this regard, the High-Level Agreements between the Cypriot parties, as well as the resolutions of the Security Council and the General Assembly and the Secretary-General's proposals must be distinguished.

1.1. *High level agreements of the Cypriot parties*

Customary international law defines an international agreement with reference to four criteria.[58] Two subjects of international law (1) must express a common will (2) to take legal commitments (3) governed by international law (4).

The high level agreements of 1977 and 1979 fall short of this definition in several ways. First, it is doubtful whether the leaders engaged in any legal commit-

[54] Bolukbasi, loc. cit. (note 45), p. 476.

[55] Report of UN Secretary-General Boutros-Ghali to the Security Council, S/1994/785 Annex.

[56] UNSC Resolution 939 of 29 July 1994, Preamble, Indent 4.

[57] Both leaders addressed open letters to the UN Secretary-General to attribute the responsibility for failure to the other side. See Clerides' letter of 8 November 1994, reprinted in Dodd, loc. cit. (note 243), Appendix 5 A, pp. 164–165, and Denktaş's letter of 21 November 1994, ibidem, Appendix 5 B, pp. 165–171.

[58] Compare Article 2 (1) (a) of the Vienna Convention on the Law of Treaties.

ments. For sure, the denomination of the High-Level Agreement of 12 February 1977 between Makarios and Denktaş as "agreement" seems to imply a legal arrangement. However, as the International Cout of Justice pointed out,[59] the title of a document is not decisive in this regard. Rather, a careful scrutiny of the text and the intentions of the parties is needed. Makarios and Denktaş declared "*We are seeking* . . .". Hence, they just referred to a common aim as guideline for their current negotiations. They did not express the will that these guidelines should be binding in case the negotiations would fail. Second, the agreement is not international in character. Neither could Denktaş claim to represent a State with the capacity to conclude treaties, nor did Makarios act as Head of State of Cyprus. Third, it can be excluded that the mutual relations between the Greek Cypriots and the Turkish Cypriots were intended to be governed by international law.

Rather, their agreement was bi-communal. However, the 1960 Constitution did not provide for a binding nature of agreements between the leaders of the two communities. It follows that the agreement was not legally binding, but a pure political document to define the framework of a settlement that could be concluded in legal forms at a later stage.

The same is true for the 10-point Agreement of 19 May 1979 between Kyprianou and Denktaş. Again, it contains some common goals for the talks at that time (§ 4: "The talks will deal with"). Like the 1977 Agreement, it is of temporary political significance, but does not bind future negotiators. Therefore, any contention that either side would "violate" the High-Level Agreements by later behaviour[60] is legally unsound.

1.2. *UN Security Council resolutions*

The Security Council addressed on a number of occasions the principles for a Cyprus settlement. It either expressed support for the two high level agreements of the parties or formulated his own detailed views on the matter.[61] The formal value of these documents must be assessed on the basis of UN law.

---

[59] ICJ, Aegean Sea Continental Shelf Case (Greece vs. Turkey), ICJ Reports (1978), p. 3, (40), § 96.

[60] Press and Information Office, loc. cit. (page 17, note 27), p. 75: "Turkish Cypriot intransigence culminated on 29 August 1994 when the illegal "Assembly" in occupied Cyprus decided with the full backing of Turkey to abandon federation as the sole form of settlement in Cyprus. This decision is in gross violation with the high-level agreements signed by the Turkish Cypriots in 1977 and 1979 (. . .)". Or Ertekün, loc. cit. (page 6, note 19), p. 84: "Nobody can seriously contend that such activities of the Greek Cypriots were not likely to "jeopardize the outcome of the talks" and were not in flagrant violation of point 6 of the Ten-Point-Agreement of 19 May 1979 to which the Greek Cypriots had agreed only a short time earlier".

[61] Starting with UNSC Resolution 649 (1990) of 12 March 1990. See above Chapter IV, A 1.2.

As the ICJ observed,

> *the language of a resolution of the Security Council should be carefully analysed before a conclusion can be made as to its binding effect. In view of the nature of the powers under Article 25, the question whether they have in fact been exercised is to be determined in each case, having regard to the terms of the resolution to be interpreted, the discussions leading to it, the Charter provisions invoked and, in general, all the circumstances that might assist in determining the legal consequences of the resolution of the Security Council.*[62]

It follows that words like "calls upon" or "demands" can, on their own, not imply that the relevant UN Security Council resolutions is mandatory.[63] Rather, it must be demonstrated that the Security Council was acting as guardian of international peace and security under Chapter VII of the UN Charter. Fulfilling the requirements of Article 39 of the Charter, the Security Council must determine that there has been a breach of the peace or that there is a threat to international peace and security.

In respect of Resolution 353 of 20 July 1974, referring to the Turkish intervention, one may discuss whether these conditions were fulfilled since the Security Council actually expressed its "grave concern about the situation that led to a serious threat to international peace and security" and called upon all parties to refrain from any action which might further aggravate the situation.[64] Similarly, a binding nature of Resolution 361 adressing the situation of internally displaced persons may not be excluded, given that the Security Council was recalling the context of Resolution 353 and "called upon all parties" to ensure the respect for fundamental human rights for everyone.[65]

However, in all resolutions on the framework for a political solution it never referred explicitly or implicitly to Chapter VII of the UN Charter.[66] Rather, it follows from the relevant discussions, the lack of invoking Chapter VII and the wording of the UNSC resolutions on the political framework of the Cyprus question that they are mere recommendations. Greek Cypriot claims that any Security Council resolution would be mandatory to the parties[67] are therefore unfounded in international law.

---

[62] ICJ, Namibia opinion, loc. cit. (note 231), ICJ Reports 1971, p. 16 (53), § 114.

[63] Inconclusive therefore Chrysostomides, loc. cit. (page 8, note 24), p. 151.

[64] UNSC Resolution 353 of 20 July 1974, Preamble, 5th recital and § 2. MacDonald, loc. cit. (page 40, note 37), pp. 35–36 finds it "plausible" that §§ 1 and 2 of Resolution 353 are binding, since the Security Council "calls upon" all parties, thus using mandatory language.

[65] Palley, loc. cit. (page xii, note 3), p. 256, note 32.

[66] Blumenwitz, loc. cit. (page 51, note 91), p. 94, as regards UN Security Council Resolution 541 of 18 November 1983.

[67] Chrysostomides, loc. cit. (page 17, note 27), p. 242; Press and Information Office, loc. cit. (note 65), pp. 18 and 80.

1.3. *UN General Assembly resolutions*

Article 10 of the UN Charter empowers the UN General Assembly to make recommendations to the Members of the United Nations or to the Security Council. Hence, in principle, the Assembly cannot take decisions that are mandatory under international law. However, some recommendations can be of greater importance if they are designed to reflect customary international law. In these cases, the resolution itself is of great assistance in identifying the relevant *opinio juris* of States.[68]

In the case of Cyprus, the Assembly's resolutions do not point in this direction. Some elements, as for example on the right to return, might be of relevance in the discussion of the customary nature of a certain rule. However, an entire Cyprus resolution of the General Assembly never reflects customary international law. Rather, it constitutes a political recommendation to the parties in which way to proceed. Turkish Cypriot attempts to escape uncomfortable General Assembly resolutions on other grounds[69] are thus starting from the wrong premise.

1.4. *UN Secretary-General's proposals*

Since the 1980ies several Secretary-Generals became more and more active in their good offices mission by formulating own proposals. They took the form of "opening statements", "non-papers", "draft agreements" or "ideas".[70] Again, the formal value of these documents can only be assessed on the basis of the UN-Charter.

Under Article 98 of the UN Charter, the Secretary-General shall perform such other functions as are entrusted to him by, *inter alia*, the General Assembly or the Security Council. In the case of Cyprus, the Security Council has explicitly mandated many good-offices missions of the Secretary-General. This mandate, however, does not confer to the Secretary-General the ability to adopt legally binding text. Good offices, as a means of friendly settlement of international disputes enumerated in Article 33 of the Charter, restrict themselves to proposals. Of course, they bear political weight since they are regarded as fair in the eyes of the highest UN administrative officer who needs the trust of a majority in the General Assembly and of the Permanent Five in the Security Council to be elected (Article 97 UN Charter). Given the Secretary-General's objectivity and experience in mediating conflicts, proposals that bear his signature reflect an important international opinion

---

[68] ICJ, Legality of the Threat or Use of Nuclear Weapons, Advisory Opinion, ICJ Reports 1996, p. 226 (254–55), § 70.

[69] Ertekün, loc. cit. (page 6, note 19), p. 76: "All U.N. resolutions which have been passed after hearing only the Greek Cypriot side and without hearing the Turkish Cypriot side, in contravention of the "audi et alterem partem" rule of the rules of natural justice, cannot be considered binding on the Turkish Cypriot side".

[70] Z. Necatigil, United Nations resolutions on Cyprus, in: Resat Arim (ed.) Cyprus and international law, p. 60 (67).

at a given moment on which kind of solution to the Cyprus Problem would be desirable and unbiased.

The same is true for good offices that have not been requested explicitly by the Security Council. The Secretary-General may bring to the attention of the Security Council any matter, which in his opinion may threaten the maintenance of international peace and security (Article 99 UN Charter). In practice, many Secretary-Generals have interpreted this provision in a broad way, undertaking many sorts of peace initiatives on their own account. From a legal point of view, these activities bear the same weight as those carried out with a special mandate from the Security Council under Article 98 of the Charter. They are not legally binding, but politically important.

1.5. *Conclusion*

Neither the High-Level Agreements between the Cypriot parties of 1977 and 1979, nor the numerous resolutions of the Security Council and the General Assembly resolutions, nor the Secretary-General's reports are legally binding. Nevertheless, the UN documents are important since they express the common political will of the parties or the international community at a given moment. As such, they bear a certain weight at a given moment as a *political framework for a settlement*. But they can also be revised easily to take into account a change of circumstances over time.

2. The UN formula on the four key issues

Conceptually, the UN's task is to reconcile two diametrically opposed aspirations of the parties: the Greek Cypriot attempt to return to a situation as close as possible to the *status quo ante* (before 1974) vs. the Turkish Cypriot objective to legalize the de facto situation established since then.[71] In an attempt to bridge these two aspirations, the UN proposals embodied several formulas on the four core issues: governance, territory, property and security.

2.1. *Governance*

2.1.1. Political equality of the two communities

The first difficult question for each UN mediator was how to treat the two parties. As has been seen above, the existence of the two communities as political entities had been constitutionally acknowledged in 1959.[72] However, this analysis contrasted with the international practice to deal only with governments. The

[71] D. Pfirter, Genesis and Key Elements of the Draft Constitution in the Comprehensive Settlement Plan of the UN Secretary-General for Cyprus (Annan Plan), in: T. Giegerich (ed.), The EU Accession of Cyprus, 2006, p. 161 (166).

[72] See above Chapter II B 2.

Greek Cypriot leader could claim to represent not only his community, but also the Republic of Cyprus, whereas the Turkish Cypriot leader was restricted to the former role. Against that background, the UN developed in the 1970s and 1980s a formula that de-emphasized the international framework of mediation, but tried to invoke the constitutional perspective. Starting with UNGA resolution 3312 (XXIX) of 1 November 1974, negotiations between the "representatives of the communities" were said to "take place on an equal footing".[73]

Later on, this concept of formal equality at the negotiation table was enhanced with more connotations of substance. In the intercommunal talks between Vassiliou and Denktaş from September 1988 to March 1990 the new formula of the "political equality of the two communities" emerged. Secretary-General Pèrez de Cuèllar, in his opening Statement on 26 February 1990, recalled this concept and its definition.[74] The Security Council endorsed it in October 1991,[75] and SG Boutrous-Ghali used the term accordingly.[76]

> *Political equality means that both communities must have equal political status and that the two federated States must have equal and identical powers and functions. Both communities must be able to participate in the political process and the equality has to be reflected by effective participation in all organs and decisions of the federal government. However, 'political equality' does not imply precise numerical equality as regards participation in all branches and administration of the federal government. It implies that approval and amendment of the federal Constitution will require approval of both communities and that there are safeguards to ensure that the federal government will not be empowered to adopt any measures against the interest of one community.*

2.1.2. Bi-communal and bizonal federation

Both in 1977 and 1979 the respective Greek Cypriot leaders subscribed to the formula of «bi-communal federation».[77] In contemporaneous discussions, there was some dispute whether Makarios, in 1977, had consented to Turkish Cypriot view that any solution must envisage two political entities, based on territory.[78] In that direction pointed at least another formulation in the Four Guidelines.[79] Under

---

[73] The Security Council adopted this formula in Resolution 367 of 12 March 1975. The GA repeated it several times (see Res 32/15 of 9 November 1977; Res 33/15 of 9 November 1978; Res 34/30 of 20 November 1979).

[74] Report of the Secretary General, of 8 March 1990, S/21183, Annex I, para. 11.

[75] UNSC Resolution 716, 11 October 1991, § 4.

[76] Report of the Secretary-General of 3 April 1992, S/23780, § 11.

[77] § 1 of the Four Guidelines of the 1977 Agreement; § 2 of the 1979 Ten-Points Agreement, confirming the Guidelines.

[78] The Turkish Cypriot side was adament in proving the Archbishop`s respective intention, but also acknowledged that the term was deliberately ommited from the text of the Four Guidelines. See Ertekün, loc. cit (page 6, note 19), pp. 45–49.

[79] § 2 of the Four Guidelines referred to "territory under the administration of each community".

Kyprianou, any mentioning of «bi-zonality» was, however, seen with great suspicion in a substantial part of the inter-communal discussions in the early 1980ies. The situation was further complicated after the auto-proclamation of the TRNC in 1983 after which «bi-zonality» could be misunderstood as legitimizing two states.

Against this background, the UN developed a position by carefully combining «bi-communalism», «bizonality» and «federation». Most clearly, the opening Statement of the Secretary-General at the intercommunal talks in February 1990,[80] uses the wording *bi-communal and bi-zonal federation*. In its endorsement,[81] the Security Council further specifies that the envisaged federation should be bi-communal as regards the constitutional aspects and bi-zonal as regards the territorial aspects.

A federation has a single international personality and sovereignty, unlike a confederation where each partner maintains its own international personality in addition to the functional international personality of the confederation (= international personality only in the fields of its competence). Under Article 2(1) UN Charter all its members have sovereign equality implying that a confederation cannot become a member of the UN. To the detriment of Turkish Cypriot demands "federation", on the one hand, excludes any option as to separation into two States and the possibility of the creation of a confederation with an implied right to secession. On the other hand, to the detriment of Greek Cypriot hesitance, "federation" has some bearing on the institutional set-up of the common state, e.g. striving for a bi-communal federal House of Representatives,[82] institutional autonomy and residuary powers of the federated entities.[83]

In the context of UN documents, 'bi-communality' reflects the set-up of the 1960 Constitution but gives room for manoeuvre. It recognises that there are two communities in Cyprus, each of which is entitled to constitutionally protected rights and powers. The acknowledgement of the existence of two communities also implies that their relationship is not one of a minority and a majority.

'Bi-zonality' refers to the *status quo* created after the Turkish intervention of 1974 and the population exchange based on the Vienna III agreement of 1975, with the north being populated by a majority of Turkish Cypriots and Greek Cypriots mainly living in the south. It means that 'each federated State will be administered by one community which will be firmly guaranteed a clear majority of the population and of the land ownership in its area'.[84] Hence, the UN accepts

[80] Report of the Secretary General of 8 March 1990, S/21183.

[81] UNSC Resolution 649 of 12 March 1991, §§ 2–3.

[82] Necatigil, loc. cit. (page 11, note 35), p. 274, note 9, observing that a uni-cameral federal legislature is not compatible with the concept of a federation.

[83] Most successful federations accept residuary powers of the federated entities. See e.g. Article 3 of the Swiss constitution of 1848, Article 30 of the German Grundgesetz, Article 15 of the Austrian Constitution, Tenth Amendment to the U.S. Constitution, Section 107 of the Commonwealth of Australia Constitution Act. Less common is that residual powers are vested in the federation (e.g. India).

[84] Report of the Secretary-General of 8 March 1990, S/21183, p. 8, Annex I.

the idea of an administration based on territory, which is one of the key concepts for the Turkish Cypriots.

2.2. *Territory*

The territorial issue refers to the percentage of the territory each community will administer in a post-settlement Cyprus. Certainly, the Turkish Cypriot part would have to be reduced from the 37%, which are currently under effective Turkish control. In the High-Level Agreement of 1977, both parties agreed to discuss territorial questions in the light of the economic viability and productivity. This implies that the territorial distribution does not need to be proportional to the strength of population and would allow the Turkish Cypriots to control more than 20 percent of the territory. The various proposals range from 80% to 70% for the Greek Cypriots and 20% to 30% for the Turkish Cypriots.

A rather crucial element of the territorial distribution concerns the selection of areas that would have to be handed over to Greek Cypriot administration. The UN Secretary-General notes that territorial adjustments should be undertaken in a manner that a "substantial number of Greek Cypriot displaced persons would be able to return to the area that would come under Greek Cypriot administration".[85]

The areas of Morphou, Varosha (a part of Famagusta) and the Karpas were usually most debated in the territorial question. Morphou touched the economic viability of the northern part. Varosha was the major tourist resort in Cyprus before 1974 and has remained practically vacant ever since. In 1984, the Turkish Cypriot side refused the so-called '5-point scenario', which would have resulted in a return of Varosha to the Greek Cypriots, because nothing was offered in return. But under any UN proposal Varosha would fall under the administration of the Greek Cypriot side. Finally, the Karpas peninsula was of great importance for the Greek Cypriots as it contained a religious site of significance in the monastery of Apostolos Andreas and also a residual Greek Cypriot population.

The most elaborate territorial proposal was contained in the 1992 'Set of Ideas'. The attached map envisaged a 28, 2% allocation for the Turkish Cypriots, thus closely meeting their initial demand of 30%. However, along with the area of Varosha, the return of the Morphou region had been proposed. Since the latter contains the northern part's main irrigable land and the majority of oranges groves held by the Turkish Cypriots as well as important water resources the proposed map was rejected by the Turkish Cypriot side. According to the leader of the Turkish Cypriot community, the principle of economic viability includes taking into account fertility and agricultural viability.

2.3. *Security*

As Makarios' attempt to terminate the Treaty of Alliance in early 1964 had failed, the traditional Greek Cypriot position at the negotiating table aimed at abrogation

[85] Report of the Secretary-General of 3 April 1992, S/23780, Part B, § 25.

of the Treaties of Guarantee and Alliance as well as full demilitarisation of the island. Remarkably, the Turkish Cypriots had agreed in the 10-points agreement of 1979 that the demilitarization of the Republic of Cyprus is envisaged, and matters relating thereto will be discussed. Nevertheless this Turkish Cypriot openness ceased, it seems, in early 1980 when the military took power in Ankara.

Faced with a strong position of the Turkish generals on that issue, the United Nations always considered the Treaty of Guarantee (together with the Treaty of Alliance) as a valid basis for discussing the security arrangements. The UN reiterated at several occasions that the 'Treaties of Guarantee and of Alliance would remain a valid framework, and that they would be updated keeping in mind the purposes and principles of the Charter of the UN'.[86] Politically, this formula must be understood as an acknowledgement of the legitimate expectation of the Turkish Cypriots that they cannot be left without a Turkish security guarantee,[87] while at the same time Greek Cypriot ideas could be channelled into a new security arrangement through a protocol to be negotiated.

Thus, the 'Set of Ideas' of 1992 provides for the presence of foreign troops, but specifies that Turkish and Greek contingents will be of equal size. Hence, it acknowledges that the "presence of Greek and Turkish contingents of reasonable and equal size is an essential feature of security in Cyprus" as mentioned earlier in the Secretary-General's Report.[88] Furthermore, the federal force will consist of a Greek Cypriot and a Turkish Cypriot unit of equal size and equipment and may not exceed the size of the Greek and Turkish contingents.

The withdrawal of foreign troops not provided for in international treaties and urged by the UN Security Council in Resolution 353 and reiterated by Resolution 360 is in line with the Greek Cypriot position and has been accepted by both sides. The timing of the withdrawal, however, is a more disputed topic. The Greek Cypriots, for example, rejected the proposal of Pèrez de Cuèllar of December 1984, and subsequently the modified proposal in March 1986 on the grounds of missing timeframes for the withdrawal of foreign troops. Instead of a gradual withdrawal parallel to the establishment of a transitory government, the Greek Cypriots urged that the withdrawal be completed before starting with the building of a transitory government. This has been taken into account in Boutros-Ghali's 'Set of Ideas'. The timetable for reduction to an agreed level of Greek Cypriot and Turkish Cypriot units and for withdrawal of all non-Cypriot forces not provided for under the Treaty of Alliance would be fully implemented prior to the establishment of the federal republic.

---

[86] Report of the Secretary-General of 8 March 1990, S/21183, p. 8, Annex I.

[87] Commenting on the stance of Kyprianou in 1985, an observer found that the Turkish Cypriots would never consent to a complete demilitarization of the island, which makes insistence on such a proposal tantamount to a strategy to produce failure. Hottinger, loc. cit. (note 26), p. 57.

[88] Report of the Secretary-General of 8 March 1990, S/21183, p. 8, Annex I.

2.4. *Property*

After the exodus of the Greek Cypriot population to the south, the Security Council, in Resolution 361 of 30 August 1974,

> *expressed its grave concern at the plight of refugees and other persons displaced as a result of the situation in Cyprus and urges the parties concerned, in conjunction with the Secretary-General, to search for peaceful solutions of the problem of refugees, and take appropriate measures to provide for their relief and welfare and to permit persons who wish to do so to return to their homes in safety.*[89]

Similarly, the General Assembly's resolution of 1 November 1974 considered that "all the refugees should return to their homes in safety" and called upon the parties concerned to undertake urgent measures to that end.[90]

However, subsequent UN formula how to implement returns, remained rather vague. The most elaborate attempt can be found in the Set of Ideas. Its fundamental principle is the recognition of the property *claims* of the displaced persons from both communities. The ownership of the property claimed is transferred to the respective agency, which exchanges titles of property on a global communal basis at the 1974 value plus inflation. The compensation paid to the displaced person will be funded from the sale of transferred property or through exchange of property and contributions from other sources. Current permanent residents of Cyprus who owned their permanent residence at the time of displacement (the cut-off dates are December 1963 for Turkish Cypriots and 1974 for Greek and Turkish Cypriots) can also opt to return to their former residence with the purpose of resuming their permanent residence. This right to return is restricted "if the current occupant is also a displaced person and wishes to remain, or if the property has been substantially altered or has been converted to public use".[91] In these cases compensation will be offered. A second limitation to the right to return derives from the concept of 'bi-zonality' of the federation. The fact that Turkish Cypriots will be guaranteed the majority in terms of population as well as land ownership in the federated State under their administration implies a ceiling of the number of displaced persons returning to their place of origin. That ceiling serves as a safeguard, if more Greek Cypriots return than expected.[92]

Whereas this concept seems to reconcile the divergent interests between those who lost their homes and those who are actually using it, the Set of Ideas was nevertheless deliberately silent on one important conceptual issue, namely on the question of ownership. The Set does not affirm that property still lies in the hands of the displaced owners, but only distinguishes between 'current occupants' and 'displaced persons who seek compensation'.

---

[89] UNSC Resolution 361 of 30 August 1974, § 4.

[90] UNGA Resolution 3212 (XXIX) of 1 November 1974, § 5.

[91] Report of the Secretary-General of 21 August 1992, S/24472, p. 19, Annex, § 84.

[92] It is uncertain how many Greek Cypriots would opt to go back to the north living under Turkish Cypriot administration. Remarkably sceptical in this regard L. G. Charalambous, Refugees: Try the reality test, Sunday Mail, 24.02.2004, p. 13.

From an international law point of view, this formula is open to criticism. Under general international law, there is a growing body of evidence suggesting an evolving customary *right* to return into one's own home. Whereas it is uncertain whether the first General Assembly Resolutions in this respect (Palestinian[93] and Pakistani refugees)[94] already expressed an *opinio juris,* the more recent UN Security Council Resolutions are more outspoken. UN Security Council Resolution 971 refers to a "right to return" for the Abkasians.[95] In the case of the local Serb population in the Croatian Krajina, it acted under Chapter VII and demanded imperatively[96]

> *that the Government of the Republic of Croatia, in conformity with internationally recognised standards and in compliance with the agreement of 6 August 1995 between the Republic of Croatia and the United Nations Peace Forces (a) respect fully the rights of the local Serb population including their rights to remain, leave or return in safety, (b) allow access to this population by international humanitarian organisations, and (c) create conditions conducive to the return of those persons who have left their homes.*

Most significantly, Article I (1) Annex VII of the Dayton-Agreement promises the refugees of Bosnia-Herzegovina a return to their homes.[97] Finally, the UN Security Council reiterated its view on a right of refugees to return home twice in the Kosovo crisis.[98]

State practice also changed over time. Whereas in the cases of the Palestinian and Greek Cypriot refugees, Israel and Turkey did not accept their return, Pakistan concluded an agreement with Afghanistan.[99] The parties to the conflict in Abchasia, i.e. Russia, Georgia and the Abchasians, also reached an agreement how to implement the return of refugees in the early 90's. The UN's call upon Bosnians nationals to come back to their homes after 1995 was widely implemented, although the "minority" return of ethnic Bosnians to predominantly Serb villages proved difficult in some instances. The quick return of Kosovars to the province was largely successful due to UN interim administration in the region under UN Security Council Resolution 1244.

---

93 UNGA Resolution 194 (III) of 11 December 1948.

94 C. Tomuschat, Das Recht auf die Heimat, Festschrift Partsch, pp. 183–214 (194 et seq.).

95 UNSC Resolution 971 of 12 January 1995, Preamble, 2nd indent: "Recalling the right of all refugees and displaced persons affected by the conflict to return to their homes in secure conditions in accordance with international law and as set out in the Quadripartite Agreement on voluntary return of refugees and displaced persons (S/1994/397, annex II), signed in Moscow on 4 April 1994."

96 UNSC Resolution 1009 of 10 August 1995, § 2.

97 Annex 7 Art. 1 Abs. 1 Satz 1 Dayton agreement states: "All refugees and displaced persons have the right freely to return to their homes of origin".

98 UNSC Resolution 1239 of 14 May 1999, § 4: "Reaffirms the right of all refugees and displaced persons to return to their homes in safety and in dignity". See also UNSC Resolution 1244 of 10 June (Preamble, 7th indent).

99 Tomuschat, loc. cit. (note 94), p. 183 (187).

It can therefore be concluded, that at least at the beginning of the 90's the right to return was not only proclaimed, but also put into some practice. It may thus be in the process of becoming customary law since then. In addition, Cyprus is bound by the standards of the First Additional Protocol to the European Convention on Human Rights.[100]

Any UN formula on property must take that status of international law into account. Nevertheless, that does not preclude that a settlement prescribes limitations to the right to return. The specific content of the evolving right to return is hard to define. Return means in the first place that there should be no entry restrictions to the disputed territory. Only exceptionally, as in the case of the Palestinians[101] and the Bosnians,[102] are property claims addressed. Under the "Bosnian rule" refugees have the right to have restored to them property of which they were deprived in the course of hostilities and to be compensated for any property that cannot be restored to them. International law, however, does not define under which circumstances compensation should be effected instead of restoration.[103] It is also silent on how to deal with those who might have acquired their actual property in good faith.

Article 1 of the First Additional Protocol ECHR neither offers much insight. In the decided cases, the Court was clear that the *non-access* to the properties in the north constituted an interference with the right to property under the first sentence of Article 1.[104] But it also scrutinised whether this interference might be justified.[105] It seemed to accept that the need to rehouse displaced Turkish Cypriots might constitute a legitimate aim for expropriating Greek Cypriots. But the Court was unable to see why this need could justify the complete negation of the Greek Cypriot property rights in the form of a total and continuous denial of access and a purported expropriation without compensation.

---

[100] See above Chapter III, B 2.3.4.

[101] UNGA Resolution 194 (III), § 11 calls for compensation for destroyed property.

[102] Dayton Agreement, Annex 7, Article 1, 2nd sentence: "They shall have the right to have restored to them property of which they were deprived in the course of hostilities since 1999 and to be compensated for any property that cannot be restored to them".

[103] Insofar questionable *Abi-Saab/Blumenwitz/Crawford/Dugard/Greenwood/Hafner/Orrego-Vicuna/Pellet/Schermers/Tomuschat*, Legal Issues arising from certain population transfers and displacements on the territory of the Republic of Cyprus in the period since 20 July 1974, Opinion of 30 June 1999, Section IV. The authors quote the Security Council Resolutions 1199, 1203 and 1239 on Kosovo to demonstrate the existence of an international law rule in favour of restitution in integrum, but do not discuss the relevant Annex VII of the Dayton Agreement which establishes a mixed system of restitution in integrum and compensation.

[104] ECHR, Loizidou v. Turkey (merits), loc. cit. (note 248), para. 63; Cyprus v. Turkey, loc. cit. (note 228), para. 187.

[105] ECHR, Loizidou v. Turkey (merits), loc. cit. (note 248), para 64; Cyprus v. Turkey, loc. cit. (note 228), para. 188.

3. Summary

The High Level Agreements of 1977 and 1979 were not legally binding between the Cypriot parties. Neither were the various resolutions from the UN General Assembly, the UN Security Council or the proposals of the UN Secretary-Generals. Although all UN efforts to bring about a settlement prior the start of accession negotiations did not bear fruit they were, for sure, not devoid of purpose. The General Assembly and the Security Council had established a political framework for a settlement. Secretary-General Boutrous Ghali had gone a long way to bridge the two positions with his set ouf ideas. The broad lines of possible "give and takes" were incorporated in the basic "UN language". The notion of a "bizonal, bi-communal Federation" is a compromise on governance and territory. "Bizonality" accepts the *status quo* of the population exchange and the idea of a Turkish Cypriot administration based on territory, to which the Greek Cypriots were opposed for a long time. The term "bi-communal" reflects the set-up of the 1960 Constitution but gives room for negotiation. In line with Greek Cypriot views, the term "federation" excludes any option as to separation into two States. But it also implies a certain institutional set-up of a united Cyprus, favourable to Turkish Cypriot ideas. The Ghali's map of 1992 made an effort to bridge the respective claims on territory at about 28,2%, whereas the UN never questioned the continued presence of Turkey's army on the island, albeit fettered by an equal number of Greek forces and a possible international force on the island. This satisfaction of Turkish Cypriot security goes hand in hand with the satisfaction of the Greek Cypriot demand to allow the return of refugees, qualified by restrictive conditions that would limit the exercise of this right.

Chapter V

Cyprus as Candidate for EU Membership

A. THE FACTS

1. EC-Cyprus relations under the 1972 Association Agreement

In 1962, one year after the British application for EC membership, Cyprus asked the European Community for an Association Agreement in order to counterbalance the prospect of losing its Commonwealth preferences with Britain.[1] However, in view of the French veto to the British entry, it withdrew this request a year later and renewed it only in 1972, when the British admission to the Community was certain.[2] The Agreement was concluded on 19 December 1972 and went into force on 1 June 1973.[3] It mainly regulated trade. Two five-year phases of liberalisation should have led to the establishment of a customs union. The Agreement also established an Association Council which decides by unanimity, including on disputes.[4]

---

[1] Joseph, loc. cit. (page 10, note 32), p. 117.

[2] Drevet, loc. cit. (page 15, note 13), p. 246.

[3] Council Regulation 1246/73 of 14 May 1973, OJ 1973, L 133, p. 1.

[4] Under Article 34 of the 1987 protocol, the dispute settlement system was strengthened. If the Association Council does not decide in a dispute, each party could designate an

Legal Aspects of the Cyprus Problem, pp. 83–96.

After 1974, the time schedule was re-arranged. Due to a cautious Community attitude,[5] the first phase of the Association was prolonged several times.[6] On 24 November 1980, the Association Council decided to start negotiating the conditions and procedures for the second phase as from 1982.[7] Following another set of interim agreements,[8] the second phase was finally agreed upon between the Community and Cyprus with the additional protocol of 19 October 1987.[9] In addition to further reductions in tariffs, both sides agreed to apply EC competition rules to the association (Article 27, 28 of the additional protocol).

Another aspect of EC-Cyprus relations prior to 1990 relates to financial co-operation. During the second meeting of the Association Council on 24 June 1975,[10] the Cypriot Minister of Foreign Affairs, Christophides, asked the Community to grant technical and financial assistance in view of the Turkish intervention. In response to the specific situation in Cyprus, and in line with its Mediterranean policy, financial protocols were concluded in 1977 (30 Mio ECU),[11] in 1984 (44 Mio ECU)[12] and in 1989 (62 Mio ECU).[13]

As regards the status of the Turkish Cypriot community, the EC followed the UN line. When, in November 1975, Turkey informed the Community that the founding of the Federated Turkish Cypriot State of Cyprus was not tantamount to partition as prohibited under the Treaty of Guarantee, it did not react officially. However, after the proclamation of the TRNC in 1983, the ten Foreign Ministers, including the new Member State Greece, issued a rather strong statement:

> *The ten Member States of the European Community are deeply concerned by the declaration purporting to establish a 'Turkish Republic of Northern Cyprus' as an independent State. They reject this declaration which is in disregard of successive resolutions of the United Nations. The Ten reiterate their unconditional support for the independence, sovereignty, territorial integrity and unity of the Republic of Cyprus. They continue to regard the Government of President Kyprianou as the sole legitimate Government of the Republic of Cyprus. They call upon all interested parties not to recognise this act, which creates a very serious situation in the area.*[14]

---

arbitrator and the Council should nominate the third (Lycorgous, loc. cit. [page 53, note 103], p. 48). The system was nevertheless "imperfect" as each side could frustrate arbitration by simply not appointing its own arbitrator or blocking the Council's decision to nominate the third one.

[5] Drevet, loc. cit. (page 15, note 13), p. 248.

[6] See the Additional Protocol of 15.09.1977, OJ 1977, L 339; Supplementary Protocol of 11.05.1978, OJ 1978, L 172; Transitional Protocol of 21.12.1979 (referred to in the Commissions answer to written question 535/79, OJ 1980, C 74, p. 4).

[7] Association Council EC-Cyprus, Decision 1/80 of 24 November 1980.

[8] Protocol of 18 March 1981, OJ 1981, L 174, 27; Protocol of 26 July 1983, OJ 1983, L 353, p. 2.

[9] Protocol of 19 October 1987, OJ 1987, L 393, p. 2.

[10] The first meeting took place on 26 November 1973 in Brussels.

[11] Financial Protocol of 15 September 1977, OJ 1978, L 332, p. 1.

[12] Financial Protocol of 7 July 1983, OJ 1983, L 85, p. 37.

[13] Financial Protocol of 30 November 1989, OJ 1990, L 82, p. 33.

[14] Declaration of 17 November 1983, EC-Bulletin 1983/11, point 2.4.1, p. 68.

The overall political situation influenced the implementation of Community aid to Cyprus. Under the first financial protocol of 1977 the infrastructure projects (projects on electricity and water supply)[15] benefited both communities.[16] In contrast, the aid under the second financial protocol of 1984 went foremost to the south, be it because the largest project concerned the upgrading of agricultural land there,[17] be it because the Turkish Cypriots did not submit projects through the Cyprus Central bank any more in order to avoid cooperation with the Republic.[18] Under the third protocol, some aid was used for the restoration of both parts of Nicosia (Nicosia Masterplan), where the mayors of both sides of the town could work together for implementation purposes.

2. The application for membership 1990

2.1. *The application*

Under the Presidency of George Vassiliou, the Cypriot Foreign Minister, Iacovou, addressed the following letter to the then President of the Council, the Italian Foreign Minister de Michelis on 3 July 1990:

> *Mr. President, on behalf of the Government of Cyprus, I have the honour to inform you that Cyprus hereby submits its application to become a member of the European Economic Community, in accordance with the provisions of Article 237 of the Treaty establishing that Community.*[19]

Apart from economic considerations, the political motivation for that move was no secret. According to a poll of April 1991, 76% of the Cypriot population in the south believed that Cypriot accession to the EU would contribute towards the solution of the political problem. On 18 December 1989, the Commission had responded negatively to the April 1987 Turkish application to join the Community, inter alia, with the reasoning that

> *The examination of the political aspects of the accession of Turkey would be incomplete if it did not consider the negative effects of the dispute between Turkey and one Member State of the Community, and also the situation in Cyprus (. . .). At issue are*

[15] Response of the Commission to written question No. 980/82, OJ 1982, C 320, 14.

[16] Lycourgos, loc. cit. (page 53, note 103), p. 40; Yesilada/Sözen, Negotiating a Resolution to the Cyprus problem, International Relations 2002, 261 (263) report that the Turkish Cypriots received 6 million ECU out of the total amount of 30 million ECU.

[17] Lycourgos, loc. cit. (page 53, note 103), p. 41.

[18] Dodd, loc. cit. (page 55, note 111), p. 37. A.-S. Jakobsson Hatay, The Contribution of European Integration to ethnic conflict resolution: the cases of northern Ireland and Cyprus, in: The Cyprus Review, Volume 13, No. 1 (2001), p. 31 (41 FN 20) claims that the Turkish Community received only 4, 5% of EC aid under the second protocol due to the declaration of statehood.

[19] In two similar letters of the same date, in the same language, applications to join EURATOM and the ECSC were made.

> *the unity, independence, sovereignty and territorial integrity of Cyprus, in accordance with the relevant resolutions of the United Nations.*[20]

This carefully drafted statement coincides with the political analysis that Greece under Prime Minister Papandreou would any way block Turkey's accession if there was no prior Cyprus settlement.[21] In diplomatic language, the European Council of Dublin, on 26 June 1990, took note of this fact and reiterated that the Cyprus problem "affects EC-Turkey relations".[22]

The Turkish Cypriot leadership reacted to the application by presenting a memorandum to the Community on 12 July 1990[23] and a supplementary note on 3 September 1990.[24] Allegedly, the application for membership was illegal because the Greek Cypriot government did not represent the Turkish Cypriots and because it violated the Treaty of Guarantee.

After lengthy discussions, COREPER proposed to the Council on 12 September 1990 to forward the application to the Commission, in order to set the accession procedure in motion. The Council agreed and reaffirmed

> *its constant position that the advantages of relations between the EC and Republic of Cyprus should be to the benefit of the whole population of the island and its full support for the independence, sovereignty, territorial integrity and unity of Cyprus.*[25]

The Commission decided not to act upon the application.[26] Under the 1991 "it-is urgent-to-wait" formula, accession negotiations should not start before the conclusion of the Maastricht Treaty at the end of that year. It was further felt that Commission fact-finding missions in Cyprus would be detrimental to the UN efforts. Consequently, the enlargement group created in September 1991 dealt with the Swedish and Austrian applications, but not with the Cypriot one. External Relations Commissioner Matutes told Foreign Minister Iacovou in March 1992 that the four freedoms could not be applied in Cyprus under the *status quo*. Neither would it be possible that only a part of the population would represent Cyprus in European institutions. Therefore, a settlement was a precondition of accession. Iacovou's response that the Commission should abstain from commenting on the political issue (which should be reserved to the Council of Ministers), but restrict its opinion to economic and social issues, was not well received in Brussels. In addition, his contention that the Greek veto could be exercised over northern enlargement did not impress the Member States. At the Lisbon summit of 26/27 June 1992 they simply stated that the "*relations* (with Cyprus) *will be*

[20] COM SEC (89) 2290 final, § 9.

[21] H. Kramer, Der türkische Beitrittsantrag und der "griechische Faktor", EA 1987, p. 605 (609).

[22] Presidency Conclusions of the European Council of Dublin, 26 June 1990, reproduced in Press and Information Office (page 17, note 27), Appendix 23, p. 186.

[23] UN Doc A/44/966–S/21398, reprinted in Ertekün (ed.), loc. cit. (note 22), pp. 39–49.

[24] UN Doc A/45/538–S/21817, reprinted in Ertekün (ed.), loc. cit. (note 22), pp. 50–53.

[25] Reprinted in Cyprus Bulletin 24.09.1990, Vol. XXVIII 19, p. 1.

[26] H.-J. Axt, Explosiver Balkan und unruhiges Mittelmeer, Konflikte im Umfeld von Griechenland als Herausforderung der EG, in: Südosteuropa 11–12/1991, p. 579.

developed and strengthened on the basis of the Association Agreements and the application for membership and by intensifying the political dialogue".

2.2. *The Commission opinion of 30 June 1993*

Only in late 1992, after the failure of Boutros Ghali's Set of Ideas, the Commission started to prepare its opinion. Two officials visited the southern part of the island. The Turkish Cypriot authorities declined to co-operate. The Cyprus Government responded to a questionnaire concerning the whole island with figures related to the south only.

In its opinion of 30 June 1993,[27] the Commission formulated no objection that the Government had applied for the whole island. It was satisfied with the situation as regards democracy and human rights. However, in the northern part of the island, opposition parties had mentioned certain constraints and restrictions in their activities, in particular as regards access to the media.[28] In the economic field, the Commission observed high disparities between the two parts. Structural reforms in the south were deemed to be necessary, but manageable.[29] The northern part could benefit from accession through financial aid for infrastructure and the opening of markets in case of a settlement.[30] As regards Cyprus' ability to implement the *acquis,* the Association Agreement could serve as a good basis for harmonisation. However,

> *as a result of the de facto division of the island into two strictly separated parts, the fundamental freedoms laid down by the Treaty, and in particular freedom of movement of goods, people, services and capital, right of establishment and the universally recognised political, economic, social and cultural rights could not today be exercised over the entirety of the island's territory. These freedoms and rights would have to be guaranteed as part of a comprehensive settlement restoring constitutional arrangements covering the whole of the Republic of Cyprus.*[31]

Furthermore, the Commission was concerned about the institutional set-up in Cyprus. A future settlement should ensure that the decision-making process of the executive and the legislature would be compatible with the Community's discussion and decision-making apparatus and would enable the Cypriot authorities to adopt the *acquis communautaire* and implement it effectively throughout the island.[32] The Commission concluded that Cyprus's integration into the Community implied a peaceful, balanced and lasting settlement of the Cyprus question.[33] Nevertheless, the prospect of significant progress in the UN talks allowed it to

[27] COM (93) 313, Bulletin EC, Supplement 5/93, Luxemburg 1993; commented by H.-J. Axt, Zypern und die Europäische Union: Beitrittsperspektiven nach der Stellungnahme der EG-Kommission. Südosteuropa-Mitteilungen, 2/1994, pp. 163–169.

[28] Commisison opinion, loc. cit. (note 27), p. 12, § 17.

[29] Commission opinion, loc. cit. (note 27), pp. 14–15, § 28 et seq.

[30] Commission opinion, loc. cit. (note 27), p. 15, §§ 37–38.

[31] Commission opinion, loc. cit. (note 27), p. 8, § 10.

[32] Commission opinion, loc. cit. (note 27), p. 12, § 21.

[33] Commission opinion, loc. cit. (note 27), p. 17, § 47.

send a "positive signal", confirming that the Community considered Cyprus as eligible for membership.[34] If, however, the UN talks were to fail the situation should be reassessed.[35]

On 19 July 1993, Denktaş wrote a letter to Commission President Delors, again stressing the illegality of the application. A unilateral entry of the Greek Cypriot side would "*cement the division of the island*". Therefore, according to his view, the unilateral application should not be processed, but the EU should facilitate the efforts of the UN Secretary-General.

3. The decision to accept Cyprus as a candidate country

3.1. *The General Affairs Council decision of 6 March 1995*

On 4 October 1993, the Council responded positively to the Commission opinion. It also

> *confirmed the Community's support for the efforts made by the United Nations Secretary-General to produce a political settlement of the Cyprus question. If, in spite of these efforts, there was no prospect of a solution in the foreseeable future, the Council agreed to reassess the situation in the light of the positions expressed by each side in the intercommunity discussions and to examine in January 1995 the question of the accession of Cyprus to the European Union in the light of this situation.*[36]

Serge Abou, a senior Commission official, should report on the political developments and the consequences for the adoption of the *acquis* as well as about the UN progress. Since TRNC authorities did not co-operate he could work only under restrictive circumstances, which was heavily deplored in the Council.[37] He submitted three reports, the last one in January 1995,[38] and conveyed the message – in frank terms[39] – that the lack of progress in the intercommunal talks was due to a lack of will of the Turkish Cypriot side.[40]

[34] Commission opinion, loc. cit. (note 27), p. 17, § 48.

[35] Commission opinion, loc. cit. (note 27), p. 18, § 51.

[36] Council conclusions on the Commission opinion on Cyprus' application for accession of 4 October 1993, EU Bulletin 10/1993, pp. 68–69.

[37] B. Zepter, Beitrittsperspektiven Maltas und Zyperns, in: European Commission (ed.), Europäische Gespräche 3/96 – Die Mittelmeerpolitik der Europäischen Union, p. 88 (91).

[38] European Observer's Report on Cyprus, 23 January 1995, reprinted in C. Dodd, Cyprus Embroglio, Appendix 6, pp. 172–180.

[39] In his last report, Abou qualified the proposals of Clerides during the informal meetings on Confidence-Building Measures in October 1994 as "extremely useful" (§ 13), whereas Denktaş's position on "land for a viable solution" was disqualified as falling outside the spirit or the letter of the Security Council resolutions on the Cyprus issue (§ 12).

[40] A. Nicolaides, Zypern auf dem Weg zum EU-Beitritt, in: European Commission (ed.), Europäische Gespräche 3/96 – Die Mittelmeerpolitik der Europäischen Union, p. 99 (101).

Assessing that the Greek Cypriot side was not responsible for the failure of the UN talks on confidence-building measures, the EU slowly changed its position regarding the necessity to reach a settlement before the start of accession negotiations. The European Council in Korfu, in June 1994, decided that the next round of enlargement should comprise Malta and Cyprus. On 6 February 1995, the Commission presented a communication to the Council providing for the "reassessment of the situation". In its view, the Community should still make sure that the institutional set-up of a future Cyprus should not be detrimental to the EU decision-making procedures. Nevertheless, accession negotiations could start six months after the conclusion of the Amsterdam Intergovernmental Conference.[41] At its meeting of 6 March 1995, the General Affairs Council endorsed this proposal and linked two important decisions.[42] First, it agreed to start accession negotiations with Cyprus together with the other candidate countries, and second it agreed to establish a customs union with Turkey. Being satisfied with the first decision, the Greek Government did not veto any more the second one, like it had done in December 1994.

3.2. *The Association Council meeting of 12 June 1995*

The "structured dialogue" with the candidate countries, introduced by the Essen summit of December 1994, was extended to Cyprus. During the 16th meeting on 12 June 1995, the EU-Cyprus Association Council started to discuss political issues, and Cyprus was allowed to associate itself with CFSP-Declarations of the 15 Member States. In addition, the Community declared its pre-accession strategy. The fourth financial protocol was concluded in the same year[43] with the express aim

> *to contribute to the economic and social development of Cyprus, facilitate its economic transition with a view to accession to the European Union, and support efforts to promote a general settlement of the Cyprus question* (Art. 1).

In practice, 7 Mio € out of the 12 Mio € could not be spent due to the non-co-operation of the Turkish Cypriot side. To use at least some money, the Commission proposed to finance civil society projects with 1,975 Mio € and the translation of some parts of the *acquis* into Turkish with 3 Mio €.

3.3. *The Luxembourg Council (December 1997)*

In December 1997, upon the recommendation of the Commission in its Agenda 2000, the Luxembourg Council decided to launch accession negotiations with

---

[41] Communication of the Commission to the Council in view of the reexamination of the question of Cyprus' accession to the European Union, SEC (95) 205 final.

[42] H.-J. Axt, Zypern – ein Beitrittskandidat der Europäischen Union – Implikationen für die Insel die Region und die Union, Südosteuropa 5/1995, pp. 259–279 (259, 263); C. Brewin, loc. cit. (page 52, note 98), pp. 137 and 140.

[43] Financial Protocol of 30 October 1995, OJ 1995 L 278, p. 23.

Poland, the Czech Republic, Hungary, Estonia, Slovenia and Cyprus. As regards the latter, the Council stated:

> *28. The accession of Cyprus should benefit all communities and help to bring about civil peace and reconciliation. The accession negotiations will contribute positively to the search for a political solution to the Cyprus problem through the talks under the aegis of the United Nations, which must continue with a view to creating a bi-community, bi-zonal federation. In this context, the European Council requests that the willingness of the Government of Cyprus to include representatives of the Turkish Cypriot community in the accession negotiating delegation be acted upon. In order for this request to be acted upon, the necessary contacts will be undertaken by the Presidency and the Commission.*

After his re-election as President, Clerides issued an invitation to the Turkish Cypriots to participate in the accession negotiations as full members of the Cypriot delegation.[44] On 12 March 1998, during the European Conference, he transmitted this invitation to the British Presidency, which conveyed it to the Turkish Cypriot leader. The latter, however, refused to accept that Turkish Cypriot representatives should be part of the delegation of the Republic.[45]

B. LEGAL EVALUATION

1. The legality of Cyprus' application to the EU

In its memorandum of 1990, the Turkish Cypriot leadership argued that Cyprus' application was illegal under international law. The Commission rejected this view in its Opinion of 1993.[46] In 1995, Turkey addressed the issue in the EU-Turkey Association Council. In a joint declaration of 28 December 1995, Turkey and the TRNC expressed their common view that Cyprus could not join "international political and economic unions to which Turkey and Greece are not members".[47] On the request of Turkey, Professor Mendelson, published a legal opinion in June/

[44] On the circumstances of the invitation see Hannay, loc. cit. (page xii, note 2), pp. 89–91.

[45] For the motivation of this refusal see E. Olgun, European Union for "Cyprus" – Pros and Cons, p. 25 (28): "If the Turkish Cypriot side accepted to discuss the subject of EU membership now, before a settlement and before a joint application, no doubt, it would, in effect, have formally recognized the legitimacy of the Greek Cypriot 'Government of Cyprus' and the validity of the unilateral membership application. This would amount to self-denial as a constituent politically equal party in Cyprus and would expose the Turkish Cypriot side to further pressure to make even more concessions".

[46] Commission opinion, loc. cit. (note 27), p. 7, § 8.

[47] Joint Declaration of the Republic of Turkey and the Turkish Republic of Northern Cyprus of 28 December 1995, § 3, reprinted in Dodd, loc. cit. (note 38), Appendix 7, p. 181 (182).

July 1997, according to which Cyprus' accession is illegal.[48] Professors Crawford, Hafner, and Pellet, rebutted this opinion in their opinion of October 1997, commissioned by Cyprus.[49] An additional Opinion prepared by Professor Mendelson in September 2001[50] provoked another counter Opinion of Professors Crawford, Hafner and Pellet in November that year.[51] The main arguments relate to the Treaty of Guarantee and to the Constitution of 1960.

1.1. *Article I (2) of the Treaty of Guarantee*

Article I (2) of the Treaty of Guarantee states:

> *The Republic of Cyprus undertakes not to participate, in whole or in part, in any political or economic union with any State whatsoever. It accordingly declares prohibited any activity likely to promote, directly or indirectly, either union with any other State or partition of the island.*

According to Article 31 (1) of the Vienna Convention, this provision shall be interpreted in accordance with the ordinary meaning to be given to its terms in their context and in the light of its object and purpose. Together with the context subsequent practice shall also be taken into account (Article 31 (3) of the Vienna Convention).

First, Cyprus' accession to a Union of 15 Member States is not creating a union between Cyprus and *one* other State. According to the opposite view, however, Article 1 (2) of the Treaty of Guarantee also prohibits EU accession because it amounts to 15 prohibited unions with any Member State of the European Union. It would thus constitute, "in particular also" an economic union with Greece.[52] Such a construction of the terms "with any State whatsoever" leaves however, its context as well as its object and purpose far behind. The history of the provision shows that unification ("*enosis*") with Greece should be outlawed, as should partitioning ("*taksim*").[53] Exactly this deal – both sides giving up their maximum positions – led to the Zurich compromise in 1959.[54] In contrast, Mendelson holds that also accession to international organisations was in principle outlawed, unless

---

[48] M. Mendelson, Opinion of 6 June 1997, loc. cit. (page 41, note 43).

[49] J. Crawford/G. Hafner/A. Pellet, Republic of Cyprus: Eligibility for EU Membership, Opinion of 14 October 1997, reprinted in: A. Markides, Cyprus and EU Membership, Important Legal Documents, pp. 13–35.

[50] M. Mendelson, Further Opinion on the Application of the "Republic of Cyprus" to join the European Union of 12 September 2001, UN Doc A/56/451/, S/2001/953.

[51] J. Crawford/G. Hafner/A. Pellet, Republic of Cyprus: Eligibility for EU Membership, Further Opinion of 17 November 2001, reprinted in: A. Markides (ed.), Cyprus and EU Membership, Important Legal Documents, pp. 36–46.

[52] Rumpf, loc. cit. (page 8, note 24), EuGRZ 1997, p. 533 (535 note 22).

[53] Crawford/Hafner/Pellet, First Opinion, loc. cit (note 49), pp. 9–11 with further references to the opinions expressed by the Greek and Turkish negotiators on 12 February 1959 after the Zurich deliberations and on 19 October 1959 during the London Joint Committee.

[54] Tzermias, loc. cit. (page 5, note 13), AöR 1959, p. 459 (473).

both Turkey and Greece were members of it or unless both Cypriot communities agreed.[55] This argument is weak, since the prohibition to accede to an international organisation of which Greece and Turkey are not members, is laid down in Article 50 of the Constitution and not in the Treaty of Guarantee. Hence a clear distinction between a "political or econonomic union with any State" on the one hand (Treaty of Gurantee), and "international organisations and pacts of alliance" on the other hand (Article 50 Constitution) was made.[56] These are different instruments: the Treaty refers to international obligations of Cyprus, whereas the Constitution sets out the internal decision-making process. The latter can thus not be used to interpret the former.[57] It is hard to see how an internal right of the Turkish Cypriot Vice-President (to veto the accession to an international organisation in which Greece and Turkey are not members at the same time) can be transformed into an international obligation of the State.

Second, even if the Treaty of Guarantee prohibited a political or economic union with other State*s* (*in plural*), membership in the European Union is not covered because Member States of the Union remain independent States. In contrast, Mendelson refers to an advisory opinion of the Permanent International Court of Justice of 1931 according to which a proposed customs union between Austria and Germany was deemed to compromise the economic independence of Austria, in violation of treaty obligations existing at that time. However, from the wording of Articles I and II of the Treaty of Guarantee and from the context in which they were negotiated it follows that the objective of the prohibition imposed on the Republic of Cyprus was to prevent its assimilation by another State as well as its partition. This finality corresponds to the founding principles of the Republic of Cyprus, namely independence, territorial integrity, and security. The accession to the European Union does not undermine the sovereignty, territorial integrity and independence of Cyprus which is shown by Article 6 (3) of the EU Treaty[58] stating that the "*Union respects the national identity of its Member States, whose systems of government are based on democratic principles*". More specifically, whereas it is true that there is a customs union between Member States (Art. 25 et seq. EC), economic policy still lies in the hands of Member States and is only co-ordinated in the EU framework (Art. 99 et seq. EC). Their decision-making would be in no way dominated by Greece.[59] Hence, the danger of economic subordination of Cyprus to Greece *via* the tools of European Union policy simply

[55] Mendelson, First Opinion, loc. cit. (page 41, note 43), § 108.

[56] Crawford/Hafner/Pellet, First Opinion, loc. cit. (note 49), p. 6.

[57] Erroneuos Mendelson that "various provisions of the Constitution bear out" his interpretation of the Treaty of Guarantee (First opinion, loc. cit. (page 41, note 43), § 108 in the beginning). Rather to the contrary, Article 185 (2) repeating that the integral or partial union of Cyprus with any other State is excluded, shows that these are two different instruments. Otherwise, the inclusion of Article 185 (2) into the Constitution would be senseless; Crawford/Hafner/Pellet, Second Opinion, loc. cit. (note 51), § 11.

[58] Crawford/Hafner/Pellet, Second Opinion, loc. cit. (note 51), § 5 (e).

[59] Filos, loc. cit. (page 5, note 16), p. 208.

does not exist. There is no specific rapprochement between Cyprus and Greece, but rapprochement between Cyprus and more than twenty other European States, excluding the possibility that Greece will hold a privileged position in Cyprus.[60]

Third, coherent subsequent practice supports the interpretation that Article I (2) of the Treaty of Guarantee does not preclude accession to the European Union. Already Article 1 of the Trade Agreement between Cyprus and Turkey of 9 November 1963 envisaged the accession of Cyprus to the EEC.[61] Such a clause would have been impossible if Article 1 (2) Treaty of Guarantee impeded the participation of Cyprus in an economic community with other States. Ten years later Turkey did not challenge the Association Agreement between Cyprus and the EEC aimed at gradually establishing a customs union with the EEC Member States on the ground that it would breach the Treaty of Guarantee. All 15 EU Member States also agreed in 1995 to enter into accession negotiations with Cyprus. The members of the UN Security Council expressly welcomed[62] this move while at the same time confirming their view that any political settlement of the Cyprus question must exclude union in whole or in part with any other country.[63] The conjuction of the two paragraphs makes it quite clear that the Security Council regards the accession of Cyprus to the EU as plainly consistent with a renewed commitment to avoid "union in whole or in part with any other country".[64] Against this background, the United Kingdom rejected Mendelson's opinion, citing the unambiguous wording of Article I (2) of the Treaty of Guarantee and "the actions and statements of other European Union Member States, the Commission and the United Nations Security Council.[65]

In sum, all accepted means of treaty interpretation lead to the result that Article I (2) of the Treaty of Guarantee does not outlaw Cyprus' accession to an international organization. Rather, as confirmed by subsequent practice of Cyprus and the Guarantor powers, this provision would prevent union of Cyprus with one other State only.

---

[60] C. Tomuschat, The Accession of Cyprus to the European Union, in: Festschrift Tsatsos, p. 672 (680).

[61] Article 1 of the Trade Agreement between Cyprus and Turkey of 9 Novemer 1963 (Official Gazette of 21 November 1963) reads:

> "The above most-favoured national treatment shall not apply
>
> (c) to privileges, exemptions from taxes (fees), preferences or concessions which each of the Contracting countries has granted or will grant in the future to other countries on account of a present or future participation, entry or association by them to a customs union, a free trade area or an economic community".

[62] UNSC Resolution 1062 of 28 June 1996, § 13; UNSC Resolution 1092 of 23 December 1996, § 17; UNSC Resolution 1117 of 26 June 1997, § 14.

[63] UNSC Resolution 1092 of 23 December 1996, § 14; UNSC Resolution 1117 of 26 June 1997, § 11.

[64] Crawford/Hafner/Pellet, First Opinion, loc. cit. (note 49), p. 13.

[65] Letter dated 5 November 2001 from the Permanent Representative of the United Kingdom of Great Britain and Northern Ireland to the United Nations addressed to the Secretary-General, A/56/612–S/2001/1059 of 9 November 2001.

1.2. *Article 50 of the Constitution*

Art. 50 (1) (a) of the Constitution reads:

> *The President and the Vice-President of the Republic, separately or conjointly, shall have the right of final veto on any law or decision of the House of Representatives or any part thereof concerning –*
> *(a) foreign affairs, except the participation of the Republic in international organisations and pacts of alliance in which the Kingdom of Greece and the Republic of Turkey both participate.*
> *For the purposes of this subparagraph, "foreign affairs" includes*
> *(i) . . .*
> *(ii) the conclusion of international treaties, conventions and agreements.*

This provision constitutes an institutional safeguard for the Turkish Cypriot community, to be exercised by the Vice-President. This provision was dispensed with after the Turkish Cypriot withdrawal from the State institutions in 1963/1964.[66] Against that finding Mendelson argues first that Greek Cypriots had not formally amended the Constitution. However, there is no legal rule according to which a Constitution must be formally changed if a provision has become temporarily obsolete. Second, Mendelson holds that Article 50 of the Constitution was meant to give a veto power to the Turkish Cypriot community as such, and not to the Vice-President *ad personam*. Drawing from the TRNC Memorandum of 1990, the Turkish Cypriot community was clearly against EU membership.[67] Apart from the fact that this argument leaves the wording of Article 50 of the Constitution far behind, it violates the principle of *dolo petit*. It is excluded that the Turkish Community can base itself on a right under a constitution from which it had withdrawn, not electing any person who could perform the function of the Vice-President of the Republic.

1.3. *Article 170 of the Constitution*

Finally, Mendelson contends that Article 170 of the Constitution would prohibit the EU accession of Cyprus. According to Article 170 (1) of the Cypriot Constitution of 1960 the Republic shall, by agreement on appropriate terms, accord most-favoured-nation treatment to Greece, Turkey and the United Kingdom. Entering the European Union would disfavour Turkey, because Greece and the United Kingdom would receive better treatment by Cyprus.

However, the provision uses a technical term of international trade law, which is reproduced in Article I GATT 1947.[68] Article XXIV (5) GATT makes it clear

---

66 See above Chapter II B 1.3.1.

67 Mendelson, First Opinion, loc. cit. (page 41, note 43), § 108.

68 Most-favoured-nation treatment is defined in Article I (1) of the GATT as follows: "With respect to customs duties and charges of any kind imposed on or in connection with importation or exportation or imposed on the international transfer of payments for imports or exports, and with respect to the method of levying such duties and charges, and with respect to all rules and formalities in connection with importation

that no state has to accord such a treatment to third States if it had joined a customs union (like the EU Single Market).[69] Indeed, such understanding was shared between Cyprus and Turkey while concluding a Trade Agreement on 9 November 1963. Article 1 of this Agreement explicitly excludes most favoured nation treatment to privileges or concessions granted on account of the participation in a customs union or free trade area. Therefore, currently, Cyprus is under no constitutional obligation to extend all rights that it grants to other EU citizens and companies by EU accession, also to Turkish citizens and companies.

2. The Power of Representation of the Cyprus Government

Turkey and the Turkish Cypriot leadership also maintained that the government of Cyprus does not represent the Turkish Cypriots.[70] Accepting an application that is made on behalf of the whole island, neglects the will of the Turkish Cypriot community that has not expressed any desire to enter the European Union. In order to demonstrate that the Greek Cypriot side does not constitute a constitutional government, Turkish Cypriots sometimes also refer to the declaration of the three Foreign Ministers of the United Kingdom, Turkey and Greece of 30 July 1974. The Ministers had agreed that negotiations should be carried out to to secure "*the re-establishment of constitutional government in Cyprus*". Citing this passage, it is argued that the three Foreign Ministers of the Guarantor powers were of the opinion that no such constitutional government exists and that "therefore, the Greek Cypriot Administration in South Cyprus cannot be that constitutional government".[71]

The legal situation is different. As observed above, since UN Security Council Resolution 186 of March 1964 the international community dealt with the Makarios government as the (only) effective government of Cyprus. In 1974, the Foreign Ministers of the three Guarantor powers addressed the situation after the coup. Their first message was to label the Sampson government as unconstitutional. Their second message did not question the constitutionality of the Makarios government at all. Rather to the contrary, for the three Ministers among the constitutional questions to be discussed was the "immediate return to constitutional legitimacy, *the Vice-President assuming the functions provided under the 1960 constitution*". For

and exportation, and with respect to all matters referred to in paragraphs 2 and 4 of Article III, any advantage, favour, privilege or immunity granted by any contracting party to any product originating in or destined for any other country shall be accorded immediately and unconditionally to the like product originating in or destined for the territories of all other contracting parties."

69 Tomuschat, loc. cit. (note 60), p. 672 (683).

70 See e.g. the "appraisal study" of C. Heinze, on the question of the compatibility of the admission of Cyprus into the European Union with international law, the law of the EU and the Cyprus Treaties of 1959/60, pp. 183 (193 et seq.) calling into question the continued existence of the Republic of Cyprus as well as the power of representation of the Cyprus government.

71 Ertekün, loc. cit. (page 6, note 19), p. 222.

the three Ministers, full constitutional legitimacy therefore required the re-establishment of the elected President (Makarios) plus the return of a Turkish Cypriot as Vice-President.

In 1997, that basic set-up had not changed. Rather, in the meantime, both the European Commission and the European Court of Human Rights affirmed that any Greek Cypriot government has international standing as the Government of Cyprus.[72] For the European Union, the only point worth discussing was whether the Turkish Cypriots were offered a sufficient practical possibility to influence the Cypriot accession course. In that context, it must be stressed that Clerides' invitation to the Turkish Cypriots of 12 March 1998 to participate in the accession negotiations was made unconditionally. The Turkish Cypriots could have freely chosen whom to appoint to the Cypriot delegation, and their nominees could have had a say on the speed and substance of the negotiations. In contrast, establishing a separate Turkish Cypriot delegation[73] would have been impossible because Cyprus would not have been able to speak with one voice in the Intergovernmental Conference between all EU Member States and Cyprus.

Treating the Cypriot government as being able to speak with effect for the territory of the whole island, and offering the Turkish Cypriots participation in a delegation of the Republic of Cyprus was therefore in conformity with international law.

3. Summary

The European Union reacted cautiously to Cyprus' application for membership of 1990. Taking into account the *de facto* division and ongoing UN efforts, the Commission issued an opinion only after three years. Member States agreed to open accession negotiations another two years later in order to secure a positive Greek vote for the EU-Turkey customs union. These steps were driven by political considerations and not due to any legal scepticism as regards the illegality of Cyprus' application. To the contrary, both the Commission and the Member States were unanimous in rejecting different claims in this regard. In particular, the allegation that membership would violate the Treaty of Guarantee was repeated several times. However, as that Treaty outlawed "*enosis*" with Greece rather than Cyprus' membership in an international organization, the efforts of the Turkish side to put Cyprus' application under legal attack rightfully did not succeed. EU accession negotiations started in 1997 with no Turkish Cypriot participation, as the leadership did not take up the invitation of the Cyprus government to be included in the Cypriot delegation.

[72] See European Commission of Human Rights, Decisions and Reports 2, 125–38 (Applications No. 6780/74 and 6950/75 – Cyprus v. Turkey) and Decisions and Reports 13, 85 (Application No. 8007/77 – Cyprus v. Turkey): European Court of Human Rights, Cyprus v. Turkey (Application No. 25781/94 – Admissibility), September 1996.

[73] M. Pabst, Zypern: UN, EU und status quo, VN 2001, 139 (142) arguing for "separate negotiations with a Turkish Cypriot delegation" (p. 143).

Chapter VI

EU Accession Negotiations and Annan Plan I–III

A. THE FACTS

1. The European Council of Helsinki and the Proximity Talks

1.1. *UN efforts 1997–1998*

In view of the June 1995 decision to open EU accession negotiations after the conclusion of the Intergovernmental Conference, the Turkish side was reluctant to start a new round of UN talks. In 1996, the tension on the island increased further in the light of the Cypriot Government's intention to deploy a set of S-300 missiles on the island. Furthermore, in August, Turkish Cypriot forces shot dead two Greek Cypriot demonstrators. At the end of the year, the UN Security Council condemned this act as unnecessary and disproportionate use of force.[1] It also reiterated grave concern about the excessive levels of military forces and armaments in the Republic of Cyprus and the rate at which they were being expanded, upgraded and modernised, including the introduction of sophisticated weaponry, as

[1] UNSC Resolution 1092 of 23 December 1996, § 2.

Legal Aspects of the Cyprus Problem, pp. 97–161.

well as the lack of progress towards a significant reduction in the number of foreign troops in the Republic of Cyprus, which threaten to raise tensions both on the island and in the region.[2] The Security Council regarded the decision of the EU concerning the opening of accession negotiations with Cyprus as "an important new development that should facilitate an overall settlement."[3]

In 1997, a new circle of Cyprus mediators emerged. Kofi Annan succeeded Boutros-Ghali, who had largely lost his interest in Cyprus, as UN Secretary-General. He appointed as his Special Envoy the Ecuadorian diplomat Diego Cordovez (1997–1999). In the United Kingdom, Lord Hannay was appointed as Special Envoy of her Majesty in May 1996, marking his presence in the region by intensive consultations. Furthermore, in June 1997, the United States government underlined its support for resumption of negotiations for a Cyprus settlement by appointing Richard Holbrooke, who had brokered the Dayton agreement for Bosnia and Herzegovina in 1995, as Presidential Special Representative.

Upon invitation of Annan, a new round of meetings between Clerides and Denktaş took place upon in Troutbeck (near New York) on 9–13 July 1997, followed by talks in Glion (near Montreux) on 11–15 August 1997. The Glion proposal submitted by Cordovez did not find the approval of Denktaş. He argued on the basis of his "two peoples-two states doctrine"[4] that no progress could be made until the Greek Cypriots publicly declared that they had no claim to rule Turkish Cypriots.[5] Furthermore, the Cordovez paper had removed the "most favoured nation clause" (subjecting Cyprus' membership to the EU to the simultaneous membership of Greece and Turkey),[6] taking account of the European Commission's Agenda 2000 of July 1997. Hence, also the UN had made clear in Glion that Cyprus could enter the EU whereas there was little mention of the Turkish aspirations. The Turkish side took the news badly and were not inclined to engage in serious Cyprus talks.[7]

After the Luxembourg Council in December 1997, where the EU showed a great restraint towards the Turkish candidature,[8] the prospects in 1998 were rather gloomy. Tensions between Greece and Turkey rose due to the ongoing arms twist in the region. A meeting between Denktaş and Annan in Geneva on 28 March 1998 did not bear fruit. Denktaş argued that the application of Cyprus to the EU violated the Treaty of Guarantee, and that under these circumstances he could not enter into negotiations.

---

[2] Ibid., § 7.

[3] UNSC Resolution 1062 of 28 June 1996, § 13; UNSC Resolution 1092 of 23 December 1996, § 17.

[4] G. Gürbey, Zypern: Hoffnung auf eine baldige Konfliktlösung, in: Südosteuropa-Mitteilungen 4/1997, p. 303.

[5] Brewin, loc. cit. (page 52, note 98), pp. 137–138.

[6] Necatigil, loc. cit. (page 11, note 35), p. 414.

[7] Hannay, loc. cit. (page xii, note 2), p. 78.

[8] See above Chapter V, A 3.3.

1.2. *The opening of accession negotiations on 31 March 1998*

As scheduled by the Luxembourg Council, the European Union convened the accession conferene with Cyprus (together with the candidate countries Poland, Czech Republic, Hungary, Estonia and Slovenia) on 31 March 1998. For the conduct of these negotiations, it adopted for each candidate country general principles. In the case of Cyprus, it was debated whether and how the unsettled political problem could probably influence the course of the negotiations. Preparing the opening date of 31 March 1998, France suggested to EU partners including the following language in the negotiation framework with Cyprus:

> *If it turns out, after the opening of negotiations, that accession could not benefit the whole of the island (...), the Commission should report immediately to the Council so that the latter can draw all consequences there from, including deciding whether it is appropriate to continue negotiations.*[9]

This proposal was countered by Greece, which tried to convince EU partners that accession negotiations would work as catalyst for a political settlement. Athens also made its intention known that it would not allow different treatment between Cyprus and other candidate countries. This hint could be understood as a Greek reservation against the whole enlargement process, if and in so far Cyprus' negotiations were to be made conditional upon a prior solution of the political problem, even if UN talks would not be restarted due to Turkish Cypriot inflexibility. The EU Member States finally agreed upon the following text in the negotiation framework:

> *A political settlement would permit the application of the Accession Treaty to the whole island. Progress that will be realized in the accession course and in the course of finding a just and viable settlement for the Cyprus problem will reinforce each other naturally. The Union reaffirms its full support for the ongoning effertos for a settlement under the auspices of the United Nations and hopes that negotiations will restart without delay.*[10]

Such hopes were, however, disappointed. In May 1998, Holbrooke visited the island and submitted a US proposal to Clerides and Denktaş. However, his plan[11] to establish three territories in Cyprus, as well as to proceed with a 24-hour recognition of the TRNC so as to enable it to conclude the settlement as an international agreement with the Republic of Cyprus, was rejected by the Greek Cypriots. Also Denktaş seems to have insisted on his well-known preconditions for negotiations.

---

[9] Council of the European Union, ELARG 6525/98 of 3 March 1998, preparation of the Intergovernmental Conference on opening accession negotiations with Cyprus, point 4, footnote 3. Translation by the author.

[10] Declaration of the EU on the occasion of the opening of accession negotiations with Cyprus, Brussels 31.3.1998. CONF-CY 2/98 of 26 March 1998, point 4. Translation by the author.

[11] J. Reuter, Zypern, Vereinte Nationen und Europäische Union – Bemühungen zur Lösung des Zypernkonflikts und Probleme des EU-Beitritts der geteilten Mittelmeerinsel, in: KAS Auslandsinformationen 9/01, p. 21 (28), with further references.

In any case, Hoolbroke's short intervention failed to create any tangible result and the American envoy effectively left the Cyprus scene.[12] Since 18 August 1998, the Turkish Cypriot position hardened by making a public proposal for a confederation for Cyprus.[13]

Against this background, the Cyprus' progress in its EU accession course was, again, subject to debate within the EU Member States. After successful conclusion of the screening process of seven negotiation chapters, the first round of effective negotiations was scheduled for 10 November 1998. At the General Affairs Council of 9 November 1998, where the relevant EU positions had to be adopted, France, Germany, Italy and the Netherlands noted in a joint declaration

> *(. . .) that it has not been possible to make any progress to date with regard to a political solution to the continuing division of Cypurs. The further negotiating progress will therefore also give rise to a number of problems that originate in the special situation of Cyprus. The Member States France, Germany, Italy and the Netherlands therefore consider that political solution is urgently needed as only this can ensure that these problems are resolved. (. . .)*

Greece countered that declaration by recalling that

> *The Luxembourg European Council stated that the eleven candidate States 'are destined to join the European Union on the basis of the same criteria and that they are participating in the accession process on an equal footing'. (. . .) The Cyprus Government has already attempted through specific proposals and initiatives to have the Turkish Cypriot side participate in the accession negotiations. Unfortunately, such efforts have so far proved fruitless. The refusal is due to the fact that Turkey, which occupies part of the island, is holding Cyprus' accession hostage. As result the actions of the European Union and its Member States must be in line with the decisions that have been taken and in no way enable third countries to stand in the way of the right of any European country fulfilling the necessary criteria to accede to the Union.*

Hence, Member States differed in their assessment of the significance of the unsettled political problem for the conduct of accession negotiations. Whereas at least four Member States were rather sceptical, Greece had again insisted on "equal treatment" for Cyprus. Notwithstanding this difference, EU Member States were unanimous in trying to include the Turkish Cypriot side as soon as possible. In each of the seven positions papers presented to Cyprus in the Accession Conference meeting of 10 November (and every paper thereafter), the European Union referred to Clerides' invitation to the Turkish Cypriots. It reserved the right to reopen each negotiation chapter, if necessary, if the Turkish Cypriots decided to participate in the negotiations.[14]

---

[12] Hannay, loc. cit. (page xii, note 2), p. 92.

[13] See R. Denktaş, Proposal for Confederation of 31 August 1998, reprinted in: (16/17) Journal of Cypriot Studies 1998, pp. 223 et seq. For an appraisal of this proposal see E. Olgun/S. Karabacak, Cyprus: An opportunity or threat, p. 17 et seq.

[14] Each EU Common Position noted "that the invitation of the Cyprus government to include representatives of the Turkish Cypriot community in the negotiations has so far not

1.3. *The preparation of UN proximity talks during 1999*

At the end of 1998, the Cyprus government earned another critical remark from the UN Security Council[15] and from the Council Presidency (Austria) as well as a large number of EU Member States[16] as regards its defence plans. The EU would not understand how the Greek Cypriots could proceed with the deployment of the missiles when negotiations were underway and efforts to broker a settlement had been started. After consultations in Athens, Clerides announced his decision not to deploy the S-300 missiles on the island, but to station them on Crete[17] – from where they could not reach the Turkish mainland.

In spring 1999, the UN Secretary-General, his newly appointed Special Advisor on Cyprus, Alvaro de Soto, and the new special envoys of the USA (Alfred Moses as the Presidential envoy/Thomas Weston representing the State Department) and the British envoy Lord Hannay prepared the ground for another effort. Since the G-8 was apparently deemed to be more acceptable to Turkey than the EU the United Kingdom and the United States decided to use this forum to launch the new initiative.[18] On 20 June 1999, the G-8 Heads of States urged the UN Secretary-General to invite the leaders of the Greek and Turkish Communities to engage in direct negotiations. Both parties should commit to set no pre-conditions, put all issues on the table, negotiate in good faith until a settlement would be reached, and to take full consideration of relevant UN resolutions and treaties.

The UN Security Council endorsed this initiative in resolution 1250 of 29 June 1999[19] in which it

> 6. *Requests the Secretary-General, in accordance with the relevant United Nations Security Council resolutions, to invite the leaders of the two sides to negotiations in the autumn of 1999;*
> 7. *Calls upon the two leaders, in this context, to give their full support to such a comprehensive negotiation, under the auspices of the Secretary-General, and to commit themselves to the following principles:*
>
> *– no preconditions;*
> *– all issues on the table;*
> *– commitment in good faith to continue to negotiate until a settlement is reached;*
> *– full consideration of relevant United Nations resolutions and treaties;*

---

been taken up, and that the Conference may therefore return to this chapter at an appropriate moment".

[15] UNSC Resolution 1217 of 12 December 1998, § 4.

[16] Compare the Commission's Regular Report on Cyprus' Accession to the EU, 1998, p. 12: "Serious concerns have been expressed, including by a large number of EU Member States, regarding the consequences of a possible deployment of the missiles on the search of a peaceful solution to the Cyprus problem".

[17] Press and Information Office, loc. cit. (page 17, note 27), p. 93.

[18] Brewin, loc. cit. (page 52, note 98), pp. 137, 139.

[19] UNSC Resolution 1250 of 29 June 1999.

> 8. *Requests the two sides on Cyprus, including military authorities on both sides, to work constructively with the Secretary-General and his Special Representative to create a positive climate on the island that will pave the way for negotiations in the autumn of 1999*
> 9. *Also requests the Secretary-General to keep the Security Council informed of progress towards implementation of this resolution and to submit a report to the Council by 1 December 1999;*

Resolution 1250 remained the basis for the negotiations in the crucial period ahead. It effectively left discretion to the UN Secretary-General to conduct the process. The Special Advisor was expected to report orally to the Security Council and to receive, from time to time, some support by the latter. However, he was not subject to a requirement of written reports, nor was it necessary to adopt new Security Council resolutions on substance. The Council had effectively given a mandate of trust to the Secretary-General. It only repeated his well-know positions, while prolonging the mandate of UNFICYP in another resolution of the same day (Resolution 1251). It reaffirmed

> *that a Cyprus settlement must be based on a State of Cyprus with a single sovereignty and international personality and a single citizenship, with its independence and territorial integrity safeguarded, and comprising two politically equal communities as described in the relevant Security Council resolutions, in a bi-communal and bi-zonal federation, and that such a settlement must exclude union in whole or in part with any other country or any form of partition or secession.*[20]

After some diplomatic activities, Annan announced on 13 November 1999 that the leaders had agreed to "start proximity talks in New York on 3 December in order to prepare the ground for meaningful negotiations leading to a comprehensive settlement of the Cyprus problem".[21]

1.4. *The Helsinki European Council 1999*

The Heads of States or Government of the European Union were ready to lend their full support to the United Nations when meeting in Helsinki in December 1999. Clearly, a new UN effort would bear the potential to overcome the negative attitude from the Turkish Cypriot leadership and Ankara surrounding Cyprus' EU accession course so far. However, facing the frequent standstills of the previous years and bearing in mind the Greek government's threat to veto the entire enlargement process if Cyprus were not admitted,[22] the European Council also addressed what would happen if a settlement were not reached in time. § 9 of the Helsinki conclusions read:

---

[20] UNSC Resolution 1251 of 29 June 1999, § 11.

[21] Press Statement of UN-Secretary-General Annan, 13 November 1999, cited in Hannay, loc. cit. (page xii, note 2), p. 110.

[22] J. Sommer, Security in Cyprus, Threat Perceptions, Possible Compromises and the Role of the EU, p. 52.

> *The European Council welcomes the launch of the talks aiming at a comprehensive settlement of the Cyprus problem on 3 December in New York and expresses its strong support for the UN Secretary-General's efforts to bring the process to a successful conclusion. The European Council underlines that a political settlement will facilitate the accession of Cyprus to the European Union.* ***If no settlement has been reached by the completion of accession negotiations, the Council's decision on accession will be made without the above being a precondition. In this the Council will take account of all relevant factors.***

Helsinki was equally important in its second conclusion as regards Turkey (§§ 11–12):

> *The European Council reaffirms the inclusive nature of the accession process, which now comprises 13 candidate states within a single framework (. . .). The European Council welcomes recent positive developments in Turkey as noted in the Commission's progress report, as well as its intention to continue its reforms towards complying with the Copenhagen criteria. Turkey is a candidate State destined to join the Union on the basis of the same criteria as applied to the other candidate States. Turkey, like other candidate States, will benefit from a pre-accession strategy to stimulate and support its reforms. This will include enhanced political dialogue, with emphasis on progressing towards fulfilling the political criteria for accession with particular reference to the issue of human rights, as well as on the issues referred to in paragraph 4 and 9 (a) (. . .)*

In addition, the Finnish Prime Minister Lipponen handed over to his Turkish counterpart Eçevit a side letter, stating, *inter alia*:

> *(. . .) I am very pleased to inform you officially of our unanimous decision to confer Turkey the status of candidate State, on the same footing as any other candidate. When, in the European Council, we discussed the draft conclusions attached to this letter, I said, without being challenged, that in § 12 of the conclusions there was no new criteria added to those of Copenhagen and that the reference to § 4 and 9a was not in relation to the criteria for accession but only to the political dialogue (. . .). Regarding Cyprus, a political settlement remains the aim of the EU. Concerning the accession of Cyprus, all relevant factors will be taken into account when the Council takes the decision.*[23]

On the one hand, the mentioning of Turkey among the other candidates by using the figure 13 (instead of 12) as well as the confirmation that it will be dealt with on the basis of the same criteria was strong encouragement for Turkey. In particular, a settlement on Cyprus was not treated as part of the accession criteria. On the other hand, the mentioning of the Cyprus issue as part of an "enhanced political dialogue" was a clear hint that it must move on the Cyprus question. Another "Cyprus package" had emerged out of the Helsinki summit that was designed to strengthen the United Nations. Both Cyprus and Turkey were expected to negotiate in good faith in view of their EU aspirations. However, the EU did neither take over the political process, nor did it seek to formally participate in the proximity talks. On an informal level, however, the Commission Chief

[23] Letter from Prime Minister Lipponen to Prime Minister Ecevit, 10 December 1999, cited in Hannay, loc. cit. (page xii, note 2), p. 115.

Negotiator for Cyprus, Leopold Maurer, was present in the proximity talks. During that period, the UN entered into first contacts with the EU Commission, leading to a regular exchange of views between the Commissioner for Enlargement, Günter Verheugen, and de Soto and their respective teams. De Soto had recruited a lawyer specialised in international and constitutional law (Didier Pfirter) and an experienced political assistant (Robert Dann). These contacts were used to exchange technical information and clarifications on matters of EU law.[24]

1.5. *The five rounds of proximity talks in Geneva and New York*

In the first round of proximity talks (3 December–14 December 1999) the UN explored the positions of the parties. The Greek Cypriot side submitted a first paper on the Constitution, but essentially the players were "waiting for Helsinki". Despite the fear that the Turkish Cypriot side would withdraw because of a Cypriot EU accession without a prior political settlement on the horizon, the second round took place from 31 January to 8 February 2000 in Geneva. The results were limited given the fact that presidential elections were scheduled for April 2000 in the TRNC (which Denktaş eventually won).

The third round was held in Geneva (4–12 July/23 July–4 August) without any significant discussion of substance between the Parties.[25] Accordingly, the UN decided to become more active. At the end of the first phase de Soto presented his preliminary thoughts on the four core issues: territory, property, security and constitution. He asked the parties to reflect on them after the adjournment on 12 July.[26] The Greek Cypriots replied by reading out a 23-page document referring to all UNSC resolutions. The Turkish Cypriot side resubmitted its August 1998 confederational proposal[27] and insisted that the status question should first be addressed before making any progress on other issues.

In his opening speech of the fourth round (12 September–26 September 2000), the UN Secretary-General tried to cut these Turkish Cypriot attempts short by making a brief statement containing two important passages. He stated that "in the course of these talks I have ascertained that the parties share a common desire to bring about, through negotiations in which each party represents each side – and no one else – as the political equal of the other, a comprehensive settlement enshrining a new partnership on which to build a better future in peace, security and prosperity on a united island." He also said "the equal status of the parties must and should be recognised explicitly in the comprehensive settlement."[28]

---

[24] Hannay, loc. cit. (page xii, note 2), p. 105.

[25] Regular Report of the European Commission on Cyprus, 8 November 2000, p. 21.

[26] "Preliminary Thoughts" of the Special Advisor on Cyprus, de Soto, of 12 July 2000, reproduced in full by Hannay, loc. cit. (page xii, note 2), pp. 125–127.

[27] J. Reuter, Zähes Ringen um Zyperns Zukunft, Die politische Meinung 2/2001, p. 71 (73).

[28] Statement of UN Secretary-General Annan of 12 September 2001, cited in the report of the Secretary-General of 1 April 2003, S/2003/398, § 25.

The Turkish Cypriot side welcomed Annan's statement of 12 September whereas the Greek Cypriot side asked for a break of three days. Clerides continued the talks after de Soto's public reassurance that this formula would not imply any move towards recognition of the TRNC.[29] At the end of the fourth round de Soto shared non-papers with the parties, outlining his bridging ideas.[30] On 11 October, the House of Representatives of the Republic adopted a resolution stating "that the opening Statement of the UN Secretary-General Mr. Kofi Annan falls outside the letter and spirit of the framework of the talks and the basis of a solution of the Cyprus problem as determined by UN principles, decisions and resolutions". The House held that the non-papers which the UN Secretary-General's representative Mr. de Soto presented to the representatives of the two communities, contain ideas and proposals which are not in line with the framework of principles and UN resolutions". It also declared that "that any proposals or ideas should be fully in line with the *acquis communautaire*". In conclusion, it called upon the President of the Republic to continue and intensify his efforts "in the direction of a full correction of the situation created by the UN Secretary-General's opening statement and of reaffirming the basis of the talks and the framework for a solution, as these are determined by the resolutions and decisions of the United Nations and the two high-level agreements".[31]

In the run-up of the fifth round (31 October–10 November), attention shifted to Brussels where the European Commission was to propose the first accession partnership with Turkey, as promised in Helsinki. The objective of this partnership is to lay down short- and medium-term goals for political and economic reforms to meet the accession criteria. The crucial question in this regard was how to integrate the Cyprus issue in this concept. Undoubtedly, the EU expected from the Turkish government to support the UN process. But could failure to do so be regarded as non-compliance with the political criteria for accession? Following the line of the Finnish letter handed over at the Helsinki summit, Commissioner Verheugen proposed to his colleagues in the Commission not to present the Cyprus issue under the rubrique "political criteria", but to include this aspect in a separate rubrique, denominated "political dialogue". However, the Greek Social Affairs Commissioner, Anna Diamantopoulou, asked the Commission to modify this approach.

---

[29] UN Press Release of 14 September 2000: "Earlier today, Mr. Alvaro de Soto, the Secretary-General's Special Avisor on Cyprus, was asked three questions by a correspondent, in connection with the statement that the Secretary-General read to Mr. Clerides and Mr. Denktaş when he met them on 12 September 2000:

1. Does the Secretary-General's statement imply recognition of the "TRNC"?
2. Does the Secretary-General's statement imply a step in the direction of the recognition of the "TRNC"?
3. Does the Secretary-General's statement imply "derecognition" of the Republic of Cyprus?

To each question Mr de Soto replied "no".

[30] For a detailed description of the non-papers see Reuter, loc. cit. (note 27), p. 71 (75–76).

[31] House of Representatives Resolution of 11 October 2001.

She favoured an explicit linkage between the Cyprus issue and the political criteria. Although the Commission adopted the proposal as foreseen (which was later endorsed by the Council in March 2001), this – well publicized debate – in Brussels fuelled some concerns at the Turkish side whether the EU would live up to its promises and whether it would make sense to support the UN process at all.

Annan's oral remarks of 8 November 2000 constituted the highlight of the fifth round. The comprehensive settlement should enshrine a new partnership on which to build a better future on a united island. The equal status of the parties in a united Cyprus must and should be recognized explicitly in the settlement. Cyprus should have a single international legal personality. There should be one sovereign, indissoluble common state. Neither side should be able to dominate the common state or the other component state. There should be a single citizenship. Human rights and fundamental freedoms should be guaranteed. The common state should have a common government, with a basic law, prescribing powers exercised by legislative, executive and judicial branches. The common government should be able to function effectively in the modern world. In the operation of the common government, the political equality of the Greek Cypriots and the Turkish Cypriots should be respected. Annan further referred to two component States, each with its own basic law, forming a common State. The component States should be largely self-governing. A comprehensive settlement would commit Cyprus to EU membership. He expressed the hope that the EU would be prepared to address special and legitimate concerns in regard to accession. Annan added that a comprehensive settlement negotiated by the UN should not present an obstacle for EU membership nor need it be re-negotiated when the terms of accession are established. On property, he considered that a solution must withstand legal challenge, but he also believed that a solution could carefully regulate the exercise of property rights by a combination of reinstatement, exchange and compensation. As regards territory, he found it hard to imagine a comprehensive settlement without return to Greek Cypriot administration of an appreciable amount of territory. Finally, he proposed a United Nations mandated force and police unit that function throughout the island to attain security for both sides. Annan asked the parties to communicate their reaction to him in due time.[32]

1.6. *The walk out of Denktaş*

Annan's remarks were immediately criticised by Papadopoulos as falling outside the UN Security Council decisions, but were accepted by Clerides as a basis for further negotiations.[33] On the Turkish side, Prime Minister Eçevit said on 11 November that the remarks were inadequate since a solution could only be found if the existence of two sovereign States were accepted. Denktaş declared that Annan's Statement did only reflect Greek Cypriot opinions. On 24 November 2000, the Turkish

[32] Statement of UN Secretary-General Annan of 8 November 2000, cited by Hannay, loc. cit. (page xii, note 2), pp. 136–140.

[33] Reuter, loc. cit. (note 11), p. 21 (34).

President Sezer and Denktaş met in northern Cyprus. They declared that the aim of the proximity talks had been to find a basis for comprehensive talks. This aim had not been reached in the five rounds. Therefore, it would not make sense to prolong the talks unless the more realistic parameter of the Turkish Cypriot side was accepted. First the existence of two States on the island had to be recognised. Denktaş accordingly informed the UN Secretary-General that he was not in favour of fixing further meetings. With the walk out of Denktaş, backed by Turkey, the proximity talks effectively came to their end.

2. The Seville European Council and direct talks 2002

2.1. *International efforts to resume talks*

Throughout 2001, many international efforts were undertaken for a resumption of the talks. In January, the UN Special Envoy, de Soto, as well as the American and British envoys, Weston and Lord Hannay visited the region. The Greek and Turkish Foreign Ministers, Papandreou and Cem, indicated in their Ankara meeting of 5–6 April that Cyprus would soon come onto the agenda of their dialogue. However, Cem reiterated during his stay in northern Cyprus on 17–19 April that the parameters of the proximity talks must be the existence of two States with equal sovereignty. The Turkish Security Council echoed this view on 29 May 2001. Upon an US/Turkish informal understanding of June 2001,[34] which caused some controversy within Turkey,[35] de Soto shared discreetly his first draft of a comprohensive settlement with the parties in July.

New optimism was spread when Denktaş met Commissioner Verheugen on 27 August 2001 in Zurich. To his satisfaction, Verheugen conveyed to him the message that the Commission could accommodate certain restrictions on the EU *acquis* on the acquisition on property, free movement and the freedom of establishment in a comprehensive Cyprus settlement.[36] A day later, on 28 August, Denktaş conferred with UN Secretary-General Annan in Salzburg. At the conclusion of his eight-day visit to the island, de Soto announced the UN's hope that "a new and re-invigorated phase of the Secretary-General's good offices would begin with separate meetings of the Secretary-General with the two leaders on 12 September 2001, in New York."[37] However, on the same day, Denktaş rejected Annan's invitation

[34] For details of the US/Turkey understanding see Hannay, loc. cit. (page xii, note 2), p. 148.

[35] L. Sariibrahimoglu, Cyprus Minister Gurel bypassed on Cyprus, Turkish Daily News 26.07.2001.

[36] J. Reuter, Schwierige Gespräche auf Zypern, Die politische Meinung 3/2003, p. 29 (31).

[37] UN Press Statement of 5 September 2001.

because common ground had yet to be established.[38] This earned him strong criticism by, *inter alia*, the European Commission[39] and the UN Security Council.[40]

In October 2001, Commission President Prodi flew to the island as part of his programme to visit each acceding State during his term of office. In a speech held at the House of Representatives, he announced publicly what Commissioner Verheugen had already told the Turkish Cypriot leader in private during their conversation in Zurich of 27 August: The Commission was prepared to accommodate a Cyprus settlement in the European legal order, as long as it is compatible with the principles on which the EU is founded. The *acquis* should, in principle, not pose additional complications when negotiating a settlement against a unique historical background. Hence, the Commission (as guardian of the EC Treaty) responded to one of the Turkish preoccupations sometimes described as condition *sine qua non*,[41] namely that a Cyprus settlement should not be undone by the application of the European *acquis*. However, at that time, it was not clear whether the same willingness would exist in all the Member States, including Greece.

2.2. *The Clerides-Denktaş meeting of 4 December 2001*

Shortly after the Prodi speech,[42] Denktaş started new initiatives to overcome the negative picture in international public opinion that he was obstructionist. He wrote to Annan and Clerides. After some initial hesitation of the latter,[43] both leaders met at the Ledra palace on 4 December 2001. Denktaş said that both leaders

[38] Anatolia News 5 September 2001.

[39] Statement of Commissioner Verheugen of 6 September 2001: "The European Commission has contributed actively to the efforts of the UN Secretary General to bring about a resumption of the talks aimed at finding a solution to the Cyprus problem. My meeting with the leader of the Turkish Cypriot community, Mr Denktaş, in Zurich on 27 August underlined the EU's clear preference for a solution to be reached before enlargement, although this is not a pre-condition for Cyprus' accession. Against this background I am very disappointed that Mr Denktaş has not accepted the UN Secretary General's invitation to talks on 12 September. The Commission considers that the window of opportunity for reaching a solution before accession remains open and encourages all interested parties to undertake all efforts with this aim in view".

[40] Statement of the UN Security Council of 26 September 2001 expressing „disappointment about the unjustified decision by the Turkish side" not to accept the UN invitation to proximity talks.

[41] H. Pazarci, Solutions juridiques pou un Chypre viable basées sur le nouveau partenariat, in: Resat Arim (ed.) Cyprus and international law, p. 134 (141–142).

[42] For Hannay, Denktaş's intiative came "completely out of the blue"; loc. cit. (page xii, note 2), p. 155.

[43] H. Kramer, Endspiel auf Zpyern – Neue Verhandlungen: die letzte Chance zur Einigung vor dem EU-Beitritt der Insel, p. 3 believes that Clerides accepted Denktaş's offer in order to avoid any bad public image for the Greek Cypriot side prior to EU accession.

should start a genuine new process based on the political equality of the two parties for negotiating the establishment of a new partnership. According to his view, there existed functioning democratic institutions on both sides, which reflect the political will of their respective peoples. They should live in harmony and cooperation under a new partnership structure based on the equal status and sovereign equality of the two Partner States. The new Partnership would have single international personality in its areas of competence. Denktaş took note of Prodi's statement that the EU will accommodate the terms of the political settlement. In this respect he would support membership of the Cyprus Partnership in the EU within the terms of a political settlement. He also proposed to set up a Bilateral Committee under the Co-Chairmanship of Clerides and Denktaş. Clerides rejected the idea of a setting up a bilateral committee. Instead both leaders agreed

> *that the (UN) Secretary General, in the exercise of his mission of good offices, would invite the two leaders to direct talks, that these talks will be held in Cyprus, starting in January 2002 on United Nations premises, that there will be no preconditions, that all issues will be on the table, that they will continue to negotiate in good faith until a comprehensive settlement is achieved, and that nothing will be agreed until everything is agreed.*

The EU General Affairs Council, on 10 December 2001 formulated the hope to see substantial progress when talks are continued in mid January under the aegis of the United Nations. The Council also called upon Turkey to continue contributing actively to the search of a political settlement for the Cyprus issue. The EU Heads of State or Government meeting in Laeken on 14/15 December 2001, welcomed the "recent meetings between the leaders of the Greek and Turkish Cypriot communities and would encourage them to continue their discussions with a view to an overall solution under the auspices of the UN consistent with relevant resolutions of the UN Security Council".[44]

2.3. *The meetings from January–April 2002*

After two private dinners on 5 and 29 December 2001 on either side of the green line, the two leaders, accompanied by two to three close aides,[45] started to meet regularly thrice a week from 16 January 2002[46] in the UN premises.

In the last two weeks of January, the meetings focused on governance. The Greek Cypriots put forward a non-paper outlining a bi-zonal, bi-communal federation.

---

[44] Conclusions of the Laeken European Council (16 December 2001), § 11.

[45] On the Greek Cypriot side, Clerides was accompanied by his Undersecretary Kouros, Spokesman Papaptetrou and Attorney-General Markides. For the Turkish Cypriot side, Denktaş was assisted by his Undersecretary Olgun and the Turkish General Ercal. Later on the Turkish constitutional lawyer Soysal was also included in the delegation.

[46] On a personal note, I will never forget this date as on the same day my daughter Jeana Hoffmeister was born.

The Turkish Cypriots replied by a paper that avoided the vocabulary of a confederation. In substance, however, the proposal stayed within the parameters of the previous confederalist proposals.[47] The Turkish Cypriots spoke of "two States entering into a Partnership", "in charge of coordination". Both States should sign the Accession Treaty to the EU, which should include permanent derogations on properties and basic freedoms. Being unable to resolve the controversy, the Parties moved on to discuss the distribution of powers. In the meetings until mid-February both sides exchanged views on security and territory, again without any tangible output.

Shortly after the leaders had resumed their meetings on 1 March, Commissioner Verheugen paid an official visit to the island (7–8 March 2002). Upon his arrival on 7 March, the Turkish Cypriots tabled a comprehensive paper, tackling all the core issues together. While remaining in the realm of "partnership", it was nevertheless remarkable that, for the first time, "European Union matters" should be "jointly exercised", indicating that EU accession would be in principle acceptable for the Turkish Cypriots. In his contacts with Clerides and Denktaş Verheugen underlined the EU timetable. The Commission would make its assessment for the 10 candidate countries in October. Delaying tactics would not help. The EU could not tell 120 million people in Eastern and Central Europe that they have to wait until a solution for a specific problem was found. The EU had a clear preference for a united Cyprus to join the Union but that was not a precondition. Finally, the EU was prepared to help the northern parts of Cyprus to catch up with a programme of over 216 Mio. € in case of a settlement.

In the second half of March, Clerides listed all his offers on security. In return, he wanted to know whether Denktaş was prepared to accept that there would be a sovereign State of Cyprus with a Constitution, a single international personality, a single citizenship and with political equality of the two component parts. Denktaş's reply of 26 March was that "the new Partnership State of Cyprus would be sovereign to the extent defined in the Constitutional Agreement, that it will have a single international personality, that citizens of the Constituent Partner States will also be citizens of the Partnership State of Cyprus, that the competences and functions to be assigned to the Partnership State of Cyprus will be mutually agreed between the two Constituent Partner States, and that residual powers will rest with the two sovereign equal Constitutent Partner States". Clerides acknowledged that a new constitution would be necessary in order to create the new partnership, but noted that sovereignty was not vested in the two communities.

These exchanges showed some common ground, in particular as the Greek Cypriots did not insist anymore that the Constitution of the Republic should be merely modified to bring about a settlement but could be abrogated and replaced by a new one. No common paper ever materialized. Upon a briefing by de Soto to the Security Council, the latter issued a statement of 4 April expressing concern that progress was slow to meet the target date of June 2002. In the subsequent April meetings

[47] Reuter, loc. cit. (note 36), p. 29 (35).

the climate deteriorated since both sides started to criticize each other heavily through lengthy papers on institutions of the Partnership state. The lowest point was reached on 29 April when the Turkish Cypriots handed in a paper insisting on decision-making in the "Partnership State of Cyprus" by consensus and involving rotation in the Partnership Council.[48] The Turkish constitutional advisor, Soysal, openly declared that the federation should be seen as a construction of two founding States as sovereign entities, implicitly securing recognition of the TRNC as founding state.[49] The paper added that membership in the EU could only be allowed after achievement of economic equilibrium and harmonisation between the two Partner States. Such ideas were unacceptable for the Greek Cypriot side. End of April therefore marked the point were the direct talks had "bogged down and were badly in need of a shot in the arm".[50]

2.4. *The mid-term review of May 2002*

On 2 May 2002, the Members of the Security Council expressed the view that the time had now come to set down on paper areas of common ground between the two sides. They urged both sides, in particular the Turkish side, to co-operate fully with the Secretary-General's special Adviser. Hence, the Security Council pointed for the first time the finger to the Turkish side. Although only referring to procedure, i.e. to the need to co-operate with de Soto, and not to substance, it was clear that the Turkish side was expected to move. In addition, the UN was ready to take over the process, as UNSG Annan announced to visit the island in mid May.

As quasi summary of their respective positions on governance, both sides submitted concise papers of 2–3 pages each on 13 and 14 May:

Issue	GC position	TC position
Foundation process	Greek Cypriots and Turkish Cypriots are co-founders through referendum	TC Partner State and GC Partner State are co-founders
Outcome of the foundation process	New State of affairs of the sovereign State of Cyprus (= State continuity of RoC)	New Partnership State of Cyprus (= State succession of New Partnerhip State to RoC)

[48] This part of the 29 April 2002 proposal was publicly explained by Olgun: "According to the Turkish Cypriot proposals, while the agreed arrangements on the substantive issues such as property, security, territory and EU membership would be final, a more evolutionary approach should be adopted for handling relationship issues like the competences, institutions and decision-making mechanisms of the "Partnership State". Rotation of the key positions and consensus decision-making arrangements would be the key pillars for translating into practical termns the equal status of the two parties in an evolving new Partnership State". E. Olgun, Cyprus: Settlement and Membership, Speech delivered on 3 June 2002, p. 7.

[49] Soysal, loc. cit. (page 17, note 28), pp. 129–130.

[50] Hannay, loc. cit. (page xii, note 2), p, 163.

cont.

Issue	GC position	TC position
Existence of a common State	One single international personality	One single international personality
Powers of the common State	All powers necessary to function as a State	– External relations – EU relations – Partnership econonomic policy – Finances
Powers of the common States	All powers not assigned to common State; common State will not be empowered to encroach on the powers of the common State	All powers not assigned to component States
Institutions of the common State	Institutions necessary to function as a State, reflecting political equality (= not numerical equality)	Institutions can be "joint" institutions from both sides (= no federal parliament or ministries); Institutions necessary to reflect the equal status and equal legitimacy of co-founder Partner States (= numerical equality)
Institutions of the component States	Excecutive, legislative, judicial organs, police and civil service in the areas of competence	Functioning democratic institutions
Guarantees	Treaty of Guarantee may be extended to cover the territorial integrity, security and constitutional order of the self-administered States.	Independence, security and territorial integrity of the Partnership State together with the constitutional order, security and territorial integrity of each co-founder Partner State will be guaranteed under the Treaty of Guarantee.
EU accession	Cyprus will accede to the EU upon referenda on both sides.	Both co-founder Partner States will support the membership of the Partnership State of Cyprus. EU will be invited to work out a transitional arrange ment which will provide Turkey with the full rights and obligations of any EU member with regard to the Partnership State until Turkey's EU accession.

Both sides agreed that there should be one common State with a single international personality, comprising two component States that are largely self-governing. They further agreed, in substance, on the distribution of powers between the levels and on external guarantees. However, the important questions of the foundation process, common institutions and the question of transitional agreements after EU accession remained controversial. No rapprochement could be recorded on territory, property and security.

Annan visited the island from 14–16 May meeting both leaders separately and jointly. He delivered a short Statement prior to his departure at the airport. His main points were that the two leaders committed themselves to negotiate in a genuine spirit of give and take; that the core issues can be resolved until the end of June provided that both sides act with the necessary political will; that de Soto will stay until the end of June and report thereafter; and Greece and Turkey should constructively support the process. Annan's insistance on the June deadline did help. Denktaş and Clerides indicated publicly that they might have to negotiate until the end of the year.[51] However, de Soto started to meet both leaders separately after the common session to explain to them where he sees signs of convergence: thus, the direct talks were complemented by a formate that ressembled the proximity talks.

On substance, the leaders negotiated in particular on security and sovereignty and got near to an agreement in June. The Treaty of Guarantee would be confirmed, extending the guarantee to the constitutional order of the two component states as well. The island would be demilitarized. The UN would impose an arms embargo and station an international military presence to operate island-wide to underpin the terms of an agreement. De Soto, with the acceptance of both sides, put down these lines on paper. However, after having produced this non-paper of 6 June, the Turkish side pulled back. Denktaş reaffirmed in public his goal that no foreign troops, especially no EU or NATO troops should be stationed in Cyprus,[52] thereby taking back what he had earlier said on the composition of a multi-national force. In return, Clerides withdrew his provisional agreement to the document as well.[53] After this failure, no more progress could be observed at the negotiation table: on 18 June the two leaders failed to even agree on the agenda. Accordingly, it became increasingly clear that the direct talks, even after a personal commitment of the UN Secretary-General, could not succeed if the UN were not allowed to prepare a comprehensive plan.[54]

2.5. *The Seville European Council of June 2002*

The Spanish Presidency followed these developments very closely. The Minister for European Affairs, accompanied by Commission officials, paid a visit to the island in Mày 2002. The Presidency reported to the other EU Member States

[51] Cyprus Press, 27 May 2002.

[52] Kibris, 6 June 2002.

[53] Hannay, loc. cit. (page xii, note 2), p. 165.

[54] H. Kramer, Verlängerung auf Zypern, p. 1.

about the slow progress in the negotiations. Against this background, the European Council in Seville of 22/23 June offered an important backing for the United Nations. The 15 EU Heads of States and Governments concluded:

> *In respect of the accession of Cyprus, the Helsinki conclusions are the basis of the European Union's position. The European Union's preference continues to be for the accession of a reunited island. The European Council fully supports the efforts of the Secretary-General of the United Nations and calls upon the leaders of the Greek Cypriot and Turkish Cypriot communities to intensify and expedite their talks in order to seize this unique window of opportunity for a comprehensive settlement, consistent with the relevant UN Security Council resolutions, hopefully before conclusion of the negotiations.* ***The European Union would accommodate the terms of such a comprehensive settlement in the Treaty of Accession in line with the principles on which the European Union is founded: as a Member State, Cyprus will need to speak with a single voice and ensure proper application of European Union law.*** *The European Union would make a substantial financial contribution in support of the development of the northern part of a reunited island.*

The statement contained three main messages to the Cypriot leaders. The EU wishes a more pro-active role of the UN-General Secretary; it prefers a settlement to be concluded before the end of the accession negotiations in December 2002; it would accommodate such a settlement in the Treaty of Accession that was likely to be signed in spring 2003, as long as the settlement stays in line with fundamental EU principles. Internally, Seville gave a firm ground for the Commission to start preparing necessary transitional arrangements that would need to be included into the Accession Treaty, following a settlement. Commissioner Verheugen accordingly started to discuss discreetly with de Soto about the practical details of this approach.

2.6. *The final rounds of the direct talks*

At the end of June 2002, territory was discussed for the first time. The Greek Cypriots submitted a paper proposing at about 24% of the territory to the Turkish Cypriots, whereas the latter were not willing to discuss a map. On 9 July, the Members of the Security Council expressed disappointment that, despite the Secretary-General's valuable personal involvement including his visit on the island in May, progress remained disappointingly slow and the June target date for agreement had not been met. They noted in this regard that the Turkish Cypriot side had been less constructive in its approach so far and had declined to support the goal of resolving the core issues by the end of June.

In the subsequent July meetings, there was no movement. In Turkey, the coalition government broke down. Gürel was appointed as successor of Foreign Minister Cem in the caretaker government until the general elections in November 2002. In the beginning of August, two irreconcilable positions on territory and property were exchanged. A Turkish Cypriot paper explained how the objective criteria for a delineation of territory between the two component states should be understood. On land ownership, one should compare and assess properties on current values and not on values of 1974 ("a legal nightmare"). Economic viability or productivity would mean that the water resources, the coastal areas, the main infrastructures in both component states should not be affected. There should only be minimal restrictions on the freedom of movement, which will not present an obstacle to the mobility of labour. Finally, the Turkish Cypriots stressed again the need to consider the security aspect of the territorial issue. The Greek Cypriot side maintained the view that justice should be done to individuals in order to have support of the settlement. In rather strong terms it attacked the Turkish Cypriot proposal to solve that question through global exchange. More specifically, it suggested that both component states should be able of sustainable development. As regards water supplies, the GC simply referred to the possibility of desalination of seawater. It insisted that there should be no separate economy for the northern "component state". Finally, the Greek Cypriot side asked again to present scenarios reflected on maps that can be discussed.

In September, after a brief discussion about citizenship between the leaders, Annan undertook a last effort to bring the direct talks forward. He met the leaders in Paris on 6 September. They should work with de Soto on the issues that he highlighted to them, and to meet him once more in New York on 3 and 4 October. He continued to believe that the gaps dividing the parties can be bridged and, on some issues, that they are quite a bit smaller than when the talks began. Effectively, the statement confirmed what was hardly any surprise: the parties themselves were unable to write any comprehensive settlement on their own by agreeing to each others's text. The direct talks had failed and were silently replaced by mediation under UN direction, which was seen as the only effective way to come to results by many observers at that time.[55]

3. Annan Plan I and II and the Copenhagen Council

3.1. *The September 2002 negotiations*

On 11 September, Denktaş submitted a revised version of the comprehensive 29 April paper.[56] It showed some flexibility on the constitutional issue, especially as regards the functioning of the executive. The Turkish Cypriots also treated EU membership in a more positive way. The paper did not address the major concerns of the Greek Cypriot side as regards property and territory. Also on security, there was no opening. On 17 September, Clerides handed over his answer. The discussions focused on the legislative and the executive of the common state. While Clerides suggested a non-executive President and rotation of the Vice-President,

[55] J. Reuter/P. Varvaroussis, Der Beitritt Zyperns zur Europäischen Union, Risiko für neue Instabilität der EU, Südosteuropa-Mitteilungen Nr. 2/2002, p. 65 (67).

[56] Ankara Anatolia News, 11.09.02.

Denktaş said he was against a system of cohabitation. Discussing territory on 24 September, Denktaş proposed a global exchange of property leaving aside the recognition of claims by both. The Greek Cypriot side refused that, considering that such a system would be incompatible with international law. Finally, on 26 September, territory was left aside contrary to de Soto's original outline.

In contrast to the limited outcome on leader's level, a working group between Markides, Soysal and Pfirter started to review which sets of legislation and international instruments of both sides could be relevant for the new Cyprus. They managed to produce a preliminary paper by 26 September 2002. In parallel, the European Commission was granted discret access to the full draft settlement in order to advise the UN on EU related questions.

3.2. *The October 2002 New York meeting*

As agreed in Paris, UNSG Annan met the two leaders in New York in early October and held intensive consultations separately and jointly. On 4 October he issued the following statement:

> *I have completed this afternoon two days of intensive consultations on Cyprus with His Excellency Mr. Glafcos Clerides, the Greek Cypriot leader, and His Excellency Mr. Rauf Denktaş, the Turkish Cypriot leader.*
>
> *I am happy to report that, since I met the two leaders in Paris, they have focused on the issues I highlighted and there has been an encouraging effort to explore ways of bridging differences pragmatically. Here in New York I tried to crystallise for the two leaders a way they could push their discussions forward to further narrow their differences with the active assistance of my Special Adviser Mr. Alvaro de Soto.*
>
> *As part of their effort to bridge differences pragmatically, the two leaders have decided to create two ad hoc bilateral technical committees to begin work immediately on important technical issues. The purpose of these committees is to make recommendations on technical matters without prejudice to the positions of the two leaders on the core issues concerned. Their work shall be ad referendum and shall focus on treaties and future "common state"* laws. The UN will assist the parties in this work.*
>
> *There is no simple solution to the Cyprus problem. For this reason, a comprehensive settlement has to be a complex, integrated, legally binding and self-executing agreement, where the rights and obligations of all concerned are clear, unambiguous and not subject to further negotiation. I hope the work of the committees will help the leaders towards this end.*
>
> *The opportunity that is at hand must be seized. In this regard, Greece and Turkey have an important role to play and I look forward to their continued support.*
>
> *As is well known, Mr. Denktaş will undergo surgery soon and he is not likely to be available for a few weeks, but work will continue in October and I have asked the leaders to clear their diaries during November, when I am looking forward to seeing them again.*
>
> * *"common state" is a provisional term.*

In the aftermath of New York, the Turkish Cypriot side did not appoint any member to the two technical committees. As a consequence they were not convened. In addition, due to Mr. Denktaş's heart surgery, there was nobody in the Turkish Cypriot side until the end of November who could effectively take over the negotiations.

3.3. *Annan I of 11 November 2002*

This standstill in the talks and the expected closing of EU accession negotiations at the Copenhagen European Council by the end of the year made an active UN involvement indispensable. After diplomatic preparation of boths sides in the October meeting, UN Secretary-General Annan unveiled his ideas for a settlement on 11 November 2002. He communicated a 138-page document to the two sides entitled "Basis for Agreement on a comprehensive settlement of the Cyprus problem" and asked both leaders to respond within a week whether they could accept it as a basis for final negotiations. For that purpose the main part of the document, the so-called "Foundation Agreement", was split into two parts: "Hard" provisions that are not due to further negotiations, and "soft" provisions that could be changed by mutual agreement no later than 28 February 2003. The Secretary-General would be invited to certify the results of the finalisation process, and to include his suggestions, if any are indispensable, to finalise the Agreement. That finalised Foundation Agreement would be submitted by each side to referendum on 30 March 2003, together with other specified matters related to the coming into being of the new state of affairs, including accession to the European Union.

The Annan plan I of 11 November consisted of a main text of four articles plus five appendices ("Appendix A–E"). Appendix A set out a "Foundation agreement" plus ten annexes ("Annex I–X"). Transitional measures to accompany and facilitate the finalization process were contained in Appendix B. Appendix C referred to a revised Treaty of Guarantee and Alliance, Appendix D enumerated matters that should be submitted to the UN Security Council for decision, and Appendix E contained requests to the EU with respect to Cyprus' EU accession.

The 14 articles of the Foundation Agreement set out the political cornerstones of the settlement. According to its Article 1, the Foundation Agreement (FA) would establish "the new state of affairs in Cyprus". It declared which laws and international treaties shall be in force and binding on Cyprus. Accession to the EU should be effected and ties of friendship with Greece and Turkey maintained. Any unilateral change of the new state of affairs was prohibited. The common State of Cyprus consisted of two equal component states (Article 2 FA). The plan conceived a single Cypriot citizenship plus internal "component state" citizenship status. A component state may tie the exercise of political rights at its level to this internal citizenship status, and may limit the establishment of residence for persons not holding this status (Article 3 FA). Under Article 4 FA human rights and fundamental freedoms were guaranteed; freedom of movement and freedom of residence would have been limited where expressly provided for in the Agreement. Article 8 FA set out the conditions of demilitarization, whereas an equal size of Greek and Turkish contingents should be stationed on the island under the Treaty of Alliance. A UN peacekeeping operation should monitor the implementation of the Agreement. Cyprus shall not put its territory at the disposal of international military operations other than with the consent of Greece and Turkey. The re-arrangement of the new boundaries between the two component states shall take place within three years (Article 9 FA). According to Article 10 (1) FA claims by dispossesed property owners shall be resolved in a comprehensive manner in accordance with international law, respect for the individual rights of dispossessed owner and current users, and the principle of bi-zonality. In areas subject to territorial adjustment, resinstatement shall take place. In other areas, the exercise of property rights shall be by way of reinstatement or compensation following certain detailed rules. Finally, a Reconciliation Committee shall promote understanding, tolerance and mutual respect between Greek Cypriots and Turkish Cypriots (Article 11 FA) and past acts shall remain valid, provided that they are compatible with the new Constitution (Article 12 FA). These cornerstones were translated into legal language in the Annexes of the Foundation Agreement.

Most importantly, Annex 1 contained the future constitution. The principles of democracy, rule of law and human rights were enshrined in Article 1 (6), 4 and 10 of the Cyprus Constitution (henceforth: CC). Part IV was dedicated to the relationship between the common state and the component states. The common state enjoys those conferred powers that are listed in Article 13 (1) CC, namely external relations, relations with the EU, central bank functions, common state finances including all indirect taxation (including customs and excise), and common state economic and trade policy, natural resources, metereology, aviation, international navigation etc., communications, Cypriot citizenship and immigration, combating terrorism, drug traficking, money laundering and organised crime, pardons and amnesties, intellectual property. Cooperation and co-ordination is possible other listed areas (Article 15 CC). Article 18 CC was fully devoted to EU membership.

The common state institutions (Part V) consisted of a legislature, an executive, independent officers and institutions, and the judiciary. The two-chamber Parliament represent the people of Cyprus and the component states under Article 21 CC. Whereas the 48 members of the Chamber of Deputies were to be elected throughout the country on the basis of proportional representation (but with a minimum of 1/4 MP's holding from each component state), the 48 members of the Senate would be elected from the people of the component states (24 MPs each). Executive power would be vested in a six-member Presidential Council (Article 25 CC) whose members are elected by Parliament for a fixed five-year term on a single list by special majority. Decisions are taken by consensus, or by majority, provided that at least one member from each "component state" has voted in favour. The alternate offices of the President and the Vice-President of the Presidential Council are rotating every ten months (Article 26 CC). Each member of the Presidential Council heads a governmental department, and the President represents the Presidential Council as Head of State (Articles 27 and 28 CC). Among the independent officers and institutions figurate the central bank and the Attorney-General and Auditor-General (Articles 31–34 CC). The Judiciary on the "common state" level is centralised in the Supreme Court. 6 members hail from each component state and three judges shall be foreigners (Article 1 of the Draft Law on Administration of Justice – Attachment 26 of Annex 3).[57] The Supreme Court has jurisdiction for disputes between the levels of government, for the determination of the constitutionality of laws, for appeals in all other disputes involving the interpretation of the Foundation Agreement, the Constitution, and international treaties binding on Cyprus. Furthermore, the Supreme Court would have the power to step in, if a deadlock arises in the political institutions of the federation, leading to a substantial default on the obligations of Cyprus as EU Member State. Finally, Parts VI and VII of the Constitution set out the rules for constitutional amendments and the transitional provisions.

The constitutional law on internal component state citizenship status and component state residency rights (Attachment 3 of Annex 2) was *sedes materiae* for several restrictions on political rights (Article 3), the right to free movement (Article 4) and residence for non-Cypriots (Article 5) and Cypriots (Article 6). In the list of common state laws the law on citizenship (Attachment 4 of Annex 3) was most relevant. It allowed in Article 3 (2) to naturalise up to 33.000 persons who received TRNC citizenship, if they are included in a list to be handed over to the UN by March 2003. Those persons that do not receive permanent residence could apply for financial assistance to relocate to their country of origin if they have lived in Cyprus for no less than five years (Article 2 (3) of the Law on Aliens, Immigration and Asylum – Attachment 5 of Annex 3). Finally, it is worth mentioning that Attachment 2 of Annex 4 contains the Draft Cooperation Agreement on EU relations, referred to in Article 18 (6) CC.

Annex VI was dedicated to the territorial arrangements. Most importantly Annan I contained two alternative maps. Both maps would have brought about an adjustment of around 9% of the territory, thereby following Boutros-Ghali's Set of Ideas. The big difference between the two maps concerned the Karpas Peninsula, which was handed over to Greek Cypriot administration in the first alternative, but not in the second which made the adjustments elsewhere.[58]

Annex VII contained detailed rules on the treatment of property affected by events since 1963. It distinguished between reinstatement and compensation and employed protection measures for current users, to be regulated by a Property Board.[59] Finally, Annex VIII established the reconciliation commission whose powers are mainly to gather information and publish reports.

In comparison to this comprehensive Foundation Agreement (Appendix A plus annexes), Appendices C-E were rather simple. Appendix C contained additional protocols to the Treaties of Guarantee and Alliance. As regards the former, the Guarantor powers now guarantee the territorial integrity, security and constitutional order of the "component States" besides the independence, territorial integrity,

---

[57] Both sides were reluctant to envisage any non-Cypriot judges; for that reason the UN foresaw that the legal basis for the appointment of foreign judges to the Supreme Court would be rooted in a simple law, not in the constitution.

[58] Hannay, loc. cit. (page xii, note 2), p. 184.

[59] For more details see Report of the Secretary-General on his mission of good offices in Cyprus of 1 April 2002, UN Doc S/2003/398, §§ 107–111.

security and constitutional order of Cyprus. As regards the latter, the level of allowed Greek and Turkish contingents to be stationed on the island were fixed between 2.500 and 7.500 soldiers. Appendix D called upon the Security Council to define the new mandate of the UN peace-keeping operation in Cyprus and to prohibit arms sale to the island. Appendix E was dedicated to "requests to the EU with respect to the accession of Cyprus". A protocol to be annexed to the Accession Treaty should contain arrangements relating to property and residency rights and safeguard measures (Articles 1 and 2). Reflecting a Turkish Cypriot proposal from the direct talks, entry and residence rights of Turkish nationals shall be granted on an equal footing to the equivalent rights of Greek nationals (Article 3). Article 4 made it clear that the European Security and Defense Policy shall not undermine the special treaty arrangements on Cyprus's security.

The whole plan would be subject to simultaneous referenda on both sides. The Referendum question combined the adoption of the plan and EU membership, thereby making it impossible to split these issuses.[60]

3.4. *Annan II of 10 December 2002*

Complying with Annan's request, Clerides reacted to the plan on 18 November after having consulted within the National Council. He wrote to Annan that he was prepared to negotiate on the basis of the proposals and seeking a number of clarifications. The latter were then pursued between the Attorney General, Markides, and the UN bilaterally.

The situation on the Turkish side was much more complicated. In early November, an electoral landslide had taken place in Turkey. All of the previous' government parties (DSP of Prime Minister Eçevit, ANAP of Deputy Prime Minister Yilmaz and MHP of Deputy Prime Minister Bahceli) did not return to the Parliament. Instead, a centre-right Islamic party, the AKP, under the former mayor of Istanbul, Erdoğan won a large majority in the single-chamber parliament. Only after the formation of the new government in Turkey under Prime Minister Gül[61] and Foreign Minister Yakis on 19 November, did the Turkish Cypriots react. Gül, who had been in charge for Cyprus affairs in the Erbakan government, had a reputation as being more flexible on the issue. Shortly before the electoral victory he had indicated his preference for the Belgian model adding that Cyprus as a national issue has to be addressed after due consideration with the Foreign Ministry, the military and other relevant agencies of the State.[62] Once in power, he coined the phrase "no solution is no solution". The AKP's "strong man" and Prime Minister to be, Erdoğan, also sent out signs of flexibility. On 27 November, Denktaş wrote a letter to Annan, expressing his willingness to negotiate on the basis of his proposals.

---

[60] Hannay, loc. cit. (page xii, note 2), p. 185.

[61] Erdoğan was prevented to head the new government since a Court had sentenced him for a non-violent public recital of an Islamic verse, thereby banning him from public office. Only after this verdict had been quashed could he take over as Prime Minister from Gül.

[62] Turkish Daily News, 02.09.2002.

Taking into account the technical comments mainly of the Greek Cypriot side, Annan tabled a slightly revised version on 10 December 2002 (Annan II). The main changes were as follows: On governance, a new paragraph empowered the Presidential Council to appoint Cypriot members for international bodies, including EU institutions. A new clause referred to representation of Cyprus in the European Parliament based on proportional representation, but reserving 2 out of the 6 seats to the Turkish Cypriots. On security, the proposal defined the possible number of troops to stay on the island between 2,500–7,500. Only one map was maintained, namely that one which gave the Karpas peninsula to the Greek Cypriots. Clarifications were introduced on the assessment of current value of the relevant properties. On settlers, the maximum number of 33.000 persons from each side was fixed, the conditions as regards naturalisation were slightly hardened, while a financial assistance scheme for persons who have to leave the island was introduced. The maximum ceiling of persons from one component state to return to the other one was decreased from 33% to 28%, but a review clause allows for a change to the system no later than 25 years. Any restriction on residence should not prevent the freedom of movement throughout Cyprus, including the right of any Cypriot citizen to temporarily (i.e. no more than an average of three nights a week) stay or holiday in their own properties or other accommodation anywhere in Cyprus. A relocation Agency should implement an efficient rehousing policy. The transitional provisions were shortened (co-presidency will exist for 2½ years instead of 3 years, substitutes allowed).

3.5. *The Copenhagen European Council 2002*

The tabling of Annan II on 10 December was closely related to the meeting of the European Council at Copenhagen on 11–12 December 2002. In the meantime, Cyprus had made good progress in the accession negotiations, the main purpose of which was to agree upon realistic timetables according to which Cyprus would implement the *acquis communautaire*. From the beginning Cyprus was very keen to proceed quickly in the negotiations. It "closed" many negotiation chapters rather early, due to, *inter alia*, the full commitment of the Chief negotiator, former President Vassiliou. In addition, as further requested by the Luxembourg Council, the EU adopted a pre-accession strategy for the candidate countries, including Cyprus.[63] For 2000–2004, Cyprus benefitted from 57 Mio €, one third of which should be dedicated to bi-communal projects.[64] The Council determined the priorities of

[63] Council Regulation (EC) No. 622/98 of 16 March 1998 on assistance to the applicant State in the framework of the pre-accession strategy, and in particular on the establishment of Accession Partnerships (OJ 1998, L 85, p. 1) and Council Regulation (EC) No. 555/2000 of 13 March 2000 on the implementation of operations in the framework of the pre-accession strategy for the Republic of Cyprus and the Republic of Malta (OJ 2000, L 68, p. 3).

[64] For the year 2000, 3 Mio. € were dedicated to the Nicosia masterplan; in 2001, 3, 3 € for the plan, 0, 3 Mio € for trade unions, 0, 2 Mio. € for the communication strategy. On the early experiences with the plan as follow-up of the common sewerage system, installed in 1980, see Demetriades, The Nicosia Master Plan, Journal of Mediterranean Studies, 1998, p. 169 et seq.

harmonisation in March 2000 and January 2002 (Accession Partnerships).[65] Cyprus was also allowed to participate in certain Community programs, such as Media II, Life II and the 5th Framework Programme on Research. However, as regards trade, no decision was taken by the Association Council to finalise the customs union. From 1998–2002 Cyprus was able to quickly close the different chapters envisaged by the Commission road map.[66] The Commission and the European Parliament[67] reported annually about steady progress. Certainly, the negotiations proved to be difficult in some sensitive areas.[68] For example, constant pressure from Brussels led to an important tax reform that touched the offshore-sector in Cyprus. Cyprus also faced criticism for rather weak measures to combat money laundering and reacted with the creation of new structures. Representing the sixth biggest fleet world wide, also the transport chapter was not an easy one since the EU insisted on the (costly) upgrading of maritime safety standards. Protectionist measures against the free flow of capital movements had to be abolished and the whole area of environmental protection needed to be revisited. Finally, as an overarching theme, Cyprus improved its administrative capacity in areas like justice and home affairs, including asylum matters. Undoubtedly, Cyprus would be able to formally conclude accession negotiation at the Copenhagen European Council in December 2002.

Against this background, the United Nations organized a Cyprus summit in Copenhagen, just 20 minutes away from the premises where the European Council met.

[65] See Council decision 248/2000 of 20 March 2000 (OJ 2000, L 78, p. 10) and Council decision 2002/84/EC of 28 January 2002 on the principles, priorities, intermediate objectives and conditions contained in the Accession Partnership with Cyprus (OJ 2002, L 44, p. 12).

[66] The chronological order of the chapters provisionally closed is the following:

Austrian Presidency (1/7/1998–31/12/1998): Science and Research; Education, Vocational Training and Youth; Culture and Audio-Visual Policy; Industrial Policy; Small and Medium-Sized Enterprises;

German Presidency (1/1/1999–30/6/1999): Telecommunications and Information Technologies; Consumers and Health Protection; Statistics; Customs Union; External Relations;

Finnish Presidency (1/7/1999–31/12/1999): Economic and Monetary Union;

Portuguese Presidency (1/1/2000–30/6/2000): Fisheries, Company Law, Social Policy and Employment; Common Foreign and Security Policy; Financial Control;

French Presidency (1/7/2000–31/12/2000): Free Movement of Goods;

Swedish Presidency (1/1/2001): Free Movement of Capital, Freedom to Provide Services, Transport Policy; Energy; Free Movement of Persons;

Belgian Presidency (1/7/2001–31/12/2001): Environment; Justice and Home Affairs;

Spanish Presidency (1/1/2002–30/6/2002): Taxation, Regional Policy, Institutions; Competition Policy;

Danish Presidency (1/7/2002–31/12/2002): Agriculture, Financial and Budgetary Provisions; Other.

[67] See the Resolutions of the European Parliament on Cyprus between 1999–2002, www.europarl.eu.int/enlargement/positionep/default_en.htm.

[68] Details can be found in the Regular Reports of the European Commission on Cyprus' progress towards membership (http://www.europa.eu.int/comm/enlargement).

At that occasion de Soto, Weston and Hannay and representatives of the two sides were present. From the beginning the involvement of the Turkish Cypriot side was badly affected by the continued absence of Denktaş. Under the TRNC constitution, the President was to be temporarily substituted by the President of the Parliament. However, the Foreign Minister Mr. Ertugruloğlu represented the Turkish Cypriot side, fuelling further incertainties as to their power to conclude the overall comprehensive settlement. Only after some pressure from Turkey, Denktaş seems to have given him full authority in writing.[69]

In any case, the negotiations of Friday 13 December did not lead to the desired result. The Danish Prime Minister Rasmussen, representing the EU Presidency, had asked the parties to inform him by 4. p.m. in the afternoon whether an agreement was signed or not. In that event, the European Council would have taken this breakthrough still into account. However, whereas the Greek Cypriot side was inclined to sign, if the Turkish Cypriot side would commit itself in the same way, Mr. Ertugruloğlu did not take a comparable position. The Turkish government did not induce the Turkish Cyriots to sign either. It was disappointed that the French-German initiative gained support among the other members in the Council, according to which accession negotiations with Turkey could only start after another report of the European Commission in December 2004. That appearing to be too late in the view of the Turkish government, there was no incentive for Ankara to press the Turkish Cypriots. Despite strong US and UK pressure to demonstrate his sincerity, Clerides decided not to sign the plan unilaterally. As a minimal result of this Cyprus summit both sides committed themselves to continue negotiations until 28 February 2003, i.e. to enter into the finalisation phase even without prior signature of the "hard core" provisions of the Foundation Agreement.

In the view of this outcome, the Copenhagen Council concluded on Cyprus:

> *As the accession negotiations have been completed with Cyprus, Cyprus will be admitted as a new Member State to the European Union. Nevertheless, the European Council confirms its strong preference for accession to the European Union by united Cyprus. In this context it welcomes the commitment of the Greek Cypriots and the Turkish Cypriots to continue to negotiate with the objective of concluding a comprehensive settlement of the Cyprus problem by 28 February 2003 on the basis of the UNSG's proposals. The European Council believes that those proposals offer a unique opportunity to reach a settlement in the coming weeks and urges the leaders of the Greek Cypriot and Turkish Cypriot communities to seize this opportunity.*
>
> *The Union recalls its willingness to accommodate the terms of a settlement in the Treaty of Accession in line with the principles on which the EU is founded. In case of a settlement, the Council, acting by unanimity on the basis of proposals by the Commission, shall decide upon the adaptations of the terms concerning the accession of Cyprus to the EU with regard to the Turkish Cypriot community.*
>
> *The European Council has decided that, in the absence of a settlement, the application of the acquis to the northern part of the island shall be suspended, until the*

[69] Hannay, loc. cit. (page xii, note 2), p. 188.

Council decides unanimously otherwise, on the basis of a proposal by the Commission. Meanwhile, the Council invites the Commission, in consultation with the government of Cyprus, to consider ways of promoting economic development of the northern part of Cyprus and bringing it closer to the Union.

After another report of de Soto to the Security Council, the President of the Council issued a statement to the press on 18 December 2002.[70] The members of the Council "regretted that the Turkish Cypriot leadership had not responded in a timely way to the initiatives to the Secretary-General; and they called for its constructive efforts to reach a settlement with the timetable proposed by the Secretary-General. (. . .) They urged both sides to work on the basis of the Secretary-General's revised proposal of 10 December".

On Turkey, the Copenhagen Council concluded:

The European Union recalls its decision in 1999 in Helsinki that Turkey as a candidate state is destined to join the Union on the basis of the same criteria as applied to the other candidate states. It strongly welcomes the important steps taken by Turkey towards meeting the Copenhagen criteria, in particular through the recent legislative packages and the subsequent implementation measures which cover a large number of key priorities specified in the Accession Partnership. The Union acknowledges the determination of the new Turkish government to take further steps on the path of reform and urges in particular the government to address swiftly all remaining shortcomings in the field of the political criteria, not only with regard to legislation but also in particular with regard to implementation. The Union recalls that, according to the political criteria decided in Copenhagen in 1993, membership requires that a candidate country has achieved stability of institutions guaranteeing democracy, the rule of law, human rights and respect for and protection of minorities.

The Union encourages Turkey to pursue energetically its reform process. If the European Council in December 2004, on the basis of a report and a recommendation from the Commission, decides that Turkey fulfills the Copenhagen criteria, the Europen Union will open accession negotiations with Turkey without delay.

In order to assist Turkey towards EU membership, the accession strategy for Turkey shall be strengthend. The Commission is invited to submit a proposal for a revised Accession Partnership and to intensify the process of legislative scrutiny. In parallel, the EC-Turkey Customs Union should be extended and deepened. The Union will significantly increase its pre-accession financial assistance for Turkey. This assistance will be from 2004 and be financed under the budget heading "pre-accession expenditure.

4. Annan Plan III and the Athens European Council

At the very day of the Copenhagen Council the rising inner Turkish Cypriot opposition to the Denktaş line culminated in large demonstrations in northern Nicosia where tens of thousands Turkish Cypriots, mobilized by more than 40 political

70 UN Press Release SC/7612 of 18 December 2002.

parties, trade unions, business men and NGO's in the Platform "This Country is ours", demonstrated for an acceptance of the Annan Plan and EU membership.[71] In Turkey, the new government and military circles were confronting each other on Cyprus.[72] The election campaign for the President's office kept the Cyprus issue high on the agenda for the Greek Cypriots.

4.1. *The resumptions of negotiations*

Against this background, both leaders resumed talks already in the second week of January 2003. The two committees on internal legislation and international instruments started working. They reviewed in particular which TRNC acts needed to apply within a unified Cyprus. The European Commission seconded an official from DG Enlargement to support the UN on EU related matters.[73] The Turkish Cypriots tried to voice their concerns on Annan I and II by handing in another series of non-papers to the UN. The most important of these was called "basic requirements for a settlement in Cyprus". Apparently written in Ankara, the 27 January paper[74] contained seven points: the map had to be renegotiated, a property moratorium should last 9 years, 50,000 Turks should stay in Cyprus for five years in addition to those are legally established there. One new idea concerned aliens: neither Turks nor Greeks should make up more than 5% of aliens in Cyprus. On governance, the one-third of senators of each constituent state would be needed for an affirmative vote. The paper suggested changes on "partnership", "peoples" "non-domination", touching the status issue. Finally, on security, the mandate of the UN force should not involve enforcement tasks. In addition, the United Kingdom offered the United Nations an "unexpected trump card" in the beginning of February. It was willing to concede 45 of the 99 square miles of the Sovereign Bases not needed for military purposes, thereby improving any UN discretion as regards the thorny territorial issue.[75]

---

[71] According to Çarkoşlu/Sözen, Turkish Cypriot General Elections of December 2003: An Appraisal, South European Society & Politics, Vol. 9, Issue 3 (2004), p. 123 (135), the idea behind the platform's slogan "This country is ours" was that Turkish Cypriots should rule northern Cyprus and that foreign – more specifically Turkish – intervention in the administration should stop.

[72] While AKP leader Erdoğan publicy referred to Denktaş as an "obstacle" to the solution (FAZ 3.01.2003), the Chief of Staff General, Özkök, critizised the government as being to lenient on Cyprus and the Annan plan, which should be rejected as a threat to the security of Turkey (NZZ 10.01.2003).

[73] Mrs. Dolores Romeo from the Cyprus team attended the meetings of the two committees in Nicosia between mid-January and end of February 2003 to advise on EU matters.

[74] Another paper of 3 February 2003, this time written in northern Nicosia, added certain well-known points on status that had already been discarded by the UN long time ago. Turkey did, however, signal to the UN that only the 27 January paper should be considered.

[75] For details see Hannay, loc. cit. (page xii, note 2), p. 207.

4.2. *Annan III of 26 February 2003*

Taking stock of six weeks of negotiations, the UN team tabled the third version of the Annan plan on 26 February (Annan III). This plan contained considerable changes to Annan II.

The "comprehensive settlement" (which constituted the overarching text of Annan I/II) was replaced by a commitment of the leaders to submit the Foundation agreement to referenda. On governance, several changes were introduced, mainly concerning denomination. Annan III baptised the two constituent states as "*the Greek Cypriot State*" and "*the Turkish Cypriot state*", thereby pleasing Turkish Cypriot demands. Furthermore these constituent states gained discretionary powers to decide on internal citizenship, thereby possibly avoiding the Greek Cypriots returning to the north would become a part of the Turkish Cypriot electorate. On the other hand, paying tribute to the Greek Cypriot's idea, the United Cyprus Republic would have a *federal government.* Easing both sides' reservations against foreign judges, a new provision ensured that these should only cast decisive votes if the Cypriot judges were not in agreement. A new Federal Court of First Instance was to be established.

On property and residence, Annan III increased the moratorium on Greek Cypriot right of residence in the north up to six years. Fifteen years after entry into force of the settlement the quota of Greek Cypriots living in the north could be restricted to 21% (as compared to 28% in the previous versions). Annan III also introduced the number of 45,000 former Turkish citizens that should have access to Cypriot citizenship. These offers to the Turkish Cypriot side were countered by the ease of restrictions for Greek Cypriots over 65 years (for whom the moratorium should only apply for two years and who would not be subject to any residence quotas). Turks not covered by the quota should only be able to claim Cypriot citizenship after nine years of residence (as compared to seven years previously). Finally, Annan III served the Greek Cypriot wish that any rules on entry and residence of Turks should be compatible with the Schengen system.

Annan III brought another territorial switch. This time, the Karpas peninsula was to remain under Turkish Cypriot administration, whereas Greek Cypriots would have an unlimited right to return to the four villages there. Overall, as result of the British offer, the Turkish Cypriot constituent state would account of 29.2% of the territory, the Greek Cypriot constituent state for 71.8%.

On security, the Annan III did not modify the mandate of the future UN force. However, addressing a Turkish Cypriot concern, the UN added a provision according to which any international military operations in Cyprus would need the consent of Greece and Turkey as well as of each constituent state. Furthermore, the plan determined the size of the Turkish and Greek troops to stay on the island to 6.000.

Finally, Annan III contained an increase of EU related provisions. As before, there was a request for the European Union to endorse the settlement. The EU should also hold a donors' conference to raise funds dedicated to projects relating to territorial adjustment and the consequences of displacement of some parts of the population. Most importantly, Annan III changed the referendum question. The link made in Annan I/II between the settlement and EU accession disappeared with the consequence that a negative vote in the referendum could not invalidate EU accession of Cyprus.

4.3. *The Hague summit of 11 March 2003*

A good month ahead of the announced April European Council in Athens, where the EU Accession Treaty was to be signed, UN Secretary-General Annan invited the leaders to meet on 11 March 2003 in the Hague. At that time he would ask them formally whether they are prepared to sign the text committing themselves to putting the proposals to a referendum on 30 March. In the meanwhile they should give him names for the transitional Supreme Court and hand in draft constitutions for the constituent states. He also waited for a decision on the flag and the anthem. The two working groups should keep on meeting. This timetable would have allowed for last-minute changes to the EU Accession Treaty whose signature was scheduled for the 16 April already.

On the Greek Cypriot side, Papadopoulos competed with Clerides in the presidential elections. It was known during the campaign that he would be less flexible than Clerides – so those who did not like the Plan were likely to vote for him. Furthermore, he seemed to have received votes from those who were dissatisfied with the aging Clerides on internal policy issues. On 16 February 2003, Papadopoulos won in the first round, receiving more than 50% of the votes. His attitude was expected to be cautious, certainly not enthuasistic about the plan. He was sworn into office on 28 February 2003 and led the Greek Cypriot delegation henceforth.

On the Turkish Cypriot side, Denktaş conferred with the new Prime Minister Erdoğan, Foreign Minister Gül, President Sezer and others in Ankara. Large parts of the Turkish diplomats and the military[76] still took an issue with the plan.[77] Although details remained unclosed, it emerged from this meeting that he had gained full support to oppose the plan – called by the British envoy Hannay as "something of a mystery".[78] Apparently, the AKP government was not decided to "give in" at this early stage where EU assurances on the accession course of Turkey remained uncertain.

---

[76] H. J. Axt/N. Neuwahl, Cyprus' EU Accession and EU-Turkey Convergence, in: Yeditepe Üniversitesi Hukuk Fakültesis Dergisi I/1, 2004, pp. 219 (221–222) reporting about the differences between the AKP government, the diplomatic circles and the military in this crucial phase.

[77] For a summary of the Turkish Cypriot objections to the Annan plan see A. Pearce, loc. cit. (page 26, note 68), p. 149 (154–155). Whereas the military was concerned with the reduction of Turkish troops in Cyprus, the diplomats seemed to relay on nationalist patterns. See e.g. G. Aktan, one leading figure in the Turkish foreign ministry at the time (in the meanwhile retired), Turkish Daily News 20.3.2003: "The EU membership as it is foreseen in the Annan plan would lead to the hegemony of the Greek Cypriots and the elimination of the Turkish Cypriot people within the EU".

[78] Hannay, loc. cit. (page xii, note 2), p. 214.

Against this background, the Secretary-General's meetings on 10 March in the Peace Palace took 19 hours, but to no avail. Annan's press statement recorded the positions of the two leaders as follows:

> *I asked each of them whether they were prepared to commit today to submit my 26 February 2003 plan to approval at separate simultaneous referenda on 30 March 2003, in order to achieve a comprehensive settlement of the Cyprus Problem.*
>
> *Mr. Papadopoulos answered that he was prepared to do so, as long as the people knew what they are being asked to vote on. To that end he wished to be sure that the gaps regarding federal legislation, as well as constituent state constitutions, would be filled. He underlined the importance of Greece and Turkey agreeing and committing to the security provisions in the plan. Furthermore, considerably more time was needed than was available for a proper, public campaing on the referendum to be carried out. These conditions need to be fulfilled before a referendum can take place. He said he was prepared not to re-open its substantive provisions if the other side was prepared to do likewise.*
>
> *Mr. Denktaş answered that he was not prepared to agree to put the plan to referendum. He said he had fundamental objections to the plan on basic points. He believed that further negotiations were only likely to be successful if they began from a new starting point and if the parties agreed on basic principles. He added that Turkey was in any case not in a position to sign the statement requested of the guarantors because this first required the authorisation of parliament.*

Despite some last ditch efforts involving the Special envoys of the United States and the United Kingdom there was no change in the position from the Turkish side. The UN Secretary General reported to the UN Security Council that his mission would now come to an end.[79] A unanimous Security Council gave "its full support to the Secretary-General's carefully balanced plan of 26 February as unique basis for further negotiations".[80]

4.4. *The Athens European Council of April 2003*

In the meanwhile, the European Union followed its strict accession timetable. On 19 February 2003, the Commission issued its favourable opinion on the applications for accession of the ten candidates, including Cyprus.[81] At its meeting of 20/21 March 2003, the European Council "regrets that the efforts of the United Nations Secretary-General to find a comprehensive settlement have failed and (. . .) urges (. . .) in particular the Turkish Cypriot leadership to reconsider its position".

[79] Report of the Secretary-General on his mission of good offices in Cyprus of 1 April 2002, UN Doc S/2003/398, §§ 144–151.

[80] UNSC Resolution 1475 of 14 April 2003, § 4.

[81] Commission opinion of 19 February 2003 on the application for accession to the European Union by the Czech Republic, the Republic of Estonia, the Republic of Cyprus, the Republic of Latvia, the Republic of Lithuania, the Republic of Hungary, the Republic of Malta, the Republic of Poland, the Republic of Slovenia and the Slovak Republic, OJ 2003, L 235, p. 3.

For the European Parliament and the European Council, the failure of the Hague meeting dispersed any uncertainty about the exact contents of the Accession Treaty. In order to keep the necessary flexibility, the Commission had prepared two options of a Protocol for Cyprus:[82] one version (version A) would have been attached to the Accession Treaty in case of unification; since 10 March it was clear that the second version (version B) had to be used by the Intergovernmental Conference. The relevant text, which translates the Copenhaguen summit language into a legal one, provides for the suspension of the *acquis* in the areas where the Cyprus government does not exercise effective control.[83]

On 9 April 2003, the European Parliament voted in favour of Cyprus' accession to the European Union (of the 562 votes cast, 507 were in favour, 29 against with 26 abstentions), in full knowledge of this version of the Protocol.[84]

On 16 April 2003, the Heads of States and governments of the European Union, meeting in Athens, took two decisions. They finalized the Union admission procedure[85] by taking a positive decision on the application[86] and they formally signed the Accession Treaty with the Cyprus Protocol attached.[87] According to Article 2 (2) of that Treaty accession was scheduled to enter into force on 1 May 2004, provided that all (25) instruments of ratification were deposited. Cyprus was thus on the eve of becoming an EU Member State as a divided island under the *status quo*.

B. LEGAL EVALUATION

From a legal perspective, it must be scrutinised what kind of measures were aimed at when the 2002 Seville Council – confirmed by all subsequent European Councils – spoke about "accommodation" of the Annan plan by the EU. Furthermore the Council defined an important legal border line: Any accommodation would have to be in line "with the principles on which the EU is founded: as a Member State, Cyprus will need to speak with a single voice and ensure proper application of European Union law". In addition, the Council demanded that any settlement should be "consistent with all relevant UN Security Council resolutions".

---

[82] M. Uebe, Cyprus in the European Union, GYIL 2004, p. 375 (382).

[83] Act of Accession, Protocol 10, Appendix 1.

[84] European Parliament Legislative Resolution on the application of the Republic of Cyprus to become a member of the European Union of 9 April 2003, OJ 2003, L 236, p. 7.

[85] On the procedural difference between the Union procedure on the application of a candidate and the accession negotiations with that candidate see F. Hoffmeister, Changing Requirements for Membership, in: A. Ott/K. Inglis, Handbook on European Enlargement, p. 90 (99 et seq.).

[86] Decision of the Council of the European Union of 14 April 2003 on the admission of the Czech Republic, the Republic of Estonia, the Republic of Cyprus, the Republic of Latvia, the Republic of Lithuania, the Republic of Hungary, the Republic of Poland, the Republic of Slovenia and the Slovak Republic of the European Union, OJ 2003, L 235, p. 15.

[87] OJ 2003, L 236, p. 955.

1. Accommodation of the Annan plan in the legal order of the European Union

1.1. *The EU principle*

Every Accession Treaty provides for the "conditions of admission and the adjustments to the Treaty on which the European Union is founded" (Article 49 (2) EU). Accordingly, an Accession Treaty including all its annexes and protocols enjoys the same rank as the founding treaties (primary law) and has the power to modify them.[88] They integrate the new Member States into the existing EU legal order. But they also incorporate agreements between the old and new member States to depart from certain established rules in order to meet the challenges that EU membership would create to both of them. It follows there from that any request to declare a provision of the Accession Treaty null and void is inadmissible before the Court of Justice, regardless of whether it is introduced by an individual under Article 230 (4) EC or by privileged claimants under Articles 230 (1–3) EC.[89]

Politically, the Intergovernmental Conference decided that such modifications should take, in principle, the form of transitional periods.[90] Transitional periods can be agreed in every policy field, including on internal market issues. Thus they can limit even the application of the four fundamental freedoms as guaranteed in Articles 28, 39, 43, 49 EC. Accordingly, the Accession Treaty 2003 provided for transitional periods up to seven years to restrict the free movement of nationals of the new Member States into the old Member States;[91] it also allowed for restrictions on the right of nationals of old Member States to purchase real estate in the new Member States,[92] going up to twelve years in the case of agricultural land in Poland.[93]

---

[88] ECJ, Joined Cases 194/85 and 241/85 Commission v. Greece (1988) ECR 1037.

[89] Hoffmeister, loc. cit. (note 85) p. 90 (102).

[90] See para. 25 of the negotiation framework of 31 March 1998, CONF-CY 2/98 of 26 March 1998. For the principles, actors and procedure of the negotiations in general see L. Maurer, Negotiations in Progress, in: Ott/Inglis (ed.), Handbook on European Enlargement, p. 113 et seq.

[91] See Article 24 of the Accession Act in conjunction with the 2nd section ("freedom of movement for persons") in the Annexes V–XIV respectively. The standard wording (e.g. Annex XII on Poland, OJ 2003, L 236, p. 876) reads: "Article 39 and the first paragraph of Article 49 of the EC Treaty shall fully apply only, in relation to the freedom of workers and the freedom to provide services involving temporary movement of workers (...) subject to the transitional provisions laid down in paragraphs 2 to 14".

[92] Article 24 of the Accession Act in conjunction with the 4th section in Annexes V–XIV respectively.

[93] See e.g. Section 4 of Annex XII on Poland: "Notwithstanding the obligations under the Treaties on which the EU is founded, Poland may maintain in force for twelve years from the date of accession the rules laid down in the Act of 24 March 1920 on the Acquisition of Real Estatet by Foreigners as amended, regarding the acquisition of agricultural land and forests".

Furthermore, there is no legal rule preventing the Member States as the treaty-makers, from accepting derogations on particular issues. In the history of the European Union some important policy areas were subject to this technique. Obvious examples are the rights of the United Kingdom and Denmark not to participate in the EURO, or the position of the United Kingdom and Ireland outside the Schengen area. Such special regimes constitute permanent derogations.

In has recently been suggested that derogations from primary law may not touch the very core of EU principles.[94] The European Court of Justice gave a small hint when finding that establishing a judicial organ of dispute settlement in the envisaged EEA agreement would diminish the role of the ECJ under Article ex 164 EC (new 220 EC) which could not have been removed even by a Treaty amendment.[95] That could be read as a guarantee that the judicial function of the Court as the guardian of EC law integrity could "never" be touched, not even by the Member States by conclusion of a new EC treaty. The idea of "untouchable" core issues is moreover present in the constitutions of some Member States[96] and in the notion of *jus cogens* in international law.

On the other hand, despite its functioning as a European constitution,[97] the EC Treaty is still subject to the intergovernmental method of treaty-making. The will of the Member States to accommodate specific economic interests has not been subject to legal limitations so far. The treaty-makers did occasionally restrict the four internal market freedoms, even permanently. One may quote the Danish prohibition for secondary residences in the Maastricht Treaty[98] or the special regime for the Aland islands attached to the Treaty of Accession of Finland, Sweden and Austria.[99]

In conclusion, even if one was to accept that a certain "hard core" of EU law could not even be changed by way a new Treaty (including an Accession Treaty) such "hard core rules" would be found foremost in the characteristics of the institutional system of the EU treaty as a quasi-constitution, protecting democracy, rule of law and human rights, as well as the supremacy and direct effect of EC law,[100] rather than in the full application of the four internal market freedoms.

---

[94] A. Ott, The 'Principle' of Differentiation in an Enlarged European Union: Unity in Diversity?, in: Inglis/Ott, The Constitution for Europe and an Enlarging Union: Unity in Diversity?, p. 103 (122 et seq.).

[95] ECJ, Opinion 1/91, ECR 1991–I 6079, § 72.

[96] Under Article 79 (3) of the German Basic law, the principles of Articles 1 and 20 GG (human dignity and certain principles of state organization) may never been modified. In France, the Republican principle is "untouchable" according to Article 89 (5) of the French constitution.

[97] ECJ, Case 294/83 (The Greens vs. European Parliament), Rec. 1986, 1339, at 1365, § 23.

[98] Protocol to the Treaty of Maastricht on the acquisition of property in Denmark, reprinted in European Union – Selected instruments taken from the Treaties, Book I, Vol. I, Luxemburg 1999, p. 459.

[99] Protocol 2 of the Act of Accession of Sweden, Austria and Finland, OJ 1994, C 241.

[100] Ott, loc. cit. (note 94), p. 123.

1.2. *Annan III*

A Draft protocol attached to Annan III (Annex IX, Attachment 2) identified those provisions, which needed to be incorporated in the Treaty of Accession. If adopted by the Intergovernemental Conference, the Protocol would then have become primary law and modified the operation of general EU norms, including internal market freedoms, for the specific situation in Cyprus. The Draft Protocol listed in particular restrictions on the right to purchase property and restrictions on residence rights. It also provided for safeguard measures that may be taken in the event that the Turkish Cypriot constituent state meets serious economic difficulties. Another point was to grant non-discriminatory access of Turkish citizens to the island, departing from the visa requirement that would otherwise be applied against them under the Schengen-*acquis*. Finally, the Draft Protocol underlined that the European Security and Defence Policy would not affect the operation of the security provisions of the Annan plan.

From an EU point of view, subjecting the possibility to purchase property in the north to a requirement of administrative licencing would conflict with the free movement of capital, as guaranteed in Article 56 EC. The case law of the Court of Justice consistently held that under the Treaty, only an appropriate notification system could be seen as proportional.[101] Accordingly, the relevant provisions of Annan III necessitated a special authorisation by primary EU law.[102] As regards the restrictions on the right to residence for Cypriots, the situation was less clear. These limitations could be seen as justifiable under Article 18 EC, in order to guarantee a settlement, operating on the basis of the bi-zonality principle.[103] Hence, the relevant article in the Draft Accession Protocol was, strictly speaking, not necessary, but certainly useful to avoid any sort of contention as regards the (dis)-proportionality of the restrictions. In contrast, restrictions for Greek citizens to enter and reside in Cyprus would have been contrary to Articles 18, 39 and 43 EC, triggering the need for special treatment in the Accession Protocol. Similarly, introducing a special economic safeguard for the Turkish Cypriots needed a basis in primary law, as well as possible deviations from current Schengen rules. Whether the provision relating to ESDP was legally necessary, seems to be less obvious.

2. Principles on which the EU is founded

The Heads of States and Government decided in Seville to accommodate a settlement "in line with the principles on which the EU is founded". This terminology

---

[101] ECJ, Joined Cases C-515/99, C-519/99 to C-524/99 and C-526/99 to C-540/99, Reisch and others, ECR I-2157, 2002, § 37 with further references.

[102] See e.g. ECJ, Case C-300/01, Salzmann, ECR 2003, I–4899. This case relates to Article 70 of the Accession Act of Austria as a special norm in that field.

[103] See in detail below section 2.3.2.

does not refer to internal market principles[104] – as demonstrated above, these are open to modification in any Act of Accession.[105] Rather the "principles on which the European Union is founded" are defined in Article 6 (1) EU reading:

> *The European Union is founded on the principles of liberty, democracy, respect for human rights and fundamental freedoms, and the rule of law, principles which are common to the Member States.*

Therefore the Annan plan had to design a United Cyprus Republic that is endowed with democratic institutions, respects the rule of law and has separated powers and effectively protects human rights and fundamental freedoms (the so-called political criterion).

2.1. *Democracy*

2.1.1. The EU principle

The democratic principle has two dimensions. According to the objective dimension, the State's decision-making body must be endowed with democratic legitimacy. The subjective dimension of democracy refers to the equal voting rights of every citizen.

The objective dimension of democracy is particularly relevant for the composition of federal parliaments. In a representative system, the level of legitimacy may vary. In theory, it might be sufficient that a federal parliament is composed of delegates from federated parliaments, if these are themselves directly elected. Such a federal Parliament would enjoy a derived democratic legitimacy. However, in practice, the lower chambers of federal parliaments in EU Member States are never composed of delegates from federated Parliaments. Rather, in Germany,[106] Austria[107] and in Belgium,[108] the lower House is always directly elected through electoral lists. In the USA, the indirect system to vote for "electors of the electoral collegue" is only applied for Presidential elections and not for parliamentary elections. Even the members of the European Parliament, which is not the parliamentary body of a State, but has law-making powers,[109] are directly elected since 1979.

The subjective dimension of democracy ensures that each citizen has, in principle, an equal voting right. The European Court of Human Rights has affirmed that Article 3 of the First Additional Protocol to the ECHR,[110] confers a subjective

---

[104] Dissenting Palley, loc. cit. (page xiii, note 3), p. 58, who equates the principles on which the EU is founded with "EU human and *economic rights standards*".

[105] See above, Chapter VI B 1.1.

[106] Artikel 38 of the Basic Law (Grundgesetz).

[107] Artikel 26 of the main Austrian Constitutional Law (B-VG).

[108] Artikel 61 of the Belgian consolidated Constitution.

[109] ECtHR, Matthews v. United Kingdom, (1999) Reports 1999–I.

[110] Article 3 of the First Additional Protocol to the ECHR reads:
"The High Contracting Parties undertake to hold free elections at reasonable intervals by secret ballot, under conditions which will ensure the expression of the free opinion of the people in the choice of the legislature".

right to the individual.[111] However, this right can be subject to implicit restrictions provided that these pursue a legitimate aim and that the employed means are not disproportionate.

Judged against this yardstick, the voting rights should have equal "counting value". It is excluded that (as witnessed for example in Prussia in the 19th century) the vote of one citizen counts for 10 votes, whereas the vote of others only counts for one vote. On other hand, equal voting rights are not synonomous to equal "success value". Electoral systems may foresee that the votes for certain candidates are "lost", for example because they belong to a political party that does not reach the national threshold, or because another candidate got more votes in a system of majority voting. Unequal success values are accepted in a proportional system because the threshold ensures parliamentary stability by excluding minor parties or candidates. In a majority voting system, the direct relationship between the electorate and the candidates is deemed to be so important that it justifies that the votes for the second best candidate are lost.

Furthermore, democratic legitimacy goes hand in hand with accountability for the exercice of public power. Whereas law-makers are directly accountable by being submitted to regular elections, judges are accountable to the people in an indirect way. They must be elected and appointed by democratically legitimised institutions (like the Parliament, the Head of State or the Government). While enjoying independence, they are bound by the law, which may set up specific rules of conduct for judges in office. They are therefore accountable in their public action for any breaches of the law. The objective dimension of the democratic principle does, however, not require that judges must be nationals. Whereas it is uncommon for European States to appoint judges of a foreign nationality to their highest Courts, there is nothing illegal about doing so, in particular in a situation where the foreign judges are conceived to help a country deciding difficult cases concerning fundamental questions for both communities. Even ardent critics of the 1960 constitution did not contend that the Republic of Cyprus was undemocratic because foreign judges were serving in Cyprus in 1960–1964. Foreigners are also currently in office for the Constitutional Court of Bosnia and Herzegovina.[112] The reliance on international support in the judicial system, especially in post-conflict situations, is therefore not incompatible with the concept of democratic accountability.

In sum, practice in EU Member States points in favour of direct elections for the members of the lower chambers of their federal Parliament. It would be also compatible with the democratic principle as enshrined in Article 6 EU to adopt a voting system that allows for a certain inequality of a vote`s success value. In contrast, the principle of democratic accountability does not forbid the appointment of foreigners as judges to the highest Courts by democratic institutions of the State.

---

[111] ECtHR, Podkolzina vs. Latvia, Appl. 46726/99, Judgement of 9 April 2002, § 33 with annotation F. Hoffmeister, AJIL 2003, p. 664.

[112] Compare further T. Grant, Internationally guaranteed constitutive order: Cyprus and Bosnia as predicates for a new non-traditional actor in the society of states, Journal of Transnational Law & Policy, 1998, p. 1 (43 et seq.).

2.1.2. *Annan III*

Under Article 1 (4) of the UCR constitution, Cyprus would have been organised "in accordance with the basic principles of (. . .), democracy, representative republican government (. . .)". The federal Parliament would have had two chambers. The seats in the Chamber of Deputies would have been attributed on the basis of the number of persons holding internal constituent state citizenship status of each constituent state; provided that each constituent state shall be attributed a minimum of one quarter of seats (Article 22 (IV) UCR constitution). The Senate would have been composed of an equal number of Turkish Cypriots and Greek Cypriots. Hence, for both chambers, the Members of Parliament would have been directly elected from the electorate, although with different quotas as regards the seats for the two communities. That would change the "success" value of a vote, but not its "counting value".

The six-member Presidential Council would receive its legitimacy from the Parliament (Article 26 I and II UCR constitution). A President, whose office would rotate on a yearly basis (Article 27 UCR constitution), would have presided over the Council. Although a government with a rotating President would be rather unusual in the practice of EU Member States, such concept reflecting a consociational model of democracy as practiced in Switzerland,[113] would have nevertheless been perfectly legal.

The Supreme Court would have been composed with three foreign judges (Article 6 (2) of the Main Articles of the Foundation Agreement). Again, while such a system would have been rather uncommon within the EU, it does not conflict with the principle of democratic accountability given that the Plan contained a number of safeguards.[114] All these foreign nationals would not have served in Cyprus against the will of the Cypriot people. Rather, like Cypriot judges, they would have been elected by the Cypriot Parliament. Furthermore, only if the six Cypriot judges were unable to hand down a decision because they are evenly split, would the three non-Cypriots cast their votes. Finally, as the appointment of foreign judges was deliberately foreseen in the statute of the court and not in the constitution the Cypriot legislative could abolish this element by an ordinary law if it became no longer necessary.

In sum, the set-up of the state institutions under Annan III did comply with the EU principles on democracy.

2.2. *Rule of Law*

2.2.1. *The EU principle*

Rule of Law means in essence the separation of powers, where the government is subordinated to the constitution and parliamentary laws (principles of constitutionality and legality), and the existence of judicial review by independent courts.[115]

---

113 A. Sözen, A Model of Power Sharing in Cyprus: From the 1959 London-Zurich Agreements to the Annan Plan, Turkish Studies, 2004, p. 61 (71).

114 Pfirter, loc. cit. (page 74, note 71), p. 161 (174–175).

115 ECJ, Case 222/84, Johnston, [1986] ECR, 1651, § 18 as to the requirement of judicial control as a general principle of law, which underlies the constitutional traditions common to the Member States.

However, the EU does not go into the detail of the internal division of powers between the branches of government.

2.2.2. Annan III

Article 3 of the UCR constitution enshrined the principle of constitutionality in clear terms. Article 4 of the UCR constitution would have fully incorporated the principle of rule of law:

> *(1) The law is the basis of and limitation for all acts of government at all levels.*
> *(2) All acts of government at all levels shall conform with the principles of public interest, proportionality and good faith.*
> *(3) . . .*

The constitution would have also foreseen the classical separation of powers by entrusting the legislative function to Parliament, the executive function to the Presidential Council and the judicial function to independent courts. One special feature was, of course, the extra-ordinary power of the Supreme Court to take measures "in lieu" of any other defaulting State institutions (Article 36 (6) of the UCR constitution): would this feature be in contradiction with the separation of powers?

In this regard, it must be recalled that many constitutional courts in Europe have certain tasks in litigation between State organs.[116] Some also have the power to declare legislation as null and void, including the power to prescribe criteria and time frames for the adoption of new ones. Admittedly, the default power of the Cypriot Supreme Court could reach even further. However, it seems to be warranted in the special situation of Cyprus, where the absence of such power was one of the reasons for the collapse of the bi-communal system in 1963/1964. Which other institution could have been entrusted with the task of breaking deadlocks? Should it be an international High Commissioner with final authority and arbitration rights over the matter causing a deadlock in decision-making?[117] In view of such alternatives, an extraordinary judicial power seems to be less intrusive for Cyprus. Allowing the Cypriot Supreme Court to step in stays within the principle of separation of powers as long as the judiciary does not replace the executive by usurping the latter's legitimate role. In that regard, it is important that the deal or breaking power can only be exercised upon application of another high state institution.[118]

[116] See e.g. the power of the German Constitutional Court (under Article 93 (1) Nr. 1 of the Basic Law) to rule "on the interpretation of this Basic Law in disputes concerning the extent of the rights and obligations of a supremce federal institution or other institutions concerned who have been vested with rights of their own by this Basic Law or by the rules of procedure of a supreme federal institution". Similar powers are vested, for example, in the Constitutional Courts of Italy and Poland, or the Cour d'Arbitrage in Belgium.

[117] See e.g. the proposal of M. Emerson/N. Tocci, Cyprus as Lighthouse of the East Mediterranean, Shaping Re-unification and EU Accession Together, p. 17, to establish an EU High Representative for Cyprus, possibly inspired by the OSCE High Representative for Bosnia and Hercegovina, who, acting under Annex X of the Dayton Agreement and the so-called "Bonn Powers", can effectively rule the country by adopting laws and regulations on behalf of defaulting institutions of the entities.

[118] Pfirter, loc. cit. (page 74, note 71), p. 175.

Moreover, Article 35 (6) of the UCR constitution is limited to cases of substantial default of EU law and calls upon the judiciary to exercise appropriate restraint. Such a system is compatible with EU requirements.

2.3. *Human Rights*

The founding principle of respect for human rights and fundamental freedoms is further spelt out in Article 6 (2) EU, which refers to the European Convention on Human Rights and the constitutional traditions common to the Member States, as general principles of Community law. It suffices to say that the Convention requires the protection of fundamental liberal rights (right to life,[119] to corporal integrity,[120] to liberty and security)[121] and of political rights (free speech,[122] right to assemble and to associate).[123] It also contains rights protecting the personal identity (right to privacy,[124] religious freedom)[125] and a due process guarantee.[126] Whereas the prohibition of torture is guaranteed in absolute terms, in general, Convention rights may be subject to proportional restrictions.[127]

Article 11 (1) of the UCR constitution declared the European Convention on Human rights and its Additional Protocols, as well as the UN Covenant on Civil and Political Rights to be an "integral part of the Constitution". There can thus be no doubt that the principle of human rights protection was generally observed in Annan III. Nevertheless, various human rights merit more attention: the right to property, the right of free movement, and the prohibtion of mass expulsions of aliens.

2.3.1. The protection of property rights

On property, Article 1 of the First Additional Protocol to the Convention provides:

> *Every natural or legal person is entitled to the peaceful enjoyment of his possessions. No one shall be deprived of his possessions except in the public interest and subject to the conditions provided for by law and by the general principles of international law.*
>
> *The preceding provisions shall not, however, in any way impair the right of a state to enforce such laws as it deems necessary to control the use of property in accordance with the general interest or to secure the payment of taxes or other contributions or penalties.*

Annan III contained certain restrictions on this right in its Annex VII ("Treatment of property"). According to Article 6 (1) of that Annex a "dispossessed owner shall be entitled to claim compensation for his/her title to property or the reinstatement of his/her property or apply for assistance in arranging the sale, long-term lease

[119] Article 2 of the Convention.
[120] Articel 3 of the Convention.
[121] Article 5 of the Convention.
[122] Article 10 of the Convention.
[123] Article 11 of the Convention.
[124] Article 8 of the Convention.
[125] Article 9 of the Convention.
[126] Article 6 and 13 of the Convention.
[127] See explicitly paragraph 2 of Articles 8–11 of the Convention.

or exchange of his/her property". A Greek Cypriot would have been entitled to claim reinstatement, unless his property is owned by institutions, used for public benefit or military purposes, used by dispossessed owners or their subsequent purchasors or has been significantly improved (Article 15 in conjunction with Articles 9–14 Annex VII). Reinstatement would be subject to certain ceilings and modalities (Articles 16–20 Annex VII). Those whose properties fall under one of the previous categories, could file claims for "full and effective" compensation. A Property Board determines the amount in accordance with international standards (Article 8 Annex 7). Decisions of the Board, composed by an equal number of members of each component state, as well as by non-Cypriot members, could be reviewed by a Property Court.

It will be recalled that previous TRNC acts on property issues are without international legal force;[128] therefore the starting point must be that Greek Cypriots are still owners of property in the north. Hence, both schemes (reinstatement under certain modalities; compensation) would have constituted interference with their respective ownership rights.

These restrictions would have aimed to foster an important public interest, namely to achieve the overall settlement of the Cyprus problem. Such settlement does not only contain these restrictions, but also a whole set of immediate guarantees for Greek Cypriots to benefit from their lost properties (return for certain categories of Greek Cypriots; compensation for others). Furthermore, both these schemes must be assessed against the necessity to achieve a peaceful co-existence of both Greek Cypriots and Turkish Cypriots over time. Hence, the relevant provisions are, *prima facie*, justified for reasons of public interest. The only real debatable question is whether such restrictions would meet the respective procedural conditions laid down in Article 1.

Those owners that would (only) be entitled to receive *compensation* are faced with a situation of expropriation. Article 1 of the First Additional Protocol requires that deprivations of one's possession must be "subject to the conditions provided for by law and by the general principles of international law". In the case law of the Court the latter requirement only applies to aliens since international law only protects them against excessive nationalisations. As regards nationals, the standard requires a fair balance between the public and the private and interest, leading to *some* compensation,[129] including for compensation for loss of use. Furthermore, matters of economic or political reform may call for less than reimbursement of the full market value. In the case of the Former King of Greece, the Court acknowledged that "less than full compensation may be equally, if not *a fortiori*, called for where the taking of property is resorted to with a view to completing such fundamental changes of a country's constitutional system as the transition from monarchy to republic".[130] Against this standard, the promise of Article 8

[128] See above Chapter III B 2.3.4.

[129] ECtHR, Lithgow v. UK, A. 102, § 120. See for a full discussion of the case law D.J. Harris/M. O'Boyle/C. Warbrick, Law of the European Convention on Human Rights, pp. 532–534.

[130] ECtHR, Former King of Greece vs. Greece, judgement of 28 November 2002, § 78.

Annex VII on "full and effective compensation", as determined by the Property Board "in accordance with international standards" and compensation for loss of use (Article 21 Annex VII) as part of a comprehensive settlement of the Cyprus problem can hardly be said to infringe Article 1 second sentence of the First Additional Protocol.

For *reinstated owners*, the situation does neither raise serious issues of human rights. First, Annan III would allow them to make use of a title that could not be enforced in practice for over 30 years, which in itself, might be regarded as an important achievement. The modalities attached to such reinstatement would, legally speaking, constitute mere conditions on the "use of property". Such interference is compatible with Article 1 second subparagraph of the First Additional Protocol for the enforcement of such laws a state "deems necessary". Although such language favours the state,[131] it also implies a "fair balance" test.[132] The modalities attached to reinstatment meet that test, given that the Plan intends to balance the conflicting interests of the owner, the current users and the public.

In sum, the Plan combined partial reinstatement with partial compensation for the dispossessed and protect current used who have made significant improvements to properties or have no alternative accommodation. These basic traits are in accordance with international and European human rights law.[133]

2.3.2. The right to free internal movement and residence

Article 2 of the fourth Protocol to the Convention contains the right to free movement and residence. It provides:

> *(1) Everyone lawfully within the territory of a State shall, within that territory, have the right to liberty of movement and freedom to choose his residence.*
> *(2) . . .*
> *(3) No restrictions shall be placed on the exercise of these rights other than such as are in accordance with law and are necessary in a democratic society in the interests of national security or public safety, for the maintenance of order public, for the prevention of crime, for the protection of health or morals, or for the protection of the rights and freedoms of others.*
> *(4) The rights set forth in paragraph 1 may also be subject, in particular areas, to restrictions imposed in accordance with law and justified by the public interest in a democratic society.*

It follows from the text that the right to free movement and the freedom to choose one's residence may be restricted in the public interest. In contrast to the protection of property rights, the standard for such legitimate restrictions is, however, stricter. Such restrictions do not only have to foster a legitimate aim. They must also be "necessary in a democratic society", hence proportional. In particular, it has to be verified whether the same policy goal cannot be achieved with less interfering means.

---

131 Harris/O'Boyle/Warbrick, loc. cit. (note 129), p. 534.

132 ECtHR, Allan Jacobsson v. Sweden, A. 163, § 55.

133 T. Giegerich, The EU accession of Cyprus and the Fate of the Annan Plan – concluding remarks, in: T. Giegerich (ed.) The EU accession of Cyprus, 2006, p. 253 (278).

Annan III (in Article 11 para. 3 UCR constitution) contained a scheme of maximum percentages of Greek Cypriot citizens to be allowed to reside in the Turkish Cypriot constituent State. Those who do not hold the northern internal citizenship status would

- not be allowed to reside there for a period of six years;
- be restricted to 7% of the population of a village or municipality between the 7th and 10th year;
- be restricted to 14% of the population there between the 11th and 15th year;
- be restricted to 21% until Turkey's accession to the European Union.

In a similar reasoning to the one put forward as regards the right to property, this scheme is intended to foster the overriding public policy goal to achieve a comprehensive settlement in Cyprus in general, and to foster inter-ethnic peace in the villages lying in the north in particular. They are designed to protect public security and political stability in a fragile situation. Hence, the restrictions serve important reasons of public policy and are covered by Article 2 (3) of the Fourth Protocol.

As to their proportionality, it must be taken into account that restrictions are transitory in character. Nevertheless, one may not say with absolute certainty whether less interfering schemes were available. Certainly, it cannot be excluded that during the negotiations a more liberal transitional scheme (higher thresholds, shorter periods) could have been agreed. However, it is precisely that background which must be taken into consideration when assessing proportionality. Unless there is manifest ignorance of a certain right which would diminish its essence substantially, any negotiated restriction between the two communities must be presumed to reflect a reasonable compromise between the individual right (interests of the Greek Cypriot community) and the need for temporary restrictions (interest of the Turkish Cypriot community) as proportional means to foster a common policy goal.

2.3.3. The prohibition of mass expulsion of aliens

As regards the treatment of aliens, the European Convention on Human Rights does not question the right of any Member State to regulate the status of illegal residents on its territory. States are, however, bound by the Convention to respect certain guarantees when they decide to expel an illegal resident. Whereas Article 1 of the Seventh Additional Protocol is not applicable since it only refers to aliens *lawfully* residing in a State, Article 8 of the Convention and Article 4 of the 4th Additional Protocol are of significance.

According to the established case law of the Court, the protection of family life and private life under Article 8 ECHR necessitates that States weighs its interests to expel an alien against the interests of the concerned to maintain his family and personal ties in the country of current residence.[134] In a more recent case, the

[134] See the early leading cases ECtHR, Berrehab v. the Netherlands, A. 138; Moustaquim v. Belgium, A. 173 and Beldjoudi v. France, A. 234–A. Since Boughanemi v. France, Judgements and Decisions 1996–II, p. 593, the Court has adopted a somewhat stricter approach.

Court highlighted the significance of a long stay of an alien on the territory of the expelling State, while stressing at the same time that expulsion was compatible with Article 8 since the applicant had preserved ties, going beyond mere nationality with his native country.[135] Furthermore, Article 4 of the 4th Protocol to the Convention prohibits collective expulsion of aliens. Collective expulsion is to be understood as any measure compelling aliens, as a group, to leave a country, except where such a measure is taken on the basis of a reasonable and objective examination of the particular case of each individual alien of the group.[136] Under this jurisprudence it might be permissible to return an alien to his country of origin, unless he can demonstrate special circumstances in his individual case. Hence, some procedure must be in place by which the individual cases can be assessed in order to avoid prohibited collective expulsion.

When Cyprus became a party to the Fourth Protocol in 1988, the Government made the following declaration:

> *The Government of the Republic of Cyprus adopts the position that, according to a proper interpretation of the provisions of Article 4 of the Protocol, they are not applicable to aliens unlawfully in the Republic of Cyprus as a result of the situation created by the continuing invasion and military occupation of the Republic of Cyprus by Turkey.*

It can be questioned whether this interpretative declaration correctly reflects the contents of Article 4. The wording "aliens" is not specifically restricted to aliens who are lawfully residing in a Member State. When the framers of the 4th Protocol felt a need to differentiate they did so, as a systematic comparison with Article 2 reveals which relates to "everyone lawfully within the territory of a State". Finally, the object and purpose of Article 4 is to prohibit collective expulsion because the very idea of a summary procedure where an alien is treated without the possibility of raising objections out of his individual situation is in conflict with basic considerations of a due process of law which a State should observe with regard to all persons in his jurisdiction, including illegal residents. Hence, Article 4 of the 4th Protocol also prohibits the mass expulsion of illegal residents, a result that the interpretative declaration of Cyprus cannot change.

Under Annan III 45,000 immigrants into northern Cyprus would have been eligible for receiving Cypriot citizenship, thereby avoiding expulsion. For the remaining mainland Turks, the plan did not foresee any mass expulsion *ex lege*. Rather, it would have been for the Cypriot authorities to apply the relevant aliens law with due regard to the individual situation of the concerned, triggering possible even benefits for the return. Those with close family links in northern Cyprus would have had the possibility to claim protection of their family life under Article 8 of the Convention.

---

[135] ECtHR, Baghli v. France (no. 34374/97), 30.11.1999 § 47–48.

[136] See ECtHR, Conga v. Belgium (No. 51564), Judgement of 5 February 2002, § 59, referring to earlier decisions of 23 Februar 1999, *inter alia*, Andric v. Sweden (No. 45917/99), unpublished, which declared a series of applications against Sweden inadmissible.

2.4. *EU collective supervision (Article 7 EU)*

2.4.1. The relationship between Article 7 EU and the Treaty of Guarantee

Any EU Member State must not only comply with the principles on which the EU is founded, but also accept some sort of collective supervision. Questions arise as regards the interaction of the Treaty of Guarantee and the collective EU guarantee under Article 7 EU. As has been demonstrated above, Article IV (2) of the Treaty of Guarantee allows for unilateral military intervention of each Guarantor power to restore the constitutional order of Cyprus.[137] In the case of a permanent and serious breach of the principles of democracy, rule of law and human rights, the EU may take sanctions under the procedure of Article 7 EU. It appears that both provisions could be triggered by the same event, for example by a military coup d'Etat abrogating the Constitution. Hence, the argument could be made that accession to the EU would be impossible for a country where the collective EU guarantee is effectively undermined by a right of military intervention of a third party. In other words: How can a country that by way of the Treaty of Guarantee has been described in legal terms as a "collective protectorate of Greece, the United Kingdom and Turkey",[138] become a member of the European Union? However, there are strong reasons for the assumption that EU law would bar the applicability of Article IV (2) of the Treaty of Guarantee during the time of an EU sanction taken under Article 7 EU so that the continued existence of the Treaty of Guarantee does not impede Cyprus' EU accession.

Insofar as Greece and the United Kingdom are concerned, they are a party to the Cyprus' Accession Treaty. In that capacity, they have agreed to put on hold their Guarantor powers to the benefit of the EU Member States by conferring to them the sanctioning power under Article 7 EU. For sure, under Article 307 (1) EC, their rights under the Treaty of Guarantee, predating their EC accession, would not have been immediately vanished. However, under Article 307 (2) EC they are under an obligation to take all appropriate action to bring their existing pre-accession commitments from international treaties in line with their membership obligations. This obligation would force them not to exercise any right under Article IV (2) of the Treaty of Guarantee, which might be incompatible with EU membership. Hence, Article 7 of the EU Treaty would be fully applicable for Greece and the United Kingdom.

As regards Turkey, the situation is more complicated. Politically, one may well subscribe to the view that EU membership weakens the Treaty of Guarantee since Turkey could hardly intervene in an EU Member State.[139] Legally, however, under Article 34 of the Vienna Convention, no treaty can be invoked to the detriment of a third party. Hence, in principle, the accession of Cyprus to the EU could not

[137] See above Chapter III B 1.2.

[138] Tzermias, loc. cit. (page 2, note 1), p. 477.

[139] Necatigil, loc. cit. (page 11, note 35), p. 411.

invalidate Turkey's rights vis-à-vis Cyprus under the Treaty of Guarantee. Nevertheless, that Treaty is itself open to interpretation as to its applicability. Article IV (2) of the Treaty of Guarantee was designed as allowing a reaction of last resort if other means prove to be ineffective. In particular, a common action by the Guarantor powers is preferred over unilateral action. This *rationale* can be transferred to the post-accession situation of Cyprus where a new, less interventionist guarantee is available through Article 7 EU. There is a presumption of first recourse to the EU for non-military intervention while maintaining as the last resort the right for a Turkish intervention after the failure of warning and sanctions of the EU intended to rectify the situation.[140] Given the actual structure of the Treaty of Guarantee, it is submitted that such a two-stage-system will be created even without formal amendments to the former after EU accession of Cyprus.

In sum, all three Guarantor powers cannot exercise their unilateral right to intervene under Article IV (2) of the Treaty of Guarantee, unless the collective EU guarantee has not been exhausted and proven to be without effect. Ineffectivenes exists where no sanctioning decision under Article 7 EU could be taken in the EU Council because one of the two EU guarantor powers has vetoed such a decision. Ineffectiveness could also be assumed if an EU sanction was actually taken but did not lead to the desired restoration of the constitutional order in Cyprus in good time, or within the timeframe eventually foreseen in the said decision.

2.4.2. Annan III

Appendix C of the Annan Plan III was silent on the relationship between the amended Treaty of Guarantee and the collective EU guarantee for Cyprus's constitutional order under Articles 7 EU. However, Appendix E on the requests to the European Union with respect to the accession of Cyprus contained a little hint in this respect. Recital vi. of the proposed Preamble for a Cyprus Protocol in the Accession Treaty reads:

> *Underlining that the political equality of Greek Cypriots and Turkish Cypriots, the equal status of the two "component states", and the prohibition of any unilateral change to the state of affairs established by the Foundation Agreement, fall within the terms of Article 6 (1) of the Treaty of the European Union.*

This reference served the purpose of offering an additional assurance to the Turkish Cypriots that the principles of democracy, rule of law and human rights are infringed if their constitutionally entrenched political equality and equal status would be put into danger. This only makes sense in order to activate the collective guarantee under Article 7 EU. The application of sanctions against Cyprus on the grounds of infringed Turkish Cypriot rights could, again, make a Turkish military intervention disproportional under the Treaty of Guarantee. Hence, the UN plan did, albeit indirectly, acknowledge the prevalence of Article 7 EU over Article IV (2) of the Treaty of Guarantee, as long as EU sanctions against Cyprus

---

[140] Emerson/Tocci, loc. cit. (note 117), pp. 64–65.

are applied. EU accession of a united Cyprus under Annan III was therefore not impeded by the existence of the Treaty of Guarantee as a competitive collective guarantee for Cyprus' constitutional order, since Article 7 EU would precede the unilateral right to military intervention of the Guarantor Powers.

3. Ability to speak with one voice

The 2002 Seville conclusions further demand that "Cyprus will need to speak with a single voice". That requirement points to all sorts of decision-making procedures in the EU. The participation of a Member State in European Council meetings and meetings of the Council of Ministers should be distinguished. The effect of an abstention also differs.

3.1. *Representation by a Head of State or Government in European Council Meetings*

3.1.1. The EU principle

Meeting at least twice a year, the European Council provides the Union with the necessary impetus for its development and defines the general political guidelines. The European Council assembles the Heads of State or Government plus the EU Commission's President, assisted by their Foreign Ministers and by another Member of the Commission. It is the choice of the individual EU Member State whether it is represented at European Council meetings either by the Head of State *or* by the Head of Government (see the wording of Art. 4(2) EU).

In practice, their Heads of Government represent most States because they exercise the political power, whereas the respective Heads of State enjoy foremost ceremonial powers. In Finland and France, the Presidents represent their country at European Council meetings.

3.1.2. Annan III

Annan III took care of this requirement at constitutional level. Article 29 IV of the UCR constitution provided:

> *The member of the Presidential Council responsible for European Union affairs shall represent the Presidential Council (in its function as Head of Government) at meetings of the European Council and shall be assisted on such occasions by the member of the Presidential Council responsible for external relations, unless the Presidential Council, deciding with separate majorities of members from each constituent state, decides otherwise.*

Hence, it was foreseen that Cyprus would always be represented at meetings of the European Council by the member of the Presidential Council who was in charge for EU affairs for reasons of visibility and effectiveness. At first sight that seems at odds with Article 4 EU that requires the representation of the Head of State. But a close look reveals that the Cypriot Presidential Council acts as collective Head of Government and may designate any of its members to represent it. Hence, for the purpose of the European Council meetings the member of the

Presidential Council responsible for EU affairs would act as Head of Government and be assisted by another member of the Presidential Council, functioning as Foreign Minister. Accordingly, Cyprus would have been properly represented in European Council meetings.

3.2. *Participation in EU decision-making procedures and institutions*

3.2.1. *The EU principle*

According to Article 203 EC, the Council of Ministers "consists of a representative of each Member State at ministerial level, authorised to commit the government of that Member State". It is not prescribed to which internal level of government that representative shall belong. Thus, even Ministers from regional governments are allowed to represent their Member State if the internal constitution so provides. The vote of that non-federal minister will be binding for the Member State as a whole.[141] According to Article 4.3 of the Council's rule of procedure "officials who assist them" may accompany members of the Council. There is no legal requirement that the official should originate from the same governmental level as the representative. Hence, it is possible to have mixed delegations of federal and regional officials. The Council can, however, restrict the number of assistants for certain meetings. The Constitutions of three Member States (Austria, Belgium and Germany) allow sending either federal or regional ministers to meetings of the Council of Ministers. The participation of the federated states depends on the subject matter that is discussed in the Council. These systems can be briefly described as follows:

Art. 23d) of the Austrian Federal Constitutional Law (B-VG) sets out how the 10 Austrian Federated States (Bundesländer) influence the Austrian vote in the EU Council. If the EU subject matter lies within the legislative powers of the Federated States, there are two options. Either Austria is represented in the Council by a federal minister who is bound to the opinion of the Federated States (this minister can only deviate from this opinion on "cogent foreign policy and European integration grounds" (Art. 23d) para. 2 B-VG)). Or the federal government authorises a representative from the Federated States to be present in the Council on Austria's behalf. This representative is bound by the common opinion of the Federated States, as expressed in a decision by the 10 Federated Prime Ministers (Landeshauptleutekonferenz). In the Council meeting he has to consult the competent federal minister who sends an associate to the representative into the Council meeting (Art. 23d) para. 2 B-VG). If the EU subject matter lies "also" in the legislative powers of the Federated States, the federal government is not bound to the opinion of the Federated States. Nevertheless, if it wishes to do so, it can authorise a representative of the Federated States to act on Austria's behalf in the Council (Art. 23d) para. 3 B-VG). If the EU subject matter lies outside the legislative powers of the Federated States, but touches on their interests, the Federation

[141] See J.-P. Pacqué, Commentary to (ex-) Art. 146 TEC, in: v.d. Groeben/Thiesing/Ehlermann, EGV, 5. Ed., 1996, § 6.

must take into account the written opinion of the Federated States and the local communities. This obligation does not stem from the Constitution, but from a constitutional agreement between the Federation and the Federated States according to Art. 23d) para. 4 B-VG.[142] In practice, there has not yet been a case in which a regional minister represented Austria.[143]

In Belgium,[144] there are three different entities: the federal government, the regions and the communities. In March 1994, they entered into a Co-operation Agreement based on three principles: consensus, mixed delegation and rotation. The so-called P-11 Committee fixes the common Belgian position. It is led by the Federal Ministry of Foreign Affairs and unites representatives from both the federal and the regional level and decides by consensus. If there is no agreement, the committee refers the question to the level of Ministers, and, as the last resort, to the Prime Ministers of the Federation and the Regions and Communities. In the exceptional case that no common position could be reached even at the highest political level, no instructions are issued to the Belgian representative in the Council. Although this is not specifically laid down in the Co-operation Agreement, customary practice has been established that he will then abstain from voting in the Council.[145] However, owing to the Belgian tradition of consensus and to the fact the Belgian influence in the Council deliberations would be otherwise completely lost, a common Belgian position is regularly reached. As far as representation of such commonly agreed positions is concerned, four categories are distinguished. In category I (all Council topics relate to federal subject matters), Belgium is represented by the federal government. In category II (a dominant share of Council topics is a federal subject matter), a system of "assistance" applies. A representative of the other levels assists the head of the delegation from the federal government. The (federal) leader votes whereas the (subnational) "assistant" politically controls his behaviour and has the right to speak. In category III (a dominant share of Council topics is subnational subject matter), the same system of assistance applies, whereas the roles of the head and assistant of the delegation change. Here, the representative of the subnational level votes under the political control of his federal assistant. In category IV (all Council topics relate to subnational subject matters), a representative from the subnational entities represents Belgium. The subnational levels (regions and communities) decide together who will represent them. The representation rotates at the same rhythm as the EU

142 BGBl. 775/1992.

143 S. Griller, The consequences of EU Membership for the organizational structure of EU Member States, A Survey with Special Regard to the Application of the Republic of Cyprus for EU Membership, p. 7.

144 Compare the overview in Emerson/Tocci, loc. cit. (note 117), pp. 23–27 and M.O. Pahl, Regionen mit Gesetzgebungskompetenzen in der Europäischen Union, p. 177 et seq.

145 According to A. Sepos, EU Policy-Making in Federal States: The Case of Belgium, Cambridge 2000, p. 37, this happened until June 2000 only three times since the creation of the system in 1994, namely as regards the e-commerce directive (1999), the television withouth frontiers directive (1997) and the municipal voting rights directive (1994).

Presidency, i.e. twice a year between the Flemish, French and German Community in Community matters (3:2:1) and between the Flemish, Wallonian and Brussels-Capital region in regional matters (1:1:1). In practice, ministers of the regions or the communities quite often represent Belgium in the Council.[146]

Art. 23 (4)–(6) of the German Basic Law regulates the relationship between the Federal Government and the 16 Bundesländer in EU affairs who are united in the Bundesrat. Each Federated State having a weighted vote, the Federal Council adopts with majority a common position of the Federated States. If the EU subject matter affects the interests of the federated states, the federal government must "take into account" the previously expressed opinion of the Federal Council. If the EU subject matter touches the legislative powers of the Federated States, the Federal Government must decisively take into account („maßgeblich berücksichtigen") the opinion of the Bundesrat (Art. 23 (5) Basic Law). If the EU subject matter predominantly lies in the legislative powers of the Federated States, a member appointed by the Bundesrat represents Germany. This minister usually has a mandate for a certain time (1–3 years).[147] In practice, Germany's representation by a regional minister designated by the Federal Council is exceptional.

In sum, if the EU subject matters lie in the legislative powers of the regional level, the representation of the Member State by a regional minister is a necessity in Belgium, a preference in Germany and a possibility in Austria. The regional level chooses its representatives on the basis of a half-year rotation in Belgium, whereas in Germany and Austria a Minister from one federated state is entrusted by all the other federated states with a longer mandate to serve their common interests. If the EU subject matter touches on the legislative powers of the regional level, Austria maintains its flexibility whether to be represented by a regional or a federal minister. In contrast, Germany sticks to federal representation whereas Belgium opts for regional representation if the regional share is dominant (category III). In practice, regional representation in the Council is common for Belgium, exceptionally exercised by Germany and has not yet been used by Austria.

3.2.2. Annan III

Annan III followed closely the Belgian model, as accepted by Clerides in the negotiations up to March 2003.[148] Articles 19 (2) and (3) of the UCR constitution stated:

> *(2) The governments of the constituent states shall participate in the formulation of the policy of Cyprus in the European Union.*
>
> *(3) Cyprus shall be represented in the European Union by the federal government in its areas of competence or where a matter predominantly concerns an area of its*

[146] See the Belgian list of Council representatives in http://www.europa.eu.int/idea.

[147] Further details can be found in the Law of 12 March 1993 on co-operation of the Federation and the Federated States in EU affairs (BGBl. 1993 I, p. 313).

[148] Palley, loc. cit. (page xii, note 3), p. 32, note 18.

> *competence. Where a matter falls predominantly or exclusively into an area of competence of the constituent states, Cyprus may be represented either by a federal government or a constituent state representative, provided the latter is able to commit Cyprus.*

Those representatives had to bring forward one Cypriot view, based on prior internal coordination. Annan III contained a detailed constitutional agreement between the Greek Cypriot and the Turkish Cypriot community to that effect.[149] This agreement provided for representation of Cyprus by a federal minister in matters of federal competence, and by a constituent state minister in matters of the constituent states. Under Annan III Cyprus would have been able to speak with one voice in the Council of Ministers of the European Union.

3.3. *Constructive participation in EU affairs*

3.3.1. The EU prinicple

In principle, an EU Member State is free to cast a positive or negative vote or to abstain from voting in the EU decision-making process. Hence, EU law cannot force a Member State to play a particular constructive role or outlaw a deliberate negative attitude. Nevertheless, it is in the EU interest to prevent that new States would block integration, if their internal set-up would prevent it from taking decisions and casting abstentions in a great number of cases. However, in the EU context the legal significance of an abstention varies according to the field of action.[150]

In the First Pillar (EC Law), which covers the most cases, an abstention does not prevent the adoption by the Council of acts which require unanimity (Art. 205 (3) EC). The abstention therefore has the same practical effect as casting a positive vote. If, to the contrary, the Council decides by qualified majority, the abstaining Member State does not add his weighted vote to the required minimum level. In this scenario, the abstention has the practical effect of a negative vote.

In the Second Pillar (EU Common Foreign and Security Policy), the abstention does not prevent the adoption of common decisions requiring unanimity (Art. 23 (1) 2nd sentence EU). In the Third Pillar (EU police and judicial co-operation in criminal matters), the abstention does not prevent the adoption of a common measure (Art. 34 (2) EU in combination with Art. 41 (1) EU referring to Art. 205 (3) EC).

Finally, in some exceptional EU affairs unanimity means the positive vote of all Member States. These areas are, the adoption of (non-binding) general political

---

[149] Cooperation Agreement between the Federal Government and the constituent states, Annan III, Annex IV, Attachment 2.

[150] Berman/Blumemwitz/Cassesse/Cot/Crawford/Dashwood/Dupuy/Fisler-Damrosch/Flintermann/Frankc/Greenwood/Hafner/Hilf/Lowe/McRae/Pellet/Rideau/Schermers/Simma/Tomuschat/Van Gerven/Wyatt: Opinion: Implications of Membership in the European Union for a Constitutional Settlement in Cyprus, § 44, allege that the failure of an EU Member State to take part in Council voting where the Council is required to act by common accord would prevent a decision to be taken. This overlooks the clear rule of Article 205 (3) EC.

guidelines by the European Council each half year (Art. 4 (1) EU), the agreement on amendments to the Treaties (Art. 48 (2) EU), the decision about admitting new members (Art. 49 EU). Furthermore, a mixed agreement between the EC and its Member States and third States can only be concluded if every Member State supports it according to its contitutional requirements.

3.3.2. Annan III

Annan III was receptive on this point. Article 19 (7) of the UCR constitution reads:

> *Any new treaty or agreement on the European Union and amendments to the treaties on which the European Union is founded or acts of accession of any applicant states to the European Union, shall be ratified by Cyprus unless this is opposed by the federal Parliament and both constituent legislatures. The President or the Vice-President of the Presidential Council shall be entitled to sign the respective instrument of ratification and hereby bind the United Cyprus Republic.*

The possible danger was effectively mitigated that Cyprus would block further important integration steps or the accession of new Member States because there is disagreement between the two constituent states. Annan III simply required a negative consensus: only if both constituent states would be against such a step, Cyprus would have been able to cast a negative vote on EU level or deny ratification of future modifications on the founding treaties. That is remarkable, if one considers that, for example, in Belgium all six (!) parliaments (Federal Parliament, Wallon regional Parliament, French community Council, Brussels-Capital Council, Council of the German-Speaking community and the Flemish Parliament)[151] have to give their positive vote to any substantial change in EU primary law affecting their competences.

4. Ability to implement and enforce EU law

The conclusions of the European Council of Seville also underlined that "Cyprus will need to . . . ensure proper application of European Union law". That is a reference to Article 10 EC, according to which an EU Member State must be able to take all appropriate measures, whether general or in particular, to ensure fulfillment of the obligations arising from this Treaty or resulting from actions taken by the institutions of the Community. This general obligation does not question the constitutional autonomy of the Member States. However, the obligation of faithful cooperation between the Community and the Member States has its bearing on the legal position of EU law in the constitutional order of Member States and on the actual administrative organization insofar as Community requirements must be effectively applied at all levels.

---

[151] See J. Beyers/B. Kerremans/P. Bursens, European Policy Preparation in the three Benelux Member States, in E. Zeff./E. Piro (ed.), Policy-Making in the European Union: The Member States, p. 32.

4.1. *Supremacy of EU law over national law*

4.1.1. The EU principle

As has been constantly held by the Court of Justice since 1964, EU law enjoys supremacy over national law.[152] Since the internal rank of national law cannot put into question the need for uniformity from an EU perspective, this principle also applies to constitutional law.[153]

Member States are free how to integrate this principle into their national law. Germany and Italy have interpreted their respective constitutional provisions[154] relating to the EU or international relations as embodying the supremacy of EU law by a "material change" of the Constitution. France and Spain require a formal change of the specific constitutional provisions before ratifying a Treaty that would otherwise entail obligations that are not compatible with those provisions.[155] A third option is to expressly incorporate the principle of supremacy directly into the constitution itself, as it has been done in Ireland[156] and was advised to the Cyprus government by a group of highly reputed international and European lawyers.[157]

4.1.2. Annan III

Article 19 (8) of the UCR constitution followed the Irish example:

> *(8) No provision of this Constitution shall invalidate laws, acts or measures by the federal government or the constituent states required by the obligations of European Union membership, or prevent laws, acts or measures by the European Union, or institutions thereof, from having the force of law throughout Cyprus.*

This provision opens the national constitutional order to supreme EU law without any reservation. In fact, such an approach was favoured by the EU Commission and coincided with the view of the Republic's Attorney-General who had publicly proposed a similar constitutional amendment for the Republic in the event that no political settlement could be reached prior to accession.[158] It was therefore beyond doubt that EU law would enjoy supremacy over Cypriot law under Annan III.

---

[152] ECJ, Case 6/64, Costa v. ENEL, [1964] ECR 585; ECJ, Case 106/77 – Simmenthal (No. 2), [1978] ECR 629.

[153] ECJ, Case 11/70, Internationale Handelsgesellschaft, [1970], ECR 1125, § 3; Case C 473/93, ECR 1996 I-3207, 3258, § 38 – Commission vs. Luxemburg.

[154] Article 23 of the German Basic Law; Article 11 of the Italian Constitution.

[155] Articles 54 and 55 of the French Constitution; Article 90 of the Spanish Constitution.

[156] Article 29 (5) of the Irish Constitution reads: "No provision in this Constitution invalidates laws enacted, acts done or measure adopted by the State which are necessitated by the obligations of membership in the European Union or of the Communities, or prevents laws enacted, acts done, or measures adopted by the European Union or by the Communities or by institutions thereof, or by bodies competent under the Treaties establishing the Communities, from having the force of law in the State."

[157] Berman/Blumemwitz/Cassesse and others, loc. cit. (note 150), p. 56 (60).

[158] A. Markides, The Constitutional Impact of Cyprus' Accession to the EU, p. 6.

4.2. *Distribution of powers between the central and the regional level*

4.2.1. The EU principle

Less evident is whether EU law establishes certain requirements as regards the internal distribution of powers. The Greek Cypriot side constantly favoured a strong central power, inter alia, by arguing that otherwise Cyprus could not effectively function in the EU. In contrast, the Turkish Cypriot side considered that EU law does not have a say on this topic at all. The latter approach is correct insofar as there is no written requirement in EC law that directly concerns the internal organization of its Member States. Nevertheless, ECJ case law and a comparison of the existing federal systems show the relevance of the European dimension in this regard.

In a case concerning the administration of EU agricultural subsidies by Germany, in which the Commission had alleged that the federal authorities did not give detailed instructions to the Länder on the type and frequency of checks to ensure the observance of the conditions laid down by the Community rules, the ECJ held:

> *It is for all the authorities of the Member States, whether it be the central authorities of the State or the authorities of a federated State, or other territorial authorities, to ensure observance of the rules of Community law within the sphere of their competence. However, it is not for the Commission to rule on the division of competences by the institutional rules proper to each Member State, or on the obligations which may be imposed on federal and Länder authorities respectively. It may only verify whether the supervisory and inspection procedures established according to the arrangements within the national legal system are in their entirety sufficiently effective to enable the Community requirements to be correctly applied.*[159]

The State should therefore be organized in such a manner that all EU obligations are effectively met. Hence, it should be scrutinized whether Article 10 EC, read together with other provisions of the Treaty, indirectly contains preferences concerning the distribution of powers.[160] According to the subsidiarity principle, the higher level should only be competent if and insofar as the objectives of government cannot be sufficiently achieved by the lower level. Article 5 (2) EC underlines this rationale in relations between the EU and its Member States. Application within the internal structure of a Member State would conform to the spirit of this principle.

One the one hand, EU membership strongly works in favour of attributing those powers to the common state, in which the EU itself functions as a single entity. The EC establishes a *common market* and an *economic and monetary union*.

---

[159] ECJ, Case C-8/88 – *Germany vs. Commission*, [1990] ECR-I 2321, § 13.

[160] From an economic perspective arguments of efficiency will play a bigger role when determining the division of competences in a federal set-up. See e.g. A. Theophanos, The political economy of a federal Cyprus, 1998, p. 53 et seq.

The monetary union can only effectively be carried out throughout the Union from the basis of national currencies and central banks. According to Article 1.2 of its Statute,[161] the European System of Central Banks consists of the European Central Bank and the central banks of Member States. This implies the existence of one currency and one single institution with authority in the field throughout the common state. The economic union calls upon the Member States to regard their economic policies as a matter of common concern and to co-ordinate them within the Council (Art. 99 EC). The common market is established by the four fundamental freedoms and an approximation of laws on EU level (Art. 28, 39, 49, 56, 95 TEC). It is not excluded that internal powers that regulate or affect the common market or the economic union originate in the regional level. However, modern economies need a reliable legal framework and a market of a certain size, which can only be created by a uniform legislation subjecting market participants to the same rules and conditions, irrespective of where they live and work.[162] In practice, even the most decentralised Member States have chosen to confer common market powers on the higher level. In Germany, the Federation is allowed to legislate in the field of the "economic law" (das Recht der Wirtschaft) under Art. 74 Nr. 11 GG. The Austrian Federation is competent in nearly all relevant fields of economy, in particular in matters of financial law, trade and industry, competition law, industrial property, labour law etc. (§ 10 para. 1 Nr. 5, 8, 11 B-VG). Even in Belgium, where the regions and communities have some economic powers, the Cour d'Arbitrage has decided that these may not endanger the principle that Belgium works under an economic and monetary union.[163]

In addition, EU Member States have established a Common Foreign and Security Policy. It runs, inter alia, a Correspondents' Network information system. Member States have to assign the post of "European Correspondent" in their Foreign Ministries. This institutional set-up argues strongly in favour of a central foreign policy power. The *acquis* leaves, however, the question open whether the treaty-making power should be monopolised at the central level,[164] or be shared

[161] Protocol (to the Treaty of Maastricht) of the European System of Central Banks and of the European Central Bank the ESCB.

[162] S. Oeter, Federal Settlements of Ethnic Conflicts as Potential Models for a Restitution of the Cyprus Conflict – Comparative Survey (Belgium, Switzerland, Canada), in: T. Giegerich (ed.), The EU accession of Cyprus, 2006, p. 69 (78).

[163] A. Alain/R. Ergec, Das föderale Belgien nach der Vierten Staatsreform 1993/1994, p. 29.

[164] Berman/Blumenwitz/Cassesse and others, loc. cit. (note 150), §§ 6 and 30 argue that the treaty-making power in a federation should be among the powers of the federation as a single subject of international law and in the light of "general practice" in federations. However, the a single international personality of the federations does not preclude them to attribute functional treaty-making powers to their federated entities (G. van der Meersch/R. Ergec, Les relations extérieures des états à système constitutionnel régional ou fédéral, Revue de droit international et droit comparé 1986, 297 (304), and "general practice" in federations is not conclusive (see next two notes).

between the central and the regional level, as this is the case in Germany (to a limited extent),[165] or in Belgium.[166]

On the other hand, Community policies as specified in Titles I–XX of Part Three of the Treaty, do not presuppose that the respective subjects are a matter for the central level. It is compatible with the *acquis* if, e.g. environmental policy, cultural policy or educational policy, falls within regional competence although a common EU policy in the field exists. However, as an exception, Community policies with financial implications should be supervised at the central level of the Member States. There is an essential interest of the EU that financial transfers to the Member States in the framework of agricultural, structural and social funds are strictly controlled. Under the *acquis*, there must be a National Authorising Officer (NAO) and a National Aid Co-ordinator (NAC) for receiving EC funds as well as a central Audit Body at government level. The same goes for trade-related own resources of the EC budget[167] that have to be collected by the Member States' customs administration, the VAT resource and the GNP rate by the general taxation administration. Again, for the sake of an effective control and proper fulfillment of its financial obligations towards the EU, a central power in these fields is preferred by the *acquis.*[168]

In sum, although each Member State is free to distribute state powers either to the central or to the regional level it would conform to the spirit of the subsidiarity principle to confer those tasks on the higher level whose objectives cannot sufficiently be achieved at the lower level. For the sake of effective implementation of EU law, the *acquis* suggests that certain minimum powers be delegated to the central level. These refer to monetary and economic policy, customs, indirect taxation (VAT), budget and foreign policy.

4.2.2. Annan III

The Annan Plan took account of these preferences. Article 14 UCR constitution defined the competences and functions of the federal government as follows:

> *(1) The federal government shall, in accordance with this Constitution, sovereignly exercise legislative and executive competences in the following matters:*
>
> *a. External relations, including conclusion of international treaties and defence policy;*
> *b. Relations with the European Union;*

---

[165] See Articles 32 (3) and 24a of the Basic Law, empowering the Länder to conclude certain kinds of international agreements.

[166] Since the 1993/1994 constitutional reform Belgium applies the principle of "*in foro interno, in foro externo*", meaning that the regions can conclude international treaties in all areas where they are internally competent. See Emerson/Tocci, loc. cit. (note 117), pp. 58–59.

[167] See Article 2 of Council Decision 2000/597/EC, Euratom of 29 September 2000 on the system of the European Communities' own resources.

[168] Berman/Blumenwitz/Cassesse and others, loc. cit. (note 150), p 63, § 27. Emerson/ Tocci, loc. cit. (note 117), p. 42.

c. Central bank functions, including issuance of currency, monetary policy and banking regulations;
d. Federal finances, including budget and all indirect taxation (including customs and excise) and federal economic and trade policy;
e. Natural resources, including water resources;
f. Metereology, aviation, international navigation and the continental shelf and territorial waters of the United Cyprus Republic;
g. Communications (including postal, electronic and telecommunications);
h. Cypriot citizenship (including issuance of passports) and immigration (including asylum, deportation and extradition of aliens);
i. Combating terrorism, drug trafficking, money laundering and organised crime;
j. Pardons and amnesties (other than for crimes concerning only one constituent state)
k. Intellectual property and weights and measures; and
l. Antiquities.

(2) . . .

(3) The federal government shall, as appropriate, entrust the implementation of its laws, including the collection of certain forms of taxes, to constituent state authorities.

(4) Obligations of the United Cyprus Republic under international treaties shall be implemented by the federal government or constituent state authority which enjoys legislative competence in the subject matter to which the treaty pertains.

The federal competences listed in paragraph 1 comprise those powers that EU law would suggest should lie on the federal levels. External relations (lit.a), monetary union (lit. c), key issues of a single market (lit. d and k.) are federal powers. Indirect taxation, which is important for the EU budget, is also regulated at federal level (lit. d), although administered at constituent state level (para. 3). The treaty-making power has been centralised (para. 1 lit. a), although implementation follows the legislative competences as regards the subject matter of the treaty (para. 4). In sum, the list of conferred powers for the common State as contained in Article 14 UCR constitution met the minimum EU suggestions in the field.

4.3. *Central default power ("droit de substitution")*

4.3.1. The EU principle

Another salient issue for effective implementation of EU law under Article 10 EC concerns the question of appropriate remedies in cases of breaches by the regional level. Whereas EU regulations apply directly in Member States, EU directives have to be implemented by legal means, leaving to the Member State the choice of form and methods (Article 249 (3) EC). Consequently, it is irrelevant at which level implementation measures are taken in the Member State as long as it results in conformity with the EU obligation. On the other hand, the State, represented by the central government, might be held responsible for non-implementation of EU obligations even if the fault lies at the regional level. The European Court of Justice repeatedly held that a Member State may not plead provisions, practices or circumstances existing in its internal legal system in order to justify a failure to comply with the obligations and time limits laid down in a directive.[169] Henceforth, it is essential that a central government has a mechanism at hand to ensure compliance with EU law in the case of a regional "blocking".[170] Here again, practical experience in the most decentralised EU Member States Austria, Belgium, Germany, Italy and Spain could serve as an example.

According to Article 23 (d) (5) B-VG there is an obligation of the Austrian federated states to implement EU obligations in their sphere of competence. If a federated state fails to meet this obligation in time, and if the European Court of Justice or the Court of First Instance has so ruled, the competence to take appropriate measures is automatically devolved to the Federation. Any Federal Statute or Decree enacted to meet the EU obligation will automatically cease to be in force once the federated state has taken the necessary measure itself. Furthermore, the law on the financial relationship between the Federation and the Federated States regulates that the Federated States have to pay the damage incurred by the Federation because of illegal behaviour of the Federated States that has led to a proceeding against Austria before the European Court of Justice.[171]

In Belgium, in case a region or a community does not implement *acquis* obligations, the federal state can use its "droit de substitution", if the ECJ has condemned Belgium beforehand (Art. 169 1st sentence of the Belgian Constitution combined with Art. 16 § 3 of the Special Law on Institutions). The federal level can adopt a law with a special majority which authorises the Parliament or the Government to take the necessary measures to comply with Belgium's EU obligations, although the subject matter normally lies within the competence of the regions or the communities.

Article 37 (1) GG authorises the German federal government to take the "necessary measures", if a federated state does not fulfill federal duties. These measures may include the enactment of the necessary legal acts for which the federation lacks general competence.[172] The provision can also apply in the case of a federated state not properly implementing EU law.[173] A decision of the federal government needs the prior approval of the Bundesrat, the common institution of the 16 federated states deciding by simple majority. Although in practice it was not necessary for the federal government to "step in", the mere existence of Article 37 GG is an important factor to ensure a law-abiding attitude of the federated states.[174] Besides, if the federal government should suffer financial damage for being held liable in the ECJ, it has a claim against the federated state under Article 104a para 5 GG for maladministration of EC law.[175]

---

[169] ECJ, Case C-107/96 – *Commission* v *Spain* [1997] ECR I-3193, § 10; Case C-323/97 – *Commission v Belgium*, [1998] ECR I-4281, § 8.

[170] Berman/Blumenwitz/Cassesse and others, loc. cit. (note 150), §§ 34–35.

[171] BGBl. I Nr. 3/2001.

[172] Bauer, in Dreier (ed.), Grundgesetzkommentar, 1998, Art. 37, note 13; Erbguth, in Sachs (ed.), Grundgesetzkommentar, 2nd edition 1999, Art. 37, note 12.

[173] E. Grabitz, AöR 1986, 1, p. 31 et seq.; K. Hailbronner, JZ 1990, pp. 149 and 157.

[174] Erbguth, in: Sachs (ed.), Grundgesetzkommentar, Art. 37, note 3.

[175] For more detail see H.-G. Dederer, Regress des Bundes gegen ein Land bei Verletzung von EG-Recht, NVwZ 2001, p. 258 et seq.

When it comes to the implementation of EU directives by the five Italian autonomous regions, the so-called "La Pergola law"[176] applies. By virtue of this law, in the matters of their exclusive competence, the autonomous Regions must implement the EU directives without waiting for intervention of the State. In the matters shared by the Regions and the central government, the Regions must implement the EU directives according to the principles and the criteria defined by a national law specifically dedicated to the enforcement of the European obligations (the so-called "legge comunitaria"). The Parliament must approve such a law each year. Since 1998, the Regions are allowed to implement EU directives directly, also in the matters shared with the State.[177] If a Region does not implement an EU directive, by virtue of "La Pergola law", the central government can use its general power of substitution,[178] if the implementation of the directive needs an administrative act from the Region. If the implementation of the directive needs a regional law, a national law can regulate the matter (even in details) until the regional law has been approved.

In Spain, if an EU obligation falls within the powers of a Spanish Community, and the Community does not properly transpose or implement it, the general provisions of control towards the communities' activity apply. The national Parliament can adopt a law obliging the Communities to harmonise their legislation provided that a general interest exists (Art. 150 § 3 of the Spanish constitution). The need to comply with EU law presumably satisfies that requirement. As a last resort, the central government – with the approval of the absolute majority in the Senate – can take all necessary measures useful to oblige the Community to behave properly (Art. 155 of the Spanish constitution).

In sum, several models exist when it comes to ensuring the proper transformation of EU law, especially directives, at the regional level. All states accept that the central power can step in. Whereas Spain has erected a material safeguard (the national law substituting the law of the autonomous province can only be adopted if there is a general interest), Belgium and Austria have introduced an external procedural hurdle (a federal substitution necessitates a prior ECJ ruling against Belgium and Austria). The Federal German government needs to take the internal procedural hurdle, which is the prior approval of the majority of federated states to step in. In Italy, the central government is free to substitute its non-compliant regions. But as a common feature, a central default power is strongly advisable to ensure the proper enforcement of the *acquis.*[179]

---

[176] L. 86/89.

[177] L. 128/98.

[178] According to governmental Decree 616/1977 the central government has a general power of substitution if a region does not implement state law.

[179] Griller, loc. cit. (note 143) reaches the same result by referring only to the Belgium mechanism.

4.3.2. Annan III

The Greek Cypriot side supported an effective system of implementation of EU obligations.[180] Article 18 (4) and (5) UCR Constitution set out the following:

> *(4) Obligations of the United Cyprus Republic arising out of European Union membership shall be implemented by the federal or constituent state authority which enjoys legislative competence for the subject matter to which an obligation pertains. Where the acquis communautaire prescribes the creation of single administrative structures, such structures and the necessary regulations will be established at federal government level. Where the acquis communautaire prescribes the creation of coordination or cooperation bodies, such bodies shall be established by Cooperation Agreements. The establishment of other administrative structures necessary for the implementation of the acquis communautaire will be decided on the basis of efficiency requirements.*
>
> *(5) If a constituent state fails to fulfill obligations of the United Cyprus Republic vis-à-vis the European Union within its area of competence and the United Cyprus Republic may be held responsible by the Union, the federal government shall, after notification of no less than 90 days (or a shorter period if indispensable according to European Union requirements) take necessary measures in lieu of the defaulting constituent state, to be in force until such time as the constituent state discharges its responsibilities.*

Clearly, Annan III incorporated the idea that EU obligations should be implemented at that level of government where the legislative power is vested (either federal or constituent state level). However, it also acknowledged that this system may put Cyprus at risk of being defaulted for non-compliance with EU obligations at the constituent state level. It provided a default power for that respect, which could be used by the federal government already after 90 days following a notification to the constituent state. In doing so, it endowed the federal level with power that could be seen as more effective than comparable powers in other federal EU Member States, which are curtailed by stricter substantial or procedural requirements.

5. Consistency with relevant UN Security Council resolutions

Finally, the European Council of Seville took the view that any settlement should be "consistent with all relevant UN Security Council resolutions". For sure, this requirement had less of an immediate impact for the EU legal order, as it was predominantly concerned with the political balance of any plan originating from the UN Secretary-General. Nevertheless, the reference was designed to remind the UN

---

[180] Markides, loc. cit. (note 158), p. 6: "It is wise to include in the future constitutional arrangements of a Federal Cyprus adequate mechanisms to cope effectively with situations which sometimes may inevitably arise by reason of the fact that those vested with the internal power of ensuring compliance with an EU obligation are not controlled by the Federal Republic".

negotiators that the EU fully subscribed to the political limits set out by Security Council Resolution 1251, namely that

> *a Cyprus settlement must be based on a State of Cyprus with a single sovereignty and international personality and a single citizenship, with its independence and territorial integrity safeguarded, and comprising two politically equal communities as described in the relevant Security Council resolutions, in a bi-communal and bi-zonal federation, and that such a settlement must exclude union in whole or in part with any other country or any form of partition or secession.*[181]

5.1. *Cyprus with a single sovereignty and international personality*

5.1.1. The principle

The Security Council requirement of statehood of Cyprus "with a single sovereignty and international personality" coincided with an obvious condition of EU accession, namely that an applicant must be a *State*. This can be inferred from the very wording of Article 49 (1) EU which refers to "any European *State* (which) . . . may apply to become a member of the Union". This criterion of statehood effectively excludes confederations, which are by the traditional international law definition no states, to become EU members.[182] Hence, sovereignty could not rest within two the two constituent States, but in the common State as the sole subject of international law.

5.1.2. Annan III

This clear-cut rule disqualified any Turkish Cypriot proposal to establish a confederation with limited international powers[183] as an EU Member State. In contrast, under Annan III, the United Cyprus Republic was defined as "an independent and sovereign state with a *single* international legal personality" (Article 1 UCR constitution). That was in line with the requirement of UN Security Council Resolution 1251 to establish only one subject of international law.[184] In compliance with

[181] UNSC Resolution 1251 of 29 June 1999, § 11.

[182] S. Griller, loc. cit. (note 143), pp. 2–3. Dissenting Neuwahl, Cyprus, Which Way – In pursuit of a confederal solution in Europe, pp. 12–14, arguing that a "Cyprus confederation" within the EU would be an attractive solution. She confounds one possible political meaning of confederation as a highly decentralised State which remains the sole subject of international law (e.g. by describing Belgium as a confederal arrangement, p. 4 and contending that the Act of accession should be concluded on behalf of the Confederation, p. 14) and the traditional legal meaning of confederation as a union of two remaining States with international capacity conferring certain powers to the confederation in specific areas (e.g. by demanding that both the TRNC and the RoC should have the right to nominate a judge to the ECJ (p. 13).

[183] Similarly P. Zervakis, Die europäische Perspektive für das geteilte Zypern: Eine neue Chance zur Lösung des Zypern-Problems?, Zeitschrift für Politikwissenschaft, 2/04, p. 451 (484).

[184] Palley, loc. cit. (page xii, note 3), pp. 28–29.

Article 49 EU this single subject UCR could have become a member of the European Union.

5.2. Establishment of UCR Statehood

5.2.1. The principle

A delicate question concerns the mode of establishment such single statehood. UN Security Council Resolution 1251 did not address this issue. The only outer limit was set by UN Security Council Resolution 541 (1983), according to which states shall not recognize the TRNC as independent state. This call upon States would also be relevant for UN negotiators. Hence, any solution could not work on the hypothesis of merger of two previously independent states. That could be construed as implying *ex post* recognition and conferring a right to secession to the Turkish Cypriot side later on, running contrary to international law principles on self-determination of the Cypriot people as a whole. On the other hand, there was no requirement flowing from any Security Council resolution that a settlement must necessarily work on the assumption of continuation of the Republic of Cyprus.[185]

EU law did neither prejudge the mode under which an applicant comes into statal existence. States with quite distinct constitutional practice as regards the foundation of their federal set-up have become EU members. Whereas there was a common nation of "the Germans" or "the Austrians" to legitimise the federal constitution, the extent of participation of the inhabitants of the sub-federal entities differed. In Germany the involvement of the *Länder* was comparatively strong in the adoption of the Grundgesetz in 1949 (the federal constitution could only be adopted with the ratification of 2/3 of the *Länder* parliaments under Article 144 (1) of the Basic Law); in Austria the Constitutional Assembly of February 1919 was composed by representatives of the *Länder*.[186] Therefore, practice in these EU Member States shows the foundation of federal states by combining a unitary (a common people) and a federal element (pre-existing federated entities).

5.2.2. Annan III

The plan adopted a "virgin birth" approach, described by the Secretary-General in the following words:

> *It was clear that the only practical way out was one that allowed both sides essentially to keep their views of the situation prior to the entry into force of the agreement (. . .) while leaving no doubt regarding the legal situation for the future. To achieve this, the settlement needed to provide elements of continuity for both sides into the new state of affairs.*[187]

---

[185] But see Chrysostomides, loc. cit. (page 8, note 24), p. 358 for an opposite view.

[186] L. Adamovich, Österreichisches Staatsrecht, Bd. 1, § 07.007.

[187] Report of the Secretary-General of 1 April 2003, S/2003/398, § 67.

Accordingly, Annan III employed a mix of central and federal elements as regards the process of building the UCR. It contained references to the Turkish Cypriots and Greek Cypriots and their respective wishes for a common future. It also gave the two constituent states, named after the relevant majority population, a prominent role. It carefully avoided referring to a pre-existing "Turkish Republic of Northern Cyprus". Rather, it included articles consistent with the interpretation of continuation (of the Republic of Cyprus) and at the same time articles consistent with the interpretation of succession (of the new Cyprus to whatever predecessors). E.g., the provisions on automatic membership of the UCR in the UN and the EU were suggestive of the continuation of the Republic of Cyprus,[188] whereas articles regarding the validity of past acts and the listing of two TRNC agreements with Turkey were suggestive of the approach of succession.[189]

However, as these provisions would only regulate the future legal situation, they could not be construed as an *ex post* recognition of the TRNC. Rather, those acts and international agreements concluded by this entity that were not acceptable from an international law point of view so far[190] would gain legal value. The will of the Cyprus people, exercised at separate simultaneous referenda, would not "heal" them for the past, but declare them of relevance *ex nunc* for the United Cyprus Republic.

In sum, the federal set-up of Annan III under the "virgin birth" approach did not imply *ex post* recognition of the TRNC. As such, it was consistent with UN Security Council Resolution 541 (1983) and as acceptable as any other federal system practiced in other Member States of the European Union.

6. Summary

The UN plan prepared by the Secretary-General on 26 February 2003 (Annan III) took full account of the EU dimension. It gave prominence to the principles of democracy, rule of law and human rights. Some features, including the powers of the Supreme Court and restrictions to the right to property and human rights, can be regarded as uncommon in the European Union, but not as contravening the common EU standard. Rather, such solutions are justifiable also from an EU perspective, given the overall need for a peaceful settlement with institutional

---

[188] See Crawford/Hafner, Opinion for the Cyprus Government, 21.11.2002, "Legal Position of Cyprus under the "Basis for Agreement on a Comprehensive Settlement of the Cyprus Problem", concluding that the membership of the UCR in the United Nations maded it clear that the State of Cyprus as it would emerge from the settlement would not be a new State. (Opinion cited by Palley, loc. cit., page xii, note 3, p. 43, note 3).

[189] K. Özersay, Separate Simultaneous Referenda in Cyprus: Was it a "Fact" or an "Illusion", Turkish Studies 2005, p. 379 (385). For a thourough analysis of these question compare further Sözen/Özersay, The Annan Plan: State succession or Continuity, Middle Eastern Studies (forthcoming), manuscript on file with the author, pp. 1 (14–23).

[190] See above Chapter III, B 2.3.

safeguards and temporary exemptions flowing from the conflict between the communities in the past. Importantly, Annan III provided Cyprus to speak with one voice, while at the same time keeping a high level of decentralisation. The EU dimension would not have stripped the constituent states of their powers, including the power of external representation in matters of their competence. From an EU point of view, the plan also contained far-reaching institutional safeguards for effective implementation of EU law at constituent state level, thereby complying with Article 10 EC. Finally, the plan was consistent with all relevant UN Security Council Resolutions. The mode of creation of the new Cyprus would not have led to ex-post recognition of the TRNC. Annan III also foresaw that Cyprus was to be a single subject of international law, thereby complying with Article 49 (1) EU. In sum, the plan met all the requirements as set out by the European Council in Seville in June 2002.

Politically, the European Council of Helsinki of December 1999 had already foreseen a situation where the Cyprus problem would not be solved during EU accession negotiations. In order not to provoke possible Greek resistance against EU enlargement to East European States but not comprising Cyprus, the Council not set the solution of the Cyprus problem as a pre-condition for its accession. From 1999 to early 2003 "all relevant factors" included the continuous demonstration of good will of the Greek Cypriot side under President Clerides. The Annan plan accordingly incorporated concessions made by the Greek Cypriot side that had never been witnessed during previous UN good offices missions. With a good degree of confidence one may argue that this was due to the constant reminder by the EU that it would prefer the accession of a reunited Cyprus rather than a divided one and that it would take account of any negative behaviour when deciding about accession.[191] However, the Turkish Cypriots under the leadership of Mr. Rauf Denktaş and the Turkish government, for a long time led by Mr. Bulent Eçevit, was not willing to make use of this opportunity prior to the signature of the Accession Treaty in April 2003.

[191] Hannay, loc. cit. (page xii, note 2), p. 46; T. Diez, The European Union and the Transformation of Conflictual Constitutional Systems: The Case of Cyprus, in: T. Giegerich (ed.), The EU accession of Cyprus, 2006, p. 219 (227) .

Chapter VII

EU Accession and Annan Plan IV–V

A. THE FACTS

After the failure to agree on Annan III at the summit in The Hague and the signature of the Accession Treaty in April 2003, in a surprising move, the TRNC government decided on 21 April 2003 to open three crossing points on the green line. Upon the invitation of the Copenhagen Council,[1] the EU Commission presented a Communication on "ways of promoting economic development in the northern parts of Cyprus and bringing it closer to the Union" on 3 June 2003.[2]

In autumn 2003, new dynamics emerged when the Turkish government under Prime Minister Erdoğan and Foreign Minister Gül made statements to the effect that the solution of the Cyprus problem would be imperative. Turkey's efforts to gain a date for the opening of its own accession negotiations were seemingly connected with an attempt to solve the Cyprus problem. Ankara became also more and more conscious of the fact that a Cyprus government would sit at the EU table as of 1 May 2004, thus being able to potentially veto any EU decision vis-à-vis Turkey.

---

[1] See above Chapter VI A 3.5.

[2] COM (2003) 325 final of 03.06.2003.

Legal Aspects of the Cyprus Problem, pp. 162–195.

Furthermore, parliamentary elections held on 14 December 2003 in northern Cyprus brought a coalition government of Mr. Talat (CTP) and Mr. Serdar Denktaş (DP) into power.[3] This Turkish Cypriot leadership took a more conciliatory view on the Annan Plan than Mr. Denktaş senior. Against this background, the European Council of Brussels (12 December 2003) concluded:

> *§ 41: In line with its relevant conclusions, the European Council reiterates its preference for a reunited Cyprus to join the Union on 1 May 2004, in order to allow all Cypriots to enjoy a secure and prosperous future and the benefits of EU accession. It considers that there is a good prospect of reaching a just, viable and functional settlement by 1 May 2004, consistent with the relevant UN Security Council resolutions. The European Council therefore again urges all parties concerned, and in particular Turkey and the Turkish Cypriot leadership, to strongly support the UN Secretary-General's efforts and, in this context, calls for an immediate resumption of the talks on the basis of his proposals. The Union reiterates its willingness to accommodate the terms of a settlement in line with the principles on which the EU is founded. In this context, the European Council welcomes the Commission's willingness to offer assistance for a speedy solution within the framework of the acquis. Following a settlement, the Union is ready to provide financial assistance for the development of the northern part of Cyprus and the Commission would be called upon to prepare all necessary steps for the lifiting of the suspension of the acquis, in accordance with Protocol 10 to the Act of Accession.*[4]

1. The February 2004 New York agreement

On the Greek Cypriot side Papadopoulos continued to signal to relevant partners from the EU and UN his preparedness to negotiate improvements to the Annan plan staying within the latter's philosophy and concept. On 14 November 2003 he addressed a formal letter to Commissioner Verheugen to that effect,[5] followed by a letter of 17 December 2003 to Annan. In Turkey, the National Security Council endorsed the policy turn proposed by the new government. During their visit to Turkey from 15–16 January 2004, Commission President Prodi, accompanied by Commissioner Verheugen, encouraged Erdoğan starting another initiative to solve the Cyprus problem prior to EU accession due in May 2004. The latter convinced Annan, while meeting in Davos on 24 January 2004 that another effort would be worthwhile. The Secretary-General invited Denktaş and Papadopoulos to New York in February 2004, where they agreed to a three-stage procedure. They would first negotiate between themselves in Cyprus on the basis of Annan III. Then Greece and Turkey would lend their collaboration. If they were unable to agree

[3] For an analysis of the election results see Çarkoğlu/Sözen, loc. cit. (page 151, note 71), pp. 133–136.

[4] European Council of Brussels, 12 December 2003, Presidency conclusions, § 41.

[5] In his letter of 14 November 2003 to Commissioner Verheugen Papadopoulos reiterated his "firm conviction to engage earnestly to substantive negotiations on the basis of the Annan Plan", making "every effort that the review and Greek Cypriot approach will move within the philosophy and the concept of the Annan plan".

on a text, Annan would have the power to finalise his plan. The finalised plan would be submitted to separate and simultaneous referenda in the Greek Cypriot and Turkish Cypriot community. One of the most contentious issues before reaching this "New York agreement" of 13 February 2004[6] was the interaction with Cyprus' EU accession course. The Greek Cypriot side insisted on a formal role of the European Union in the negotiations. However, taking into account Turkish sensitivities on this point, Commissioner Verheugen signalled to the UN that such role was not deemed necessary. The Commission would be prepared to offer technical assistance to the United Nations to ensure compatibility of the plan with EU requirements.[7]

2. The negotiations in Cyprus

From 19 February to 22 March 2004, the negotiations were conducted in Cyprus. The United Nations reactivated their conference centre in the buffer zone. They also mobilized considerable staff. De Soto was equipped with a core UN team and a range of international advisors, assigned to him by several governments (the United States, the United Kingdom, Canada, Switzerland, Germany, the Netherlands, Luxembourg), the European Commission, the World Bank, the International Monetary Fund, the European Central Bank, UNDP and UNHCR. The parties agreed to the following structure:

- the leaders of the communities would discuss amendments to the Plan;
- the Committee on Laws should elaborate as many federal laws as possible that would have to be compatible with the plan and be annexed to it;
- the Committee on International Treaties should review the list of instruments that are compatible with the plan and could be declared binding upon the united Cyprus;
- the Economic Committee should review the financial and property implications of the plan.

Each meeting would be chaired by the United Nations. Decisions would require consensus of the parties. If a Committee is stuck, the United Nations would refer the question to the leaders committee for decision. The Committees could establish Sub-Committees.

On substance, the two sides publicy announced certain of their negotiation objectives. For the Greek Cypriots, ensuring the implementation of the plan,

[6] The agreement can be found on the UN homepage: http://www.cyprus-un-plan.org. under "negotiations".

[7] UN Secretary-General Annan stated this agreement in the following terms: "I welcome (...) the assurances of the European Union to accommodate a settlement and the offer of technical assistance by the European Commission. I look forward to drawing on this assistance as well as that of others in the course of the negotiations". (New-York agreement of 13 February 2004, see preceding footnote).

improving the functionality, workability and viability of the settlement as well as smooth participation in the EU was essential. They were also interested in completing the list of international agreements binding on the united Cyprus and working out as many federal laws as possible. Financial aspects should be analysed closer and the judiciary should be strengthended by creating a federal Court of First Instance. The security provisions should be improved. Finally, the issue of settlers and immigration should be renegotiated. The Turkish Cypriots called for strengthening of bi-zonality (lesser returns of Greek Cypriots, straightening of the inter-entity line), derogations on the property issue and securing Turkish military presence in accordance with its guarantor rights.

2.1. *The Leader's meetings*

The two leaders, assisted by three main aides each,[8] came together in the Buffer Zone for a ceremonial opening of the talks in 19 February with de Soto. They also met Commissioner Verheugen who had flown to the island to show the EU's support for the final phase. In the coming weeks they gathered at least three times a week. Usually they spent the morning hours in the presence of de Soto and his core team[9] following the UN's agenda to address different "clusters". These were structured to address in an organized way the points that both leaders had presented to Kofi Annan in New York on 10 February as their negotiating goals.

The Turkish Cypriot side presented on 24 February a comprehensive paper listing textual changes of the plan on many issues (with the exception of territory). The paper had the merit of working directly with the plan and seemingly addressing all negotiable issues. However, some proposals fell outside the philosophy of the plan (especially reintroducing inacceptable language on the foundation process) in the view of the UN.[10] Acting upon profound Greek Cypriot disapproval, De Soto therefore spent some time convincing Denktaş to withdraw the most far-reaching proposals. It took until 9 March, the day after the EU troika with Solana and Verheugen had met Erdoğan and Gül in Ankara that he decided to do so.

The Greek Cypriot side produced separate detailed papers on each cluster. The Turkish Cypriots complained that not all cards were on the table, effectively preventing any "give and take" negotiations. Practically, they nevertheless engaged on some Greek Cypriot proposals and discussed textual amendments to the Annan Plan. In particular, they were ready to look at the division of competences

[8] The Turkish Cypriot delegation consisted of Mr. Denktaş senior, Mr. Talat, Mr. Denktaş junior and Mr. Olgun; the Greek Cypriot delegation was headed by Mr. Papadopoulos, assisted by Mr. Tzionis, Mr. Mavroyiannis and Mr. Emiliou.

[9] Mr. de Soto was assisted by his Legal Advisor, Mr. Pfirter, his political advisor, Mr. Dann, his advisor for property issues, Mrs. Jones, his security advisor, Mr. Hutter, and his advisor for EU affairs, Mr. Hoffmeister.

[10] Report of the UN-Secretary-General of 28 May 2004 on his mission of good offices in Cyprus, S/2004/437, § 19.

between the federation and the constituent states and the shape of federal institutions. Several proposals from the Greek Cypriot side to establish certain bodies at the federal level (e.g. a competition commission or a telecommunications regulator) were found to be acceptable, after having been advised that, following the Belgian model, these bodies could nevertheless be composed of representatives from both federated entities. The Turkish Cypriots also agreed to some modifications to the "cooperation agreement" between UCR and the constituent States on EU affairs. The Greek Cypriot side insisted on full satisfaction of their demands, with the effect that virtually no amendment to the text of the Annan plan was ever agreed in the leaders' meetings.[11]

The process ended on 22 March 2004 without tangible result. Since Mr. Denktaş senior had already announced that he would not participate in the next phases of the negotiations, that meeting carried the weight of the last "official" appearance of the Turkish Cypriot leader. He and Papadopoulos had a long private walk there after.

2.2. *The Committee on Laws*

The Committee on Laws had before it the task to draft the federal legal framework for the UCR. In the preparations for Annan III in 2003, it had been envisaged to complete 44 essential laws and to complete the remaining laws after the referenda. The outcome of the early 2003 meetings had not managed to reach that aim: in 2003 only a few laws of a technical character (e.g. weights and measures; intellectual property rights) had been largely agreed.

Upon the wish of the Greek Cypriots that timetable was changed in 2004. In order to achieve as much legal certainty as possible that Cyprus meets its EU obligations, they asked the UN[12] to prepare 136 federal laws *before* the referenda. To respond to the new task, the Committee split into several sub-committees, dealing principally with justice and home affairs, economic affairs, maritime affairs and others. UN staff in every subcommittee included experts from the European Commission[13] whose input on *acquis*-related questions was vital for the process.

[11] The only exception relates to Draft Article 19 (7) of the UCR constitution. The Turkish Cypriot side agreed on 4 March 2004, at the ninth leaders's meetings, to the proposal of the Greek Cypriot side that Cyprus shall ratify not only amendments to the founding EU treaties, unless such amendment is opposed by the federal parliament and both constituent state legislatures, but also so-called "mixed agreements" concluded by the EC and the Member States of the one part, and a third state, of the other part.

[12] The Committee on Laws was chaired by Mr. Satya Tripathi. The delegations of the two parties were headed by Mr. Petros Clerides and Mr. Ergun Olgun.

[13] The Commission seconded Mr. Bernd Biervert and Mr. Thomas Zerdick (both DG Enlargement) on a permanent basis to the Technical Committees. The UN appointed them to chair certain sub-committees. In addition, experts from many other Directorate-Generals helped the relevant Sub-Committee on particular acquis related laws, when such law was about to be discussed.

Every Subcommittee went through a draft, most often proposed from the Greek Cypriot side. These drafts bore the presumption of being compatible with the *acquis communautaire* as they should have been screened before in the accession process. The Turkish Cypriot side presented modifications, mostly related to the competent administrative authorities. Both sides, under UN chairmanship tried to reconcile the draft with the list of federal competences and the federal system of administration as provided for in the Annan plan. Through extraordinary efforts the Committee on Laws finalized 131 laws, comprising 4 constitutional laws, 124 federal laws and 3 cooperation agreements by 26 March 2004.[14]

2.3. *The EU sub-committee*

In addition, the European Commission used this occasion to start closer working relations with the Turkish Cypriot administration as regards the legislation in the future Turkish Cypriot federated State. Commissioner Verheugen convinced the Turkish government as well as the Greek and Turkish Cypriots that a fifth UN subcommittee should focus on issues concerning their legislation with the EU *acquis*.[15] Hence, those Commission experts from several Directorate-Generals who were helping to screen the federal laws explained the *acquis* in the Ledra Palace to representatives of the Turkish Cypriot side in presence of their Greek Cypriot counterparts. This exercise was designed to meet particular concerns of the Turkish Cypriots. Starting with regional policy, the Commission went through many fields of EU law where an immediate impact on the ground could be expected after a settlement. The Head of the Commission Delegation, van der Meer, actively continued these contacts and was able to establish good working relations with the Turkish Cypriot side. This policy turn certainly had the effect of creating more trust in the European Commission, whose efforts to explain the *acquis* in northern Cyprus had been treated with suspicion and obstruction for a long time.

---

[14] Report of the UN-Secretary-General of 28 May 2004, loc. cit. (note 10), Annex II, § 4.

[15] The terms of Sub-Committee 5 were as follows:

1. The objective of the sub-committee is to prepare the future United Cyprus Republic for membership of the EU in line with the provisions of Article 19 of the draft Constitution of United Cyprus Republic.
2. The subcommittee shall examine issues concerning the harmonisation of federal and constituent state legislation with the obligations of the future United Cyprus Republic as a member of the European Union.
3. This task will be carried out on the basis of an analytical examination of the acquis on a chapter-to-chapter basis.
4. The findings of the subcommittee may be the basis of recommendations for the process of harmonization and implementation by the future federal government or the constituent according to their competences.

2.4. *The Committee on International Instruments*

The Committee on international instruments started from scratch. Since there was merely no output from the 2003 sessions the list of applicable instruments binding on the UCR, as contained in Annan III had to be reworked completely. The UN[16] asked both sides to present a list of those international instruments they sought to be eligible to bind the United Cyprus Republic. For the Greek Cypriots, that meant producing a list of over 1400 bilateral and multilateral treaties in force for the Republic. For the Turkish Cypriots, many of their 256 presented instruments were concluded between the TRNC and Turkey; very rarely they could also point to a bilateral or multilateral treaty with other States, where the TRNC was said to be a party (such as an agreement on cooperation in the field of education, sports and culture with Azerbaijan). After having exchanged the texts (and translations), both sides commented on the each other's proposals.

The Greek Cypriot side objected to 247 of the Turkish Cypriot instruments on the ground that they either did not constitute international treaties or would be in contravention to the UN plan or the EU *acquis*. In common sessions, these objections were discussed between the two sides and the UN. In some 80 instances, the Turkish Cypriot side agreed to withdraw their request, in particular relating to those documents containing merely political language or not being concluded by political institutions. In other instances the UN decided to accept Greek Cypriot objections on EU incompatibility, holding however, that most of the objections based on incompatibility with the plan were not founded. In particular, the objection of the lacking TRNC capacity to conclude international agreements was rejected as this question was deemed to be irrelevant according to the "virgin birth" approach of the plan.[17] As a result of this exercise, a restricted list of Turkish Cypriot instruments was found eligible to bind the future UCR. These concerned in particular cultural, education or social affairs, providing for certain cooperation mechanisms with Turkey. The UN also kept the TRNC-Turkey agreements on civil aviation, on coastal security and on search and rescue at sea on the list. Both Committee chairmen did not share the Greek Cypriot contention that these instruments would be incompatible with the Foundation Agreement by allowing the participation of Turkish military units to operate in Cyprus' jurisdiction for the limited purposes described in these agreements.[18]

The Turkish Cypriot side objected to 12 Greek Cypriot proposals. Some of these objections referred to Cypriot-Greek arrangements to promote Hellenism or other sorts of language incompatible with the UN plan. The UN eliminated these treaties. In addition, after the UN had raised the issue, the Greek Cypriot side removed 81 agreements, mainly with EU Member States, from the list. These had

[16] The Committee on Treaties was chaired by Mr. Chris Harland and Mr. Frank Hoffmeister. The delegations of the two parties were headed by Dr. Lycourgos and Dr. Özersay.

[17] See above Chapter VI B 5.2.

[18] For the Greek Cypriot point of view see Palley (loc. cit., page xii, note 3), pp. 110–111.

been superseded by EU membership. There remained, however, two great controversies. One strong Turkish Cypriot objection related to the agreement between Cyprus and Egypt on the delimitation of the continental shelf of 2003. The second objection was levelled against the 1936 Montreux Convention on the Turkish Straits, which, according to the Greek Cypriot view, was binding on the Republic of Cyprus by way of succession to the United Kingdom in 1960. Since both objections could not be resolved at the level of the Technical Committee, it was decided to come back to the issue as part of the Bürgenstock negotiations.

2.5. *The Economic Committee*

Upon a proposal from the Greek Cypriot side in New York, this new Committee[19] looked into the economic and financial viability of the Annan plan. It made recommendations for changes in the plan, inter alia on the central bank, the public finance sector, and property and relocation issues. Several working groups also looked at budgetary issues, the non-banking financial sector, insurance, pensions, social security, education, energy, agriculture and natural resources and other harmonization issues. With the support of both sides the Committee concluded that the Annan Plan would, if implemented in accordance with its recommendations and with international financial support, represent a solid economic basis for the reunification of Cyprus and its future stable economic growth.[20]

2.6. *The Committees on State institutions and symbols*

The UN organized competitions for the design of the flag and the anthem of the UCR, attracting over 1,500 and 100 entries respectively. Two technical committees, composed of three Greek Cypriots and Turkish Cypriots each, made a single recommendation that was accepted by the political leadership on both sides. Finally, another two technical committees were set up in mid-March to determine the initial structure and staffing of the federal government. These committees produced the relevant staffing lists and identified buildings on each side of the green line to house the relevant transitional institutions.[21] Finally, both leaders had agreed to identify three international judges and a registrar for the Supreme Court upon proposals from the UN.

---

[19] The Economic and Financial Committee was chaired by Mr. Roger Manring and Mr. Alexander Italianer, Director at the Directorate-General Economic and Financial Affairs of the European Commission. The delegations of the parties were headed by Mr. M. Kyprianou and Mrs. A Dönmezer.

[20] Report of the UN-Secretary-General of 28 May 2004, loc. cit. (note 10), Annex II, § 9.

[21] Report of the UN-Secretary-General of 28 May 2004, loc. cit. (note 10), Annex II, §§ 8 and 10.

2.7. *Constituent state constitutions*

As it had been laid down in Annan I–III, the constituent states would work according to their own constitution, provided that they do not contravene the Plan. For that purpose it was necessary to establish the respective texts as early as possible. Fulfilling the New York agreement, the Greek Cypriots submitted a draft constitution before 12 March. The Turkish Cypriots did not. Curiously, Denktaş argued that writing such a constitution would be tantamount to high treason against the TRNC since it implied its abrogation. Such unwillingness was clearly politically motivated and legally without substance – drafts cannot violate the constitution. Furthermore, the TRNC Constituent Assembly had already adopted in 1985 a declaration according to which the acceptance of the TRNC constitution will not hinder, but facilitate the establishment of a federal republic of Cyprus.[22]

3. The negotiations in Bürgenstock on Annan IV

In Bürgenstock (Switzerland), from 22–31 March 2004, the scene was set for four-party negotiations. The Greek Cypriot was represented by President Papadopoulos, accompanied by most members of the National Council consisting of the party leaders. Prime Minister Talat and Foreign Minister S. Denktaş, who had been formally authorized to negotiate with full powers, led the Turkish Cypriot delegation. The Foreign Ministers of Turkey and Greece were also present, to be joined by the two respective Prime Ministers and Kofi Annan on 28 and 29 March. The special envoys of the United Kingdom and the United States were granted informal access. The negotiations did not follow any agreed structure. De Soto tried in vain to organize serious negotiations by all the four parties. Partly due to Greek Cypriot resistance, he was only able to organize some rather meaningless social gatherings.[23]

On 25 March, the UN communicated to the two sides the main ideas for the final version of the plan and asked for reactions. In became clear that no settlement could be concluded by agreement. Whereas the Turkish side presented a rather short and operational list of "essentials" to the UN, the Greek Cypriot side came up with a consolidated list of demands, comprising 44 pages.[24] In this climate, Kofi Annan put forward, in the morning of 30 March, a version of how he intended to finalize the plan (Annan IV). These bridging proposals concerned the main text of the plan as well as a few outstanding issues in the work of the laws and treaties committees.

---

[22] The declaration is referred to in Necatigil, loc. cit. (page 11, note 35), p. 298.
[23] Report of the UN-Secretary-General of 28 May 2004, loc. cit. (note 10), §§ 33–35.
[24] Report of the UN-Secretary-General of 28 May 2004, loc. cit. (note 10), § 37.

3.1. *Changes in the main plan*

3.1.1. Modifications inspired by Greek Cypriot concerns

For the Greek Cypriots, the revised version addressed the functionality of the federation in several ways. The Presidential Council was enlarged (from 6 to nine members) and rotation of the office of President would only alternate between one Greek Cypriot and one Turkish Cypriot member (and not among all members of the Council) every 20 months. Furthermore, the UN took up most of the proposals of the previous discussions in the leaders meetings to streamline the cooperation agreement on EU affairs. Annan IV also created a Court of Primary Federal Jurisdiction and revised the structure of the Central Bank.[25] Finally, the federal constitution now contained a fully-fledged human rights catalogue modelled along the lines of the European Convention on Human Rights and its Additional Protocols.

On security, Annan IV added a reference to the commitment of Cyprus and the Guarantor powers to international law and the principles of the UN Charter. That took up the old discussion about the limits of intervention under Article IV (2) of the Treaty of Guarantee. It also reduced the ceiling of Turkish and Greek troops to stay on the island below 6,000 which was the figure used in Annan III. It did not foresee a total withdrawal of Turkish troops, not even after Turkey's possible accession to the European Union.

The UN also made some important changes in the field of property rights, responding, *inter alia*, to recommendations from the international experts from the Economic and Financial Committee. Annan IV removed the ceilings on property reinstatement, thereby doubling the number of Greek Cypriots who could expect to be reinstated although their property would continue to lie in the Turkish Cypriot constituent state. Restrictions on the establishment of secondary residences by Cypriot citizens anywhere in Cyprus were also removed.[26]

Finally, the UN committed to assume the territorial responsibility over areas subject to territorial adjustment *in the last phase* before transfer. This move fell short of the Greek Cypriot request to take over such responsibility immediately upon the entry into force of the Plan, but was designed to improve the overall confidence on the implementation of the plan.

3.1.2. Modifications inspired by Turkish Cypriot concerns

Annan IV also contained a number of modifications inspired by Turkish Cypriot concerns. The repeated request to strengthen bi-zonality led to the establishment of a safeguard clause related to the establishment of residency in the Turkish Cypriot state. Second, the voting mechanism for the Senators in the second house of the federal Parliament was changed. Addressing the fear that over time many Greek Cypriots would take up residence and internal citizenship status in the

[25] Report of the UN-Secretary-General of 28 May 2004, loc. cit. (note 10), § 44.

[26] Report of the UN-Secretary-General of 28 May 2004, loc. cit. (note 10), § 48.

north, thereby voting for the Senators from the north, voting rights for these Senators was now reserved to those of Turkish mother tongue.[27]

In the field of security, the Turkish request to keep a minimum contingent on the island was accommodated by a reference to the force levels under the 1960 Treaty of Alliance. Accordingly, Greece and Turkey would be allowed to keep 950 and 650 troops on the island, even after EU accession of Turkey.[28]

Finally, the practically important question of relocation of Turkish Cypriots – hitting approximately one fourth of the Turkish Cypriot population – was given more attention. Under Annan IV, the Relocation Board activities were enlarged, the time period for adjustment of territory was extended by six months, and the Turkish Cypriot State would be entitled, for a transitional period, to maintain a slightly larger number of federated police than under the previous version of the plan.[29]

3.2. *Proposals on laws*

Annan IV also incorporated 131 finalised federal laws stemming from the Technical Committee on Laws. These corresponded largely to the relevant Greek Cypriot draft. In a few instances, like on the Law on the judiciary, final drafting was necessary to properly reflect the latest version of the main plan. Taking up a proposal from the Turkish Cypriot side, the UN also prepared a framework federal law, allowing for special transitional periods for some federal laws transposing the *acquis communautaire* in order to allow the gradual catch-up of the Turkish Cypriot State.[30] During these transitional periods the federal law would temporarily not be applied in the Turkish Cypriot State – the length of the relevant periods were decided by the EU experts in the UN team upon a recommendation from the Chairmen of the Economic and Financial Committee.

3.3. *Proposals on treaties*

A list of 1,134 international treaties was annexed to the plan. These were considered to be binding on the UCR. The list corresponded to the provisional result of the Committee on Treaties. The UN took a final decision on the two outstanding issues in Bürgenstock.

The continental shelf agreement between Cyprus and Egypt was considered to be binding on the UCR. Even if the Turkish objection that this convention applied the equidistance method for determining the continental shelf in the region in contravention to Turkish rights were correct, such presentation could not invalidate the agreement itself. Any disputes on that matter could be taken up between the UCR and Turkey after the entry into force of the settlement. In order to safeguard

[27] Report of the UN-Secretary-General of 28 May 2004, loc. cit. (note 10), § 52.

[28] Report of the UN-Secretary-General of 28 May 2004, loc. cit. (note 10), § 55.

[29] Report of the UN-Secretary-General of 28 May 2004, loc. cit. (note 10), § 56.

[30] Foundation Agreement, Anenx III, Attachment 3, Law 2: "Federal law on the application of certain federal laws transposing the European Union acquis".

the Turkish legal view, the UN introduced a footnote to that effect into the list.[31] Accordingly, the Turkish ratification of the settlement would not have had any influence on the Turkish legal position in this issue.[32]

The 1936 Montreux Convention was not kept in the list of applicable treaties. As was clear from its Article 27, this Convention regulating the passage through the Turkish straits was not open to universal participation, but only to signatories of the Lausanne Peace Treaty of 1923. Accordingly, Cyprus was prevented from becoming a party to that Convention against the will of Turkey. Could it have nevertheless become a party as a matter of treaty succession in 1960, when it became independent from the United Kingdom, which is a signatory to the Montreux Convention? Article 8 (1) of the Treaty of Establishment provided that international *obligations and responsibilities* of the UK Government are assumed by the Cyprus Government "in so far as they may be held to have application to the Republic of Cyprus". Under paragraph 2 of that provision, international *rights and benefits* enjoyed by the UK Government "in virtue of their application to the territory of the Republic of Cyprus" were taken over by the Government of the Republic Cyprus. The Montreux Convention of 1936 did not fall within the ambit of this latter provision since the rights granted to the UK as regards the Turkish straits did not apply to "the territory of the Republic of Cyprus", as required under Article 8 (2) of the Treaty of Establishment.[33]

Hence Cyprus could have only become party to the Montreux Convention by applying the general rules of state succession. Responding positively would mean that all former UK dominions like e.g. India could claim such a legal entitlement. That seems to be in contravention with the will of the signatory states in 1936 to keep the circle of the participating states restricted. Nevertheless, the silence of the Convention on the matter of becoming a party by succession cannot be equated with an absolute prohibition in this regard. Therefore, subsequent practice, which is a respected method of treaty interpretation (Article 31 (3) (b) of the Vienna Convention), is of importance. From the evidence produced by the depository, the French government, it materialized that the Cyprus declaration of succession of 1969 was circulated to all signatories of the Convention, including Turkey. Turkey did not object at the time, but delivered yearly reports about the

[31] Annex V to Annan V, p. 117, note 2.

[32] Palley (loc. cit. page xii, note 3) comments critically that the Treaty on the New State of Affairs was not supposed to be subject to any reservations. However, the cited footnote in the list of treaties does not constitute a reservation within the meaning of Article 2 (1) (d) of the Vienna Convention. The listed Cyprus-Egypt treaty did not create any obligations for Turkey to which it could make reservations. Rather, the footnotes records the Turkish legal view on the international validity of that agreement, thereby preserving Turkey's right to make this view known in appropriate circumstances also after the entry into force of the Foundation Agreement ("Rechtsverwahrung").

[33] Dissenting Palley (loc. cit., page xii, note 3), p. 109, presenting Article 8 of the Treaty of Establishment as a rule on succession of Cyprus to all international rights, benfits and obligations of the United Kingdom. She omits, however, the crucial qualifiers contained in both paragraphs of that provision.

application of the Convention under Article 24 to all States including Cyprus from 1969–1973. It excluded Cyprus from this flow of information thereafter. In April 1983 a meeting in Paris examined the Turkish decisions of 16 November 1982 and 28 February 1983 to raise fees and taxes collected from merchant vessels passing through the Straits. Upon invitation of the French government Cyprus participated, Turkey did not. After the meeting, Turkey summoned the French and the British Ambassador to Turkey and raised an official protest, *inter alia*, on the ground that Cyprus could not be considered to be a State party to the Convention. Other parties did not take any view on the matter. Since the period of non-objection from 1969–1973 seems to be too short for acquiescence, the more recent Turkish objections against Cyprus' attempts to be treated as a State party to the Convention bears decisive weight. Hence, there are good grounds for the view that the Republic of Cyprus did not become a party to the Montreux Convention by way of succession.

That view also leads to practical results: one the one hand, Cyprus ships did not lose the right to innocent passage guaranteed under customary international law from the exclusion of the Montreux Convention from the list of applicable treaties for the UCR;[34] on the other hand, if the Convention had been included in the list even with a footnote preserving the Turkish legal position to the contrary, the maintenance of Turkey's position in practice would have been rendered significantly more difficult. After the entry into force of the plan Turkey would have had to seek the consent of the UCR government for bringing the question of the UCR's membership to the Montreux Convention before the International Court of Justice or an *ad hoc* arbitration tribunal. That being rather theoretical, inclusion of the Convention into the list of applicable treaties for the UCR would have effectively overruled the Turkish legal position on the issue without preserving a practical possibility for Turkey to challenge this decision.

Finally, the plan modified the procedure of reviewing the list after the entry into force of the Foundation Agreement (Article 48 UCR constitution). It was clarified that the constituent state's right to object to a particular treaty having been listed in Annex V includes objections on the ground of EU incompatibility of any agreement (new footnote 25). Furthermore, the UN had discovered during the establishment of the list that certain agreements may only be relevant or interesting for one constituent state (e.g. an agreement on cultural exchanges). It would be convenient to apply it only with respect to the territory of one constituent state. However, such reduction of territorial applicability would need the consent of the other contracting party. Hence, Article 48 (6) UCR put forward a new procedure, according to which each constituent state may initiate a request by the Council of

[34] In the referendum campaign the Minister of Industry, Commerce, Trade and Tourism, Mr. Lilikas, claimed that Cypriot-flagged ships would no longer have access through the Bosphorus Straits under the Annan Plan, because the Montreux Convention was not annexed to it. This did not accurately reflect the legal situation and was even criticized by his permanent secretary (Cyprus Mail 24 April 2004).

Ministers to the other High Contracting party to a listed treaty to reduce the territorial scope of a treaty.

3.4. *Constitutions of the constituent states*

In Bürgenstock, a well-written draft Greek Cypriot constitution had been communicated to the Turkish Cypriots. Their rather limited comments were mostly of a technical character and could be accommodated by the UN with the consent of the Greek Cypriot side. Furthermore, the UN removed several provisions of this constitution, which were at odds with the Foundation Agreement. Not touching upon the carefully drafted human rights catalogue as such,[35] it was necessary to bring especially Articles 24 and 25 (Freedom of Movement and Residence; Right to Property) in line with the UCR constitution. Furthermore, Article 3 on the relationship between the Constituent State and the federal State was revised; in particular a new formulation of Article 3 (4) in the Greek Cypriot constitution introduced the concept of fidelity to the constitution of the United Cyprus Republic. The Greek Cypriot side contended[36] that this was an unnecessary degree of editing, introducing some theoretical German federal concepts which were not warranted by the Foundation Agreement. While it is true that the term "fidelity" did not explicitly form part of the Annan plan, Article 3 (2) of the UCR constitution required that "each constituent State shall fully respect and not infringe upon powers and functions of the federal government". In order to specify this federal obligation in a coherent way for both constituent States,[37] a modification of the Greek Cypriot constitution was an important element of the vetting process. The procedure for the Turkish Cypriot constitution was more cumbersome. Since there was no draft from their side, the UN undertook the laborious work to prepare a first draft on their own.[38] Upon consultation with Mr. Talat and Mr. Denktaş junior in Bürgenstock, some modifications were integrated into the text, which was then submitted to the Greek Cypriot side for comments. They put into question several formulations relating to the character of the Turkish Cypriot constituent state and cautioned against using terms to close to sovereignty.[39] Some comments were also made on the ground of incompatibility with the EU

[35] But see Palley, loc. cit. (page xii, note 3), p. 140, saying that the UN disputed the need for a comprehensive statement of Human Rights in the Greek Cypriot Constitution. However, the Human Rights Catalogue in Title II of the Constitution of the Greek Cypriot State (Articles 10–41) remained intact.

[36] Palley, loc. cit. (page xii, note 3), p. 140.

[37] Compare the similar wording in Article 4 of TCCS Constitution.

[38] De Sotos Legal Advisor, Pfirter, had mandated two Swiss constitutional law experts (in the first phase on the island) and the present author (in Bürgenstock) with that task.

[39] For example, the Greek Cypriot side objected against the use of the phrase "national security" as a ground for limiting human rights. Accordingly, the relevant phrases were replaced by the wording "public security" (see, inter alia, Article 28 (4) on the freedom of thought, speech and expression or Article 30 (3) on the freedom of the press of the TCCS Constitution).

acquis.[40] The UN modified the TCCS Constitution in view of several acceptable Greek Cypriot comments.[41]

4. The finalisation by the Secretary-General (Annan V)

Annan IV of 30 March 2004 was perceived with frustration on the Greek Cypriot side, reluctance from the Greek government and with satisfaction on the Turkish Cypriot and Turkish side. In the remaining less than 48 hours, Kofi Annan heard the view of each side in closed sessions. At that stage, the Greek Cypriot side came up with specific proposals, most importantly on territory. The Greek government expressed concern on certain security aspects of the plan and asked to shorten the transitional period in which acquisition of property in the north could be restricted. The Turkish Cypriot and Turkish side was still concerned with the procedure on how to accommodate the settlement in the EU *acquis* and presented certain elements on strengthening bi-zonality. In the remaining short time, the UN could effectively only address the territorial and constitutional questions.

Dealing with the interest of the Greek Cypriot side in the Karpas region, the UN faced a dilemma. On the one hand, the negative stance in the Greek Cypriot community had become so widespread that acceptance of the plan in the referendum was seriously at risk. It would have been almost imperative to come up with a last minute success for the Greek Cypriot side with a high appeal on Greek Cypriot voters. But the relevant trade-offs were contained in other parts of the Annan plan, where the UN bridging proposal had already been finalised.[42] Accordingly, any last minute negotiations on the territorial issue, including soundings from the US and UK envoys with both sides, did not bear fruit. To the disappointment of the Greek Cypriots Annan V therefore did not change the map.

Commissioner Verheugen, accompanied by a Member of his Cabinet, Mrs. K. Schreiber, a Director of the Legal Service, P.J. Kuijper, the Chief Negotiator on Cyprus, L. Maurer, and a member of the Cyprus team, M. Uebe, joined the efforts of the four parties to reach an agreement on 29 March, shortly before the Secretary-General tabled the fourth version of the Plan. He was charged to broker a deal as regards the two EU related issues: the scope of EU exemptions in the plan, and the form under which these would be incorporated into EU law.

[40] As an anecdote it suffices to quote the Greek Cypriot objection that Turkish Cypriot Presidents should not take an oath on the principles of Ataturk (Article 106 of the Draft Turkish Cypriot constitution) since the latter refers to a sort of State planning economy in contravention of EU competition law.

[41] Palley, loc. cit. (page xii, note 3), p. 140 alleged that Greek Cypriot comments were rejected in the next morning after the comments had been handed over to the UN the previous night. This is mis-representation of the facts. As can be demonstrated from the difference between the draft TCCS and the final TCCS attached to Annan V (see, *inter alia*, footnote 99), several Greek Cypriot comments were accepted.

[42] Report of the UN-Secretary-General of 28 May 2004, loc. cit. (note 10), § 59.

4.1. *Scope of EU related exemptions*

The scope of EU related exemptions were laid down in a "Draft Act of Adaptation". This Act followed broadly the former Draft Protocol to the Accession Treaty in Annan III but differed in some important details. Starting from the premise that permanent derogations should be avoided as far as possible, the Commission had already made it known to the UN during the preparatory phase of Bürgenstock that the exceptions on property and residence rights should be clearly framed as transitional.

4.1.1. Acquisition of property

The negotiations on turning the derogation in former Article 1 of the Draft Accession Protocol of Annan III into a transitional period for the acquisition of property (Article 1 of the Draft Act of Adaptation of Annan IV) were particularly difficult. The UN had prepared a revised formula which allowed for the application, on a non-discriminatory basis, of restrictions in the Turkish Cypriot constituent state for as long as the gross domestic product per capita in that constituent state does not reach the level of 90% of the gross domestic product capita in the Greek Cypriot state. For the Commission, the approach to compare the macroeconomic output of the two constituent states was in principle acceptable. However, it estimated that the period of economic discrepancy would last rather long. Accordingly, the Commission favoured to set the comparative index at 85% of GDP, accompanied by an absolute cut-off date. The former was accepted by the UN, which accordingly included it in Annan IV. However, as regards the latter, the UN did not foresee any time cap, but rather sought to hear the views of the parties. Whereas the Turkish side had in mind periods from 20 years on, the Greek Cypriot side found such a long period unacceptable, and, on the second last day of the negotiations, Greece formally asked for the reduction of the period to 15 years. Commissioner Verheugen, acting in line with guidance from Commission President Prodi, had been less outspoken. However, after the college of Commissioners met, he defined 15 years as his bottom line. After some last-minute confirmations, the UN finally opted for a 15 years transitional period for the acquisition of property (Article 1 of the Draft Act of Adaptation of Annan V) to secure the Commission's support of the plan.

4.1.2. Right of residence

Less controversial was the 19-year long lasting special regime for residence rights of Cypriots or Greeks and Turks, combined with a special identity safeguard clause (Articles 2 and 3 of the Draft Act of Adaptation of Annan IV). Here, the Commission did not ask for changes, as it was foreseen that safeguards against further immigration of Turks or Greeks upsetting the demographic ratio of Cypriot permanent residents speaking either Greek or Turkish as mother tongue should be taken by the United Cyprus Republic (the federal level) and in consultation with the Commission.

4.1.3. Safeguards

On Article 4 of the Draft Act of Adaptation of Annan IV (safeguard measures) the Commission felt no need to intervene in the negotiations either. The application of economic safeguards by the Turkish Cypriot constituent state, if any, would be strictly limited to three months, and any prolongation would have to be authorised by the Commission. Hence, such safeguard would be rather limited in its effect and not pose a threat to the internal market.

4.1.4. Entry and residence rights for Greeks and Turks

Article 5 of the Draft Act of Adaptation touched a more sensitive issue. It foresaw equivalent rights for Greeks and Turks regarding entry and residence rights. That formula meant effectively that Cyprus would have to allow the entry and residency of Turkish citizens in the same way as the entry and residency of Greek citizens. Neither the Schengen *acquis* (requiring visa for Turkish citizens) would apply, nor could Cyprus prevent that Turkish workers use the relevant EC freedom to apply for jobs in Cyprus. The Greek Cypriot side read this provision as implying that Cyprus could never participate in the Schengen system. They pointed to the awkward situations that Cypriot citizens would then have to be treated as "non-Schengen-citizens" when they travel to other EU Member States and wanted to be reassured that granting such rights to Turkish nationals would not impede future Cyprus participation in the Schengen system. The UN took this concern on board. Accordingly, Draft Article 5 of the Act of Adaptation (Annan IV) contained the sentence: "Rules of implementation of such entry and residence rights for Turkish citizens, compatible with the above principles and the participation of Cyprus in the Schengen area, shall be negotiated between the European Community and Turkey within six months". For the European Commission, this approach was acceptable. First, this provision of Annan IV referred to "equivalent rights" of Turkish nationals, and not to "equal treatment" as Article 3 of the Draft Accession Protocol under Annan III. That already made sure that these rights of Turkish nationals should have the same effect, namely to guarantee non-discriminatory access to the territory of Cyprus, but would not necessarily mean that the measures to achieve such effect would be identical. Second, it would be for the European Community to agree with Turkey on the rules of implementation, thereby giving it the possibility to derogate itself from some Schengen rules, e.g. by introducing a special entry right for Turkish citizens into Cyprus, but restricted to that very territory (and not enabling them to migrate further to other Schengen participating States). For all these reasons, there was no need for the Commission to discuss Draft Article 5 of the Act of Adaptation as contained in Annan IV. Indeed, the provision remained unchanged in Annan V.

4.1.5. European Defense and Security Policy

Article 6 of the Draft Act of Adaptation in Annan IV took over the relevant provisions of the Draft Accession Protocol in Annan III. The provision provided for a declaratory statement that participation of Cyprus in the European Defence and Security Protocol should fully respect the relevant security provisions of the Cyprus settlement. It was apparently designed to reassure the Turkish side that at no instance, Cyprus could participate in an ESDP action that would be conceived in Ankara as contrary to the Treaty of Guarantee.

4.1.6. Representation in the European Parliament

Article 7 repeated the special provision already contained in Annan III that representation of the Cypriot people in the European Parliament should be proportional, but with a special guarantee that the one third of the Cypriot MEPs should be elected from the Turkish Cypriot constituent state. That is another way of saying that 2 of the 6 Cypriot MEPs should be Turkish Cypriots. The Commission did not see any ground to negotiate on these two respective domains (ESDP and special rule of representation in the European Parliament for Turkish Cypriots).

4.1.7. Turkish as official EU language

Annan IV contained finally a new clause as regards the Turkish language. According to Article 8 of the Draft Act of Adaptation, it could be treated as an official language of the European Union at the latest after five years. In Bürgenstock, the Commission showed itself a bit sceptical of such a deadline, especially drawing from the experience that finding adequate staff for the translation of EU texts into the languages of the new Member States is difficult. Accordingly, Commissioner Verheugen asked for a more flexible formula. Annan V was receptive to this demand. Article 8 (2) of the Draft Act of Adaptation was accordingly modified to read as follows: "The Council shall decide on the effective application of paragraph 1 upon fulfillment of the necessary personnel and technical requirements. In the period preceding this decision, the Turkish language may be used in European Council and Council meetings".

4.2. *Incorporation of EU related exemptions into EU law*

Commissioner Verheugen also discussed with the Turkish Cypriots and the Turkish Government the question how the EU exemptions contained in the Annan plan could, if accepted in the referendum, be incorporated into EU law despite the fact that the Accession Treaty was already signed. After some tough exchanges, he finally agreed to the following double-track procedure. In the words of the UN Secretary-General he

> *confirmed that the European Commission is committed to submitting the appended Draft Act of Adaptation of the terms of accession of the United Cyprus Republic to the European Union for consideration by the Council of the European Union prior to 24 April 2004, and for its adoption after successful outcome of the separate simultaneous referenda before 1 May 2004. Furthermore, the European Commission is also committed to bringing about a final outcome, without delay, which will result in the adaptation of primary law and ensure legal certainty and security within the European Union legal system for all concerned.*[43]

[43] Letter of UN Secretary-General Annan of 31 March 2004 to the leaders of the Greek Cypriot and the Turkish Cypriot Community, Turkey, Greece and the United Kingdom. This

On 7 April 2004, Commissioner Verheugen put the Draft Act of Adaptation before the European Commission. The entire college of Commissioners supported the approach of the Enlargement Commissioner and adopted the Draft Act on the basis of Article 4 Protocol 10 to the Accession Treaty.[44] The Act reproduced, in essence, the relevant text contained in Annan V.[45] The Commission forwarded the Draft Act to the Council of Ministers for immediate adoption after an eventual successful outcome of the referenda.

5. The referenda

After the tabling of Annan V in the late hours of 31 March 2004, both sides started their respective referendum campaigns.

On the Turkish Cypriot side, President Denktaş senior continued his negative stance; his son remained neutral as a party leader, but said that he would vote "no" as an individual. Prime Minister Talat spoke strongly in favour of the plan. He was supported by Ankara, where Prime Minister Erdoğan made it clear that this plan was in the interest of Turkey.

On the Greek Cypriot side, President Papadopoulos made a lengthy and emotional television presentation on 7 April 2004.[46] His essential message was that the UN plan was unworkable and unbalanced. The finalization of the plan had mainly satisfied Turkish (Cypriot) concerns, but not Greek Cypriot ones. He feared that the Republic of Cyprus would come to an end with no equitable compensation. The Greek Cypriots could not be certain whether Turkey would keep its promises to implement the plan ("we buy hope and all we get in return is a hope for goodwill"). Papadopoulos added that the functional weaknesses of the Plan could endanger the smooth activity and participation of Cyprus, with one voice, in the European Union. As a member of the European Union the prospects for the Greek Cypriots to achieve a good solution were far better because the Greek Cypriots would have achieved the strategic goal to upgrade and shield politically the Republic of Cyprus. Also AKEL, traditionally the most conciliatory among the Greek Cypriot political forces, did not support the plan. A few days before the referendum, AKEL leader Christofias sought better guarantees for the implementation of the plan and security guarantees.[47] However, upon the report of the Secretary-General in New York,[48] a draft UN Security Council resolution to obtain security

passage is reproduced in the Report of the UN-Secretary-General of 28 May 2004, loc. cit. (note 10), § 53.

[44] COM (2004) 189 final of 7 April 2004. See Appendix 2.

[45] Annan V of 31 March 2004, Appendix D: "Draft Act of Adaptation of the terms of accession of the United Cyprus Republic to the European Union".

[46] The speech can be found at http://www.moi.gov.cy/moi/pio/pio.nsf.

[47] Papadakis, loc. cit. (page 10, note 33), p. 249; on the threat perception of Greek Cypriots and their demands compare further Sommer, loc. cit. (page 102, note 22), pp. 32–38.

[48] Report of the Secretary-General on Cyprus of 16 April 2004, S/2004/302.

arrangements prior to the adoption of the plan was vetoed by Russia. Accordingly, the Security Council did not endorse the Foundation Agreement.[49] In view of that failure, AKEL called for a "soft no" in the referendum. From the other political parties, only former President Clerides' Demoratic Rally and Vassilious liberal party campaigned for a yes. Also the Greek government under Prime Minister Costas Karamanlis supported the plan.

Nevertheless, the overall mood was negative to the plan. Particularly disturbing was the discussion of the plan in the electronic mass media. Already during the negotiations on the island, prominent Greek Cypriots including the Presidential Advisor Tzionis were given every opportunity to attack the plan[50] whereas neither the United Nations nor the European Commission could actively participate in the public debate held in the electronic media. The board of the state-owned broadcasting corporation, CyBC, decided to ban all members of the international community from its TV shows.[51] While de Soto was given space in leading newspapers, he was declined air time on television after Bürgenstock.[52] A request of Commissioner Verheugen to explain the EU view was turned down by CyBC and one private station.[53] Commissioner Verheugen reacted in a speech before the European Parliament on 24 April 2004, stating:

> *I feel personally cheated by the government of the Republic of Cyprus. For months, I did like all the others my best in good faith to establish conditions that will enable the Greek Cypriots to vote for this plan. Unfortunately, that has not become true now. The minimum what can now be expected from a country that wants to accede to the European Union in less than 10 days is that it ensures fair and balanced information about the goal and content of this plan. In the history of the European Commission it has not yet occurred that a member of the Commission was prohibited to explain a central European question in a Member State, because such explanation would constitute interference in domestic matters. I call upon President Papadopoulos to ensure that the principles of freedom of information and free speech are strictly observed in his country. And that from today on also those have the possibility to voice their view in the Cypriot media, who can deliver a full explanation of the plan in line with the intentions of the United Nations. I am still ready to do that.*[54]

---

49 UN Press Release SC/8066 of 21 April 2004.

50 See e.g. the critique of these interventions as "a classical example of political duplicity" from Loucas G. Charalambous, Cyprus Mail, 14 March 2004. The author "cannot think anyone is stupid enough to swallow the ludicrous claim that these people (i.e. Tzionis and most of Papadopoulos' party's deputies) are supposedly expressing their personal opinions when they are railing against the plan".

51 Cyprus Sunday Mail, 18 April 2004, p. 13.

52 Report of the UN-Secretary-General of 28 May 2004, loc. cit. (note 10), § 71.

53 Palley, loc. cit. (page xii, note 3), p. 207, note 207, claims that the decision of the TV facilities on Verheugen were purely commercial since "not all politicians are favoured with telegenic personalities, and channels transmitting in German (or even English) with Greek sub-titles would rapidly have been switched".

54 Intervention of Günter Verheugen on 21 April 2004 in the European Parliament on Cyprus (translation by the author).

Only Kofi Annan was allowed to record an address to the people of Cyprus, which was covered on both sides.

On 15 April 2004, the European Commission organized a preparatory Donor's conference in Brussels. Interested governments and International Organizations made financial commitments, amounting to 800 million Euros. This amount was primarily designed to support Cyprus after a settlement in relocation issues.

The separate simultaneous referenda took place on 24 April 2004. The voters in the TRNC, i.e. all TRNC citizens who were registered as electors in December 2003,[55] voted with 64,9% in favor of the plan; 75,8 % of the voters in the government controlled areas of the Republic voted against it. Accordingly, the Annan plan did not enter into force. The Republic of Cyprus entered the European Union as a divided island under the *status quo* on 1 May 2004.

B. LEGAL EVALUATION

1. Legality of the Referenda

After the referenda, some criticism was directed against the process. The international right to self-determination would prevent the participation of Turkish settlers in the referendum carried out in the north; only the original population of the territory should be empowered to express its will on its political future.[56]

This issue raises difficult questions of determining the scope of electors in an act of self-determination. As seen above,[57] UN General Assembly Resolution 1541 refers to the "will of the territory's peoples" (la volonté des populations du territoire), but gives not further guidance on the actual composition of these peoples. Also the International Court of Justice did not further specify this issue in its advisory opinions on Western Sahara[58] and the Israeli wall.[59] Hence, further guidance must be sought from UN and State practice.

For the Southern Cameroon plebiscite of 1960, the General Assembly recommended that only persons born in the Southern Cameroons or persons where one of the parents was born in the Southern Cameroons should vote in the plebiscite.[60] Similarly, in the case of East Timor, Indonesia and Portugal agreed that persons

[55] Article 5 of TRNC Law No. 2/2004 of 22 March 2004 on Referendum with Regard to the Solution of the Cyprus Problem.

[56] Palley, loc. cit. (page xii, note 3), pp. 74–75; Auer/Bossuyt/Burns/de Zayas and others (International Expert Panel for a European Solution of the Cyprus problem), A principled basis for a just and lasting Cyprus settlement in the light of international and European Law, § 14.

[57] Part I, B I 2.

[58] ICJ, Western Sahara, Advisory Opinion, ICJ Reports 1975, p. 12.

[59] ICJ, Legal Consequences of the Construction of a Wall in the Occupied Palestinian Territory, Advisory Opinion, 9 July 2004, at: http://www.icj-cji.org, § 88.

[60] UNGA Resolution 1352 (XIV) of 16 October 1959, § 3.

born in East Timor as well as persons born outside East Timor but with at least one parent having been born in East Timor were entitled to vote in referendum of 30 August 1999.[61] In addition, voting rights were granted to "persons whose spouses fall under either of the two categories above".[62] On that basis, the United Nations Mission in East Timor established by Security Council Resolution 1246 (1999) organised a registration process, which was reviewed and certified as legitimate basis for the conduct of the consultation by an Independent Electoral Commission.[63] As regards Western Sahara, Morocco and the Frente POLISARIO gave their agreement in 1988 to the proposal from the UN Secretary-General and the Chairman of the OAU that all Saharans counted in the 1974 census taken by the Spanish authorities will have the right to vote in the referendum. In addition, an identification commission was charged with the task to update that census, taking into account the real growth of the Saharan population (births and deaths) as well as the movements of the Saharan population.[64] On the basis of this plan, which was endorsed by the Security Council[65] and the General Assembly,[66] the United Nations Mission for the Referendum in Western Sahara initiated the process, collecting applications and appeals of potential voters and established a provisional voters list in 1999. A renewed effort driven by the Secretary-General's Special Envoy Baker, led to a peace plan for self-determination in 2003, also endorsed by the Security Council[67] and the General Assembly.[68] Under that plan, not only the persons identified by the identification Commission or those who are listed on the repatriation lists of the UNHCR would be entitled to vote, but also those "who have resided continuously in Western Sahara since 30 December 1999".[69]

It appears from these three cases that a considerable margin of appreciation is left to the parties of a conflict to take account the specific circumstances of their case, when determining the right to vote. First, birth in the concerned territory or

[61] Agreement between the Republic of Indonesia and the Portugeuse Republic regarding the modalities for the popular consultation of the East Timores through direct ballot, contained in the Report of the UNSG of 5 May 1999, A/53/951/–S/1999/513, Annex II, Section C. "Entitlement to vote", lit. (a) and (b).

[62] Modalities agreement, loc. cit (note 684), Section C, lit (c).

[63] Report of the UNSG of 13 December 1999 to the UNGA, A 54/654, §§ 17, 26–27.

[64] Settlement plan of 30 August 1988, reproduced in UNSG Report of 18 June 1990 on the Situation concerning Western Sahara, S21360, Part I, §§ 24–27.

[65] UNSC Resolution 658 (1990) of 27 June 1990; UNSC Resolution 690 (1991) of 29 April 1991.

[66] UNGA annual resolutions on Western Sahara; most recently UNGA Resolution 59/131 of 25 January 2005, recital No. 5.

[67] UNSC Resolution 1495 (2003) of 31 July 2003.

[68] UNGA annual resolutions on Western Sahara; most recently UNGA Resolution 59/131 of 25 January 2005, § 2.

[69] Peace plan for self-determination of the people of Western Sahara, contained in the UNSG Report on the situation concerning Western Sahara of 23 May 2003, Annex II, § 5.

descendance from persons born there was always used as primary criterion to identify the eligible voters. Second, being married with an eligible voter (East Timor) or continous residence on the territory (Western Sahara) may also become relevant. The UN always took account of such views when involved in a popular referendum concerning the future political status of a territory.

Against that background, the referenda in Cyprus in April 2004 were not falling outside the international law framework. First, the persons born in Cyprus or descendant from a Cyprus-born person were entitled to vote, be it the Greek Cypriots in the south or the Turkish Cypriots in the north. Second, in so far as the eligible voters in the north comprised settlers of Turkish origin, they must have been in possession of TRNC citizenship. Acquisition of that citizenship may have occurred by way of marriage to a Turkish Cypriot or by way of permanent residence, both legitimate criteria – the Cyprus government itself had acknowledged that fact in the negotiations leading up to Annan III, under which 45,000 settlers may be regarded as Cypriot citizens after the settlement. Therefore, the only contentous point may be that the TRNC did not eliminate from the voter lists an unknown number of remaining settlers. Only as regards these, it may be argued that the prohibition of forcible transfer of settlers under Article 49 (6) of the Fourth Geneva Convention is undermined, if they may participate in an act of self-determination of the Cypriot people.

However, it must also be taken into account that the United Nations did not assume a formal role of organizing the referenda. Neither was the UN required to exercise any supervisory role in the referendum process or scrutiny of elector's rolls.[70] Rather, in their 13 February 2004 agreement, both leaders had accepted to carry out simultaneous and "separate" referenda. That could only have meant that each side organizes its own referendum according to its own procedural requisites. Despite formal representations to the UN Secretary-General about this fact,[71] the Greek Cypriot side never announced its intention to reject the results of the referenda as "illegal" in the event of a double "yes".[72] Accordingly, the Greek Cypriot side merely maintained its position that settler's voting conflicts with international law. But it also acknowledged that settler voting in the TRNC does not nullify the results of the separate referenda, which have been the result if there had been a breach of the right to self-determination.

In sum, the settler's participation in the referendum in the north did not question the international legality of the separate and simultaneous referenda as an act of self-determination.

---

[70] Letter of UNSG Annan to President Papadopoulos, cited at Palley, loc. cit. (page xii, note 3), p. 75, footnote 18.

[71] Letter of President Papadopoulos to UNSG Annan of 7 June 2004, p. 4, UN Doc S/2004/493–A/58/543, Annex.

[72] Özersay, loc. cit. (page 160, note 189), Turkish Studies 2005, 379 (390).

2. Adaptations to the Terms of Cyprus' Accession

The European Council of Seville (June 2002)[73] made the political promise to accommodate a UN settlement in the EU's legal order in line with the principles on which the EU is founded. However, with the signature of Accession Treaty in April 2003, the possibility to attach a Cyprus protocol did not exist any more. Hence, the Bürgenstock debates focused on the form and the scope of such adaptations. These two issues shall be reviewed separately.

2.1. *The form of adapting the terms of Cyprus' Accession*

The first controversy focused on the interpretation of Article 4 of Protocol 10.

> *In the event of a settlement, the Council, acting unanimously on the basis of a proposal from the Commission, shall decide on the adaptations to the terms concerning the accession of Cyprus to the European Union with regard to the Turkish Cypriot Community.*

For the Turkish side, any accommodation by way of a Council Act could not ensure legal security.[74] In the Turkish view, such an act would not amount to primary law. Primary law is only created when EU governments conclude an amending treaty to the foundation Treaty that is ratified according to their respective constitutional requirements. Only such acts of primary law could not be challenged before the European Court of Justice.

Article 4 of Protocol 10 enables the Council to decide on the basis of a proposal by the Commission. That the European Parliament is not involved is rather uncommon, but also not unheard of in the EC's decision-making procedures.[75] Therefore, at first sight, Article 4 Protocol 10 reminds of ordinary procedures for the adoption of secondary law. At second sight, however, Article 4 of Protocol 10 must be read in its special context. The accommodation of a political settlement into the European legal order is an important political matter that transcends usual "law-making" by the Council. Article 4 of Protocol 10 was designed to avoid convening another Intergovernmental Conference in the event of a Cyprus settlement after entry into force of the Act of Accession. The history and the intention behind the enabling clause (namely to allow accommodation also at a later stage) supports this purpose.[76] Hence, it contained a simplified procedure for modifying the Act. In other words, Member States delegated treaty-making power to the Council. Such an enabling clause, whereby a Council decision may change the Act of Accession,

---

[73] See above Chapter VI A 2.5.

[74] Compare e.g. H. Kabaalioğlu, Lessons learnt from the Greek Cypriot Rejection of the Annan Plan, in: T. Giegerich (ed.), The EU accession of Cyprus, 2006, p. 233 (238).

[75] For example, for acts adopted on the basis of Article 133 EC, the European Parliament is not involved.

[76] Uebe, loc. cit. (page 129, note 83), GYIL 2004, p. 389 (p. 398) et seq.

is not new. On the basis of a comparable clause, the Council had to adjust the previous Act of Accession due to the Norwegian failure to ratify it.[77]

In any event, even if a Council decision adopted on the basis of Article 4 of Protocol 10 were to be regarded by the Court of Justice as an act amenable to judicial review under Article 230 EC, the Court would have to take account of the broad margin of appreciation vested in the Council. A decision of the Council under Article 4 of Protocol 10 concerns "the adaptations to the terms concerning the accession of Cyprus to the European Union". Accordingly, any judicial control of the European Court of Justice would, if at all, be restricted to the question whether the Act would contain "adaptations with regard to the Turkish Cypriot Community" only or go beyond.

2.2. *The scope of the adaptations*

2.2.1. *Property*

With the cut-off date of 15 years in Article 1 of the Draft Act of Adaptation (DAA), any restrictions on the acquisition of property rights in the Turkish Cypriot constituent state were designed as a transitional period. As such, it could be compared with other transitional periods in the Accession Treaty on the acquisition of property. Cyprus itself had been granted a transitional period for restricting the acquisition of secondary residences by EU foreigners of 5 years;[78] other new Member States enjoyed a transitional period for restrictions in the field of agricultural property for seven years; Poland had even managed to receive a transitional period up to 12 years.[79] Therefore, it can be fairly concluded that this adaptation would have remained in the general framework of the Accession Treaty.

2.2.2. *Restrictions on residence rights*

The same applies for the restrictions on residence rights for Cypriot citizens (Article 2 (1) DAA) or Greek and Turkish nationals (Article 3 (1) DAA). Both restrictions are clearly framed as transitional with a maximum period of nineteen years.

As regards the special identity safeguards in Article 2 (2) and 3 (2) DAA,[80] the situation may be less obvious. First, these safeguards have the potential to be applied without any temporal limitation and do therefore not appear to be of a

[77] Decision of the Council of 1 January adjusting the instruments concerning the accession of new Member States to the European Union, on the basis if Article 2 (2) of the Act of Accession for Austria, Sweden, Norway and Finland (OJ 1995, L 1, 1).

[78] Annex VII related to Article 24 of the Accession Treaty – Cyprus; OJ 2003, L 236, p. 819.

[79] Annex VII related to Article 24 of the Accession Treaty – Poland; OJ 2003, L 236, p. 878.

[80] See above Chapter VII A 4.1.2.

transitional nature.[81] Second, identity safeguards that may be applied in order to protect the demographic ratio of a new Member States' main communities have no precedent in previous Accession Treaties or counterpart in the present one.

Yet, such safeguards are not at odds with the EU legal order. In the previous enlargement round, the EU had agreed that the Åland islands could apply certain permanent restrictions on the right to residence in order to protect the Swedish identity of this Finnish island.[82] In the 2003 Accession Treaty, the EU accepted a derogation from the freedom of capital for Malta. Under Protocol 6 to the Act of Accession, the EU "bore in mind the very limited number of residences in Malta and the very limited land available for construction purposes, which can only cover the basic needs created by the demographic development of the present resident".[83] Accordingly, Malta was allowed to keep certain restrictions for reasons of objectively justified national needs. Similarly, under draft Preambular paragraph 7 DAA the Commission recognised the "*particular national identity* of Cyprus and the need to protect the balance between Greek Cypriot and Turkish Cypriots in Cyprus, the bi-zonal character of the United Cyprus Republic and the distinct identity and integrity of the constituent states. That was a hidden reference to Article 6 (3) of the EU Treaty according to which the EU respects the national identity of its Member States. In other words, the special safeguards in Articles 2 and 3 DAA could be regarded as implementing the respect the EU accords to the needs of a bi-communal Member State in a post-conflict situation. Even though the relevant safeguards would have no limitation in time, their (hypothetical) use would still be compatible with fundamental principles of EU law and therefore a legitimate subject for a Council decision on the "adaptation of the terms of Cyprus accession".

2.2.3. Safeguards

The economic safeguard in Article 4 DAA was limited in time and concerned only a very small territory of the Union's internal market.

2.2.4. Entry and residence rights for Greeks and Turks

The tension between granting equivalent entry and residence rights to Turks and the Schengen system under Article 5 DAA has already been described.[84] Certainly, according to Article 8 of the Schengen protocol (1997), "for the purposes for the admission of new Member States to the European Union, the Schengen *acquis* and further measures taken by the institutions within its scope shall be regarded as an *acquis* which must be accepted in full by all States candidates for admission". However, Article 5 DAA may be seen as *lex specialis* for Cyprus, which does not result in an opting-out of Cyprus (which Article 8 of the Schengen protocol

[81] Palley, loc. cit. (page xii, note 3), p. 170.

[82] Protocol 2 to the Act of Accession of Sweden, Austria and Finland, OJ 1994, C 241.

[83] Protocol No. 6 on the acquisition of secondary residences in Malta, OJ 2003, L 236, p. 947.

[84] See above Chapter VII A 4.1.4.

intended to prevent), but to a special regime. Furthermore, if there were certain safeguards, to be agreed between Turkey and the European Community, under which conditions Turkish nationals could exercise a right to entry into Cyprus, the presence of these Turks in a future Schengen country could not be perceived as a possible immigration threat to other Member States. Accordingly, it would have been possible that Cyprus participates in the Schengen system allowing free travel of those staying in Cyprus to other EU countries without border controls.

2.2.5. European Security and Defence policy

The ESDP clause (Article 6 DAA) had a merely declaratory significance. That Cyprus should not jeopardize its commitments under the Annan plan by participating in ESDP operations follows already from the general rule of *pacta sunt servanda* (Article 26 of the Vienna Convention). Whether it was actually necessary for the European Union, to reproduce such a clause in its own legal order is doubtful: the provision does not depart from any other EU legal instrument. Nevertheless, it could not have been harmful to reproduce such a symbolic clause, if that was deemed necessary for political reasons to fully implement the relevant provision in the Annan plan.

2.2.6. Representation in the European Parliament

On representation of Cyprus in the European Parliament, Article 7 DAA would have laid down a specific quota for MEPs to be elected from the Turkish Cypriot constituent state. As primary EU law does not require a strict proportional electoral system for EP elections (the relevant act of a uniform procedure for EP elections under Article 190 (4) EC not yet adopted), this rule would not even have derogated from any EC norm. However, it cannot be excluded that in the future, such a uniform procedure for EP elections would be adopted. It was therefore safe to include Article 7 of the Draft Act of Adaptation as a possible derogation from that EU wide procedure on the election of MEPs.

2.2.7. Turkish as EU language

Finally, the Turkish language clause (Article 8 DAA) would have touched upon its status as an official language of the EU. However, as Article 290 EC enables the Council to lay down the relevant rules for the use of official languages in the institutions, it would have been perfectly possible that the Council, by way of a decision under Article 4 of Protocol, would have laid down certain specific rules for Turkey as official language, taking account of the fact that the Cyprus' government had not requested to include this language as EU official language before, but only after the approval of the settlement.

2.3. *Conclusion*

During the final phase of negotiations on the Annan plan, the question of adapting the terms of Cyprus' EU accession could have developed into a main stumbling block. However, close coordination between the UN and the EU led to a "double track" solution. As a first step, the EU Council would have immediately adopted an Act of Adaptation on the basis of Article 4 Protocol 10, introducing the necessary special conditions of the Cyprus settlement into the EU legal order. Such conditions, including the identity safeguard clause, were in accordance with EU primary law because the latter is respectful of national identities of its Member States to which the bi-communal and bi-zonal character of the UCR would have been added. As a second step, these adaptations would have been formally incorporated into primary law in order to bring about legal security within the EU's legal system.

3. Compatibility with the EU requirements

Some Greek Cypriot criticism on Annan V refers to its relationship to EU requirements. In a letter to UN Secretary-General Annan, President Papadopoulos maintained "serious doubts on whether the final plan is compatible with the *acquis* communautaire", alleging that the European Commission simply examined Annan I, but not subsequent versions.[85] As demonstrated above, Annan III had complied with EU requirements, as laid down by the European Council of Sevilla (2002). Accordingly, it must only be assessed whether the changes introduced into the fourth and fifth version of the plan fundamentally alter the above analysis.

3.1. *Democracy, rule of law, human rights*

3.1.1. Democracy and rule of law

Under Annan V, the Senators would not be elected from "each constituent state" anymore. Rather Greek Cypriot and Turkish Cypriot senators were to be elected on a proportional basis by the citizens of Cyprus, voting separately as Greek Cypriots and Turkish Cypriots (Article 22 (3) UCR constitution).

One author[86] attacked this provision of Annan V as "using racist criteria". According to his view, "all citizens of Cyprus, irrespective of their ethnic origin belong to one and the same electoral body that elects its representatives to state office; Representatives must emanate from the same electoral roll". Granting political rights on the basis of ethnic origin would not be recognised by contemporary democratic states.

As seen above, differentiation in the electorate was already organized in bi-communal Cyprus under the 1960 Constitution. There were two electoral rolls for the elections to the House of Representatives, and the communal chambers with competences for certain affairs were also elected separately. It is not unheard of that certain entities are not elected by all citizens, but only by a group of citizens

[85] Letter of President Papadopoulos to Secretary-General Annan, 7 June 2004, page 5, second paragraph, UN Doc S/2004/493–A/58/543, Annex.

[86] L. Loukaides, Cypriot judge of the European Court of Human Rights, Cyprus Weekly, 20 April 2005.

organized along ethnic or linguistic lines: in Belgium, the French, Dutch and German speaking communities have their own entities ("les Communautés"), administering public power in areas of interest for the personal status of Belgium citizens. Many European States grant persons belonging to a national minority privileged political rights: e.g. the Danish minority in Germany does not have to pass the 5% threshold to have elected representatives in the regional Parliament of Schleswig Holstein). Accordingly, separate voting by the communities to the Senate, as well as some over-representation of Turkish Cypriots is well compatible with democratic principles, as practiced in contemporary Europe.

Annan V also kept the provision that three foreigners may be appointed to the Supreme Court, ensuring a final decision in cases where the Cypriot judges would be unable to form a majority on their own. Furthermore, foreigners would sit in some property related institutions (Relocation Board, Property Court, Property Board), the Central Bank and the Reconciliation Committee. This set-up has been criticised as being "in stark contradiction" to the principle of democracy since the foreign nationals would not be accountable to the people of Cyprus.[87] However, as has been already demonstrated with regard to Annan III,[88] also foreign judges are accountable to the Cypriot people since they would have been appointed by democratic institutions of the Cypriot State.

A similar reasoning can be put forward against the critique that Annan V was "nothing short of disaster" since the default power of the Supreme Court "would violate the basic norms of the separation of powers".[89] Since Annan I, it had been a Greek Cypriot wish to improve the workability of governance and to provide for an effective deadlock mechanism. As has demonstrated above, constitutional courts may generally well interfere with the powers of the legislative or executive branches of government, and an extraordinary judicial power to take measures "in lieu" of blocked political institutions is the less intrusive variant of such a deadlock-meachnism.[90] In Annan V, the important default power remained untouched, and the respective role of the Supreme Court was fully preserved. And precisely that role of the Supreme Court was even strengthened by introducing the federal First Instance Court, upon proposal from the Greek Cypriot side. The UN accepted that some 'ordinary' competences of the Supreme Court should be devolved to another body. This would have diminished the threat that it could be overloaded with cases and not exercise his truly constitutional functions effectively. Hence, these constitutional changes in Annan IV and V did not violate the separation of powers.

---

[87] International Expert Panel for a European Solution in Cyprus, loc. cit. (note 56), §§ 8 and 18.

[88] See Chapter VII B 2.1.

[89] T. Papadopoulos, Why Greek Cypriots wisely said "no" to Solomon's Justice, Cyprus Mail, 05.04.2005.

[90] See Chapter VII B 2.2.

3.1.2. Human Rights

On human rights, the incorporation of a fully-fledged catalogue into the federal constitution was certainly an important improvement. Furthermore, the restrictions on acquisition of property were shortened to 15 years. The special safeguard clause on residence rights could, if applied, interfere with the individual right to chose one's own residence throughout the country. However, as explained above,[91] this clause is compatible with the EU legal order for reasons of public policy and the protection of a particular Cypriot identity. Some details of the elaborate system on the return of Greek Cypriots were modified, but did not overstep the discretion of the legislature to limit property rights by combining the offer of restitution or compensation depending on the location and current use of the affected property.[92]

Accordingly, any contention that Annan IV and V lessened the protection of human rights for Cypriots below the level of EU requirements[93] must be firmly rejected.

3.2. *Ability to speak with one voice*

Some Greek Cypriots attacked Annan V on the account that a Cyprus representative in the EU would be forced to abstain from voting, if there were no agreement between the two constituent states whether to vote "Yes" or "No". It is maintained that Annan V betrayed a profound ignorance of the European process, since it would give either party an incentive to block decision-making so as to achieve its desired outcome (namely whether a Cypriot abstention is harmless or effectively operates as a no) through abstention.[94] One author goes so far as claiming that Cyprus would not have been able to speak with one voice under Annan V.[95]

As compared with Annan III, the technical modifications to resolve deadlocks by introducing a swifter procedure in the cooperation agreement on EU affairs under Annan V did strengthen and not weaken Cyprus' ability to speak with one voice in the EU. The only valid critique may therefore be directed against the fact that in a final deadlock situation, where disagreement would persist between the constituent states on the highest level, Cyprus would still (like under Annan III) have had to abstain in Brussels. However, this situation could not have occurred in federal matters, where the federal government decides alone on the Cypriot position. A possible deadlock could only have been detrimental to the exercise of Cyprus' vote in the EU Council on non-federal matters. This threat of "abstention" as means of policy-making has not proven true in Belgium, where only very rare positions were actually not internally agreed between the regions after intervention on ministerial level. In any event, the plan provided for the *ability* of Cyprus to

[91] See Chapter VII B 1.2.2.

[92] On the relevant standards under the European Convention see above Chapter VII B 1.3.1.

[93] International Expert Panel, loc. cit. (note 56), § 16. The experts create the misleading impression that the right to return could not be restricted under international law.

[94] Papadopoulos, loc. cit. (note 89).

[95] Palley, loc. cit. (page xii, note 3), p. 113, note 14.

speak with one voice by providing for a sophisticated system of internal decision-making and adequate presentation: whether the political culture in the island would develop so as to actually exercise this ability, is not a legal matter.

3.3. *Ability to implement the* acquis

With respect to Cyprus' ability to implement the *acquis*, Papadopoulos maintained that the proposed United Cyprus Republic would not have been entitled and able to assume its full rights and duties. He pointed to restrictions on free movement and the need for Cyprus to become a member of the Schengen area with Turkish agreement only.[96] Free movement and participation in the Schengen area were policy areas where specific rules had been agreed early on since Annan I. These rules did not put at risk Cyprus' general ability to take part in the European legal order.

On the other hand, at the level of ordinary law, the new framework law, allowing the suspension of some *acquis* related federal laws in the Turkish Cypriot state could be seen as being in variance with this principle. However, it must be kept in mind that harmonisation to EU standards had not been carried out throughout the whole accession negotiations. Immediate implementation of the *acquis* in northern Cyprus would have created a situation of economic hardship that all the accession countries tried to avoid by asking for transitional periods. Clearly, separate transitional periods for the Turkish Cypriot state could not have been held after the conclusion of the settlement both for political and for practical reasons. In that situation some sort of ad-hoc transitional periods, which had been worked out by the relevant economic and financial experts, including from the European Commission, were a practical way out to solve this dilemma. The temporary suspension of some *acquis* related federal laws must therefore been seen as some sort of special transitional periods that would not have put at stake the general ability of Cyprus to implement the *acquis*.

3.4. *Consistency with relevant UN Security Council Resolutions*

Finally, in his speech of 8 April 2005, Papadopoulos questioned several aspects of the plan relating implicitly to the requirements as laid down in Security Council Resolutions 541 (non-recognition of the TRNC) and 1251 (single international personality of Cyprus). In particular, he stated:

> *We are called upon to abolish the Republic of Cyprus, the only foothold of our people and the guarantee of our historic character. Shall we do away with our internationally recognized state exactly at the very moment it strengthens its political weight with its accession to the European Union? We have to assess seriously the dangers from a possible collapse of the new state of affairs, because the facts that will be created will be irreversible. Collapse of the Federal State would mathematically lead to what we all want to avoid: partition through the international recognition of the constituent states.*

[96] Papadopoulos, loc. cit. (note 89).

The statement makes reference to partition by international recognition of the constitutent states as a possible consequence of a collapse of the United Cyprus Republic. Annan V does not contain any such provisions. The constituent states shall organize themselves within the limits of the federal constitution, and shall only exercise those powers that are not vested by the Constitution in the federal government (Article 15 (1) UCR Constitution). Furthermore, also Annan V followed the virgin birth approach, to which the Greek Cypriot side under Clerides had consented as early as September 2002.[97] Hence, no provision in the Annan Plan spoke of the TRNC as a "founder" of the UCR or alike, which could have been read as *ex post* recognition of that entity.

Neither can it be inferred from Article 12 of the Foundation Agreement on the continuing validity of past acts (including those taken in northern) that the TRNC is "legitimised"[98] – the provision is simply concerned with the future validity of state acts under domestic law of the UCR and not the international validity of certain TRNC acts in the past. Also the listing of further TRNC treaties (in addition to the two ones already contained in Annan III) in Annex V of Annan V does not point to that direction. Rather, the constructive ambiguity of the "virgin birth" doctrine remained intact. Listing such TRNC treaties may well be explained on the basis of traditional approaches state succession. However, Annan V also reiterated the automatic membership of the United Cyprus Republic in the European Union (Article 19 (1) UCR Constitution) and the United Nations (Article 13 (3) Foundation Agreement). Only on the basis of State continuity such membership could be brought about without being obliged to start a new accession procedure to both organizations.[99]

This last point also speaks against the thesis that Annan V required the "abolishment of the Republic of Cyprus":[100] it continued to combine elements of State succession and continuity as a way of compromise how to interpret the past, but at the same time creating legal certainty for the future. Under Annan V, as in previous versions, the future was built on the United Cyprus Republic as an independent and sovereign state with a single international legal personality (Article 1 (1) of the UCR Constitution).

In sum, Annan V respected the limits set by UN Security Council Resolutions 541 (no recognition of the TRNC) and 1251 (single international personality of Cyprus), as required by the European Union.

---

[97] Palley, loc. cit. (page xii, note 3), p. 25.

[98] International Expert Panel, loc. cit. (note 56), § 14.

[99] See Crawford/Hafner, loc. cit. (page 160, note 188), on the relevant prosision in Annan II. Annan V did not modify this approach.

[100] See Papadopoulos, loc. cit. (note 89) and International Expert Panel, loc. cit. (note 56), §§ 6 and 22.

3.5. *Conclusion*

The changes from Annan III to Annan V are in line with the fundamental EU principles. Also under Annan V, the United Cyprus Republic would have adhered to the principles of democracy, rule of law and human rights. It would have been able to speak with one voice under a strengthened cooperation agreement modelled along the Belgian example and it would have kept the rather unique guarantees that non-implementation of the *acquis* by the constituent states could be sanctioned by the federal level. The new framework law allowing for the suspension of some *acquis* related laws in the Turkish Cypriot State contained some sort of special transitional periods that would not have put at stake the general ability of Cyprus to implement the *acquis*. Accordingly, Greek Cypriot critique against Annan V on these issues in the No-campaign could not refer to the changes introduced since Annan III. Rather, such critique hit the fundamentals of the UN's approach, thereby undermining Papadopoulos' credibility to have negotiated about the UN plan in good faith already at the Hague in March 2003.[101]

4. Summary

The EU closely followed the developments from Annan III to V, by providing for experts to the UN team throughout the process and by personal involvement of the Enlargement Commissioner Verheugen at the final stage of the Bürgenstock negotiations. Sticking to the Seville formula of the European Council of June 2002, the Commission adopted on 7 April 2004 a Draft Act of Adaptation, in order to accommodate Annan V in the EU legal order. At the same time, the principles on which the EU is founded would have continued to be respected. The modifications as compared to Annan III did neither put Cyprus' ability to speak with one voice nor to implement the acquis communautaire at risk. Finally, autodesignation of entitled voters by both sides for the separate and simultenous referenda did not encroach on the right to self-determination.

Therefore, respective criticism with legalistic undertones, trying to justify the Greek Cypriot rejection of the plan with shortcomings as regards its EU compatibility or procedural defects under international law, is not well founded. Such attempts rather show the unwillingness of the Greek Cypriot leadership to accept the basic features of the Annan plan in a situation where EU accession was already secured for Cyprus under the *status quo*, namely after the signature of the Accession

[101] Report of the UN-Secretary-General of 28 May 2004, loc. cit. (note 10), § 66: "Likewise, given what he had said to me in The Hague in March 2003, I was concerned that the Greek Cypriot leader's speech appeared to call into question many fundamental aspects of the plan, even while acknowledging that the final version contained improvements"; Hannay, loc. cit. (page xii, note 2), p. 245; Verheugen, Speech before the European Parliament of 21 April 2004.

Treaty in April 2003. There is nothing to add to the observation of the UN Secretary-General in this respect:

> *The prospect of accession to Cyprus to the European Union and the opening of Turkey's path towards that goal provided a context of balanced incentives. The leadership of the Turkish Cypriots and Turkey did not seize that opportunity while it existed. By the time they were willing and able to seek a compromise solution, the incentives on the Greek Cypriot side had substantially weakened, the Greek Cypriot leadership was pursuing a less flexible policy, and time was running very short.*[102]

[102] Report of the UN-Secretary-General of 28 May 2004, loc. cit. (note 10), § 79.

Chapter VIII
Cyprus as EU Member State

A. THE FACTS

On 1 May 2004, the Accession Treaty entered into force after having been ratified by the fifteen old Member States and the ten new ones, including Cyprus.[1] Besides its general provisions the Treaty contains two important Protocols that deal with specific legal issues arising out of Cyprus' EU membership.

1. Rights and obligations of the Republic of Cyprus

According to Article 2 of the Act of Accession, the provisions of the original Treaties and the acts adopted by the institutions and the European Central Bank became binding on Cyprus as from that date "under the conditions laid down in those Treaties and in this Act". These bodies of law contain rights and obligations for Cyprus.

---

[1] The Cypriot House of Representatives ratified the Accession Treaty in an extra-ordinary session on 14 July 2003. The instrument of ratification was submitted to the EU Presidency on 5 August 2003.

Legal Aspects of the Cyprus Problem, pp. 196–222.

1.1. *Rights*

Under the Accession Treaty Cyprus received the right to take part in the internal market and EU policies. As EU citizens, Cypriots may derive individual rights from primary Community law, including the four freedoms and the right not be discriminated against on the basis of nationality. In addition, many rights flow from pieces of secondary EC law, including entitlements to agricultural subsidies, regional funds or structural aid. Sometimes, these rights are subject to specific conditions over time. Such conditions are contained, inter alia, in Annex VII listing the transitional periods for Cyprus under Article 24 of the Act.

From an institutional perspective, Cyprus may elect six representatives for the European Parliament (Article 11 AA). When the Council takes decisions by qualified majority, the Cyprus government votes with 4 votes (like Latvia, Estonia, Slovenia and Luxembourg). Cyprus may nominate a judge for the European Court of Justice and the Court of First Instance (Article 13 AA). One Cypriot national is eligible for the European Commission (Article 45 AA). Cyprus has six members in the Economic and Social Committee and the Committee of Regions. The transitional periods agreed for Cyprus are laid down in Article 24 AA in combination with the relevant Annexes.

The Cyprus government nominated Mr. M. Kyprianou for the Commission. During the interim period from May 2004 to November 2004 he assisted Mrs. Schreyer in the portfolio on budget. As from December 2004 he holds the portfolio on public health and consumer protection in the Barroso Commission. The six Cypriot Members of Parliament were duly elected in June 2004, among them the former Foreign Minister, Mr. Y. Kassoulides. The Cypriot judges at the European Court of Justice and the Court of First Instance are Mr. G. Arestis and Mr. S.S. Papasavvas.

1.2. *Obligations*

Cyprus also committed under the Accession Treaty to respect primary and secondary EC law. It shall contribute to the EC budget, implement EC policies and treat other EU citizens in conformity with Communtiy law.

On 8 November 2005, the Supreme Court had to decide about the transferral of a Cypriot national, suspected of tax evasion in the United Kingdom, under the procedures foreseen in the EU arrest warrant.[2] It held that Article 14 of the Cypriot constitution[3] forbids such transferral, notwithstanding Cyprus' obligation under EU law. As a reaction to that judgment, the Attorney General prepared a constitutional amendment to be adopted in the House of Representatives in 2006.

[2] Framework decision No. 2002/584/JHA of 13 June 2002 on the European arrest warrant and other surrender procedures between Member States, OJ 2002, L 190, p. 1.

[3] Article 14 of the 1960 Constitution reads: "No citizen shall be banished or excluded from the Republic under any circumstances".

Furthermore, some controversy arose in relation to the treatment of Turkish Cypriot property in the government controlled areas. Under the Turkish Cypriot Properties Law No. 139/91, the Minister of Interior manages Turkish Cypriot property in the south as a Custodian as long as the "abnormal situation" since 1974 prevails. According to the law, the primary aim of such custody is to meet the needs of Greek Cypriot refugees. Practice until-mid 2003 was to permit restitution of property to Turkish Cypriot who had returned to the government-controlled areas and who gave 6 months notice.[4] After the opening of the green line in April 2003 that policy was, however, changed. Upon advice of the new Attorney General, Mr. Nikitas, restitution to Turkish Cypriots was henceforth denied, pointing to approximately 25,000 Greek Cypriot refugees housing in about 5,500 Turkish Cypriot-owned homes. The Turkish Cypriot Human Rights Foundation claims that applications from Turkish Cypriot owners claiming restoration are not even considered by the Custodian, awaiting a final solution of Cyprus problem.[5] Furthermore, it is contended that Turkish Cypriot property is also used for public purposes, such as roads, bridges, car-parkes, military camps or the Larnaca airport. Finally, it seems that no compensation has been paid for those properties, which were compulsorily acquired (with resultant loss of title for the Turkish Cypriot owner).[6]

Against that background, the application and interpretation of Law No. 139/91 was subject to judicial review. In September 2004, a judge from the Supreme Court handed down a landmark decision. He held that the Turkish Cypriot Arif Mustafa, who had returned to the south, could claim his property in Episkopi back, even though currently occupied by a Greek Cypriot refugee family.[7] The Attorney General Nikitas filed an appeal against this decision in early October 2004, arguing that guardianship did not end by the fact that a Turkish Cypriot owner had returned to live permanently in the south. Rather, under Article 3 of the Law, it was for the Council of Ministers to determine whether the unsettled situation in Cyprus was actually over.

2. Suspension of the *acquis communautaire* in the northern part of Cyprus

One of the special conditions derived from the Accession Treaty is regulated in Protocol 10 on Cyprus. Article 1 (1) of this Protocol provides that the application of the *acquis* shall be "suspended in thoses areas of the Republic of Cyprus in

[4] Palley, loc. cit. (page xii, note 3), p. 176.

[5] Statement of the Chairman of the Turkish Cypriot Human Rights Foundation of 14 September 2005, leaflet, p. 2.

[6] Palley, loc. cit. (page xii, note 3), p. 177, note 37.

[7] Supreme Court, Hadjihambis J., Judgment of 24 September 2004, Arif Mustafa v. Minister of Interior, through Limassol District, Case 125/2004.

which the Government of the Republic of Cyprus does not exercise effective control".[8] Soon after the 1st May 2004 several situations arose where the interpretation of this provision was of importance.

Against the background of a building boom in the north, in part managed by UK real estate agents and involving customers from EU Member States, the government of the UK, Germany and France and other states issued warnings not to buy Greek Cypriot properties in the north or at least to seek a legal opinion prior to any purchase. Furthermore, several legal actions by Greek Cypriots against transactions in the north were introduced.

At the level of civil law, a Greek Cypriot requested before the Cypriot courts the demolition of a house built on his property in the north ("the Orams case").[9] The applicant intends to execute it in the United Kingdom, based on the Regulation 44/2001[10] on jurisdiction and enforcement of judgements in civil and commercial matters.

As regards criminal law, the Parliament of the Republic of Cyprus amended section 281 of the criminal code in early 2005. In particular, the penalty for "illegal use of property" was raised to over 2 years. On the basis of this amendment, the authorities of the Republic of Cyprus started to issue EU arrest warrants in May 2005 for illegal use of Greek Cypriot owned properties in the northern part of the island. Two of these arrest warrants against UK real estate agents were transferred to the authorities of the United Kingdom; others against Turkish citizens were handed over to Interpol.

3. The Green Line Regulation of 29 April 2004

Article 2 of Protocol 10 enabled the Council to lay down a special regime for the green line. On that basis the Council adopted on 29 April 2004 the relevant "Green Line Regulation".[11] According to its recital 7, the green line does not constitute an external border of the EU. Special rules concerning the crossing of goods, services and persons need to be established as the application of the acquis is suspended in the areas north of the green line. The Regulation is intended to facilitate trade and other links from the north to the south, whilst ensuring that appropriate standards of protection of the security of the EU should be maintained. Such standards relate to illegal immigration and threats to public order. Furthermore, EU's economic interests as far as the movement of goods is concerned should be protected.

---

[8] Appendix 1.

[9] Nicosia District Court, Judgment of 9 November 2004, Apostolides v. Orams.

[10] Council Regulation (EC) No. 44/2001 of 22 December 2000 on jurisdiction and the recognition and enforcement of judgements in civil and commercial matters, OJ 2001, L 12, p. 1.

[11] Council Regulation (EC) No. 866/2004 of 29 April 2004, OJ 2004, L 161, p. 128 with corrigendum at OJ 2004, L 206, p. 51.

3.1. *Crossing of persons*

Title II on "crossing of persons" obliges the Republic of Cyprus to carry out checks on all persons crossing the line with the aim to combat illegal immigration of third country nationals and to detect and prevent any threat to public security and public policy. Under Article 2 (2) of the regulation all persons have to undergo an identity check. Third country nationals shall only be admitted if they have a residence permit or a valid visa and do not represent a threat to public policy or public security. The regulation further identifies those crossing points through which the traffic shall be channelled (Ledra Palace and Agios Demetrios); in April 2005 two more crossing points were added (Ledra Street and Zodia – not yet operating in practice),[12] followed by another two immediately operational crossing points in August 2005 (Kokkina and Kato Pyrgos).[13]

In practice, the crossing of persons at the operational crossing points is running smoothly. According to the Commission, thousands of Cypriots from either side cross the line daily without any incidents. EU nationals may move freely. As regards third country nationals, surveillance does not seem to be very effective, as in some areas it is possible to cross the green line without any controls. Accordingly, illegal immigration took place and Cyprus witnessed a significant increase of asylum applications between 1 May 2004 and 30 April 2005.[14]

3.2. *Crossing of goods*

The Green Line Regulation also governs trade of goods (live animals and animal products are currently excluded) from the northern parts into the southern parts of Cyprus. Under Article 4 of the regulation, it is necessary to prove origin of goods arriving from the north. The relevant documents are issued by the Turkish Cypriot Chamber of Commerce, which had been enabled by the Commission in agreement with the Government of Cyprus for that purpose.[15] In addition, certain goods need to comply with veterinary, phytosanitary and food safety requirements and checks. Under these conditions, the goods may enter into the southern parts of Cyprus, not being subject to customs duties or charges having equivalent effect. Only agri-

---

[12] Commission Regulation (EC) No. 601/2005 of 18 April 2005, amending Annex I to Council Regulation (EC) No. 866/2004 on a regime under Article 2 of Protocol No. 10 to the Act of Accession, OJ 2005, L 99, p. 10.

[13] Commission Regulation (EC) No. 1283/2005 of 3 August 2005 amending Annex I to Council Regulation (EC) No. 866/2004 on a regime under Article 2 of Protocol 10 to the Act of Accession, OJ 2005, L 203, p. 8.

[14] It is estimated that more than 50% of the over 10.000 asylum seekers in Cyprus illegally crossed the green line. Communication from the Commission of 14 July 2005: Report on the implementation of Council regulation (EC) 866/2004 and the situation resulting from its application; COM (2005), 320 final, Section Two on crossing on persons.

[15] Article 4 (5) of the Green Line Regulation and Commission Decision of 7 July, OJ 2004, L 272.

cultural goods that are eligible for export refunds or intervention measures are subject to duties (Article 4 (2) Green Line Regulation).[16] No import tax is due, provided goods arriving from the north are destined for consumption in the Republic of Cyprus and are not transported to other EU Member States (Article 4 (7) of the regulation). Importantly, these goods shall have the status of Community goods, once they have entered the Government controlled areas (Article 4 para. 11 of the regulation).

Upon enactment of specific implementation rules by the Commission on 10 August 2004,[17] trade from the northern parts over the green line remained at a low level, reaching an average volume of approximately 100.000 € per month in the first year. The Commission identified several obstacles. The Republic of Cyprus did not accept the roadworthiness certificates for lorries or taxis, issued by the TRNC authorities. Neither were driving licences of drivers for such vehicles recognized as fulfilling the requirements of the Republic's legal prescriptions. Instead the Republic of Cyprus organizes examinations for Turkish Cypriots, so that they may receive professional driving licences provided they already worked as bus or truck drivers and pass an oral test.

Trade of Turkish Cypriot products over the green line into the territory of other Member States does virtually not exist. It seems that the main obstacle lies in the fact that for such goods import VAT is due (Article 4 (7) of the regulation), rendering such trade economically uninteresting.

4. Relations with the Turkish Cypriot Community

Two days after the outcome of the referenda on Annan V, on 26 April 2004, the EU Council (still consisting of 15 Ministers) was *"determined to put an end to the isolation of the Turkish Cypriot community and to facilitate the reunification of Cyprus by encouraging the economic development of the Turkish Cypriot community"*. The Council therefore *"invited the Commission to bring forward comprehensive proposals to this end, with particular emphasis on the economic integration of the island and on improving contact between the two communities and with the EU"*.[18]

Already at the time of the enactment of the green line regulation, most observers estimated that its effect would be limited to overcome the isolation of the Turkish Cypriot Community. It was therefore crucial to envisage further measures. Accordingly, the Commission proposed two regulations on 7 July 2004.

[16] See also Council Regulation (EC) No. 293/2005 of 17 February 2005, amending the Green line regulation, in order to facilitate trade in certain agricultural goods; OJ 2005, L 50, p. 1.

[17] Commission Regulation (EC) 1480/2004 of 10 August 2004, OJ 2004, L 272, p. 3.

[18] General Affairs Council of 26 April 2004.

4.1. *The financial aid regulation*

Under the proposal for a financial aid regulation,[19] 259 Mio € were earmarked for the years 2004–2006 to engage in infrastructure projects, social and economic development, bi-communal events, the harmonisation of the Turkish Cypriot legal system with the *acquis communautaire* and other purposes. The Commission would mandate the European Agency for Reconstruction (Thessaloniki), which carries out EU aid for Serbia and Montenegro and the former Yugoslav Republic of Macedonia, to cover also northern Cyprus. The Council finalised its preparatory work successfully in November 2004. Nevertheless, it did not adopt the regulation at the time because of persisting disagreement as regards the second Commission proposal. Whereas the Government of Cyprus supported the adoption of this regulation only, other Member States led by the United Kingdom insisted that the two proposals should be adopted simultaneously. Also the Turkish Cypriot leadership called for the "package", stating several times not to support the implementation of the financial regulation in the absence of direct trade. Since the Council did not adopt the draft aid regulation by the end of 2005, 120 Mio € were lost for budgetary reasons. However on 27 February 2006, the Council finally agreed to use the maintaining 139 Mio € for the Turkish Cypriot community.[20] A few statements were recorded in the Council minutes. With respect to the management of the assistance (ad Article 3), the Commission declared its readiness to consult the Cyprus government about the major aspects of implementation and if feasibility studies leave doubt as to whether actions to be financed might affect property rights. The Commission also promised to establish any operational centre needed by the Agency for implementing the assistance in the areas under effective control of the Government of the Republic of Cyprus (statement ad Article 5). Finally, ad Article 9 on the right to participate in tenders and contracts, the Council noted that the term "natural or legal persons of member States of the European Union" includes those residing or established in the areas. The Commission complemented that statement by recalling that the main objective of the financial instrument was to encourage the economic development of the Turkish Cypriot community. It therefore understands the same term to include all genuinely existing domestic legal persons residing or established in the areas. The Commission declared that this understanding will be specified in the tenders and that this does not imply recognition of any public authority in the areas often than the Government of the Republic of Cyprus.

4.2. *The draft direct trade regulation*

That proposal provided for privileged conditions for direct trade between northern Cyprus and EU Member States.[21] Certain goods arriving from the areas where

[19] COM (2004) 465 final of 7 July 2004.

[20] Council Regulation (EC) No. 389/2006 of 07 February 2006, of 2006, L 655. Appendix 4.

[21] COM (2004) 466 final of 7 July 2004. Appendix 5.

the Government does not exercise effective control would be exempt from customs duties and charges having equivalent effect within yearly tariff quotas. The Turkish Cypriot Chamber of Commerce would issue the necessary certificates of origin. Independent experts would be charged to carry out phytosanitary inspection and reporting so that plants and other products covered by EC Directive 2000/29/EC could also enter the common customs territory. Once those northern Cypriot products enter into another Member State they could be released for free circulation into the customs territory of the Community. This special regime would not cover feedingstuff, certain agricultural goods or goods subject to trade defence measures (draft Article 1 (4)-(6)).

In the Council, at ambassador level (COREPER), the Cypriot government argued that the legal basis of that proposal (Article 133 EC, triggering qualified majority in the Council) was inacceptable. For Nicosia, supported by an opinion of the Council Legal Service of 25 August 2004, direct trade amounted to a partial reintroduction of the *acquis* for northern Cyprus. Such decision could only be based on Article 1 (2) of Protocol 10, requiring unanimity in the Council. The Government also argued that direct aid would undermine its sovereign decision of 1974 to close all northern ports and airports for international traffic. According to its view, the regulation would therefore violate international law.[22] Given that fundamental resistence by Nicosia on the one hand and the request of some member States to couple the aid and trade regulations on the other hand, the Dutch Presidency decided in October 2004 to put the respective discussions on hold, also in view that the decision of the European Council on the opening of Turkey's accession negotiations was scheduled for December that year.

In the first half of 2005, the Luxemburg Presidency made an attempt to deblock the situation. In the north, Mehmet Ali Talat had been elected President in February 2005, backed by a parliamentary majority of his CTP party after the April 2005 elections. Inspired by an old confidence-building proposal from Boutros-Ghali and working on a proposal submitted by the Cypriot government in August 2004 on the "return of Varosha to its lawful inhabitants and the re-opening of Famagusta port", the EU Presidency held a series of bilateral political meetings with both sides on the island. Having received positive signals, the Luxembourg Deputy Foreign Minister Nicolas Schmit, assisted by the Commission, invited the Greek Cypriots and Turkish Cypriots for three rounds of confidential talks in June 2005 in Brussels. The central idea was to allow for direct trade through the port of Famagusta. For that purpose the Cypriot Government could revoke its decision of 1974 to close the port for international traffic. In return, the Turkish Cypriots would make an effort to protect Greek Cypriot property in the north and, possibly, engage to discuss the return of Varosha. The Commission would be prepared to supervise customs, taxation and phytosanitary matters on the ground in Famagusta. However, no such deal could be struck. For the Turkish Cypriots any commitment on the return of Varosha had to be combined with the opening of other ports and airports as well. The Greek Cypriots were only prepared to discuss the

[22] The Government relied in particular on a legal opinion of Professors Vaughan Lowe and Derrick Wyatt of 19 May 2004.

modalities of opening Famagusta. Accordingly, no progress on the direct trade regulation could be recorded under the Luxemburg Presidency.

5. The Sovereign Base Areas of the United Kingdom in Cyprus

Protocol 3 to the Accession Treaty relates to the Sovereign Base Areas of the United Kingdom in Cyprus. According to the Treaty of Establishment the two bases (Dhekelia and Akrotiri) remained part of the United Kingdom when Cyprus became independent in 1960. At the time the UK government declared that one of the main objectives to be achieved is the protection of the interest of those resident or working in the Sovereign Base Areas (SBA's). The United Kingdom had agreed that the Republic of Cyprus administers a wide range of public services in the SBA's, including in the fields of agriculture, customs and taxation.

After Cyprus' accession, Community law regulates some of these subject matters with respect to Cyprus. *Inter alia*, the Community would grant benefits to Cyprus' agriculture, there would be uniform rules how to deal with imported goods etc. In order to maintain the special regime of the SBAs, the United Kingdom agreed – in parallel negotiations to the accession negotiations with the European Commission and the Cyprus government – to modify Article 299 (6) (b) of the EC Treaty.[23] In its amended version, Article 299 (6) (b) EC provides for the application of EC law to the SBA's to the extent necessary to ensure the implementation of the arrangements of Protocol 3 to the Accession Treaty.[24]

Under that protocol, the SBA's are included within the Community customs territory, but the UK may maintain certain reliefs and exemptions from duties and taxes on supplies to its forces and associated personnel, which are granted by the Treaty of Establishment. Community payments under the common agricultural policy could be paid to Cypriot farmers living on the SBA's. Persons resident or employed there are covered by the social security schemes under EC law when they are migrating to another EU Member State. Most importantly, no checks on persons crossing from the SBA's to the territory of the Republic need to be introduced because the UK guarantees to exercise such controls on the external borders of the SBA's. Finally, the Protocol determines the system of implementation as divided between the autorities of the SBA and the Republic of Cyprus, thereby continuing established practices.

---

[23] When the United Kingdom became a member of the European Community, Article 299 (6) (b) EC was inserted into the EC Treaty and read as follows: "This Treaty shall not apply to the Sovereign Base Areas of the United Kingdom of Great Britain and Northern Ireland in Cyprus".

[24] Protocol No. 3 on the Sovereign Base Areas of the United Kingdom of Great Britain and Northern Ireland in Cyprus, OJ 2003, L 236, p. 940.

B. LEGAL EVALUATION

I. Rights and Obligations of the Republic of Cyprus

1.1. *Application of the acquis communautaire*

Cyprus undertook the obligation to implement the *acquis* in the areas under its effective control (Article 2 Act of Accession). This is not the appropriate occasion to review the legal consequences that flow therefrom for the entire Cypriot legal order. It suffices to refer to the regular reports of the European Commission which set out in details the enormous efforts of harmonization that were successfully carried out. Indeed, Cyprus prepared well to apply the *acquis* by amending existing legislation or enacting new one. Therefore, it is most probable that EU law will generally be implemented properly in the government-controlled areas.

Nevertheless, one field of conflict was not properly tackled. Under Article 169 (3) of the constitution treaties, conventions and agreements shall have superior force to *any municipal law*. In Malachtou v. Armefti,[25] the Supreme Court specified that the term 'municipal law' refers to parliamentary statutes, but not to the Constitution as such which has the highest rank under Article 179 of the constitution. Hence, the hierarchy of norms in Cyprus is the following: Constitution, international treaties, national statutes.[26] It follows therefrom that, under Cypriot constitutional law, EU law would only precede the application of national laws, whereas constitutional law itself remained the supreme law of the Republic. Such a situation is not in conformity with the principle of EU law supremacy. Some writers had raised this point already at a time when Cyprus was still negotiating, calling for an amendment of the Cypriot constitution.[27] The then Attorney-General Markides, as early as in May 2002, joined these voices. Pointing to the fact that Article 179 of the Constitution is not listed among the unamendable provisions a modified Article 169 could state that no provision of the Constitution invalidates EU law. Furthermore, an amendment to Article 179 could specify that the Constitution is the supreme law of the Republic "subject to the provisions of

---

[25] 1 CLR 207, at p. 217.

[26] N. Emiliou, Cyprus, in: A. Ott/K. Inglis (ed.), Handbook on European Enlargment, p. 239 (241).

[27] C. Patsalides, The Accession of Cyprus to the EU: Constitutional Problems and Complexities, pp. 98 et seq; Emiliou, loc. cit. (note 26), p. 239 (245–246). For the opposite view see K. Chrysostomides, Issues under Constitutional and International Law in the Path of Cyprus towards Accession to the EU, (Manuscript on file with the author), p. 5, arguing that the doctrine of necessity could be sufficient in this regard. For historical and practical reasons it appears, however, that such an important decision should not be left to the discretion of the Supreme Court, working with rather vague criteria that have been developed to cope with a completely different problem.

Article 169".[28] This acceptance of EU law supremacy should have been decided by a 2/3 majority in Parliament for constitutional changes and be made subject to a popular referendum.[29]

Unfortunately, this very lucid proposal did not see the day. Pointing to the ongoing negotiations on a settlement, neither Clerides nor Papadopoulous attempted to tackle this issue. Against this background, it came as no surprise that the Supreme Court upheld in November 2005 the supremacy of Cypriot constitutional law in the case concerning the EU arrest warrant. For sure, the obligations flowing from a Framework decision adopted under Article 34 of the EU Treaty do not enjoy the same prinipled supremacy as Community law adopted on the basis of the EC Treaty. Nevertheless, under Article 11 (2) of the EU Treaty, Cyprus is under an obligation to carry out Framework decision and to adapt its national legal order accordingly. It remains to be seen, whether and how the proposals of the new Attorney General Petros Clerides will pass through the House of Representatives until spring 2006, when Parliament will be dissolved. At the present stage it is too early to assess whether the prepared amdendment will indeed remove the potential conflict between Community law and Cypriot constitutional law.

1.2. *Compliance with the principles on which the EU is founded*

The treatment of Turkish Cypriot property by the Law 139/91 poses several important questions under Article 1 of the First Additional Protocol to the European Convention on Human Rights. That norm forms part of the human rights on which the EU is founded[30] and which Cyprus must generally observe. It may also become relevant in individual cases, provided a national measures falls into the scope of Community law, e.g. if an EU citizen of Turkish Cypriot origin would be impeded to exercise his right to free movement within the European Union. One could imagine cases where the return of EU citizens to Cyprus would face severe difficulties through restricted access to their property in the Republic.[31]

First, the law puts all Turkish Cypriot property in the south under custody, as long as the "abnormal situation" in the island prevails. Although drafted as a temporal requirement, the practical effect of this approach is to pre-empt restoration or even compensation to Turkish Cypriot owners. In line with the Loizidou case law of the European Court of Human Rights, the denial of access for Turkish Cypriots to their property cannot be justified under Article 1 of the First

[28] Markides, loc. cit. (page 150, note 158), p. 10.

[29] Markides, loc. cit. (page 150, note 158) p. 16.

[30] See above Chapter VI B 2.3.1.

[31] See *mutatis mutandis* ECJ, Case C-60/00, Mary Carpenter, Judgment of 11 July 2002, para. 39. The Court srutinized whether the impugned British measure to separate Mr. Carpenter from his wife would be detrimental to the conditions under which Mr. Carpetner exercises a fundamental freedom. It held that the case fell into the scope of Community law because the freedom to provide services abroad could not be fully effective if Mr. Carpenter were to be deterred from exercising it by obstacles raised in his country of origin to the entry and residence of his spouse.

Additional Protocol with the absence of a political settlement or the deprivation of Greek Cypriot property by Turkish Cypriot authorities.[32] Such practice under Law 139/91, effectively turning the Turkish Cypriot ownership titles to empty shells, constitutes a continuing violation of the Convention's standard.

Second, it is unclear whether the law provides for an effective remedy, as required by Article 13 of the Convention in conjunction with the right to property. If the allegations of the Turkish Human Rights Foundations were true, it seems that applications may be formally be made, but are postponed *sine die*, pending a solution of the Cyprus problem. Such non-treatment of applications can only be acceptable under the Convention's standards if the failure to act can be attacked under the Cypriot legal system before independent Courts. In this regard, it remains to be seen how the pending Arif Mustafa case will be finally adjudicated.

Third, it seems that some Turkish Cypriot property has not been allocated for the temporal use of Greek Cypriot refugees, but rather for public use. Such decisions can only be effected in a formal procedure of expropriation, if a reasonable cause for public acquisition can be demonstrated. In any event, in such cases, prompt and adequate compensation is due to the former Turkish Cypriot owners of that property upon their application. Since formal decisions do not seem to have been taken, nor does compensation seem to have been paid, the Republic of Cyprus is infringing its obligations under Article 1 of the First Additional Protocol of the Convention.

2. Suspension of the *acquis* in the northern part of Cyprus

Many practical legal questions relate to the suspension of the *acquis* in the northern part of Cyprus, which is a real novelty in EU law.

2.1. *The principle*

Some general introductory remarks on "suspension" seem appropriate. The term refers to international treaty law as codified in the Vienna Convention. Under Article 61 of that Convention, "supervening impossibility of performance" may invalidate a treaty or be invoked as a reason for its suspension. This provision does not encompass initial impossibility of a government to perform its obligations. Nevertheless, it may well be argued that impossibility to perform always has its bearing on a treaty, whether it existed before the conclusion of a treaty or thereafter. Or put even stronger: What sense does it make to conclude a treaty when both sides know that one side cannot honour it, at least for parts of its territory?

It was well known to the negotiatiors that the Cyprus Government would be unable to implement European law in the northern parts, pending a settlement. Accordingly, at least a tacit understanding would have limited the territorial reach

[32] Palley, loc. cit. (page xii, note 3), p. 245, note 10, emphasizing that a policy of "a wrong for a wrong" is inconsistent with the observance of human rights.

of the accession treaty and suspended the application of the *acquis* in the northern parts of Cyprus' territory.[33] Against this background Article 1 (1) of the Act merely spells out the application of international treaty law to the peculiar situation of Cyprus.

This situation is different from the German experience.[34] Although the western Allies recognized the West German government as the sole legitimate government of Germany as a whole it never acted with legal effect for the territory of the German Democratic Republic. Accordingly, upon membership in the then European Coal and Steel Community and the European Economic Community, European law only applied to the territory governed by the Basic Law of the Federal Republic of Germany.[35] For Cyprus, however, Article 1 (1) of Protocol 10 makes clear that European law extends in principle also to the northern parts of the island. Nevertheless, taking account of the factual situation, its actual application is temporarily suspended.

2.2. *Rights of Turkish Cypriots*

Are Turkish Cypriots EU citizens? If so, what consequences does the temporal non-application of EU law in the northern parts of Cyprus have for the Turkish Cypriots living there?

2.2.1. *Turkish Cypriots as EU citizens*

Under Article 17 (1) EC, every person holding the nationality of a Member State shall be a citizen of the Union. EU citizenship shall complement and not replace national citizenship. Turkish Cypriots, which can demonstrate that they are Cypriot nationals under the relevant citizenship law of 1967,[36] are therefore EU citizens. In practice, the Republic regularly issues a passport upon application. Those who fulfil the material requirements of the citizenship law, but cannot present this document may only derive rights from EU citizenship if and in so far it had been impossible for them to obtain the official passport for reasons that are outside their control.

2.2.2. *Rights linked to territorial application of EU law*

Although being EU citizens, Turkish Cypriots living in the north cannot rely on EU rights *there* because of their lack of territorial application. That means, that

[33] Tomuschat, loc. cit. (page 93, note 60), p. 672 (684); Chrysostomides, loc. cit. (page 10, note 24), p. 466.

[34] Necatigil, loc. cit. (page 11, note 35), p. 344, note 27.

[35] See Article 229 EC of the Treaty of Rome (1957). C. Tomuschat, EWG und DDR, Völkerrechtliche Überlegungen zum Sonderstatus des Außenseiters einer Wirtschaftsunion, Europarecht 1969, pp. 298–332 (300–305); ECJ, Case 14/74, ECR 1974, p. 899, § 6.

[36] Law No. 43/1967 of 28th July 1967, as amended in 1972 and 1983. For a description of the relevant requirements see N. Skoutaris, Differentiation in European Union citizenship law – the Cyprus problem, in: A. Ott/K. Inglis (ed.), The Constitution for Europe and an Enlarging Union: Unity in Diversity?, p. 160 (168).

nobody may invoke against TRNC authorities any rights derived from primary or secondary EU law.

2.2.3. Elections to the European Parliament

According to Article 190 EC, the people of each Member State shall elect representatives to the European Parliament. Pending a uniform electoral system, the Member States are entitled to choose the appropriate system. Usually, they opt for applying an analogous system to the one used in national elections.[37]

Articles 62 and 63 of the 1960 Cypriot Constitution foresee the enrolment of Greek Cypriots in one electoral list (voting for 70% of the parliamentarians), and enrolment of Turkish Cypriots in another one (voting for 30 %). However, the implementing legislation of 1979[38] does not provide for any separate electoral list for Turkish Cypriots in view of the factual situation after 1974. Since only approximately 1.100 Turkish Cypriot voters live in the south, providing them with a separate list would enable a very small margin of the actual population to elect 30 % of the Members of Parliament. Accordingly, a different system must be sought of to include the Turkish Cypriots in the democratic process in the government-controlled areas. Just ignoring their existence falls foul of the very essence of the democratic right to vote under Article 3 of the First Additional Protocol ECHR and Article 190 EC.[39] To comply with these standards, those Turkish Cypriots residing in the south must be included in the Greek Cypriot electoral system, as the European Court of Human Rights has decided with respect to national Cypriot elections.[40] The fact that the Turkish Cypriot Community as a whole rejected to participate in elections organized by the Republic cannot deprive an individual Turkish Cypriot the right to do so, disagreeing with the policy

---

[37] The situation is therefore different from the representation of Cyprus in the Parliamentary Assembly of the Council of Europe to which the national Parliaments send delegates. For an account of relevant – inconcise – practice of the Strasbourg organ (not) to accept only Greek Cypros delegates see Necatigil, loc. cit. (page 11, note 35), pp. 242–245.

[38] Law 72/79.

[39] In 2001, the European Commission, in its Regular Report 2001 on Cyprus' progress towards EU accession, noted with criticism that Turkish Cypriots living in the south were not allowed to vote (Regular Report 2001, p. 17). See also Özgür, loc. cit. (page 10, note 34), p. 139, describing his (vain) efforts, in 1990, to convince the Greek political party leaders that the denial of voting rights for Turkish Cypriots violates human rights standards.

[40] ECtHR, Aziz v Cyprus, Application No. 69949/01, Judgement of 22 June 2004, §§ 29–30: "(The Court) observes that, despite the fact that the relevant constitutional provisions have been rendered ineffective, there is a manifest lack of legislation resolving the ensuing problems. Consequently, the applicant, as a member of the Turkish Cypriot community living in the Government-controlled area of Cyprus, was completely deprived of any opportunity to express his opinion in the choice of the members of the House of Representatives of the country of which he is a national and where he has always lived. The Court considers that, in the light of the above circumstances, the very essence of the applicant's right to vote, as guaranteed in Article 3 of Protocol No. 1, was denied".

choice of the majority. The same rationale applies to elections for the European Parliament: Turkish Cypriots residing in the south have a right to participate in these elections – the suspension of the *acquis* in the north does not alter this analysis.

The more difficult question is whether Turkish Cypriot living in the north should be allowed to vote for the European Parliament under Article 190 EC. Is this right linked to territory and therefore "suspended" under Article 1 (1) Protocol 10? On the one hand, one may argue that voting is a personal a right, not dependent on actual residence. To provide for an institutional balance and to respect the democracy principle, there must be room for Turkish Cypriot representation in the EU.[41] On the other hand, the European Union must ensure that the elections are conducted in a fair and free manner, and that registration and the actual voting process comply with the principles of European Law. Since European law is suspended in the north, these preconditions cannot be met. Hence, Turkish Cypriots living in the north are excluded from EP elections in so far as they would ask for exercising this right at their place of residence. However, Article 1 (1) of Protocol 10 does not preclude Turkish Cypriot to cross the green line at election-day and to vote in the south provided they had been registered there. Indeed, as foreseen by the Cypriot legislation, as amended in October 2003, Turkish Cypriots residing in the north are allowed to cast their ballot in an election facility in the south. At the elections for the European Parliament on 13 June 2004, approximately 500 Turkish Cypriots had been registered, out of which 97 actually voted. A Turkish Cypriot independent candidate received 681 votes.

One author contends that such elections put the democratic content of Community law into jeopardy given that the Turkish Cypriots do generally not accept to be represented through organised elections that are unilaterally dictated by the Republic.[42] This line of argument is, however, not convincing. There is no democratic deficit caused by the Republic of Cyprus if Cypriot citizens of Turkish Cypriot origin do not participate in elections that are formally open to them. Furthermore, non-participation of a majority Turkish Cypriots in EP elections would not lead to "non-democratic foreign rule" in the north since EU law is effectively suspended in this area.

Nevertheless, such representation would fall foul of the EU principle of representativeness in the event of a settlement. Therefore, the mandates of the current Members of the European Parliament are conditional on the absence of a settlement. In order to make this known to the elected MPs, the Council already issued a decision in advance of the EP elections of 13 June 2004.[43] That decision puts

[41] A. Berramdane, Chypre entre adhésion à l'Union européenne et réunification, 2003/1, revue trimestrielle de droit européen, p. 87 (106).

[42] Neuwahl, loc. cit. (page 158, note 182), p. 9 (note 14).

[43] Council Decision of 10 June 2004 concerning the representation of the people of Cyprus in the European Parliament in case of a settlement of the Cyprus problem, OJ 2004, L 211, p. 22.

an early end to the elected parliamentarians and provides for new extraordinary elections in the whole of Cyprus in the event of a settlement.

2.2.4. *Rights not linked to territory*

In contrast, suspension of the *acquis* in northern Cyprus does not have any effect on the exercise of personal rights of Turkish Cypriots (possessing the passport of the Republic of Cyprus) not linked to that territory. In particular, they are entitled, as Cypriot citizens to exercise their fundamental freedoms in other EU Member States or to work in the institutions of the European Union.[44] Furthermore, they may also participate in Community programs.

With respect to legal persons, participation in Community programs is less evident. Although the Cyprus company law inherited from British rule is still applied in the whole of the island, companies registered in the north after 1974 may not qualify as legal persons under the law of the Republic. Nevertheless, Article 9 of the financial regulation provides that "participation in the award of procurement of grants financed under this regulation shall be open to all natural and legal persons of the Member States". In statements made at the time of adoption on 27 February 2006 the Council of Ministers and the Commission noted that the term "natural or legal persons of Member States of the European Union" includes those residing or established in the areas. Therefore, their eligibility under that regulation does not depend on registration in a company or association register of the Republic of Cyprus. The same rationale applies to participation of such companies in Community programmes. However, due to the non-application of the acquis in the north, projects implemented in those areas cannot be funded by those Community programs if and in so far the project would be basically situated there.

2.3. *Rights of Greek Cypriots*

A difficult question is whether the suspension of the *acquis* for the northern part of Cyprus affects the legal actions brought in the Republic of Cyprus for the protection of properties in the north.

2.3.1. *Recognition of civil judgements*

Those Greek Cypriots, who were forced to leave their property lying in the north behind, still enjoy ownership rights under Cypriot civil law and are protected by international human rights law. Accordingly, they may bring legal action against those who are using their property unlawfully. However, any court judgement rendered

[44] In the first recruitment competition after Cyprus' EU accession, the European Commission required that examinations should be passed in the Greek language (EPSO/A/1/03). Two Turkish Cypriots brought on 18 November 2004 an action before the Court of First Instance against the Commission, arguing that this requirement constituted unlawful discrimination against Cypriot citizens whose mother tounge is not Greek. The case is pending before the Court of First Instance (T-455/04). In the meantime, new recruitment competitions for Cypriots may be passed in any official Community language.

in the Republic cannot be enforced in the northern parts, due to the factual circumstances. If the respondent of such an action is a UK citizen, it may therefore be interesting to execute the judgement in the United Kingdom.

In principle, judgements in civil and commercial matters shall be executed under Article 33 of Regulation 44/2001[45] in other Member States without any special procedure being required. The regulation does not differentiate whether the original judgement relates to facts occurring within the jurisdiction of the original court or elsewhere. If for example, a Cypriot court renders a judgement on a tort committed against a Cypriot national in a non-EU Member State, that judgement may be executed in the United Kingdom without the UK court inquiring in the case. Similarily, a Cypriot judgement on torts against a Greek Cypriot occurring in north Cyprus may also be enforced in the United Kingdom. The fact that the *acquis* does not apply in northern Cyprus does not matter in this regard.

However, Article 35 (1) of the regulation prohibits the recognition if it conflicts with, *inter alia*, Section 6 of Chapter II of the regulation. This section provides for several grounds of exclusive jurisdiction. Under Article 22 No. 1 of the regulation, "in proceedings which have as their object rights *in rem* in immovable property, the courts of the Member State in which the property is situated, shall be the only competent court". For example, a UK court shall not recognize a German judgement, if it relates to immovable property situated in another Member State because the courts there should have been competent. It is not clear what Article 22 No. 1 of the regulation means for properties lying in northern Cyprus: should a UK court reject recognition of a Cypriot judgement rendered in the Republic of Cyprus relating to property in the north, because only courts situated in the TRNC are competent? From the wording of Article 22 No. 1 of the regulation such interpretation is not cogent, since courts in the TRNC are not courts "of a Member State". The object and purpose of the provision may, however, point to the opposite direction. Article 22 No. 1 of the regulation grants exclusive jurisdiction to those courts where the property actually lies because only those courts have the possibility to ascertain all relevant facts with regard to that property. In view of the findings of the European Court of Human Rights that TRNC courts could be relied on for the purpose of exhaustion of local remedies in a human rights context on a case-to-case basis, it is not excluded that they could also ascertain exclusive jurisdiction for property issues in the north.[46] On the other hand, such exclusivity rests on the assumption of objectivity and neutrality of the courts in property matters. That may not be generally assured, given that such Courts apply the legal order of the TRNC, which could be at odds with the claims of the Greek Cypriots. Therefore, Article 35 in conjunction with Article 22 No. 1 of the regulation would not seem to exclude recognition of judgements rendered in the Republic Cyprus relating to properties lying in the north.

[45] Council Regulation (EC) No. 44/2001 of 22 December 2000 on jurisdiction and the recognition and enforcement of judgements in civil and commercial matters, OJ 2001, L 12, p. 1.

[46] See above Chapter III, B 2.3.4.

Finally, a UK court may refuse to recognise a Cypriot judgement on the ground that such recognition is "manifestly contrary to public policy in the Member State in which recognition is sought". Hence, the court would have to verify relevant UK policy as regards the property issue. It may easily arrive at the conclusion that the UK counselled for caution in dealings with Greek Cypriot property in the north. Accordingly, there is no public UK policy that would stand in the way of recognition of judgements rendered in the Republic on these matters.

2.3.2. *Execution of European arrest warrants*

As regards criminal cooperation, the starting point is similar because the Council Framework decision of 13 June 2002 on the European arrest warrant is also built on the underlying idea of mutual recognition.[47] Again, the fact that the *acquis* is suspended for northern Cyprus is not decisive. For the application of Cypriot penal law, it is sufficient that the victim of the offence is of Cypriot nationality and not that the offence is committed in an area where the *acquis* applies.

Cypriot judicial authorities are therefore entitled to issue decisions with a view to the arrest and surrender by another Member State or a requested person, for the purposes of conducting a criminal prosecution or executing a custodial sentenced or detention order (Article 1 of the Framework decision). Such a request triggers an obligation of other Member States to carry it out, provided that they cannot invoke a ground for mandatory or optional non-execution. As regards the latter category, Article 4 Nr. 1 of the Framework decision grants discretion to the executing authority of an executing State of a European arrest warrant, if the crime is not included in the list of Article 2 Nr. 2 of the Framework decision and does not constitute an offence under the law of the executing Member State. Accordingly, execution of a Cypriot arrest warrant based on "illegal use of property" depends on the question whether the executing state knows of a comparable crime. If that is not the case, the European arrest warrant may not be effective.

2.4. *Rights of EU citizens*

How does the suspension of the *acquis* in northern Cyprus affect EU citizens? In principle, the answer must be categoric. They cannot invoke any rights derived from EU law in their dealings with the administration in northern Cyprus. Accordingly, they neither benefit from the fundamental freedoms or other EU rights such as the right to vote in municipal elections,[48] when entering into or staying in northern Cyprus.

However, the situation changes if they enter into the government controlled areas. Here, EU citizens may freely exercise their rights as guaranteed by EU law. This particular situation has practical consequences on the ground in the following

---

[47] See Recital 6 of Council Framework Decision of 13 June 2002 on the European arrest warrant and surrender procedures between Member States, OJ 2002, L 190, p. 1.

[48] Directive 94/80/EC of 19 December 1994.

situation. An EU citizen travels from Turkey to northern Cyprus and then crosses the green line into the government controlled areas. Under Article 12 (1) of the Cypriot Alien's and Immigration law, such entry is illegal as the EU citizen used an "illegal entry point" to arrive to Cyprus. On the other hand, under EU law, the EU citizen enjoys a right to free movement in the Union, including a right to entry into Cyprus, under Article 18 EC and relevant secondary law.[49] Therefore, any restrictions under Cypriot law must pursue a legitimate policy goal and be proportional.[50] Recital 7 of the Green line regulation observes in this regard:

> *While taking into account the legitimate concerns of the Government of the Republic of Cyprus, it is necessary to enable EU citizens to exercise their rights of free movement within the EU and set the minimum rules for carrying out checks on persons at the line (. . .).*

Article 2 of the regulation prescribes identity checks for persons entering into the government controlled areas, but does not foresee checks as regards the previous travel route. On the other hand, the green line regulation does neither outlaw such checks. Rather it sets out "minimum rules". Accordingly, Cyprus may well inquire whether EU citizens actually entered into Cyprus via an entry point of the north. Such checks would follow the legitimate policy goal to exercise some control of international traffic relating to its borders in order to prevent illegal immigration. However, Cypriot regulations that foresee criminal penalties (including imprisonment) for illegal entry into Cyprus would seem to be disproportional.[51] Such offences are clearly of administrative character only. Fortunately, some unpleasant events occurring in late 2003, where several EU citizens were threatened with imprisonment by Cypriot judges, did not continue after May 2004, when Article 18 EC became fully binding on Cyprus. The Nicosia District Court ruled on 20 August 2004 as last instance in this case[52] that a Greek Cypriot travelling via the Ercan airport in the north to Istanbul, and coming back to the south on the same route was *not* guilty of criminal charges, pointing to the free movement principle embodied in the Green line regulation. Moreover, the Cyprus government adopted a Code for the implementation of Regulation 866/2004, stating the EU citizens may cross the line from and to the Government controlled areas "irrespective of their point of entry into the territory of the Republic".

Similarly, Article 18 EC is of direct benefit for EU citizens when they cross the green line from the government-controlled areas into northern Cyprus. Their right to free movement cannot be disproportionately restricted by imposing arbitrary

[49] See Directive 2004/38/EC of the European Parliament and the Council of 29 April 2004 on the right of the citizens to move freely within the territory of the Member States amending (Regulation No. 1612/68 and repealing Directives 64/221/EEC, 68/360/EEC, 72/194/EEC, 73/148/EEC, 75/35/EEC, 90/364/EEC, 90/365/EEC and 93/96/EEC.

[50] See e.g. ECJ, Case C-100/01, Ministry of Interior vs. Olazabal.

[51] Uebe, loc. cit. (page 129, note 82), GYIL 2003, p. 375 (395).

[52] An appeal from the Attorney-General against the judgement was rejected by the Supreme Court of Cyprus on 8 September 2004.

requirements on the length of their stay. For example, it may not serve any legitimate goal of public policy to require a return to the government-controlled areas on the same day or even within some days. Such restrictions, if enforced by administrative or even penal law, would not be compatible with Cyprus' obligation to ensure the free movement of EU citizens, which includes the possibility to decide freely when to enter and re-enter into Cyprus at the recognized posts of entry.

2.5. *Conclusion*

The suspension of the *acquis* for the northern part of Cyprus under Article 1 of Protocol 10 has several legal consequences. Turkish Cypriots living in the north and possessing a passport of the Republic of Cyprus may not exercise EU rights linked to territory, but they still enjoy personal rights under EU law. They may also participate in the elections to the European Parliament provided that they are enrolled in the voter's list of the Republic and cross the green line at electionday. For Greek Cypriots, the suspension of the *acquis* does not mean that they cannot try to enforce civil or criminal law decisions relating to illegal property dealings in the north. However, the authorities in other EU Member States may check whether all conditions for recognition in their own national systems under the civil judgements regulation and the European Arrest warrant framework decision are fulfilled. EU citizens cannot exercise rights stemming from EU law when dealing with the Turkish Cypriot administration in the north. But Article 18 EC protects them when entering into the government controlled via the north against a disproportional application of Cyprus' rules on illegal border crossing.

3. The Green Line Regulation

Under Cypriot law, goods coming from the north into the south circulate in the same country. For the European Union, however, they come from an area outside the customs union, and enter into it only by passing the green line. Under normal circumstances, the EU would therefore apply customs, taxation, phytosanitary rules on those goods as if they were foreign goods. From this perspective, Article 2 of Protocol 10 and the Green line regulation adopted thereunder constitute the legal basis for a preferential regime for Turkish Cypriot products. That situation is comparable to the former Protocol on Inter German Trade,[53] which allowed goods from Eastern Germany to enter into Western Germany without complying with ordinary EU formalities for third country goods. The EU institutions enjoy a broad margin of discretion, which goods may benefit from these preferences. Legally, there is no obligation to keep the green line regulation as it is, or to extend it to other goods.

[53] Bundesgesetzblatt 1957 II, p. 984.

4. Relations with the Turkish Cypriot Community

4.1. *Direct Trade*

Goods circulating from the north to other EU Member State come from outside the EU customs union and have to be cleared upon entry into one Member State, subject to the external customs tariff and other requirements of import. The Community may, however, enact rules to facilitate such trade by granting privileged access. Three legal questions need to be addressed in this context: Which is the correct legal basis for such facilitation in EU law? Would facilitation of direct trade between northern Cyprus and EU Member States be compatible with international law? Or would it at least conflict with the duty of loyalty under EC law (Article 10 EC)?

4.1.1. Legal basis in EC law

The Cypriot government and the Council Legal Service consider Article 1 (2) of Protocol 10 to the Act of Accession to constitute the appropriate legal basis.[54] It reads:

> *The Council, acting unanimously on the basis of a proposal from the Commission, shall decide on the withdrawal of the suspension referred to in paragraph 1.*

The wording of this provision refers to "the withdrawal of the suspension referred to in paragraph 1". Recital No. 4 provides that "in the event of a solution to the Cyprus problem this suspension shall be lifted". Accordingly, Article 1 (2) of Protocol 10 was foremost designed to allow for a *complete* integration of the northern parts of Cyprus into European Law after a comprehensive settlement. Nevertheless, "*a maiore ad minus*", it may be arguable that such empowerment also covers *partial* withdrawal of the suspension,[55] reflecting the political possibility that only partial solutions of certain aspects of the Cyprus problem are found over time.

More decisive is therefore whether the proposed direct trade regulation foresees the "partial withdrawal of the suspension of the *acquis*" for northern Cyprus as regards free circulation of goods. The Commission defined the term *acquis* in its opinion on Cyprus's accession to the EU. *Acquis* comprises the Treaty on European Union and all its objectives, all decisions taken since the entry into force of the Treaties establishing the European Communities and the Treaty on European Union and the options taken in respect of the development and strengthening of those Communities and of the Union.[56] This definition may also serve as proper yardstick for interpreting the same term when used in the Act of Accession.[57]

[54] Palley, loc. cit. (page xii, note 3), p. 250 with further references.

[55] Uebe, loc. cit. (page 129, note 82), p. 375 (386).

[56] COM (2003) 79 final of 19 February 2003, point (9).

[57] Uebe, loc. cit. (page 129, note 82), p. 375 (384).

As regards primary law, the application of articles 28–30 EC is *not* extended to northern Cyprus. First, the regime does not cover all goods, but exempts a substantial part. Second, the covered goods are systematically made subject to tariff quotas, constituting an entry regime like the one in place for other privileged access of third country products. These products are only released for free circulation in the internal market after clearance by the respective EU Member State. That is fundamentally different to free circulation of goods in the EU where such clearance is not necessary. Third, under Article 28–30 EC a strong safeguard provision as the one provided for in Article 7 of the draft regulation would be impossible. Finally, extension of articles 28–30 EC to northern Cyprus would mean that the Republic of Cyprus would responsible for the administration of free circulation, whereas under the proposal that is not the case.

If adopted, the regulation would constitute secondary law. Would not its own application be extended to northern Cyprus, thereby triggering Article 1 (2) of Protocol 10 as the legal basis? Again, the answer must be negative. First, such an understanding would turn Article 1 (2) of Protocol 10 into a *lex specialis* for all measures concerning northern Cyprus. This would effectively abrogate the condition that it shall be used for "withdrawal of the suspension" (only). For example, if this understanding were correct, also the financial aid regulation would constitute *acquis* whose application were to be extended to the north. The Council did not follow such a broad interpretation of Article 1 (2) of Protocol 10 in the relevant discussions on that regulation accepting Article 308 EC as its legal basis. Second, even if the trade regulation were to constitute "*acquis*" within the meaning of that provision, it would not apply "in" northern Cyprus. Rather, the Member States would apply it when dealing with goods from northern Cyprus. In order to take decisions on entry formalities and customs duties, they would rely on certificates drawn up by the Turkish Cypriot Chamber of Commerce (for the proof of origin) and experts appointed by the Commission (for the phytosanitary certificates). For sure, these certificates would have been established in northern Cyprus. But, like relevant certificates drawn up in third countries that certain goods fulfil the conditions laid down in the regulation, such preparatory action for administrative acts of Member States' authorities cannot be equated with "application of the regulation" in northern Cyprus.

For all these reasons, Article 1 (2) of Protocol 10 cannot constitute the legal basis for the direct trade regulation. In such a situation, Article 3 (1) of Protocol 10 refers back to the general provisions of the EC Treaty: "*Nothing in this Protocol shall preclude measures with a view to promoting the economic development of areas referred to in Article 1*". Introducing a special regime for direct trade from northern Cyprus to EU Member States would constitute such a measure. Article 133 EC Treaty provides for the adoption of any sort of trade measures, including unilateral opening (privileged access). The only *caveat* in this regard concerns the special status of the areas: they do not belong to a third country, but to a Member State. At first sight, it may therefore seem odd to base such a regime on a legal basis, which is primarily used to address international trade relations. However, as can be seen from Article 299 EC, there are certain areas in each Member States where the *acquis* does either not apply, or only applies with certain modifications. In EU practice, the relations between other Member States and such special areas, lying outside the customs union, have been regularly dealt with under Article 133 EC. For example, Ceuta, Melilla and Gibraltar are subject to trade rules adopted under Article 133 EC.[58] For Büsingen, Campione d'Italia and Helgoland, the relevant third country rules apply. They are equally based on Article 133 EC. Comparably, Article 133 EC is the correct legal basis to provide for a special direct tade regime for goods originating in the areas not subject to effective control of the Cypriot government.

4.1.2. Compatibility with international law

Moreover, the argument was made that the European Union could not unilaterally establish trade relations with the areas, thereby disregarding the decision of the Cypriot government of 1974 to close all ports outside its control.[59] That would run contrary to the international law principle that only the (lawful) Government may decide which ports are open to international traffic. If closing of the ports could be disregarded, the Government would be exposed to a risk of incurring international liability for acts that it cannot control.

This line of argument may be challenged on several grounds. First, it is doubtful whether the Government of Cyprus would indeed bear responsibility for acts in a northern port/airport under international law. As has been confirmed by the European Court of Human Rights, Turkey exercises effective control over northern Cyprus. Accordingly, acts occurring in ports and airports of northern Cyprus that are contrary to international law obligations (e.g. negligence in port state control) could hardly be imputed to the Government of Cyprus (but to Turkey). Second, it is hard to see, why the establishment of a preferential trade regime with northern Cyprus undermines the sovereign decision of the Cyprus governments to close all ports and airports in the north. The trade regulation does not purport to "open" such ports. Hence, there is no legal conflict with the 1974 decision of the Government to close such ports to international traffic. Third, creating an incentive for Turkish Cypriots to use ports/airports closed by the Government, is not illegal under international law. Otherwise, every State that accepts goods arriving from these ports/airports would bear international responsibility just by operating its customs regime. Such a far-reaching thesis is not supported by any practice: goods arriving from northern Cyprus since 1974 have been accepted by the EU Member States until 1994 under the privileged conditions as laid down in the EC-Cyprus Association Agreement. Nobody ever claimed that such practice was contrary to international law because it would undermine the sovereign decision of

[58] See Council Regulation (EC) No. 2501/2001 applying a scheme of generalised tariff preferences (OJ 2001, L 346) and Council Regulation (EC) No. 1140/2004 of 21 June 2004 suspending the autonomous Common Customs Tariff duties on certain fishery products originating in Ceuta and Melilla (OJ 2004, L 222, p. 1).

[59] Order by the Council of Ministers declaring the ports closed as from 3rd October 1974, communicated to the International Maritime Organization on 12th December 1974 for distribution to its Member States.

the Cypriot government to close the ports in the north. Rather, the European Court of Justice struck down such privileged entry due to the fact that the certificates of origin issued by authorities in the north could not be verified.[60] It did not hold that allowing privileged trade with northern Cyprus would undermine the decision of the Cypriot government to close relevant ports and airports. Finally, the direct aid regulation would not contravene Security Council Resolution 541 (1983), calling upon states not to recognize the TRNC and not to facilitate or in any way assist it. Rather than consolidating the TRNC as such, would direct trade benefit individual Turkish Cypriots. As stressed in the first recital of the draft regulation putting an end to be isolation of the Turkish Cypriot community is deemed to facilitate the unification of Cyprus. Such a measure, which is neither intended nor likely to deepen the division of Cyprus, but creates a new privileged system of entry into the European Union for goods originating from northern Cyprus is compatible with international law.[61]

4.1.3. Duty of loyalty (Article 10 EC)

Finally, it has been argued that fostering trade with northern Cyprus would run counter to the duty of loyalty of the Community to Cyprus as Member State and encroach on its sovereign rights to administer trade relations with other Member States itself.

The second plea is connected with the role of the Turkish Cypriot Chamber of Commerce, a legal entity created in 1959. Can the EU entrust this Chamber with the task of issuing certificates of origin, in a situation where the Republic of Cyprus does not agree? In that regard, it must be recalled that certificates issued by that body are not binding on Member States. Accordingly, the Chamber would not be entrusted with exercising public authority (which could encroach on sovereign rights of Cyprus). It follows from the above that the sovereign right of the Republic of Cyprus to decide which of its organs set "*acta iure imperii*" is not challenged.

The first plea is of a broader political character. For sure, Article 10 EC does not only require Member States to act in loyalty to the Community, but also puts certain obligations on EU institutions vis-à-vis the Member States.[62] However, the Community does not set aside the sovereign decision of Cyprus to close its ports. Rather, it would not follow a Cypriot policy to discourage any international trade via these ports. Article 3 of Protocol 10 (which has been accepted by Cyprus as well by signing the Accession Treaty) explicitely ensures that measures promoting the economic development of northern Cyprus are permitted. It would be odd if implementation of this article would constitute at the same time a breach of loyalty vis-à-vis Cyprus. It has not been demonstrated so far which other "more loyal" means of applying Article 3 Protocol 10 is at the disposal of the EU.

---

[60] ECJ, Anastasiou I, loc. cit. (note 236).

[61] Giegerich (page 139, note 133) loc. cit., p. 253 (263).

[62] See e.g. ECJ, Cases 2/88, ECR 1990, I-3365 (3372); – Zwartveld and others; C-339/00, ECR 2003, I-11757, §71 – Ireland v. Commission.

Consequently, fostering trade with northern Cyprus does neither breach the duty of loyality vis-à-vis Cyprus, incumbent on the Community institutions under Article 10 EC.

4.2. *Financial aid*

4.2.1. Legal basis in EC law

Under Article 3 of Protocol 10, measures to promote the economic development of northern Cyprus shall not be precluded. Accordingly, under general EC law, financial aid may be granted. In parallel to the argument developed as regards Article 133 EC, provisions on external EC policies may constitute the appropriate legal basis for adopting such a financial aid regulation. As regards northern Cyprus, whose economic development may not be equated with a typical developing country, the appropriate legal basis would therefore be Article 181a EC (and not Article 308 EC as proposed by the Commission and acted upon by the Council).

4.2.2. Compatibility with international law

On substance, the financial aid regulation can only be meaningfully implemented with some sort of cooperation between the Commission (via the Agency) and TRNC authorities. Any doubt as to whether that could amount to implied recognition can be erased, since the Community legislator explicitly stated its intention in recital No. 10 not to do so. Accordingly, the financial aid regulation does not contravene Security Council Resolution 541 (1983) on non-recognition of the TRNC. In a similar vain, it does not interfere with property right of Greek Cypriots guaranteed under Article 1 of the First Additional Protocol of the European Convention of Human Rights, since the Commission is put under an obligation to observe the Strasbourg case law when implementing the regulation (Article 7 (1)).

4.3. *Conclusion*

The circulation of goods between northern and southern Cyprus could be regulated on the basis of Article 2 Protocol 10. Although not being obliged to do so, the EU granted preferential entry conditions for Turkish Cypriot goods to the south, which can later be exported to other EU Member States. However, already the actual intra-Cyprus trade volume is rather modest; the Green Line regulation may only seen as indirectly fostering trade between northern Cyprus and the EU. Responding to the call of the Council in April 2004, the Commission proposed two regulations to overcome the economic isolation of the Turkish Cypriot community. Whereas the financial aid regulation did not meet political resistance of Nicosia since the Commission proposed Article 308 EC (triggering unanimity in the Council) and not Article 181a EC (leading to qualified majority voting), the proposal on direct trade under Article 133 EC provoked legal objections from the Cyprus government, supported by the Council Legal Service. However, these objections do not withstand legal scrutiny, since the trade regulation would neither embody partial withdrawal of the *acquis* (for which Article 1 (2) of Protocol

10 would indeed be a *lex specialis*), nor contravene international law or the duty of loyalty under Article 10 EC. Accordingly, the non-adoption of the direct trade regulation in the Council seems to be due more to political resistance than to legal reasoning. In turn, the Council did neither adopt the financial regulation for a long time because of the political "coupling" of the two proposals, which was mainly supported by the United Kingdom government. Although the financial aid regulation could have been adopted on the basis of Article 181a EC (triggering qualified majority rating in the Council) the Council finally reached unanimity which is required under Article 308 EC. Carefully avoiding implied recognition of the TRNC or interference with property rights, the financial aid regulation is compatible with international law.

5. The Sovereign Base Areas of the United Kingdom in Cyprus

The old version of Article 299 (6) (a) EC had exempted the Sovereign Base Areas of the United Kingdom from the realm of EU law. Only vis-à-vis Cyprus did the United Kingdom bear international obligations concluded by virtue of the Treaty of Establishment. Hence, from a legal point of view, the United Kingdom had to adopt an approach how such commitments could be honoured after Cyprus' EU accession in a practical way. In that regard, it was felt that allowing for the partial application of the *acquis* to the SBA's would minimise the need to adopt practical changes on the ground. The correct way to implement this goal was to modify Article 299 (6) EC. Since Accession Treaties bear the force of primary law,[63] this result could be properly achieved by annexing Protocol 3 to the Accession Act.

6. Summary

The EU Member State Cyprus will have to treat the *acquis* as a supreme source of law in its internal legal order. Whereas it took all necessary preparations during the accession negotiations to align its legislation, it did not yet revise Article 169 (3) of its constitution in order to avoid that EU law will be declared to be of lower rank than Cypriot constitutional law. Furthermore, Cyprus is under a duty to implement EU standards on human rights, including on the protection of property. In this regard, the treatment of Turkish Cypriot property to deny reinstatement or compensation to the legal owners, even if they had moved to the south, raises serious concern.

On the other hand, the Cypriot government cannot be held responsible for non-application of the *acquis* in the northern parts, since Article 1 (1) of Protocol 10

[63] See above Chapter VI B 1.

provides for its suspension there. This temporary non-application of the *acquis* to the territories not under the effective control of the Government has the effect that those EU rights and obligations linked to territory cannot be invoked by Turkish Cypriots, Greek Cypriots or EU nationals when dealing with the north. Nevertheless, certain personal rights of Turkish Cypriots (provided that they are nationals of the Republic of Cyprus), the operation of mutual recognition schemes in the EU with regard to property dealings in the north, and the right to free movement of EU citizens into the territory under effective control of the Government are not affected by suspension. Relations with the Turkish Cypriot Community may be further fostered when the EU adopts measures, as requested by the Council conclusions of April 2004 and legally possible under Article 3 of Protocol 10 referring back to the EC Treaty. However, mainly because of political resistance from Nicosia against the direct trade regulation this instruments has not yet been adopted by the Council. On the other hand, London gave up its insistence to link it with the financial aid regulation, so that the latter was finally adopted in February 2006, more than one and a half year after the positive vote of the Turkish Cypriot community on the Annan plan.

Chapter IX

Relations between Cyprus and Turkey

A. THE FACTS

After Cyprus' accession to the European Union, Nicosia needed to position itself vis-à-vis Turkey. The next steps in Turkey's accession course were due and the question how to achieve normalization of the economic relations between Cyprus and Turkey came up.

The initial bone of contention was the smooth implementation of the EU-Turkey customs union. The new Member States, having become part of the EU customs territory, would participate in such union. However, Article 29 of the Ankara Agreement of 1963 had listed the European territory of the individual Member States as "territorial scope" of the Agreement instead of using a dynamic territorial clause. Such a clause would have referred to the territory covered by the EC Treaty, thereby allowing for automatic extension of the Ankara Agreement after each EU enlargment. In the absence of such a dynamic territorial clause, the Ankara agreement had to be adapted to take account of the new Member States in the European Union. Turkey took a first step when it unilaterally extended the territorial scope of the customs union to all new Member States except Cyprus on

Legal Aspects of the Cyprus Problem, pp. 223–232.

12 May 2004.[1] In October 2004, "Cyprus" was included as well,[2] not specifying whether that would cover the Republic of Cyprus. In practice, Turkey upheld restrictions such as the prohibition for ships under Cypriot flag to land in Turkey, in force since 1987.[3]

1. The European Council of Brussels of December 2004

At the European Council meeting of 16/17 December 2004 the Heads of States and Governments of the EU 25 took several decisions on Turkey. Upon the recommendation of the Commission, they concluded that Turkey fulfills the political accession criteria after having enacted another very impressive reform package in summer 2004. Therefore, accession negotiations could start in October 2005. However, this promise was made subject to further conditions. Turkey was expected to bring into force six specific items of legislation, including a liberalised Penal Code, as to make the political reform progress irreversible. The Council also underlined the need for unequivocal commitment to good neighbourly relations (Agean Sea, Armenia). As regards Cyprus, the Council concluded:

> *§ 19: The European Council welcomed Turkey's decision to sign the Protocol regarding the adaptation of the Ankara agreement, taking account of the accession of the ten new Member States. In this light, it welcomed the declaration of Turkey that "the Turkish Government confirms that it is ready to sign the Protocol on the adaptation of the Ankara protocol prior to the actual start of the accession negotiations and after reaching agreement on and finalising the adaptations which are necessary in view of the current membership of the European Union".*

The Government of Cyprus declared "that it consents to the commencement of accession negotiations with Turkey on the clear understanding that the Protocol referred to in paragraph 19 of the Conclusions of the Presidency of 17 December 2004 will have been signed into force and implemented by 3 October 2005".

2. The signature of the Protocol to the Ankara agreement

On 18 May 2005, the European Commission presented to the Council the text of the protocol on the adaptation of the Ankara Agreement, together with a proposal

[1] Decision amending the Decision concerning the principles of implementation of the customs union established between Turkey and the European Union, 12 May 2005, Official Gazette Nr. 25460.

[2] Decision amending the Decision concerning the principles of implementation of the customs union established between Turkey and the European Union, 2 October 2005, Official Gazette Nr. 25601. The relevant list includes "Kibris" (Cyprus).

[3] A. Akçakoca, Cyprus – Looking to a Future Beyond the Past, p. 18.

for signature and conclusion.[4] The 25 Member States (including Cyprus) and the European Community, of the one part, and the Republic of Turkey, of the other part, agree that the ten new Member States become a party to the Ankara Agreement (Article 1 para. 1). The protocol also provides that the Association Agreement applies to the territory where the EC Treaty applies, in accordance with the conditions set out in the EC treaty and to the territory of the Republic of Turkey (Article 1 para. 3). Furthermore, the protocol adapts some technical provision on the rules of origin and other administrative issues pertaining to the functioning of the EU-Turkey customs union.

2.1. *The Turkish declaration of 29 July 2005*

Roughly two months later, after intensive discussions, a representative of the EU Presidency and a representative of the Turkish government signed the Protocol. On that occasion of 29 July 2005, the Turkish government made the following declaration:

1. *Turkey remains committed to finding a political settlement of the Cyprus issue and has clearly demonstrated its resolve in this regard. Accordingly, Turkey will continue to support the efforts of the UN Secretary-General towards achieving a comprehensive settlement, which will lead to the establishment of a new bi-zonal partnership state. A just and lasting settlement would greatly contribute to peace, stability and harmonious relations in the region.*
2. *The Republic of Cyprus referred to in the Protocol is not the original partnership state established in 1960.*
3. *Turkey will thus continue to regard the Greek Cypriot authorities as exercising authority, control and jurisdiction only in the territory south of the buffer zone, as is currently the case, and as not representing the Turkish Cypriot people and will treat the acts performed by them accordingly.*
4. *Turkey declares that signature, ratification, and implementation of this Protocol neither amount to any form of recognition of the Republic of Cyprus referred to in the Protocol nor prejudice Turkey's rights and obligations emanating from the Treaty of Guarantee, the Treaty of Alliance and the Treaty of Establishment of 1960.*
5. *Turkey reaffirms that its existing relationship with the Turkish Republic of Northern Cyprus remains unchanged by becoming a party to this Protocol.*
6. *Pending a comprehensive settlement, the position of Turkey on Cyprus will remain unchanged. Turkey expresses its readiness to establish relations with the new partnership State which will emerge following a comprehensive settlement in Cyprus.*

2.2. *The EU Counter-Declaration of 21 September 2005*

In their initial reactions, both the British Government as EU Presidency and Enlargement Commissioner Rehn welcomed the Turkish signature to the Protocol. In early August, the French Prime Minister de Villepin publicly raised concern

[4] COM (2005), 191 final. Council doc. 9042/05 of 18 May 2005.

whether Turkey could start accession negotiations without having formally recognized the Republic of Cyprus.[5] In early September, the United Kindgom and France agreed between themselves that the EU should call upon Turkey to recognise Cyprus "as soon as possible". During intensive discussions between all EU Member States, the Cyprus Government favoured stronger wording on early recognition. With the support of Greece it also tried to delink this question with eventual renewed UN efforts for a comprehensive settlement. For the UK Presidency and several other Member States such mentioning of the UN as the appropriate forum for settlement negotiations was, however, indispensable. Having recourse to an Opinion of the Council's Legal Service, the elements of "counter-declaration" were finalised on 21 September 2005. It reads as follows:

1. *The European Community and its Member States acknowledge the signature by Turkey of the Additional Protocol to the Agreement establishing an Association between the European Community and its Member States on the one part and Turkey on the other, in accordance with the conclusions of the European Council of December 2004. They regret that Turkey felt it necessary to make a declaration regarding the Republic of Cyprus at the time of signature.*
2. *The European Community and its Member States make clear that this declaration by Turkey is unilateral, does not form part of the Protocol and has no legal effect on Turkey's obligations under the Protocol.*
3. *The European Community and its Member States expect full, non-discriminatory implementation of the Additional Protocol, and the removal of all obstacles to the free movement of goods, including restrictions on means of transport. Turkey must apply the Protocol fully to all EU Member States. The EU will monitor this closely and evaluate full implementation in 2006. The European Community and its Member States stress that the opening of negotiations on the relevant chapters depends on Turkey's implementation of its contractual obligations to all Member States. Failure to implement its obligations in full will affect the overall progress in the negotiation.*
4. *The European Community and its Member States recall that the Republic of Cyprus became a Member State of the European Union on 1st May 2004. They underline that they recognise only the Republic of Cyprus as a subject of international law.*
5. *Recognition of all Member States is a necessary component of the accession process. Accordingly, the EU underlines the importance it attaches to the normalisation between Turkey and all EU Member States, as soon as possible.*
6. *The Council will ensure a follow-up on the progress made on all these issues in 2006.*
7. *In the context of this declaration, the European Community and its Member States agree on the importance of supporting the efforts of the UN Secretary-General to bring about a comprehensive settlement of the Cyprus problem in line with relevant UN Security Council resolutions and the principles on which the EU is founded, and that a just and lasting settlement will contribute to peace, stability and harmonious relations in the region.*

[5] On the French position, primarily inspired by reasons of domestic French policy, see H. Kramer, Türkei-Verhandlungen als Spielball der Interessen, p. 1 (4–5).

On 28 September 2005, the European Parliament decided to delay its vote on the protocol, showing its dissatisfaction with the Turkish declaration of 29 July 2005.

3. Start of Turkey's EU accession negotiations on 3 October 2005

Together with the draft protocol to amend the EU-Turkey Customs Union the Commission also proposed to the Council the negotiating framework how to conduct accession negotiations. The proposal followed closely the text of the 2004 Brussels European Council. In particular, it emphasized that the opening and closing of negotiations on each chapter of the acquis depends on actual progress. Member States decide unanimously. Furthermore, accession negotiations as whole could be suspended by a decision taken with qualified majority in the Council in cases of serious and persistent breaches of the principles on which the EU is founded.

The framework document was acceptable to all Member States but Austria. At the meeting of the Foreign Ministers in Luxemburg on 2/3 October 2005, the Austrian Foreign Minister Plassnik insisted to add a formulation according to which the common aim of the negotiations should include other possible statuses than full membership for Turkey. Later, Austria presented the view that the absorption capacity of the European Union should be mentioned in the document more prominently. Furthermore, Cyprus requested that Turkey should give up its resistance against Cypriot membership in some international organizations. That led to a debate whether the negotiating framework could have a possible bearing on NATO membership (where Turkey is a member, but Cyprus not). An intervention from the American Secretary of State, Rice, reassured Turkey and some EU Member States that it remained up to NATO countries to decide unanimously about NATO's membership. Against that background, § 5 of the negotiating framework contained a paranthesis that Turkey "will be required to progressively align its policies towards third countries and its positions within international organisations *(including in relation to the membership by all EU Member states of those organisations)* with the policies and positions adopted by the Union and its Member Sates".

After last minute contacts between the British Foreign Minister Straw and the Turkish Prime Minister Erdogan, these compromise formulas were agreed on 3 October in Luxemburg. The British Presidency formally opened the negotiations, followed by statements of Commissioner Rehn and the Turkish Foreign Minister Gül. Mr. Straw recalled the EU's acknowledgment of the Turkish signature of the Protocol regarding the adaptation of the Ankara Agreement and the EU's declaration of 21 September 2005. Mr. Rehn repeated that Turkey should implement fully its commitments under the Association Agreement and the customs union.

B. LEGAL EVALUATION

What were the expectations from Turkey by the European Council in December 2004? What is the significance of the EU counter-declaration of September 2005? These two issues must be distinguished for the legal analysis.

1. The duty to implement the customs union vis-à-vis Cyprus

1.1. *The significance of the December 2004 conclusions of the European Council*

The European Council, in § 19 of the Presidency conclusions of December 2004 expected Turkey to "sign" the enlargement Protocol to the Ankara agreement. As the 25 Member States were aware that Cyprus and Turkey would have to be a party to this agreement, the question comes up whether the Council asked for recognition of the Republic of Cyprus by Turkey.

Under general international law, recognition may be expressed formally by way of declaration or in the form of unilateral acts or conduct. On the one hand, no recognition is implied by conclusion of a multilateral treaty to which the unrecognized entity is also party.[6] On the other hand, the conclusion of a bilateral treaty may be seen as implied recognition of the other side since the governments concerned were at full liberty to enter into treaty relations or not. However, even in a bilateral context, concluding a treaty does not imply recognition if and insofar a State makes an opposite declaration. Then, treaty relations are established, but these do not amount to implied recognition.[7]

The European Union did not take an unequivocal position on the issue in December 2004. The enlargement protocol is to be concluded between the 25 Member States and the EC "of the one part" and Turkey "of the other part". As a "mixed agreement" it is treated like a bilateral agreement. Accordingly, the Council conclusions could be read as if the EU asked Turkey for implied recognition of Cyprus by signing this protocol. However, the Council did not say expressly so. It did neither rule out that the any opposing declarations could be be made.

Furthermore, the Council conclusions are also ambiguous in another matter: they asked Turkey to "sign" the Ankara protocol. Under the Vienna Convention, this term may have two meanings. It may denote an expression by a State to be bound by a treaty (Article 11, 12 of the Vienna Convention). It may also refer to

[6] I. Brownlie, Principles of International Law, p. 93.

[7] Brownlie, loc. cit. (note 6), pp. 89 and 91, emphasizing the intent of a government in the context of all relevant factors and rules of law must be scrutinized.

an act by government, according to which consent to be bound may only be expressed at a later stage, namely after internal ratification or approval (Article 14 of the Vienna Convention). Against this background, the understanding of the Cyprus government that it expects the agreement to be "signed into force" clearly refers to the first alternative. However, this declaration constitutes a unilateral understanding of one member of the Council only. It does not reflect the consensus at the table. Accordingly, the EU did not seem to ask Turkey to declare its will to be bound by the agreement prior to the start of accession negotiations; rather it asked for the signature of the Protocol to the Ankara Agreement as a preparatory act in treaty-making. This understanding is confirmed by the EU's declaration of 21 September 2005, whereby it acknowledged Turkey's signature to the Protocol. As the Council did not regret that Turkey did not yet complete its internal (ratification) procedures to express its consent to be bound, it made again clear that it had asked for signature (only) of that protocol prior to 3 October 2005.

Finally, one must ascertain what scope such recognition would have. In this regard, it must be kept in mind that signature of the protocol to the Ankara agreement shall ensure the proper application of the customs union between the EU and Turkey. After signature of the enlargement protocol Turkey is under an obligation not to defeat the object and purpose of that agreement pending its entry into force (Article 18 of the Vienna Convention). In particular, it may not take measures that impede the functioning of the customs union between Cyprus and Turkey. Article 1 (3) of the enlargement protocol makes clear that the customs union applies only to the territories of the Member States where EC law applies. This includes a reference to Article 1 Protocol 10 of the Accession Act. Hence, the Ankara agreement itself is suspended in northern Cyprus. Accordingly, Turkey is under an obligation to ensure the proper functioning of the customs union vis-à-vis the territory that is under the effective control of the Cyprus government. In particular, it may not close its ports to ships under the Cypriot flag, refuse documents originating from the Cyprus government or introduce physical barriers for free trade under Articles 5 and 6 of Decision 1/95.[8] § 3 of the EU's counter-declaration of 21 September 2005 focused exactly on that point, when it called upon Turkey to remove all obstacles to the free movement of goods, including on means of transport.

On the other hand, the December 2004 conclusions do not contain an obligation for Turkey to recognize that the Government of Cyprus is entitled to govern over the northern parts of Cyprus. Such recognition is not necessary to ensure the proper application of the customs union between Turkey and the parts of the European Union covered by the *acquis*.

---

[8] The ECJ already decided in relation to the corresponding Articles 28 and 29 EC that physical barriers to the free circulation of goods are incompatible with European law. See e.g. ECJ, Case C-112/00, ECR 2000 I-5659 para. 51 – Schmidberger.

1.2. *The Turkish declaration of 29 July 2005*

Against this yardstick, it must be assessed whether the Turkish declaration of 29 July met the expectations from the European Council of December 2004.

§§ 1 and 6 refer to the UN process. The declared will to support the efforts of the UN Secretary-General is in line with the long-standing EU policy, as laid down in the Accession Partnerships. That Turkey thrives for the "establishment of a new bi-zonal partnership State" reflects its long-standing policy and carries no legal significance for the operation of the EU-Turkey customs union.

§ 2, according to which the Republic of Cyprus referred to in the Protocol "is not the original partnership state established in 1960", deserves more attention. Two readings appear possible. If, on the one hand, it were to mean that – in the view of Turkey – the Republic of Cyprus does not enjoy statehood under international law, then this would be a contradiction in terms. A contracting party to the enlargement Protocol must have legal capacity to enter into international obligations. Every state fulfills this criterion (Article 4 of the Vienna Convention). Accordingly, Turkey cannot sign the agreement with the Republic of Cyprus and at the same time contend that it is not a state. On the other hand, the phrase denies that the Republic is "*the original partnerhip*" state. That could also be read as a reference to constitutional law, namely that the Republic of Cyprus exists as a state, but is constitutionally different from 1960 because it lost its characteristics as partnership. In that reading, § 2 does not question the statehood of the Republic of Cyprus, but points to the Turkish view that the current Cyprus government is different from the one foreseen under the 1960 constitution.

Under § 3 the latter view seems to be confirmed. Turkey recognises that "Greek Cypriot authorities are "exercising authority, control and jurisdiction (only) in the territory south of the buffer zone". Accordingly, Turkey deals with the Republic of Cyprus as a state, governed by a Greek Cypriot government with a restricted territorial reach to the south. In contrast, Turkey does not accept that this State may govern the Turkish Cypriots in the north. Insofar it clarifies that its signature, ratification and implementation of the Protocol does not amount to recognition of the Republic of Cyprus with a territorial reach over the whole island (§ 4). It follows therefrom that Turkey still regards the TRNC as endowed with statehood to which it continues to deal with on this basis (§ 5).

These three paragraphs do not coincide with the European view, according to which there is only one State in Cyprus, namely the Republic of Cyprus whose *de jure* jurisdiction over the whole of the island is only *de facto* restricted to the south. However, as demonstrated above, the European Council did not expect from Turkey to take over this legal view, but to implement the EU-Turkey customs union properly. For this purpose, §§ 3–5 do not harm provided that the phrase in § 3 that Turkey "*will treat the acts performed by them* (i.e. the Cyprus government) *accordingly*" is not meant to keep the *status quo* of not accepting Cypriot ships in Turkish ports, denying legal value to certificate issued by Cypriot authorities. Such meaning would defeat the object and purpose of the Turkish signature to the enlargement protocol. However, that phrase is used in the context of defining the relationship between the Cyprus government and the Turkish Cypriots. Hence, the phrase does not question the proper implementation of EU-Turkey customs since northern Cyprus is not included in the operation of it under Article 1 of Protocol 10.

2. The duty to recognize the Republic of Cyprus during the accession negotiations

A legally different matter from implementing the customs union vis-à-vis the enlarged EU is the conduct of accession negations. Under Article 49 (2) EU, these are held by an Intergovernmental Conference between all 25 Member States on the one hand, and Turkey on the other hand. At the end of such conference, an Accession Treaty with Turkish accession conditions will be signed. Full membership in the European Union will necessarily require full recognition of all EU Member States including the Republic of Cyprus.

The question is therefore pertinent whether such full recognition is a necessary prerequisite for opening the accession negotiations, or whether such recognition is only due at the very end of the Intergovernmental Conference. From a strictly legal point of, Article 49 (2) EU does not offer any guidance in this respect. It rather leaves it to the political discretion of Member States at what stage in time, full recognition of all Member States by a candidate country is expected.

Against this background, § 5 of the EU's counter-declaration of 21 September 2005 can be understood. The EU reiterated first the legal situation that recognition of all Member States is a necessary component of the accession process. As regards timing it called for a normalisation between Turkey and all EU Member States "as soon as possible". This diplomatic phrase is itself open to interpretation and leaves enough flexibility for the EU negotiators to assess a potential progress towards finding a comprehensive settlement under UN auspices. Nevertheless, it may also be seen as strengthening Cyprus' position in UN talks. A possible full recognition of the Republic of Cyprus prior to a Cyprus settlement may exclude any settlement on the basis of the "virgin birth" concept, but lead to fully-fledged continuity from the Republic of Cyprus to any Cypriot entity arising out of a future settlement.

3. Summary

The European Council of December 2004 asked Turkey to sign the enlargement protocol to the Association Agreement. For the smooth operation of the EU-Turkey customs union, Turkey was required to recognize that those parts where the *acquis* applies in the Republic of Cyprus form part of that union, leading, *inter alia*, to the removal of certain restrictions for ships sailing under the Cypriot flag to Turkish ports. Turkey was, however, not required to recognize that the Republic of Cyprus legally governs the entire island. Although not free from political ambiguities, the Turkish declaration of 29 July 2005 conforms to these expectations. Nevertheless, it provoked a counter-declaration from the EU, in which the latter set out a new element. In view of the opening of the accession negotiations in an Intergovernmental Conference Turkey was now asked to recognize the Republic of Cyprus (including its claim to legally govern the whole island) "as soon as possible" in the accession process.

Chapter X
Conclusion

In the introduction, two different types of questions had been raised. From an international relations perspective, it is important to know why Cyprus could accede to the European Union without a prior settlement. Equally important is to understand how the United Nations and the European Union coordinated their efforts to bring about a comprehensive Cyprus settlement. As a foremost legal study, I concentrated, however, on the related questions about the significance of international law and European law when international actors dealt with the Cyprus problem. Dwelling on the factual accounts for the first set of questions, and on the analytical exercise for the second one, I therefore wish to present as an overall conclusion some responses to these two complexes.

A. EU-UN RELATIONS AND CYPRUS' EU ACCESSION WITHOUT A PRIOR SETTLEMENT

Upon the Cypriot application for membership in 1990, the EU opted not to take a formal role to broker a comprehensive settlement prior to eventual accession. It took account of the fact that the UN had developed over time a substantial corpus of formula describing the political framework for a settlement.[1] The EU also

[1] See above Chapter IV, B 2.

Legal Aspects of the Cyprus Problem, pp. 233–240.

preferred not to interfere with the ongoing mediation of UN Secretary-General Boutros-Ghali, culminating in his Set of Ideas of 1992. From 1990 to 1995, the EU therefore remained in a waiting mode.[2]

In 1997, the EU started the accession negotiations in the same way as with other candidate countries, thereby giving priority to ensure harmonisation of Cyprus' legal order with the *acquis communautaire*. This role naturally led to close contacts between the Commission and the Cyprus government only, whereas political initiatives as regards the political problem were not warranted. Upon European pressure Clerides invited the Turkish Cypriots to participate in the accession negotiations. This offer was rejected by Denktaş *sr.*

With the Helsinki Council conclusions of 1999 the EU assigned to itself a more active stance. The Council's proclamation to take into account all relevant factors when deciding about Cyprus' membership also meant to build up capacity for a fair assessment of the efforts of all sides to solve the political problem. The Council was also aware that the whole accession process could face obstacles in Athens, if Cyprus were not dealt on an equal basis with other candidate countries and excluded from EU membership in the event of a continuing uncompromising stance of the Turkish Cypriot leadership backed by Ankara.

Accordingly, since the start of the proximity talks in 1999 the EU supported the good offices missions of the UN-Secretary General, knowing that Turkey would place more trust in the UN than in the EU with Greece being a Member State. UN priority was also in the interest of the British and the American governments, which, as permanent members of the UN Security Council and through their special envoys could exercise direct influence on the Secretary-General's Special Advisor. The European Union did not confine its support to periodical verbal proclamations by the Heads of States and Governments only, meeting as European Council four times a year. Rather, the Member States gave Enlargement Commissioner Verheugen a free hand to actively coordinate Cyprus policy with the United Nations. The Chief Negotiator on Cyprus, Maurer, established contacts with the UN Special Advisor on Cyprus, de Soto, by regular presence during the UN proximity talks (1999–2000). He prepared the ground for an exchange of view between the Commissioner and de Soto on questions of substance, including legal matters. Such coordination led to the famous Council conclusions of June 2002, according to which the EU was ready to accomodate a settlement in line with the principles on which the EU is founded. Furthermore, the European Commission could make its views known to the UN team when preparing the first drafts of the Annan plan.[3]

The first procedural climax occurred at the European Council of Copenhagen in December 2002. The UN Secretary-General opted to present the first two versions of his plan prior to that meeting. It was felt that in Copenhagen the political

[2] See above Chapter V, A 2.

[3] See above Chapater VI, A 2 and 3.

pressure on both sides would be at its peak. The Greek Cypriots could endanger their successful EU accession negotiations when showing a rejectionist attitude and Turkey could have seized the chance to improve substantially its own aspirations in that regard. However, the orchestration of EU/UN efforts stuck in the face of the immovable position of Denktaş and the Turkish establishment. Even under the newly elected Prime Minister Erdoğan Ankara allowed a second chance to slip away when Annan presented the third version of his plan in The Hague in March 2003.[4]

After signature of the EU accession treaty in April 2003, the Greek Cypriot side under the newly elected President Papadopoulos affirmed its readiness to negotiate on the basis of the UN plan. Responding to a policy change in Turkey, the UN again took advantage of the EU calendar. With the assistance of EU Member States and the United States, Annan brought about final negotiations between the parties just before that date. The European Commission continued its policy not to ask for a formal role in this process, while providing de Soto with technical support. In an unprecedented move, Commissioner Verheugen seconded a substantial number of Commission officials to the UN offices in Nicosia, advising the UN team on matters of the *acquis communautaire* related to the constitution, federal laws and international agreements as well as to the economic viability of the plan. In response, de Soto invited Verheugen to be present in the Bürgenstock diplomatic conference end of March 2004, negotiating especially with Turkey on crucial EU issues. Thanks to his personal involvement, the transitional period for restrictions on the acquisition of property in northern Cyprus could be lowered to 15 years. He also gave reassurances to Turkey to bring about legal security as regards accommodation of the settlement in the EU legal order. These two moves removed a potential stumbling block where the EU dimension could have endangered the Annan plan.[5]

Overseeing the process of EU-UN cooperation on the Cyprus issue, it may thus be concluded that the relations between the two organizations were working very well. The EU deferred to the technical expertise and the reputation of the UN; the UN took advantage of the political pressures and calendars that Cyprus' EU accession course offered. In crucial questions of substance, a common understanding was developed. Even though the concerted UN/EU efforts did not bring about acceptance of the Annan plan by the two communities, the Cyprus experience may well be recorded positively in the annuaries of the two organizations. Or, as Kofi Annan put it in his good offices mission report:

> *I wish to thank the European Union, including the European Commission, for the truly exemplary assistance and support it provided, in what was a model of European Union/United Nations cooperation.*[6]

---

[4] See above Chapter VI, A 4.

[5] See above Chapter VII, A 2 and 3.

[6] Report of the UN-Secretary-General of 28 May 2004, loc. cit. (note 638), § 94.

This calendar of events also explains why the Republic of Cyprus was able to accede to the European Union without a prior settlement. The decision of the 1999 Helsinki European Council employed a policy of carrot and sticks in particular vis-à-vis the Greek Cypriots. The formula worked well, as the flexibility of the Greek Cypriot side under Clerides in the proximity talks 1999–2000 and the direct talks on the island in 2002 was greater than ever before. However, movement on the Turkish side towards a settlement was, if at all, far more limited at the time when Eçevit and Denktaş were still in power in Ankara and northern Nicosia. After the signature of the Accession Treaty in April 2003 and the election of Papadopoulos as Cyprus President the roles slowly changed. Now, the Turkish government under Prime Minister Erdoğan and the newly elected Turkish Cypriot Prime Minister Talat were signalling there intention to subscribe to a Cyprus settlement, whereas the Greek Cypriot side was trying to secure far better terms in the Annan plan, knowing that EU accession was not to be altered even in the event of a Greek Cypriot rejection of the plan. In short: if in the process leading up to Annan III in 2003 the Turkish and Turkish Cypriot side had been more forthcoming, or if in 2004 the Greek Cypriot leadership had supported Annan V, the situation on the island would most probably differ today.

B. THE SIGNIFICANCE OF INTERNATIONAL LAW AND EUROPEAN LAW IN THE CYPRUS PROBLEM

The Cyprus problem raised an unusual variety of legal questions, relating to international, European and constitutional law for Cyprus' accession to the EU. Both sides usually presented their respective positions with a legal undertone. As demonstrated throughout this study, assessing the merits of these positions sometimes necessitates a deep look into past events as well as detailed knowledge of the body of applicable law and international practice. My results are, in a nutshell, as follows.

In 1959, the people of Cyprus, comprising of two communities, exercised self-determination by accepting the London/Zurich agreements. The 1960 Cyprus Treaties and constitution created a Republic where power was shared between the Greek Cypriot community and the Turkish Cypriot community. Both were constitutionally recognised as distinct legal entities.[7] An international right to separate self-determination of either Greek Cypriots or Turkish Cypriot did, however, not exist.

The political and military confrontation of 1963/1964 led to a breakdown and a partially unconstitutional hellenisation of the Republic. Although the Greek Cypriot leadership bears some responsibility for the criminal attacks against Turkish Cypriot civilians, the orchestrated absence of Turkish Cypriots from their offices in the executive and parliament was a terrible mistake from their side. It

[7] See above Chapter I, B 3.

allowed the Makarios government to represent the Republic (which continued to exist as a subject of international law) internationally and to apply the doctrine of necessity internally. Starting with UN Security Council Resolution 186 of 1964, the international community treated any Cyprus government only consisting of Greek Cypriots as legitimate. Accordingly, the EU, from 1990 onwards, correctly rejected any objection from the Turkish Cypriot side that the application for EU membership of Cyprus with effect for the whole island was not presented by a legitimate government.[8]

The coup d'Etat of 1974 inspired by Greece was a clear breach of the Treaty of Guarantee by virtue of which the three powers had promised to safeguard the independence and bi-communal system of Cyprus. The removal of President Makarios by Greek officers in the National Guard triggered the Turkish military intervention and its continued presence in northern Cyprus. Against the view of many authors, Article IV (2) of the 1960 Treaty of Guarantee allows for the employment of military force by a Guarantor power. *Ius cogens* or Article 103 of the UN-Charter do not override this provision, since it contains the ex-ante invitation of the Cypriot government for the Guarantor powers to intervene under sufficiently precise conditions. Therefore, the first phase of the intervention was justified. However, the second phase was not because the Turkish forces did not re-establish the *status quo ante*, but took northern Cyprus with a view of exercising territorial control there for the benefit of Turkey and the Turkish Cypriots. That purpose is at odds with the Treaty, which explicitly prohibits acts aimed at partition.[9] Legally, the Turkish presence did neither destroy the sovereignty of the Republic of Cyprus nor individual property rights of Greek Cypriot displaced persons. In the same vain, the Turkish Cypriot efforts to legalize the *de facto situation* since 1974 by founding the TRNC in 1983, describing this move as an act of self-determination, must fail. With the exception of Turkey, there is near unanimity in international theory and practice that the Turkish Cypriots are not entitled under international law to claim secession. Nor can the TRNC be regarded as an effective state because it is lacking independence from Turkey. Nevertheless, some legal acts issued from TRNC authorities are valid, if and insofar they are benefitting the population.[10]

Against the background of the 1974 events, the European Union was politically not very impressed by a Turkish attempt to stop Cyprus' accession by quoting the very same Treaty of Guarantee, which had been so bluntly violated by both Greece and Turkey in 1974. But also from a legal view there was no doubt that accession to the European Union (an international organization comprising of many states) is not outlawed by Article I (2) of that Treaty prohibiting *enosis* in the disguised formulation of "union with any other State whatsoever".[11]

Whereas all these international law analyses refer to past events shaping the status and practical dealings of the EU with the two sides after 1990, new questions

---

[8] See above Chapter V, B 2 and Chapter II, B 2.

[9] See above Chapter III, B 1.

[10] See above Chapter III, B 3.

[11] See above Chapter V, B 1.

of foremost European law came up in the elaboration of the Annan plan in 2002–2004. With the Seville formula of June 2002 the European Council officialised the relevant legal yardstick. As the Treaty of Accession could incorporate deviations from the *acquis*, the EU promised to accommodate the settlement. At the same time, the settlement should respect the principles on which the EU is founded and ensure Cyprus' ability to speak with one voice and to implement the *acquis communautaire*. Working on these criteria, Annan III put forward a governmental system based on democracy and the rule of law. Several restrictions to human rights and fundamental EU freedoms were found acceptable for reasons of public policy, namely to allow for transitional periods in the implementation of the settlement and to safeguard bi-zonality. Although not expressly laid down in Annan III, the sanctioning powers of the European Union under Article 7 EU would have superseded the rights of the Guarantor powers to intervene in Cyprus in cases of serious and persistent breaches of the founding EU principles.[12] Annan III further foresaw dealings of Cyprus with EU institutions along the lines of the Belgian model. That meant close coordination of the two communities in the decision-making on issues with importance for the federal and federated level, but designating one representative to express the previously agreed Cypriot position.[13] The third version of the Annan plan also distributed state powers between the federal level and the federated states following relevant suggestions rooted in European law and comparative constitutional law of federal States in Europe. Moreover, the plan provided for a federal default power in cases when the constituent states do not implement EU law and a special role for the Supreme Court in cases of a deadlock at the federal level. Together with a clause of supremacy of EU law over national constitutional law, Annan III would have enabled the proper implementation of EU law in the envisaged United Cyprus Republic.[14] Finally, Annan III established the United Cyprus Republic with a single international personality. It combined elements of state continuity and succession, labelled as "virgin birth" approach, falling short of *ex post* recognition of the TRNC. The plan was therefore also consistent with all relevant UN Security Council resolutions.[15]

In the negotiations on Annan IV and V, these basic features of the plan were not altered.[16] Any Greek Cypriot legal contention that Annan V does not comply with principles of EU law or were inconsistent with relevant UN Security Council resolutions is therefore not convincing. Rather, the Bürgenstock negotiations needed to focus on the different question of how to ensure accommodation of the settlement in the EU order in a situation where the Accession Treaty was already signed. In that situation, the European Commission favoured the flexible approach to enact an Act of Adaptation under Article 4 of Protocol 10. However, since the

[12] See above Chapter VI, B 2.
[13] See above Chapter VI, B 3.
[14] See above Chapter VI, B 4.
[15] See above Chapter VI, B 5.
[16] See above Chapter VII, B 2.

Turkish side did not believe that such act would indeed produce the legal security it sought, Commissioner Verheugen agreed to bring the matter to the attention of the European Council with a view of adopting another Protocol (with the undoubtable force of primary law) in due time.[17]

Since May 2004, EU membership of the Republic of Cyprus created another series of legal controversies. The hitherto unsettled question of the relationship between EU law and Cypriot constitutional law[18] has come up already within 2005, when the Supreme Court faced the conflict between the prohibition to extradite Cypriot citizens and the requirements of the EU arrest warrant. Issues related to the suspension of the *acquis* for the northern parts became practical in many instances. It has been shown that a difference must be made as regards to EU rights and obligations related to territory and personal rights.[19] The isolation of the Turkish Cypriot community has not yet been overcome, since the relevant proposals from the European Commission on financial aid and direct trade are still pending before the Council. However, it is hard to see why direct trade with northern Cyprus would amount to a partial application of the *acquis* in the north or violate the decision of the Cyprus government to close the ports there.[20] Hence, again, legal arguments seem to be put forward to justify an essentially political position. Finally, the "recognition battle" between Cyprus and Turkey prior to the beginning of the Turkish accession negotiations in October 2005 may serve as another demonstration how legal arguments are overstretched. Under the EU-Turkey customs union, Turkey is required to deal with the Republic of Cyprus as EU Member State where the *acquis* only applies to the areas under the effective control of the government. There is no requirement to accept – for the time being – that the Republic of Cyprus exercises legal jurisdiction over the north.[21] Nevertheless, as a matter of policy, the European Council expects from Turkey to recognize the Republic of Cyprus during its accession course, since full recognition must be brought about at the date when Turkey's accession eventually will take place.

C. CLOSING REMARK

The Cyprus problem is unique. In view of the failure of the concerted EU/UN effort, will Cyprus continue to be a "diplomat's grave" – and if I may add – an "international and European lawyer's goldmine"?[22]

---

[17] See above Chaptert VII, B 1.
[18] See above Chapter VIII, B 1.
[19] See above Chapter VIII, B 2.
[20] See above Chapter VIII, B 3.
[21] See above Chapter VIII, B 4.
[22] I cannot count how many legal opinions by reknowned international lawyers, commissioned by both sides, I have read for the preparation of this book. Their number seems to outnumber by far legal opinions on other international conflicts.

In this study, it was demonstrated that international law and European law provided for the *framework parameters* of a Cyprus settlement, in which political negotiations involving give-and-take may occur. On the one hand, I am deeply convinced that the Annan plan in all its versions respected these outer limits for any settlement proposal. On the other hand, I refrained from assessing the political balance of the Annan plan or from commenting politically on the negotiation positions of the actors involved.

Hence, one lesson from this book may be not to overestimate any legal reasoning stemming from both sides. In a not unsubstantial number of cases it could be shown that the references to international or European law standards merely served to cover a political position that would otherwise be open to negotiation. In other words: the potential for successful negotiations on the Cyprus problem is significantly increased when both sides are urged to express their political will openly, rather than to hide behind legal formulas, historical excursions or allegedly binding standards.

The elements of compromise are on the table. The start of Turkey's EU accession negotiations on the 3rd of October 2005 may well offer opportunities for a renewed UN initiative to assist the Cypriot parties in their search for a comprehensive settlement on the basis of the Annan plan. The European Union's willingness to accommodate a comprehensive settlement is still valid. Article 4 of Protocol 10 to the Accession Act reflects this continuing political promise legally. When the time will be ripe, Cypriots may hopefully solve the Cyprus problem by political means, turning most of the legal aspects dealt with in this book to history as well.

Appendices

Appendix 1

Protocol 10 to the Act of Accession[1]

Protocol 10 on Cyprus

"The High Contracting Parties,

reafirming their commitment to a comprehensive settlement of the Cyprus problem, consistent with relevant United Nations Security Council Resolutions, and their strong support for the efforts of the United Nations Secretary General to that end,

considering that such comprehensive settlement to the Cyprus problem has not yet been reached,

considering that it is, therefore, necessary to provided for the suspension of the application of the *acquis* in those areas of the Republic of Cyprus in which the Government of Cyprus does not exercise effective control,

considering that, in the event of a solution to the Cyprus problem this suspension shall be lifted,

considering that the European Union is ready to accommodate the terms of such a settlement in line with the principles on which the EU is founded,

[1] OJ 2003, L 236, p. 33, 955.

Legal Aspects of the Cyprus Problem, pp. 241–273.

considering that it is necessary to provide for the terms under which the relevant provisions of EU law will apply to the line between the abovementioned areas and both those areas in which the Government of the Republic of Cyprus exercises effective control and the Eastern Sovereign Base Area of the United Kingdom of Great Britain and Northern Ireland,

desiring that the accession of Cyprus to the European Union shall benefit all Cypriot citizens and promote civil peace and reconciliation,

considering, therefore, that nothing in this Protocol shall preclude measures with this end in view,

considering that such measures shall not affect the application of the acquis under the conditions set out in the Accession Treaty in any other part of the Republic of Cypurs,

have agreed upon the following provisions:

Article 1

1. The application of the acquis shall be suspended in those areas of the Republic of Cyprus in which the Government of the Republic of Cyprus does not exercise effective control.
2. The Council, acting unanimously on the basis of a proposal from the Commission, shall decide on the withdrawal of the suspension referred to in paragraph 1.

Article 2

1. The Council, acting unanimously on the basis fo a proposal from the Commission, shall define the terms under which the provisions of EU law will apply to the line between those areas referred to in Article 1 and the areas in which the Government of the Republic of Cyprus exercise effective control.
2. The boundary between the Eastern Sovereign Base Area and those areas referred to in Article 1 shall be treated as part of the external borders of the Sovereign Base Areas for the purpose of Part IV of the Annex to the Protocol on the Sovereign Base Area of the United Kingdom of Great Britain and Northern Ireland in Cyprus for the duration of the suspension of the acquis according to Article 1.

Article 3

1. Nothing in this Protocol shall preclude measures with a view to promoting the economic development of the areas referred to in Article 1.

2. Such measures shall not affect the application of the acquis under the conditions set out in the Accession Treaty in any other part of the Republic of Cyprus.

Article 4

In the event of a settlement, the Council, acting unanimously on the basis of a proposal from the Commission, shall decide on the adaptations to the terms concerning the accession of Cyprus to the European Union with regard to the Turkish Cypriot Community."

Appendix 2

The Draft Act of Adaptation[1]

Commission Proposal for an Act of Adaptation on the terms of the United Cyprus Republic to the European Union of 7 April 2004

THE COUNCIL OF THE EUROPEAN UNION

Having regard to Protocol No. 10 of the Act of Accession 2003, and in particular Article 4 thereof,

Having regard to the proposal from the Commission,

(1) Taking into account the approval of the Foundation Agreement by the Greek Cypriots and the Turkish Cypriots on 24 April 2004,
(2) Taking into account the Treaties of Guarantee and Alliance, the Additional Protocol thereto, and the Treaty of Establishment,
(3) Bearing in mind and respecting the demilitarisation of Cyprus,
(4) Considering that the Act of Accession shall not prevent the implementation of the Foundation Agreement, and shall accommodate its terms in line with the principles on which the European Union is founded,
(5) Recalling that the European Union's mission is peaceful cooperation of states and citizens, founded on the principles of liberty, democracy, respect for human rights and fundamental freedoms and the rule of law, principles which are common to the Member States and which have found their expression in

[1] COM (2004) 189 final of 7 April 2004.

the Foundation Agreement which introduces a new state of affairs in Cyprus and allows its peaceful integration into the Union,

(6) Underlining that the political equality of Greek Cypriots and Turkish Cypriots, the equal status of the two constituent states, and the prohibition on any unilateral change to the state of affairs established by the Foundation Agreement, fall within the terms of Article 6(1) of the Treaty of the European Union,

(7) Recognizing the particular national identity of Cyprus, and the need to protect the balance between Greek Cypriots and Turkish Cypriots in Cyprus, the bi-zonal character of the United Cyprus Republic and the distinct identity and integrity of the constituent states, which require certain safeguards and temporary restrictions on the right of residence of Cypriot citizens as well as citizens of Greece and Turkey,

(8) Considering that the main articles of the Foundation Agreement form part of the national identity of the United Cyprus Republic, which the European Union shall respect,

(9) Bearing in mind that the United Cyprus Republic shall take all appropriate measures, whether in general or in particular, to ensure the fulfilment of the obligations arising out of European Union membership, in line with the specifications of the Act of Accession and this Act.

(10) Underlining that accession to the European Union shall benefit Greek Cypriots and Turkish Cypriots alike and promote development to help reduce economic disparities,

(11) Recalling that, in accordance with the Presidency Conclusions of the Brussels European Council of 12 December 2003, the Union is ready to provide financial assistance for the development of the northern part of Cyprus following a settlement,

(12) Being convinced that the economic disparities between the Turkish Cypriot constituent state and European Union Member States as well as between the two constituent states necessitate authorisation procedures for the acquisition of property in the Turkish Cypriot constituent state in order to avoid unacceptable sudden price increases and large scale buy-out of land,

(13) Being further convinced that the economic situation in the Turkish Cypriot constituent state may also necessitate the adoption of special safeguard measures for a limited period of time in order to protect certain sectors of its economy,

(14) Taking into account the special relations and strong ties of Greek Cypriots and Turkish Cypriots with Greece and Turkey respectively,

(15) Bearing in mind that, as a European Union Member State, Cyprus shall fulfil its obligations arising from the Association Agreement between Turkey and the European Communities of 1963, its additional Protocol and the decisions taken by the Association organs including the decision establishing a Customs Union between Turkey and the European Union, thereby according European Union treatment to Turkey in the fields where this is provided for,

(16) Wishing to accord, to the extent possible with the European Union membership of Cyprus, similar rights to Greek and Turkish nationals vis-à-vis Cyprus,
(17) Considering that the Foundation Agreement foresees equivalent entry and resident rights for Greek and Turkish nationals vis-à-vis Cyprus. The implementation of this principle requires derogations from Community law in the case of Cyprus. Unlimited immigration can, however, not be accorded to either Greek or Turkish nationals in the interest of the internal balance of population in Cyprus,
(18) Underlining that all necessary preparations should start immediately so that Turkish shall become and operate as an official and working language of the European Union as soon as possible

HAS ADOPTED THIS ACT OF ADAPTATION OF THE TERMS OF ACCESSION

Article 1
Property

1. Notwithstanding existing provisions of Community law, the application of restrictions, on a non-discriminatory basis, on the right of natural persons who have not been permanent residents for at least three years in the Turkish Cypriot constituent state, and of legal persons, to purchase immovable property in the Turkish Cypriot constituent state without permission of the competent authority of that constituent state, for fifteen years or for as long as the gross domestic product per capita in that constituent state does not reach the level of 85% of the gross domestic product per capita in the Greek Cypriot state, whichever is the earlier, shall not be precluded.
2. The authorisation procedure for the acquisition of immovable property applied by the competent authorities of the Turkish Cypriot constituent state shall be based on published, objective, stable and transparent criteria and shall be applied in a non-discriminatory manner.
3. The Commission shall report every five years to the European Parliament and the Council on the application of the provisions of paragraphs 1–2. The Commission may at that time recommend to the Turkish Cypriot constituent state to abolish in total or in part the restrictions, if it considers that the political, economic and social conditions in Cyprus so allow.

Article 2
Residence of Cypriot citizens

1. Notwithstanding existing provisions of Community law, the application of restrictions, on a non-discriminatory basis, on the right of a Cypriot citizen to reside in a constituent state of which he does not hold the internal constituent state citizenship status shall not be precluded,

   a) in the form of a moratorium, during the first five years following the date of the entry into force of this Act;
   b) if the percentage of such residents of the total population of a municipality or village has reached 6% between the 6th and 9th years and 12% between the 10th and 14th years following the date of entry into force of this Act; and
   c) if the percentage of such residents of the total population of a constituent state has reached 18% for a period of up to nineteen years following the entry into force of this Act or until Turkey joins the European Union, whichever is the earlier.

2. Thereafter, either constituent state may, with a view to protecting its identity, take safeguard measures to ensure that no less than two-thirds of its Cypriot permanent residents speak its official language as their mother tongue.

Article 3
Residence of Greek and Turkish nationals

1. Notwithstanding existing provisions of Community law, the application of restrictions, on a non-discriminatory basis, on:

   a) the right of Greek nationals to reside in Cyprus, if the number of resident Greek nationals has reached 5% of the number of resident Cypriot citizens who hold the internal constituent state citizenship status of the Greek Cypriot constituent State and who are not dual nationals;
   b) the right of Turkish nationals to reside in Cyprus, if the number of resident Turkish nationals has reached 5% of the number of resident Cypriot citizens who hold the internal constituent citizenship status of the Turkish Cypriot constituent State and who are not dual nationals;
   c) shall not be precluded for a transitional period of up to 19 years after the entry into force of this Act or until Turkey joins the European Union, whichever is the earlier.

2. Thereafter, the United Cyprus Republic, in consultation with the Commission, may take safeguard measures to ensure that the demographic ratio between Cyprus's permanent residents speaking either Greek or Turkish as mother tongue is not substantially altered.

Article 4
Safeguard measures

1. Without prejudice to Articles 37 and 38 of the Act of Accession, if until the end of a period of up to six years after the entry into force of this Act, the operation of the European Union's internal market causes, or threatens to cause, difficulties which are serious and likely to persist in any sector of the economy, or which could bring a serious deterioration in the economic situation in the Turkish Cypriot constituent state, the competent Cypriot authorities may take appropriate safeguard measures which shall be applicable for a period of three months. These measures shall be proportional and shall not constitute disguised restrictions on trade and shall take account of the interests of all parties concerned.
2. On request, the Commission may prolong these measures, in total or in part, or adopt different measures of which it shall determine the time of application within the six years period set out in paragraph 1.

Article 5
Equivalent rights of Greek and Turkish nationals

Without prejudice to the restrictions applied under Articles 1–3 and rules applying to entry and residency rights of Turkish nationals in other Member States, Cyprus is authorised to accord to Turkish nationals equivalent treatment with Greek nationals regarding entry and residency rights. Rules of implementation for such entry and residency rights for Turkish citizens, compatible with the above principles and the participation of Cyprus in the Schengen area, shall be negotiated between the European Community and Turkey within six months.

Article 6
The European Security and Defence Policy

The participation of Cyprus in the European Security and Defence Policy shall fully respect the provisions of the Foundation Agreement and the provisions of the Treaties of Guarantee and Alliance and the Additional Protocols thereto, and in no sense undermine those provisions.

Article 7
Representation in the European Parliament

Cyprus will be represented in the European Parliament according to proportional representation, provided that each constituent state is attributed no less than one third of the Cypriot seats in the European Parliament.

Article 8
Turkish as official language of the European Union

1. Turkish shall be an official and working language of the institutions of the European Union.
2. The Council shall decide on the effective application of paragraph 1 upon fulfilment of the necessary personnel and technical requirements. In the period preceding this decision, the Turkish language may be used in European Council and Council meetings.
3. The texts of the acts of the institutions and the European Central Bank, adopted before paragraph 1 takes effect, and drawn by the Council, the Commission or the European Central Bank, in Turkish shall, from that date be authentic under the same conditions as the texts drawn in the other official languages. They shall be published in the Official Journal of the European Union if the texts in the other official languages were so published.

Article
Application

This Act shall be published in the *Official Journal of the European Union* and become applicable the same day.

Done at Brussels, [. . .]

For the Council
The President
[. . .]

Appendix 3

The Green Line Regulation[1]

COUNCIL REGULATION (EC) No 866/2004 of 29 April 2004 on a regime under Article 2 of Protocol 10 to the Act of Accession

THE COUNCIL OF THE EUROPEAN UNION,

Having regard to Protocol 10 on Cyprus to the Act concerning the conditions of accession of the Czech Republic, the Republic of Estonia, the Republic of Cyprus, the Republic of Latvia, the Republic of Lithuania, the Republic of Hungary, the Republic of Malta, the Republic of Poland, the Republic of Slovenia and the Slovak Republic and the adjustments to the Treaties on which the European Union is founded(1), and in particular Article 2 thereof,

Having regard to Protocol 3 on the Sovereign Base Areas of the United Kingdom of Great Britain and Northern Ireland in Cyprus(2) to the said Act of Accession, and in particular Article 6 thereof,

Having regard to the proposal from the Commission,

Whereas:

(1) The European Council has repeatedly underlined its strong preference for accession by a reunited Cyprus. Regrettably, a comprehensive settlement has

---

[1] OJ 2004, L 161, p. 128 with corrigendum at OJ 2004, L 206, p. 51.

not yet been reached. In conformity with paragraph 12 of the conclusions of the European Council in Copenhagen, the Council on 26 April 2004 outlined its position on the current situation on the island.

(2) Pending a settlement, the application of the acquis upon accession has therefore been suspended pursuant to Article 1(1) of Protocol 10, in the areas of the Republic of Cyprus in which the Government of the Republic of Cyprus does not exercise effective control.

(3) Pursuant to Article 2(1) of Protocol 10, this suspension makes it necessary to provide for the terms under which the relevant provisions of EU law shall apply to the line between the abovementioned areas and those areas in which the Government of the Republic of Cyprus exercises effective control. In order to ensure the effectiveness of these rules, their application has to be extended to the boundary between the areas in which the Government of the Republic of Cyprus does not exercise effective control and the Eastern Sovereign Base Area of the United Kingdom of Great Britain and Northern Ireland

(4) Since the abovementioned line does not constitute an external border of the EU, special rules concerning the crossing of goods, services and persons need to be established, the prime responsibility for which belongs to the Republic of Cyprus. As the abovementioned areas are temporarily outside the customs and fiscal territory of the Community and outside the area of freedom, justice and security, the special rules should secure an equivalent standard of protection of the security of the EU with regard to illegal immigration and threats to public order, and of its economic interests as far as the movement of goods is concerned. Until sufficient information is available with regard to the state of animal health in the abovementioned areas, the movement of animals and animal products will be prohibited.

(5) Article 3 of Protocol 10 explicitly states that measures promoting economic development in the abovementioned areas are not precluded by the suspension of the acquis. This regulation is intended to facilitate trade and other links between the abovementioned areas and those areas in which the Government of the Republic of Cyprus exercises effective control, whilst ensuring that appropriate standards of protection are maintained as set out above.

(6) Regarding persons, the policy of the Government of the Republic of Cyprus currently allows the crossing of the line by all citizens of the Republic, EU citizens and third-country nationals who are legally residing in the northern part of Cyprus, and by all EU citizens and third country nationals who entered the island through the Government Controlled Areas.

(7) While taking into account the legitimate concerns of the Government of the Republic of Cyprus, it is necessary to enable EU citizens to exercise their rights of free movement within the EU and set the minimum rules for carrying out checks on persons at the line and to ensure the effective surveillance of it, in order to combat the illegal immigration of third country nationals as well as any threat to public security and public policy. It is also necessary to define the conditions under which third-country nationals are allowed to cross the line.

(8) Regarding checks on persons, this Regulation should not affect the provisions laid down in Protocol 3, and in particular Article 8 thereof.

(9) This Regulation does not affect in any way the mandate of the United Nations in the buffer zone.

(10) Since any change in the policy of the Government of the Republic of Cyprus with regard to the line may pose problems of compatibility with the rules established by this Regulation, such changes should be notified to the Commission, prior to their entry into force, in order to allow it to take the appropriate initiatives so as to avoid inconsistencies.

(11) The Commission should also be allowed to amend Annexes I, and II to this Regulation with a view to responding to changes which may occur and require immediate action,

HAS ADOPTED THIS REGULATION:

TITLE I GENERAL PROVISIONS

Article 1
Definitions

1. For the purpose of this Regulation the following definitions shall apply:

   1. the term «line» means:

      (a) for the purpose of checks on persons, as defined in Article 2, the line between the areas under the effective control of the Government of the Republic of Cyprus and those areas in which the Government of the Republic of Cyprus does not exercise effective control;

      (b) for the purpose of checks on goods, as defined in Article 4, the line between the areas in which the Government of the Republic of Cyprus does not exercise effective control and both those areas in which the Government of the Republic of Cyprus exercises effective control and the Eastern Sovereign Base Area of the United Kingdom of Great Britain and Northern Ireland;

2. the term «third-country national» means any person who is not a citizen of the Union within the meaning of Article 17(1) of the EC Treaty.

References in this Regulation to areas in which the Government of the Republic of Cyprus does not exercise effective control are to areas within the Republic of Cyprus only.

TITLE II CROSSING OF PERSONS

Article 2
Check on Persons

1. The Republic of Cyprus shall carry out checks on all persons crossing the line with the aim to combat illegal immigration of third-country nationals and to detect and prevent any threat to public security and public policy. Such checks shall also be carried out on vehicles and objects in the possession of persons crossing the line.
2. All persons shall undergo at least one such check in order to establish their identity.
3. Third-country nationals shall only be allowed to cross the line provided they:
   (a) possess either a residence permit issued by the Republic of Cyprus or a valid travel document and, if required, a valid visa for the Republic of Cyprus, and
   (b) do not represent a threat to public policy or public security.
4. The line shall be crossed only at crossing points authorised by the competent authorities of the Republic of Cyprus. A list of these crossing points is laid down in Annex I.
5. Checks on persons at the boundary between the Eastern Sovereign Base Area and the areas not under effective control of the Government of the Republic of Cyprus shall be carried out in accordance with Article 5(2) of Protocol 3 to the Act of Accession.

Article 3
Surveillance of the line

Effective surveillance shall be carried out by the Republic of Cyprus all along the line, in such a way as to discourage people from circumventing checks at the crossing points referred to in Article 2(4).

TITLE III CROSSING OF GOODS

Article 4
Treatment of goods arriving from the areas not under the effective control of the Government of the Republic of Cyprus

1. Without prejudice to Article 6, goods may be introduced in the areas under the effective control of the Government of the Republic of Cyprus, on condition

that they are wholly obtained in the areas not under effective control of the Government of the Republic of Cyprus or have undergone their last, substantial, economically justified processing or working in an undertaking equipped for that purpose in the areas not under the effective control of the Government of the Republic of Cyprus within the meaning of Articles 23 and 24 of Council Regulation (EEC) No 2913/92(4).

2. These goods shall not be subject to customs duties or charges having equivalent effect, nor to a customs declaration, provided that they are not eligible for export refunds or intervention measures. In order to ensure effective controls, the quantities crossing the line shall be registered.
3. The goods shall cross the line only at the crossing points listed in Annex I and the crossing points of Pergamos and Strovilia under the authority of the Eastern Sovereign Base Area.
4. The goods shall be subject to the requirements and undergo the checks as required by Community legislation as set out in Annex II.
5. Goods shall be accompanied by a document issued by the Turkish Cypriot Chamber of Commerce, duly authorised for that purpose by the Commission in agreement with the Government of the Republic of Cyprus, or by another body so authorised in agreement with the latter. The Turkish Cypriot Chamber of Commerce or other duly authorised body will maintain records of all such documents issued to enable the Commission to monitor the type and volume of goods crossing the line as well as their compliance with the provisions of this Article.
6. After the goods have crossed the line into the areas under the effective control of the Government of the Republic of Cyprus, the competent authorities of the Republic of Cyprus shall check the authenticity of the document referred to in paragraph 5 and whether it corresponds with the consignment.
7. The Republic of Cyprus shall treat the goods referred to in paragraph 1 as not being imported within the meaning of Article 7(1) of Council Directive 77/388/EEC(5) and Article 5 of Council Directive 92/12/EEC(6), provided the goods are destined for consumption in the Republic of Cyprus.
8. Paragraph 7 shall not have any effect on the European Communities' own resources accruing from VAT.
9. The movement of live animals and animal products across the line shall be prohibited.
10. The authorities of the Eastern Sovereign Base Area may maintain the traditional supply of the Turkish Cypriot population of the village of Pyla with goods coming from the areas which are not under the effective control of the Government of the Republic of Cyprus. They shall strictly supervise the quantities and nature of the goods in view of their destination.
11. Goods complying with the conditions set out in paragraphs 1 to 10 shall have the status of Community goods, within the meaning of Article 4(7) of Regulation (EEC) No 2913/92.
12. This Article shall apply immediately as from 1 May 2004 to goods wholly obtained in the areas not under the effective control of the Government of the Republic of Cyprus and complying with Annex II. In respect of other goods, the full implementation of this Article shall be subject to specific rules that

take full account of the particular situation in the island of Cyprus on the basis of a Commission decision to be adopted as soon as possible and at the latest within two months of the adoption of this Regulation. For such purpose, the Commission shall be assisted by a Committee and Articles 3 and 7 of Council Decision 1999/468/EC(7) shall apply.

Article 5
Goods sent to the areas not under the effective control of the Government of the Republic of Cyprus

1. Goods which are allowed to cross the line shall not be subject to export formalities. However, the necessary equivalent documentation shall be provided, in full respect of Cypriot internal legislation, by the authorities of the Republic of Cyprus upon request.
2. No export refund shall be paid for agricultural and processed agricultural goods when crossing the line.
3. The supply of goods shall not be exempt under Article 15(1) and (2) of Directive 77/388/EEC.
4. The movement of goods, the removal or export of which from the customs territory of the Community is prohibited or subject to authorisation, restrictions, duties or other charges on export by Community law, shall be prohibited.

Article 6
Facilities for persons crossing the line

Council Directive 69/169/EEC shall not apply, but goods contained in the personal luggage of persons crossing the line, including a maximum of 20 cigarettes and 1/4 litre of spirits, shall be exempt from turnover tax and excise duty provided they have no commercial character and their total value does not exceed EUR 30 per person. Exemptions from turnover tax and excise duty on tobacco products and alcoholic beverages shall not be granted to persons crossing the line under 17 years of age.

TITLE IV SERVICES

Article 7
Taxation

To the extent that services are supplied across the line to and from persons established or having their permanent address or usual residence in the areas of the Republic of Cyprus which are not under the effective control of the Government of the Republic of Cyprus, these services shall for VAT purposes be deemed to have been supplied or received by persons established or having their permanent address or usual residence in the areas of the Republic of Cyprus under the effective control of the Government of the Republic of Cyprus.

TITLE V FINAL PROVISIONS

Article 8
Implementation

The authorities of the Republic of Cyprus and the authorities of the Eastern Sovereign Base Area in Cyprus shall take all appropriate measures in order to ensure full compliance with the provisions of this Regulation and to prevent any circumvention of them.

Article 9
Adaptation of Annexes

The Commission may, in agreement with the Government of Cyprus amend the Annexes to this Regulation. Prior to amending the Annexes, the Commission shall consult the Turkish Cypriot Chamber of Commerce or other body duly authorized by the Government of the Republic of Cyprus as referred to in Article 4(5), as well as the United Kingdom if the Sovereign Base Areas are affected. When amending Annex II the Commission shall follow the appropriate procedure referred to in the relevant Community legislation relating to the matter being amended.

Article 10
Change of policy

Any change in the policy of the Government of the Republic of Cyprus on crossings of persons or goods shall only become effective after the proposed changes have been notified to the Commission and the Commission has not objected to these changes within one month. If appropriate, and after consultation with the United Kingdom if the Sovereign Base Areas are affected, the Commission may propose modifications to this Regulation in order to secure compatibility of national and EU rules applicable to the line.

Article 11
Review and monitoring of the Regulation

1. Without prejudice to Article 4(12), the Commission shall report to the Council on an annual basis, starting not later than one year after the date of entry into force of this Regulation, on the implementation of the Regulation and the situation resulting from its application, attaching to this report suitable proposals for amendments if necessary.
2. The Commission shall examine in particular the application of Article 4 of this Regulation and the patterns of trade between the areas under the effective control of the Government of the Republic of Cyprus and the areas not under its effective control, including the volume and value of trade and products traded.
3. Any Member State may request the Council to invite the Commission to examine and report back to it within a specified time frame on any matter of concern arising from the application of this Regulation.
4. In the event of an emergency creating a threat or risk to public or animal and plant health, the appropriate procedures as set out in EU legislation in Annex II shall apply. In the event of other emergencies or where other irregularities or exceptional circumstances arise which require immediate action, the Commission may in consultation with the Government of the Republic of Cyprus apply forthwith such measures as are strictly necessary to remedy the situation. The measures taken shall be referred to the Council within 10 working days. The Council may, acting by qualified majority vote, amend, modify or annul the measures taken by the Commission within 21 working days from the date of receipt of notification from the Commission.
5. Any Member State may invite the Commission to provide details of the volume, value and products crossing the line to the appropriate standing or management committee, provided it gives one month's notice of its request.

Article 12
Entry into force

This Regulation shall enter into force on the day of accession of Cyprus to the European Union.

This Regulation shall be binding in its entirety and directly applicable in all Member States.

Done at Luxembourg, 29 April 2004.

Appendix 4

The financial aid regulation[1]

Council regulation (EC) No. 389/2006 of 27 February 2006 establishing an instrument of financial support for encouraging the economic development of the Turkish Cypriot community and amending Council Regulation (EC) No. 2667/2000 on the European Agency for Reconstruction

THE COUNCIL OF THE EUROPEAN UNION,

Having regard to the Treaty establishing the European Community, and in particular Article 308 thereof,

Having regard to the proposal from the Commission,

Having regard to the Opinion of the European Parliament,

Whereas:

(1) The European Council has repeatedly underlined its strong preference for accession by a reunited Cyprus. As yet, a comprehensive settlement has not been reached.

(2) The Council of 26 April 2004, considering that the Turkish Cypriot community had expressed their clear desire for a future within the European Union, recommended that the funds earmarked for the northern part of Cyprus in the event of a settlement should be used to put an end to the isolation of that community and to facilitate the reunification of Cyprus by encouraging the

[1] OJ 2006, L 65, p. 5.

economic development of the Turkish Cypriot community, with particular emphasis on the economic integration of the island and on improving contact between the two communities and with the EU.

(3) Following the accession of Cyprus, the application of the *acquis* is suspended pursuant to Article 1 (1) of Protocol No 10 of the Act of Accession 2003 in the areas of the Republic of Cyprus in which the Government of the Republic of Cyprus does not exercise effective control (hereinafter referred to as 'the areas').

(4) Pursuant to Article 3 (1) of Protocol No 10, nothing in this Protocol shall preclude measures with a view to promoting the economic development of the Areas.

(5) Measures to be financial under this Regulation are of an exceptional and transitional nature and are intended in particular, to prepare and facilitate, as appropirate, the full application of the *acquis* communantaire in the areas following a solution to the Cyprus problem.

(6) With a view to allocating the financial support in the most efficient and rapid way, it is desirable to provide that assistance can be supplied directly to the beneficiaries.

(7) In order to supply assistance in accordance with the principles of some financial management, the Commission should be in a position to delegate to the European Agency for Reconstruction implementation of assistance under this Regulation. Therefore, Council Regulation (EC) No. 2667/2000 on the European Agency for Reconstruction needs to amended accordingly.

(8) The development and restructuring of infrastructure, in particular in the areas of energy and transport, the environment, telecommunications and water supply should take account of island-wide planning, where appropriate.

(9) In the implementation of actions financed under this Regulation, the rights of natural and legal persons, including the rights to possessions and property, should be respected.

(10) Nothing in this Regulation is intended to imply recognition of any public authority in the areas other than the Government of the Republic of Cyprus.

(11) In accordance with Article 2 of Council Decision 1999/468 laying down the procedures for the exercise of implementing powers conferred on the Commission, measures for the implementation of this Regulation should be adopted by use of the procedure provided in Article 4 of that Decision.

(12) Implementing this Regulation contributes, as set out above, to the achievement of Community objectives, but the Treaty provide, for no powers other than those referred to in Article 308, thereof for the adoption of this Regulation.

HAS ADOPTED THIS REGULATION:

Article 1
Overall Objective and Beneficiaries

1. The Community shall provide assistance to facilitate the reunification of Cyprus by encouraging the economic development of the Turkish Cypriot community with particular emphasis on the economic integration of the island, on improving contacts between the two communities and with the EU, and on preparation for the *acquis communautaire*.
2. Assistance shall benefit *inter alia* local bodies, cooperatives and representatives of the civil society, in particular organisations of the social partners, business support organisations, bodies carrying out functions in the general interest in the areas of local or traditional communities, associations, foundations, non-profit organisations, non-governmental organisations, and natural and legal persons.
3. The granting of such assistance shall not imply recognition of any public authority in the areas other than the Government of the Republic of Cyprus.

Article 2
Objectives

Assistance shall be used to support *inter alia*:
- the promotion of social and economic development including restructuring, in particular concerning rural development, human resources development and regional development,
- the development and restructuring of infrastructure, in particular in the areas of energy and transport, the environment, telecommunications and water supply,
- reconciliation, confidence building measures, and support to civil society,
- bringing the Turkish Cypriot community closer to the Union, through *inter alia* information on the European Union's political and legal order, promotion of people to people contacts and Community scholarships,
- preparation of legal texts aligned with the *acquis communautaire* for the purpose of these being immediately applicable upon the entry into force of a comprehensive settlement of the Cyprus problem,
- preparation for implementation of the *acquis communautaire* in view of the withdrawal of its suspension in accordance with Article 1 of Protocol No 10 to the Act of Accession.

Article 3
Management of Assistance

1. The Commission shall be responsible for administering the assistance.
2. The Commission shall be assisted by the Committee provided for in Article 9 (1) of Council Regulation (EEC) No 3906/89, composed of representatives of the Member States and chaired by a representative of the Commission.

3. The Committee shall give its opinion on draft financing decisions, where they are in excess of EUR 5 million. The Commission may approve, without seeking the opinion of the Committee, financing decisions on supporting activities falling under Article 4 (3) of this Regulation, and amendments to financing decisions complying with the objective of the programme and not exceeding 15% of the financial envelope of such a financing decision.
4. Where, in accordance with paragraph 3, the Committee is not consulted on financing decisions, the Commission shall inform it no later than one week after the decision is taken.
5. For the purposes of this Regulation, the management procedure laid down in Article 3 of Decision 1999/468/EC shall apply, in compliance with Article 7 (3) thereof.

Article 4
Types of Assistance

1. Assistance under this Regulation may, *inter alia*, finance procurement contracts, grants, including interest rate subsidies, special loans, loan guarantees and financial assistance.
2. Assistance may be financed in full by the budget where it is justified and necessary to achieve the objectives of this Regulation.
3. Assistance may also be used to cover in particular the costs for supporting activities such as preliminary and comparative studies, training, activities linked to preparing, appraising, managing, implementing, monitoring, controlling and evaluation of assistance, activities linked to information and visibility purposes as well as costs for supporting staff, renting of premises and supply of equipment.

Article 5
Implementation of Assistance

1. Actions under this Regulation shall be implemented according to the rules set down in Title IV of part 2 of Council Regulation (EC, Euratom) No 1605/2002 of 25 June 2002 on the Financial Regulation applicable to the general budget of the European Communities. All individual legal commitments relating to assistance under this Regulation shall be concluded no later than three years following the date of the budgetary commitment.
2. Without prejudice to any decision taken in accordance with Article 2(5) of Regulation (EC) No 2667/2000, the Commission may, within the limits established in Article 54 of Regulation (EC, Euratom) No 1605/2002, decide to entrust tasks of public authority, and in particular implementation tasks, to the European Agency for Reconstruction or other bodies listed in Article 54(2) of

that Regulation. The selection criteria for the bodies listed in Article 54(2)(c) are the following:

- internationally recognized standing,
- compliance with internationally recognized systems of management and control, and
- supervision by a public authority of a Member State or by an international organisation/institution.

3. Actions under this Regulation may be implemented by shared management according to the rules set down in Title I and II of part 2 of Council Regulation 1605/2002.

Article 6

In Article 2 of Regulation (EC) No 2667/2000 the following paragraph shall be added:

1. The Commission may entrust the Agency with the implementation of assistance for encouraging the economic development of the Turkish Cypriot community within the framework of Council Regulation (EC) No 389/2006 of 27 February 2006 establishing an instrument of financial support for encouraging the economic development of the Turkish Cypriot community and amending Regulation (EC) No 2667/2000 on the European Agency for Reconstruction.*

Article 7

Protection of Rights of Natural and Legal Persons

1. The Commission shall ensure that in the implementation of actions financed under this Regulation the rights of natural or legal persons including the rights to possessions and property shall be respected. In this context, the Commission shall act in accordance with the case law of the European Court of Human Rights.

2. In order to allow the Member States to convey to the Commission any information on possible violations of property rights, the Commission shall submit any draft financing decision which might affect property rights to the Committee referred to in Article 3(2) two months before the financing decision is to be taken.

Article 8
Protection of Community's financial interest

1. The Commission shall ensure that, when actions financed under this Regulation are implemented, the financial interests of the Community are protected against fraud, corruption and any other irregularities in accordance with Council Regulation (Euratom, EC) No 2988/95 of 18 December 1995 on the protection of the European Communities' financial interests[5] and Council Regulation (Euratom, EC) No 2185/96 of 11 November 1996 concerning on-the-spot checks and inspections carried out by the Commission in order to protect the European Communities' financial interests against fraud and other irregularities, and with Regulation (EC) No 1073/1999 of the European Parliament and *of* the Council of 25 May 1999 concerning investigations conducted by the European Anti-Fraud Office (OLAF).[7]
2. For the Community actions financed under this Regulation, the notion of irregularity referred to in Article 1(2) of Regulation (Euratom, EC) No 2988/95 shall mean any infringement of a provision of Community law or any breach of a contractual obligation resulting from an act or omission by an economic operator, which has, or would have, by an unjustified item of expenditure, the effect of prejudicing the general budget of the Communities or budgets managed by them.
3. Any agreements with the beneficiaries shall expressly provide for the Commission and the Court of Auditors to have the power of audit, on the basis of documents and on the spot, over all contractors and subcontractors who have received Community funds. Those agreements shall also expressly authorise the Commission to carry out on-the-spot checks and inspections in accordance with the procedural provisions of Regulation (Euratom, EC) No 2185/96.
4. All contracts resulting from the implementation of assistance shall ensure the rights of the Commission and the Court of Auditors as provided for in paragraph 3, during and after the implementation of contracts.

Article 9
Participation in tenders and contracts

1. Participation in the award of procurement or grant contracts financed under this Regulation shall be open to:

   - all natural or legal persons of Member States of the European Union,
   - all natural or legal persons who are nationals of, or legally established on the territory of another Member State of the European Economic Area,
   - all natural or legal persons who are nationals of, or legally established on the territory of Candidate Countries for Accession to the European Union.

2. Participation in the award of procurement or grant contracts financed under this Regulation shall be open to all natural or legal persons who are nationals of,

or legally established on the territory of, any other country than those referred to in paragraph 1 in cases where reciprocal access to their external assistance has been established.

3. Participation in the award of procurement or grant contracts financed under this Regulation shall be open to international organisations.
4. All supplies and materials purchased under a contract financed under this Regulation must originate from the Community customs territory, the areas, or a country eligible under paragraphs (1) and (2).
5. The Commission may, in duly substantiated cases and on a case-by-case basis, authorise the participation of natural and legal persons from other countries or the use of supplies and materials of different origin.

Article 10
Reporting

Each year the Commission shall send to the European Parliament and the Council a report on the implementation of Community assistance under this instrument. The report shall contain information on the actions financed during the year and on the findings of monitoring work, and shall give an assessment of the results achieved in the implementation of the assistance.

Article 11
Event of a settlement

In the event of a comprehensive settlement of the Cyprus problem, the Council shall, on the basis of a proposal from the Commission, decide unanimously on the necessary adaptations to this Regulation.

Article 12
Event into force

This Regulation shall enter into force on the third day following its publication in the *Official Journal of the European Union.*

This Regulation shall be binding in its entirety and directly applicable in all Member States.

Done at Brussels, 27 February 2006.

For the Council
The President
[. . .]

Appendix 5

Commission proposal for a direct trade regulation

Commission Proposal for a Council regulation on special conditions for trade with those areas of the Republic of Cyprus in which the Government of the Republic of Cyprus does not exercise effective control[1]

THE COUNCIL OF THE EUROPEAN UNION,

Having regard to the Treaty establishing the European Community, and in particular Article 133 thereof,

Having regard to the proposal from the Commission,

Whereas:

(1) The European Council has repeatedly underlined its strong preference for accession by a reunited Cyprus. As yet a comprehensive settlement has not been reached. Having in mind that the Turkish Cypriot community in the referendum on a comprehensive settlement of the Cyprus problem as proposed by the UN Secretary General has expressed its clear desire for a future within the European Union, the Council on 26 April 2004 expressed its determination to put an end to the isolation of the Turkish Cypriot community and to facilitate the reunification of Cyprus by encouraging the eco-

[1] COM (2004) 466 final of 7 July 2004.

nomic development of the Turkish Cypriot community. The Council invited the Commission to bring forward comprehensive proposals to this end.

(2) Pending a settlement, the application of the acquis has been suspended pursuant to Article 1(1) of Protocol No 10 of the Act of Accession 2003 in the areas of the Republic of Cyprus in which the Government of the Republic of Cyprus does not exercise effective control, hereafter referred to as "the Areas".

(3) Pursuant to Article 3(1) of Protocol No 10, measures to promote the development of the Areas are not precluded by the suspension of the acquis. The development of trade with the Areas would contribute to the process of economic development of the above-mentioned Areas. Special rules to facilitate trade between those areas and Member States other than Cyprus may therefore be devised. They should not undermine the standard of safety protection in the EU, in particular the EC rules on health, safety, environmental and consumer protection and on the prohibition on the bringing in of counterfeit and pirated goods, or lead to unacceptable risks to plant health in the Community and should not harm its economic interests.

(4) The Commission should determine annual tariff quotas for products in such a way as to encourage the development of trade, while avoiding the creation of artificial trade patterns or facilitating fraud.

(5) In the interest of safeguarding Community interests, the measures should in particular be accompanied by provisions allowing for their temporary or permanent withdrawal, in whole or in part, in cases where fraud or other irregularities are suspected or established.

(6) Until adequate veterinary and public health standards are achieved, the movement of animals and animal products should be prohibited.

(7) Entitlement to benefit from these measures is conditional on the involvement of the Turkish Cypriot Chamber of Commerce or any other body duly authorized for that purpose by the Commission, in effective cooperation with the Commission and the customs authorities of the Member States in order to prevent any risk of fraud. This authorisation should be subject to prior written commitments by the authorized body and should be revoked if this body fails to fulfil one or more of these commitments in such a way as to endanger the correct application of this Regulation.

(8) The provisions of this Regulation, in particular when terms taken from the acquis are used should be interpreted in the light of the special circumstances prevailing in the Areas.

(9) Certain provisions of Council Regulation (EEC) No 2913/92, Commission Regulation (EEC) No 2454/93 and Commission Regulation (XX) on the implementation of Article 4 of Council Regulation (EC) No 866/2004 ought also to apply in the framework of this Regulation.

(10) These arrangements should be reviewed in light of the experience gained in the implementation of this Regulation.

(11) To the extent that this Regulation does not determine special conditions, the general rules governing the Community's external trade are applicable.

(12) This Regulation is without prejudice to the requirements which have to be fulfilled in order to comply with the international rules on the security and safety of maritime and air transport.
(13) The measures are part of the abovementioned comprehensive proposals in a response to a specific situation in Cyprus. They will not constitute a precedent for the Community's trade policy,

HAS ADOPTED THIS REGULATION

Article 1
Treatment of goods arriving from the Areas

1. Products that, within the meaning of Articles 23 and 24 of Council Regulation (EEC) No 2913/92, originate in the Areas and are transported directly there from, may be released for free circulation into the customs territory of the Community with exemption from customs duties and charges having equivalent effect within the limits of annual tariff quotas fixed in accordance with Article 4, provided that they are accompanied by the document referred to in Article 2(2) and provided that they are not eligible for export refunds or intervention measures. This is without prejudice to indirect taxes due on importation.
2. By derogation from the above, the Commission may, in accordance with the relevant management committee procedure established under the common agriculture policy, determine preferential conditions and modalities of access for products eligible for export refunds or intervention measures.
3. The entry into the Community of live animals and animal products which are subject to Community legislation on veterinary requirements from the Areas shall be prohibited until an adequate veterinary and public health standard can be ensured. The lifting of this prohibition shall require the adoption of Commission decisions pursuant to Article 58 of Regulation (EC) No 178/2002 of the European Parliament and the Council laying down the conditions applicable for trade.
4. For food safety reasons, the entry into the Community of feedingstuff from the Areas shall be prohibited.
5. For food safety reasons, the entry into the Community via the Areas of goods of a type falling under the Commission Decisions listed in Annex IV shall be prohibited. The same shall apply to goods covered by similar decisions adopted in future safeguard measures under Directive 93/43/EC or Regulation 178/2002/EC. For other foodstuffs the testing and checks of food safety requirements as set out in measures adopted under Article 95 of the EC Treaty shall be fully observed.
6. The entry into the Community of goods which are subject to EU trade defence measures, including goods incorporating materials subject to such measures, shall

be prohibited. This is without prejudice to the application of the Community's anti-dumping, anti-subsidy, safeguard or other trade defence instruments.

Article 2
Conditions for special treatment

1. The arrangements referred to in Article 1 shall be conditional on no new or increased duties or charges having equivalent effect, no new quantitative restrictions or measures having equivalent effect, nor any other restrictions, being applied in the Areas on the entry of goods of Community origin from the day of entry into force of this Regulation.
2. The Turkish Cypriot Chamber of Commerce or another body duly authorised for that purpose by the Commission in conformity with Article 5, shall issue an accompanying document certifying that the goods referred to in Article 1(1) originate in the Areas within the meaning of Articles 23 and 24 of Council Regulation (EEC) No 2913/92. The accompanying document shall be made out on forms corresponding to the specimen given in Annex I.
3. Operators who wish to request an accompanying document shall submit a written application to the issuing bodies referred to above. The application form shall be made out on forms corresponding to the specimen given in Annex II.
4. The Turkish Cypriot Chamber of Commerce or another body duly authorized shall communicate to the Commission on a monthly basis the type, volume, and value of goods for which it has issued the documents referred to in Article 2 (2), and details of any irregularities discovered and any sanctions applied.

Article 3
Rules of origin

1. The origin of any product to which this Regulation applies shall be determined in accordance with the provisions in force in the Community concerning the definition of non preferential origin.

Article 4
Tariff Quotas

1. The Commission shall, in accordance with the procedure set out by Article 248 of Council Regulation (EEC) No 2913/92, determine the annual tariff quotas for products referred to in Article 1 (1) in such a way as to encourage the development of trade, while avoiding the creation of artificial trade patterns or facilitating fraud. When defining categories of products and the levels of tariff quotas for such categories, the Commission shall collect and take into account

information from the Turkish Cypriot Chamber of Commerce or other appropriate bodies on the existing production capacities and their potential growth, traditional consumption patterns and any other relevant data.

2. The tariff quotas shall be managed by the Commission in accordance with Articles 308a to 308c of Regulation (EEC) No 2454/93.

Article 5
Authorisation

1. The authorisation referred to in Article 2 (2) shall be in particular subject to the prior written commitment by the Turkish Cypriot Chamber of Commerce or any other duly authorised body to apply correctly, and supervise the correct application by the requesting operators, the Community legislation concerning the definition of non preferential origin according to Articles 23 and 24 of Council Regulation (EEC) No 2913/92 and its implementing provisions, including the commitments, *inter alia*:

   (a) to carry out controls as necessary to ascertain that the specifications given by the requesting operator on the application form as referred to in Article 2 (3) are accurate;
   (b) to issue the accompanying document and to certify unambiguously that the goods to which it relates originate in the areas as defined in Article 1(1) of Protocol No 10 of the Act of Accession 2003 according to Articles 23 and 24 of Council Regulation (EEC) No 2913/92 and its implementing provisions;
   (c) to send to the Commission specimen impressions of the stamps used for the issue of the accompanying document;
   (d) to undertake to keep available for at least three years the application form for the accompanying document and all supporting documents;
   (e) to co-operate with the Commission and the competent authorities of the Member States as to the verification of the authenticity and correctness of the accompanying document as well as to prevent any risk of fraud or other irregularities;
   (f) to carry out on its own initiative or at the request of the Commission or the administration of a Member State, appropriate enquiries when any information appears to indicate that the provisions of this Regulation are being contravened;
   (g) to accept checks, audits or investigations on the spot within the body and facilitate those checks, audits or investigations in the premises of operators having requested the establishment of an accompanying document as to the validity of such document;
   (h) to communicate to the Commission on a monthly basis the type, the volume and the value of goods for which it has issued accompanying documents, and details of any irregularities discovered and any sanctions applied.

2. Where the authorised body fails to fulfil this commitment, and this failing is such as to endanger the correct application of this Regulation, the Commission shall revoke the authorisation.

Article 6
Phytosanitary Inspection and Reporting

1. Where the goods consist of plants, plant products and other objects covered by Part B of Annex V to Council Directive 2000/29/EC, independent phytosanitary experts appointed by the Commission and operating in coordination with the Turkish Cypriot Chamber of Commerce or any other duly authorised body, shall inspect the goods at the stage of production and again at harvest and at the stage of preparation for marketing.
   In the case of potatoes, the above experts shall verify that the potatoes in the consignment were grown directly from seed potatoes certified in one of the Member States or from seed potatoes certified in any other country for which the entry into the Community of potatoes intended for planting is not prohibited pursuant to Annex III to Directive 2000/29/EC.
   In the case of citrus fruits, the above experts shall verify that the fruits have been found to be free from leaves and peduncles and bear the appropriate origin mark.
2. If the above experts, to the best of their knowledge and as far as can be determined, establish that the relevant plants, plant products or other objects in the consignment are considered to be free from the harmful organisms in Annex I and, where applicable, Annex II to Directive 2000/29/EC as amended, and comply with the provisions of the second and third subparagraph of paragraph 1, they shall report their findings, using the model form of "Report of Phytosanitary inspection" under Annex III. The "Report of Phytosanitary inspection" shall be added as a supplement to the accompanying document as referred to in Article 2 (2).
   The experts shall not issue "Reports of Phytosanitary inspection" in respect of plants intended for planting, including tubers of Solanum tuberosum (L.) intended for planting.
3. The experts shall seal or close the packaging of the consignment or the means of transport used for the consignment in such a way that the products concerned cannot cause infestation or infection during their transport and that their identity remains unchanged. No commodities covered by the provisions of this Article shall be moved to the customs territory of the Community unless the said report form is filled in completely and duly signed by at least one of the above mentioned phytosanitary experts.
4. Upon arrival in the customs territory of the Community, the competent authorities shall examine the consignment. Where applicable, the report of Phytosanitary inspection shall be replaced by a plant passport, issued in conformity with the provisions of Commission Directives 92/105/EEC and 93/51/EEC.

5. If the consignment consists of or contains potato lots, an appropriate part of these lots shall be examined in respect of *Ralstonia solanacearum* (Smith) Yabuuchi et al. and *Clavibacter michiganensis* ssp. *sepedonicus* (Spieckermann et Kotthoff) Davis et al., in accordance with the Community established methods for the detection and diagnosis of those harmful organisms.

Article 7
Temporary suspension

1. Without prejudice to the Commission's power to revoke the authorisation referred to in Article 5 (2), the Commission may temporarily suspend the special arrangement provided for in this Regulation, where it has made a finding, on the basis of objective information, allowing the presumption of irregularities or fraud.
2. For the purpose of this Article a finding of irregularities or fraud may be made, *inter alia*, where there is a rapid increase, without satisfactory explanation, in the entry of goods originating in the Areas in the customs territory of the Community exceeding the usual level of production capacity of the Areas that is linked to objective information concerning irregularities or fraud.
3. The application of a temporary suspension shall be subject to the following conditions:

   (a) When the Commission has made a finding, on the basis of objective information, of the irregularities or fraud, it shall without undue delay inform the Customs Code Committee instituted by Article 247 of Council Regulation (EEC) No 2913/92 of its findings together with the objective information.
   (b) Temporary suspensions under this Article shall be limited to that necessary to protect the financial interests of the Community. They shall not exceed a period of six months, which may be renewed as appropriate.

4. The Commission shall publish a notice to economic operators in the *Official Journal of the European Union*. The notice to economic operators should indicate that there is a finding, on the basis of objective information, of the irregularities or fraud.

Article 8
Implementing Rules

The Commission may adopt implementing rules in accordance with the procedure set out in Article 4 (12), last sentence of Council Regulation (EC) No 866/2004; with regard to Article 4, 5 and 7 implementing provisions may be adopted in accordance with the procedures set out in Council Regulation (EEC) 2913/92.

Article 9
Review, Monitoring and Cooperation

1. The Commission shall report to the Council on an annual basis, starting not later than one year after the date of entry into force of this Regulation, on the implementation of the Regulation and the situation resulting from its application, attaching to this report suitable proposals for amendments if necessary.
2. The Commission shall examine in particular the patterns of the trade which will develop under this Regulation, including the volume and value of trade and products traded.
3. The Member States and the Commission shall closely cooperate to ensure compliance with this Regulation.

Article 10
Entry into force

This Regulation shall enter into force on the 10th day following that of its publication in the *Official Journal of the European Union*.

This Regulation shall be binding in its entirety and directly applicable in all Member States.

Done at Brussels, [. . .]

For the Council
The President
[. . .]

(Annexes omitted).

Bibliography

I. Books and Articles

Abi-Saab, Georges/Blumenwitz, Dieter/Crawford, James/Dugard, John/Greenwood, Christopher/ Hafner, Gerhard/Orrego-Vicuna/Pellet, Alain/Schermers, Henry/Tomuschat, Christian, Legal Issues arising from certain population transfers and displacements on the territory of the Republic of Cyprus in the period since 20 July 1974, Opinion of 30 June 1999, http://www.pio.gov.cy/docs/other/opinion_en.htm.

Adamovich, Ludwig K., Österreichisches Staatsrecht, Bd.1, Vienna/New York, 1997.

Akçakoca, Amanda, Cyprus – Looking to a Future Beyond the Past, European Policy Centre, Issue Paper No. 32, Brussels, May 2005.

Akehurst, Michael/Malanczuk, Peter, Modern Introduction into International Law, 7th edition, London, 1997.

Aksoy, Muammar, Zur Zypernfrage, Alte und neue Tatsachen, Frankfurt/M., 1974.

Alain, A. /Ergec, Rustem, Das föderale Belgien nach der Vierten Staatsreform 1993/1994, Brussels, 1994.

Auer, Andreas/Bossuyt, Mark/Burns, Peter/De Zayas, Alfred/Silvio-Marcus, Helmons/Kasimatis, George/Oberdoerfer, Dieter/Shaw, Malcolm, A principled basis for a just and lasting Cyprus settlement in the light of international and European Law, Paper of the International Expert Panel, committed by the Committee for a European solution in Cyprus, presented to members of the European Parliament, 12.10.2005, on file with the author.

Axt, Heinz-Jürgen, Zypern und die Europäische Union: Beitrittsperspektiven nach der Stellungnahme der EG-Kommission, Südosteuropa-Mitteilungen 2/1994, p. 163.

Axt, Heinz-Jürgen, Zypern – ein Beitrittskandidat der Europäischen Union – Implikationen für die Insel die Region und die Union, Südosteuropa 5/1995, p. 259.

Axt, Heinz-Jürgen/Neuwahl, Nanette, Cyprus' EU Accession and EU-Turkey Convergence, in: Yeditepe Üniversitesi Hukuk Fakültesi Dergisi I/1, 2004, p. 219.

*Bermann, George/Blumenwitz, Dieter/Cassesse Antonio/Cot, Jean-Pierre/Crawford, James/Dashwood, Allan Dupuy, Pierre-Marie/Fisler-Damrosch, Lori/Flintermans, Cees/ Franck, Thomas M/Greenwood Christopher/Hafner, Gerhard/Hilf, Meinhard/Lowe, Vaughan/McRae Donald M./Pellet, Alain/Rideau, Joel/Schermers, Henry G./Simma,

Bruno/Tomuschat, Christian/Van Gerven, Walter/Wyatt, Derrick, Opinion of 29 March 2001: Implications of Membership in the European Union for a constitutional settlement in Cyprus, in: Markides (ed.) Cyprus and EU Membership, Important Legal Documents, Nicosia 2002, p. 56.

Berner, Uwe, Das vergessene Volk, Der Weg der Zyperntürken von der Kolonialzeit zur Unabhängigkeit, Pfaffenweiler (Dissertation Freiburg), 1992.

Berramdane, Abedelkhaleq, Chypre entre adhésion à l'Union européenne et réunification, 2003/1, Revue trimestrielle de droit européen, p. 87.

Bertrand, Gilles/Rigoni, Isabelle, Turcs, Kurdes et Chypriotes devant la Cour européenne des droits de l'homme: une contestation judiciaire de questions politiques, in: Revue Etudes internationales 2000, p. 413.

Besler, Ayse Füsun, Die völkerrechtliche Lage Zyperns unter besonderer Berücksichtigung des Selbstbestimmungsrechts, (Dissertation Munich), 1973.

Blumenwitz, Dieter, The legal status of Greek Cypriots and Turkish Cypriots as parties of a future agreement for Cyprus, Opinion of 19 June 1991, in: Ertekün (ed.), The Status of the Two Peoples in Cyprus – Legal Opinions, 2nd edition, Nicosia, 1997, p. 85.

Bolukbasi, Suha, Boutrous-Ghali's Cyprus Initiative in 1992: Why did it fail?, in: Middle Eastern Studies, 1995, p. 460.

Bouony, Lazhar, The status of the Turkish Republic of Northern Cyprus and its adherence to the Organization of the Islamic Conference, Opinion of 6 June 1991, in: Ertekün (ed.), The Status of the Two Peoples in Cyprus – Legal Opinions, 2nd edition, Nicosia, 1997, p. 112.

Brewin, Christopher, The European Union and Cyprus, Huntingdon, 2000.

Brewin, Christopher, The G8 Initiative and the status of northern Cyprus in Europe, Marmara Journal of European Studies 2001, p. 137.

Brownlie, Ian, Principles of International Law, 6th edition, Oxford, 2003.

Çarkoğlu, Ali/ Sözen, Ahmet, Turkish Cypriot General Elections of December 2003: An Appraisal, South European Society & Politics, Vol. 9, Issue 3 (2004), p. 123.

Chrysostomides, Daphne, Les requêtes chypriotes contre la Turquie devant la Commission et la Cour européenne des droits de l'homme et leur importance, Nicosie, 1998.

Chrysostomides, Kypros, The Republic of Cyprus, A Study in International Law, The Hague, 2000.

Chrysostomides, Kypros, Issues under Constitutional and International Law in the Path of Cyprus towards Accession to the EU, Speech at the Conference – Federalizing Europe – Federations within Europe and the path of Cyprus, Nicosia 29–30 June 2001 (Manuscript on file with the author).

Clogg, Richard, Griechenland und die Zypernkrise, Europa-Archiv 1974, p. 633.

Crawford, James, The Creation of States in International Law, Oxford, 1979.

Crawford, James/Hafner, Gerhard/Pellet, Allain, Republic of Cyprus: Eligibility for EU Membership, Opinion of 14.10.1997, in: Markides, A. (ed.), Cyprus and European Union Membership, Important Legal Documents, Nicosia 2002, p. 13.

Crawford, James/Hafner, Gerhard/Pellet, Allain, Further Opinion: The Eligibility of the Republic for EU Membership, Opinion of 17.11.2001, in: Markides, A. (ed.), Cyprus and European Union Membership, Important Legal Documents, Nicosia 2002, p. 36.

Crawshaw, Nancy, Zypern in der Sackgasse, Europaarchiv 1979, p. 82.

Dederer, Hans-Georg, Regress des Bundes gegen ein Land bei Verletzung von EG-Recht, Neue Zeitschrift für Verwaltungsrecht 2001, p. 258.

Diez Thomas, The European Union and the Transformation of Conflictual Constitutional Systems: The Case of Cyprus, in: T. Giegerich (ed.), The EU Accession of Cyprus – Key to the Political and Legal Solution of an "Insoluble" Ethnic Conflict? Baden-Baden 2006, p. 219.

Dodd, Clement, The Cyprus Embroglio, Huntingdon, 1998.

Dodd, Clement, Storm over Cyprus, A briefing, Huntingdon, 2001.

Dodd, Clement, The Annan Plan and the Cyprus Conflict, in: Yeditepe Üniversitesi Hukuk Fakültesi Dergisi I/1, 2004, p. 99.

Doswald-Beck, Louise, The Legal Validity of Military Intervention by Invitation of the Government, British Yearbook of International Law 1985, p. 189.

Drevet, Jean-Francois, Chypre en Europe, Paris, 2000.

Elbe, Viktor, Der Gebietswechsel, insbesondere die Abänderung der Europäischen Gebietsordnung seit dem Wiener Kongress, Zeitschrift für ausländisches öffentliches Recht und Völkerecht 1929, p. 368.

Ehrlich, Thomas, International Crisis and the Role of Law, Cyprus, 1958-1967, London, 1974.

Emerson, Michael/Tocci, Nathalie, Cyprus as Lighthouse of the East Mediterranean, Shaping Re-unification and EU Accession Together, Center for European Policy Studies, Brussels, 2002.

Emiliou, Nicholas, The Prohibition of the Use of Force in International Law and the Cyprus Problem, in: Modern Greek Studies Yearbook. University of Minnesota, Bd. 10/11, Minneapolis, 1994/1995, p. 171.

Emiliou, Nicholas, Cyprus, in: A.Ott/K. Inglis (ed.), Handbook on European Enlargement, The Hague 2002, p. 239.

Ertekün, Necati Münir, Inter-Communal Talks and the Cyprus Problem, Nicosia, 1977.

Ertekün, Necati Münir, In Search for a negotiated settlement, Nicosia, 1981.

Ertekün, Necati Münir (ed.), The status of the two peoples in Cyprus – Legal Opinions, 2nd edition, Nicosia, 1997.

Evriviades, Marios L., The Legal Dimension of the Cyprus Conflict, in: Texas International Law Journal, Band 10, No. 2 (spring 1975), p. 227.

Filos, Altana, Die Entwicklung der Zypern-Frage unter besonderer Berücksichtigung der geplanten EU-Mitgliedschaft der Republik Zypern, Zeitschrift für ausländisches öffentliches Recht und Völkerrecht 1999, p. 185.

Franck, Thomas, Postmodern Tribalism and the Right to Secession, in: Brölmann/Lefeber/Zieck (eds.), Peoples and Minorities in International Law, Boston, 1993, p. 3.

Ganshof van der Meersch, W.J./Ergec, R., Les relations extérieures des états à système constitutionnel régional ou fédéral, Revue de droit international et droit comparé 1986, p. 297.

Grabitz, Eberhard, Die Rechtsetzungsbefugnis von Bund und Ländern bei der Durchführung von Gemeinschaftsrecht, Archiv des öffentlichen Rechts 1986, p. 1.

Grant, Thomas D., Internationally guaranteed constitutive order: Cyprus and Bosnia as predicates for a new non-traditional actor in the society of states, Journal of Transnational Law & Policy, Vol. 8:1, 1998, p. 1.

Giegerich, Thomas, The EU Accession of Cyprus and the Fate of the Annan Plan, in: T. Giegerich (ed.), The EU Accession of Cyprus – Key to the Political and Legal Solution of an "Insoluble" Ethnic Conflict? Baden-Baden 2006, p. 253.

Griller, Stephan, The consequences of EU Membership for the organizational structure of EU Member States, A Survey with Special Regard to the Application of the Republic of Cyprus for EU Membership, Manuscript, Vienna 2002 (on file with the author).

Gürbey, Gülistan, Zypern – Konflikt ohne Ende?, Südosteuropa 1997, p. 618.

Gürbey, Gülistan, Zypern: Hoffnung auf eine baldige Konfliktlösung, in: Südosteuropa-Mitteilungen 1997, p. 301.

Hailbronner, Kay, Völker- und europarechtliche Fragen der deutschen Wiedervereinigung, Juristenzeitung 1990, p. 149.

Hale, William M./Norton, J.D., Die Türkei und die Zypern-Krise, EA 1974, p. 639.
Hannay, David, Cyprus, The Search for a Solution, London, 2005.
Harris, David/O'Boyle, Michael/Warbrick, Chris, Law of the European Convention on Human Rights, London, 1995.
Heinze, Christian, The position of the Greek and Turkish Communities under the Cyprus Constitution of 1960, in: ders. (ed.), Cyprus 2000, Nicosia, 2001, p. 22.
Heinze, Christian, The present stage of the Cyprus conflicts with special reference to the principle of self-determination, in: ders. (ed.) Cyprus 2000, Nicosia, 2001, p. 30 (reprint from the Zeitschrift für Politik 1991, p. 406).
Heinze, Christian, On the question of compatibility of the admission of Cyprus into the European Union with international law, the law of the EU and the Cyprus Treaties of 1959/60, in: Necati Münir Ertekün (ed.), The Status of the Two Peoples in Cyprus, 2nd edition, Nicosia, 1997, p. 181.
Hoffmeister, Frank, Changing Requirements for Membership, in: Ott, A./Inglis, K. (ed.) Handbook on European Enlargement, The Hague, 2002, p. 90.
Hoffmeister, Frank, Case note on ECtHR, Cyprus v. Turkey, American Journal of International Law 2002, p. 445.
Hoffmeister, Frank, Case note on ECtHR, Podkolzina vs. Latvia, American Journal of International Law 2003, p. 664.
Hottinger, Arnold, Das ungelöste Zypern-Problem, Europaarchiv 1986, p. 51.
Jakobsson Hatay, Ann-Sofi, The Contribution of European Integration to ethnic conflict resolution: the cases of northern Ireland and Cyprus, in: The Cyprus Review, Volume 13, No. 1 (2001), p. 31.
Joseph, Joseph S., Cyprus, Ethnic conflict and International Politics, From Independence to the Threshold of the European Union, 2nd edition, London, 1997.
Kabaalioğlu, Lessons to be Learnt from the Greek Cypriot Rejection of the Annan Plan, in: T. Giegerich (ed.), The EU Accession of Cyprus – Key to the Political and Legal Solution of an "Insoluble" Ethnic Conflict? Baden-Baden 2006, p. 233.
Karaosmanoglu, Ali L., UNFICYP and the problem of consent, in: R. Arim (ed.), Cyprus and International Law, Ankara, 2002, p. 104.
Kazancigil, Ali, Die Türkei und die Entwicklung im östlichen Mittelmeer, Europaarchiv 1973, p. 413.
Kohlhase, Norbert, Der griechisch-türkische Konflikt in der Sicht der Europäischen Gemeinschaft, Europa-Archiv 1981, p. 161.
Kokott, Juliane/Rudolf, Beate, Case Report: Loizidou v. Turkey (Admissibility), American Journal of International Law 1996, p. 98.
Kramer, Heinz, Der türkische Beitrittsantrag und der "griechische Faktor", Europaarchiv 1987, p. 605.
Kramer, Heinz, Endspiel auf Zpyern – Neue Verhandlungen: die letzte Chance zur Einigung vor dem EU-Beitritt der Insel, Stiftung Wissenschaft und Politik, SWP-Aktuell, Berlin, 2002.
Kramer, Heinz, Verlängerung auf Zypern, Stiftung Wissenschaft und Politik, Berlin, 2002.
Kramer, Heinz, Zypern, Ende der Hoffnung, Stiftung Wissenschaft und Politik, Berlin, 2003.
Kramer, Heinz, Türkei-Verhandlungen als Spielball der Interessen, Stiftung Wissenschaft und Politik, Berlin 2005.
Kranidiotis, Jannos N., Relations between Cyprus and the European Community, in: Modern Greek Studies Yearbook, University of Minnesota, Vol. 8, Minneapolis, 1992, p. 165.
Laffert, Gerd van, Die völkerrechtliche Lage des geteilten Zypern und die Fragen seiner staatlichen Reorganisation, Frankfurt/M., 1995.

Lauterpacht, Elihu, The Right of Self-determination of the Turkish Cypriots, Opinion of 9 March 1990, in: Ertekün (ed.), The Status of the Two Peoples in Cyprus – Legal Opinions, 2nd edition, Nicosia, 1997, p. 9.

Lauterpacht, Elihu, The Turkish Republic of Northern Cyprus – The Status of the Two Communities in Cyprus, Opinion of 10 July 1990, in: Ertekün (ed.), The Status of the Two Peoples in Cyprus – Legal Opinions, 2nd edition, Nicosia, 1997, p. 15.

Lauterpacht, Elihu/Leigh, Monroe, On sovereignty and its relationship to proposals for a solution of the Cyprus problem along federal lines, Opinion of 31 May 1991, in Ertekün (ed.), The Status of the Two Peoples in Cyprus – Legal Opinions, 2nd edition, Nicosia, 1997, p. 69.

Leigh, Monroe, The legal status in international law of the Turkish Cypriot and the Greek Cypriot communities in Cyprus of 20 July 1990, in: Ertekün (ed.), The Status of the Two Peoples in Cyprus – Legal Opinions, 2nd edition, Nicosia, 1997, p. 54.

Lycourgos, Constantinos, L'Association de Chypre à la CEE, Travaux et recherches de l'université de droit, d'économie et de sciences sociales de Paris, Paris, 1989.

MacDonald, R. St., International Law and the Conflict in Cyprus, The Canadian Yearbook of International Law 1981, p. 1.

Markides, Alecos (ed.), Cyprus and European Union membership, Important Legal Documents, Nicosia, 2002.

Markides, Alecos, The Constitutional Impact of Cyprus` Accession to the EU, Speech delivered 21 May 2001 in Nicosia, (Manuscript on file with the author).

Maurer, Leopold, Negotiations in Progress, in: Ott. A/Inglis K. (ed.), Handbook on European Enlargement, The Hague 2002, p. 113.

Meinardus, Reinhard, Eine neue Phase im Zypern-Konflikt, Europaarchiv 1984, p. 297.

Melakopides, Costas, EU enlargement in the Mediterranean: Human Rights and the resolution of the Cyprus Turkey legal and political conundrum, Cyprus Journal of European Studies, 2001, p. 1.

Mendelson, Maurice H., The application of the "Republic of Cyrus" to join the European Union, Opinion of 6 June 1997, reprinted Ertekün (ed.), The Status of the Two Peoples in Cyprus – Legal Opinions, 2nd edition, Nicosia, 1997, p. 137.

Mendelson, Maurice H., Further Opinion on the Application of the "Republic of Cyprus" to join the European Union of 12 September 2001, UN Doc A/56/451/, S/2001/953.

Murswieck, Dietrich, The Issue of a Right of Secession – Reconsidered", in: C. Tomuschat, (ed.) Modern Law of Self-Determination, Dordrecht et alt., 1993, p. 21.

Nanopoulos, David Kimon, L'adhésion de la République de Chypre et de la Turquie à l'Union européenne et les perspectives de résolution du conflit, Note de recherches présentée pour l'obtention du DEA du Droit International Public, Université Robert Schuman, Strasbourg, 2001.

Necatigil, Zaim, M., The Cyprus question and the Turkish Position in International Law, Revised 2nd edition, Oxford, 1996.

Necatigil, Zaim, United Nations resolutions on Cyprus, in: Resat Arim (ed.) Cyprus and international law, Ankara, 2002, p. 60.

Neuwahl, Nanette, Cyprus – Which Way? – In Pursuit of a Confederal Solution in Europe, Harvard Jean Monnet Working Paper 4/00, Harvard Law School, 2000; http://www.jeanmonnetprogram.org/papers/00/000401.html.

Nicolaides, Andros A., Zypern auf dem Weg zum EU-Beitritt, in: European Commission (ed.), Europäische Gespräche 3/96 – Die Mittelmeerpolitik der Europäischen Union, Bonn, 1996, p. 99.

Oeter, Stefan, Federal Settlements of Ethnic Conflicts as Potential Models for a Resolution of the Cyprus Conflict – Comparative Survey (Belgium, Switzerland, Canada), in: T. Giegerich (ed.), The EU Accession of Cyprus – Key to the Political and Legal Solution of an "Insoluble" Ethnic Conflict? Baden-Baden 2006, p. 69.

Ott, Andrea, The Principle of Differentiation in an Enlarged European Union: Unity in Diversity?, in: K. Inglis/A. Ott (ed.), The Constitution for Europe and an Enlarging Union: Unity in Diversity?, Groningen 2005, p. 103.

Özersay, Kudret, The validity and scope of the 1959-1960 Cyprus Treaties, in: Resat Arim (ed.) Cyprus and international law, Ankara, 2002, p. 11.

Özersay, Kudret, Separate Simultaneous Referenda in Cyprus: Was it a "Fact" or an "Illusion", Turkish Studies 2005, p. 379.

Özgur, Özdemir A., Cyprus in My Life – Testimony of a Turkish Cypriot Diplomat, Mannheim and Möhnsee, 2001.

Olgun, Ergün, European Union for "Cyprus" – Pros and Cons, in: UN Association of Northern Cyprus (ed), Cyprus and the European Union: The Turkish view and some selected articles, Nicosia, May 1996, p. 25.

Olgun, Ergün, Confederation: The Last Chance for establishing a New Partnership in Cyprus, Perceptions – Journal of international Affairs, March–May 2001, p. 1.

Olgun, Ergün, Cyprus: Settlement and Membership, Speech delivered on 3 June 2002 at the conference of the Europe-Turkey Foundation and the Turkish Economic and Social Studies Foundation, at the venue of the European Parliament, Brussels, Manuscript on file with the author, pp. 1–18.

Olgun, Ergün/Karabacak, Sülen, Cyprus: An opportunity or threat, Contribution of 15 October 2001 for the Round Table Quarterly, London, (Manuscript on file with the author).

Pabst, Martin, Zypern: UN, EU und status quo, Vereinte Nationen 2001, p. 139.

Pahl, Marc-Oliver, Regionen mit Gesetzgebungskompetenzen in der Europäischen Union, Eine rechtsvergleichende Analyse ihrer Mitwirkung an der EU-Rechtsetzung, Baden-Baden 2004.

Papadakis, Yiannis, Echoes from the Dead Zone – Across the Cyprus divide, London 2005.

Pazarci, Hüseyin, Solutions juridiques pou un Chypre viable basées sur le nouveau partenariat, in: Resat Arim (ed.) Cyprus and international law, Ankara, 2002, p. 134.

Pearce, Anthony, Is a settlement in Cyprus still possible? Yeditepe Üniversitesi Hukuk Fakültesi Dergisi I/1, 2004, p. 149.

Pernthaler, Peter, Some critical aspects regarding the UN Secretary-General's proposal for a comprehensive settlement of the Cyprus problem, Yeditepe Üniversitesi Hukuk Fakültesi Dergisi I/1, 2004, p. 119.

Pfirter, Didier, Genesis and Key Elements of the Draft Constitution in the Comprehensive Settlement Plan of the UN-Secretary-General for Cyprus (Annan Plan), in: T. Giegerich (ed.), The EU Accession of Cyprus – Key to the Political and Legal Solution of an "Insoluble" Ethnic Conflict? Baden-Baden 2006, p. 161,

Press and Information Office of the Republic of Cyprus, The Cyprus Problem, 2nd edition, Nicosia, 1999.

Press and Information Office of the Republic of Cyprus, Resolutions by the United Nations on the Cyprus Problem 1964–1999, Nicosia, 1999.

Reddaway, John, Burdened with Cyprus – the British Connection, 3rd edition, London, 2001.

Reuter, Jürgen/Varvaroussis, Paris, Der Beitritt Zyperns zur Europäischen Union, Risiko für neue Instabilität der EU, Südosteuropa-Mitteilungen 2002, p. 65.

Reuter, Jürgen, Zähes Ringen um Zyperns Zukunft, Die politische Meinung 2/2001, p. 71.

Reuter, Jürgen, Zypern, Vereinte Nationen und Europäische Union, Konrad-Adenauer-Stiftung/Auslandsinformationen 9/2001, p. 21.

Reuter, Jürgen, Schwierige Gespräche auf Zypern, Die politische Meinung 3/2002, p. 29.

Rousseau, Ch., Grèce, Royaume Uni et Turquie, Conclusion des accords des 11 et 19 février 1959 relatifs au statut du Chypre, Revue Générale de Droit International Public 63 (1959), p. 522.

Rousseau, Ch., Chypre, Conclusion du traité d'établissement du 6 juillet 1960 relatif au statut des bases britanniques et proclamation de l'indépendence de l'île (16 août 1960); RGDIP 64 (1960), p. 792.

Rudolf, Beate, Case Report: Loizidou v. Turkey (Merits), American Journal of International Law 1997, p. 532.

Rühl, Lothar, Der Zypernkonflikt von 1974 und der griechisch-türkische Interessenkonflikt, Europaarchiv 1975, p. 699.

Rühl, Lothar, Der Zypernkonflikt, die Weltmächte und die europäische Sicherheit, Europaarchiv 1976, p. 19.

Rumpf, Christian, Die Staats- und völkerrechtliche Lage Zyperns, Europäische Grundrechtezeitschrift 1997, p. 533.

Rumpf, Christian, Comments on the Legal Status of Cyprus: Issues of Conflict and their Causes, in: T. Giegerich (ed.), The EU Accession of Cyprus – Key to the Political and Legal Solution of an "Insoluble" Ethnic Conflict? Baden-Baden 2006, p. 37.

Savvides, Phillipos K., Cyprus at the Gate of the European Union – Scenarios, Challenges and Prospects, Hellenic Foundation for European and Foreign Policy, Policy Paper No. 1, Athens, June 2002.

Sepos, Angelos, EU Policy-Making in Federal States: The Case of Belgium, Faculty of History-Centre of International Studies, Cambridge, July 2000.

Shaw, Malcolm N., International Law, 5th edition, Cambridge 2003.

Skoutaris, Nikolaos, Differentiation in European Union citizenship law - the Cyprus problem, in: K. Inglis/A. Ott (ed.), The Constitution for Europe and an Enlarging Union: Unity in Diversity?, Groningen 2005, p. 160.

Sommer, Jerry, Security in Cyprus – Threat perceptions, possible compromises and the role of the EU, Bonn International Centre for Conversion, Bonn 2005.

Soysal, Mumtaz, Inequality of status: impediment to a solution in Cyprus, in: R. Arim (ed.), Cyprus and International Law, Ankara 2002, p. 121.

Sözen, Ahmet, A Model of Power Sharing in Cyprus: From the 1959 London-Zurich Agreements to the Annan Plan, Turkish Studies, Vol.5: 61–77, Issue 1 (2004), p. 61.

Sözen, Ahmet, Turkish Cypriot Early General Elections of February 2005: The Rise of CTP/BG" South European Society & Politics, Vol. 10, Issue 3 (2005), Manuscript on file with the author, pp. 1–11.

Sözen, Ahmet/Özersay, Kudret, The Annan plan: State succession or Continuity, Middle Eastern Studies (forthcoming), Manuscript on file with the author, pp. 1-26.

Suvarierol, Semin, La question de l'adhésion de Chypre à l'Union Européenne et Problème de la République Turque de Chypre-Nord, www.ceri-sciences-po.org, Septembre 2001.

Steinbach, Udo, Das Zypernproblem, in: Südosteuropa-Mitteilungen 2/1975, p. 1.

Talmon, Stephan, The Cyprus Question before the European Court of Justice, European Journal of International Law 2001, p. 727.

Tatli, Suzan, Der Zypernkonflikt, Pfaffenweiler 1986.

Theophanous, Andreas, The Political Economy of a federal Cyprus, Nicosia, 1996.

Tomuschat, Christian, EWG und DDR, Völkerrechtliche Überlegungen zum Sonderstatus des Außenseiters einer Wirtschaftsunion, Europarecht 1969, p. 298.

Tomuschat, Christian, Das Recht auf die Heimat, Festschrift für Karl-Josef Partsch, J. Jekewitz (ed.), Berlin, Duncker & Humblot, 1989, p. 183.

Tomuschat, Christian, The Accession of Cyprus to the European Union, in: P. Häberle/ M. Morlok, V. Skouris (ed.), Festschrift für Dimitris Th. Tsatsos, Baden-Baden 2003, p. 672.

Tsoutsos, A.G., La Question internationale de Chypre, in Revue Générale due Droit International Public 1955, p. 423.

Tzermias, Pavlos, Der neue Status Cyperns, Archiv des öffentlichen Rechts 1959, p. 459.

Tzermias, Pavlos, Die Entstehung der Republik Zypern, Jahrbuch des öffentlichen Rechts 1960, p. 245.

Tzermias, Pavlos, Die Verfassung der Republik Zypern, Jahrbuch des öffentlichen Rechts 1961, p. 485.

Tzermias, Pavlos, Geschichte der Republik Zypern, 3rd edition, Tübingen, 1998.

Tzermias, Pavlos, Die Zypernfrage – Geschichte und Perspektiven, in: Südosteuropa, 11/1997, p. 610.

Varvaroussis, Paris, Deutschland und die Zypernfrage, Eine Dokumentation, 1954–1994, München, 1995.

Verdross, Alfred/Simma, Bruno, Universelles Völkerrecht, 3rd edition, München 1984.

Uebe, Max, Cyprus in the European Union, German Yearbook of International Law, 2003, p. 375.

United Nations Association of Northern Cyprus (ed.), Cyprus and the European Union: the Turkish Cypriot view and some selected Articles, Nicosia, May 1996.

Woodhouse, Christopher Montageu, Das Zypernproblem und die Abkommen von 1959, in: Europa-Archiv 1960/3, p. 63.

Wouters, Pas, Der belgische Föderalismus: Die Verfassungen von Flandern und Wallonien, in: Diesener, G./Rochtus, D. (ed.), Verfassungsgebungsprozesse im Vergleich, Leipzig 2002, p. 12.

Yesilada, Birol A./Sozen, Ahmet, Negotiating a Resolution to the Cyprus Problem: Is Potential European Union Membership a Blessing or a Curse?, in: 7 International Negotiations (2002), p. 261.

Zepter, Bernhard, Beitrittsperspektiven Maltas und Zyperns, in: European Commission (ed.), Europäische Gespräche 3/96 – Die Mittelmeerpolitik der Europäischen Union, Bonn 1996, p. 88.

Zervakis, Peter A., Die europäische Perspektive für das geteilte Zypern: Eine neue Chance zur Lösung des Zypern-Problems?, Zeitschrift für Politikwissenschaft, 2/04, p. 451.

II. UN Documents

A. *UN Security Council Resolutions*

Resolution 186 of 4 March 1964
Resolution 187 of 13 March 1964
Resolution 193 of 8 August 1964
Resolution 244 of 22 December 1967
Resolution 247 of 18 March 1968
Resolution 353 of 20 July 1974
Resolution 354 of 23 July 1974
Resolution 357 of 14 August 1974
Resolution 358 of 15 August 1974
Resolution 359 of 15 August 1974
Resolution 360 of 16 August 1974
Resolution 361 of 30 August 1974
Resolution 364 of 13 December 1974

Resolution 367 of 12 March 1975
Resolution 370 of 13 June 1975
Resolution 440 of 27 November 1978
Resolution 541 of 18 November 1983
Resolution 550 of 11 May 1984
Resolution 649 of 12 March 1990
Resolution 716 of 11 October 1991
Resolution 750 of 10 April 1992
Resolution 774 of 26 August 1992
Resolution 789 of 25 November 1992
Resolution 939 of 29 July 1994
Resolution 971 of 12 January 1995
Resolution 1009 of 10 August 1995
Resolution 1062 of 28 June 1996
Resolution 1092 of 23 December 1996
Resolution 1117 of 26 June 1997
Resolution 1239 of 14 May 1999
Resolution 1250 of 29 June 1999
Resolution 1251 of 29 June 1999
Resolution 1475 of 14 April 2003

B. ***UN Secretary-General Reports***

Report of 29 April 1964, S/5671
Report of 10 June 1966, S/7350
Report of 29 July 1965, S/6569
Report of 12 December 1984, S/16585
Report of 8 March 1990, S/21183
Report of 8 October 1991, S/23121
Report of 19 December 1991, S/23300
Report of 3 April 1992, S/23780
Report of 21 August 1992, S/2447
Report of 11 November 1992, S/24830
Report of 1 April 2003, S/2003/398
Report of 16 April 2004, S/2004/302
Report of 28 May 2004, S/2004/437

Table of Abbreviations

AA	Act of Accession
Annan I	Comprehensive Settlement of the Cyprus Problem, presented by UN Secretary-General Annan, on 11 November 2002
Annan II	Revised Comprehensive Settlement of the Cyprus Problem, presented by UN Secretary-General Annan, on 10 December 2002
Annan III	Revised Comprehensive Settlement of the Cyprus Problem, presented by UN Secretary-General Annan, on 26 February 2003
Annan IV	Revised Comprehensive Settlement of the Cyprus Problem, presented by UN Secretary-General Annan, on 30 March 2004
Annan V	Revised Comprehensive Settlement of the Cyprus Problem, presented by UN Secretary-General Annan, on 31 March 2004
B-VG	Bundes-Verfassungsgesetz
CC	Cyprus Constitution (under Annan I–II)
CFSP	Common Foreign and Security Policy
COREPER	Committee of Permanent Representatives of the EU Member States
DDA	Draft Act of Adaptation
DG	Directorate-General
EC	European Community; or Treaty establishing the European Community
ECHR	European Convention on Human Rights
ECJ	European Court of Justice
ECtHR	European Court of Human Rights
EOKA	Ethniki Organosis Kyprion Agoniston
ESDP	European Security and Defense Policy
EU	European Union; or Treaty establishing the European Union
FA	Foundation Agreement
GG	Grundgesetz
MP	Member of Parliament
MEP	Member of European Parliament
NATO	North Atlantic Treaty Organization
OAU	Organization of African Union
SBA	Sovereign Base Area

TMT	Türk Mukavemet Teşkilati
TRNC	Turkish Republic of Northern Cyprus
UCR	United Cyprus Republic (under Annan III–V)
UK	United Kingdom
UN	United Nations
UNDP	United Nations Development Programme
UNFICYP	United Nations Force in Cyprus
UNHCR	United Nations High Commissioner for Refugees
UNGA	United Nations General Assembly
UNSC	United Nations Security Council
UNSG	United Nations Secretary-General
Vienna Convention	Vienna Convention on the Law of Treaties (1969)

Index

Nijhoff Law Specials

50. K. Wellens (ed.): *Resolutions and Statements of the United Nations Security Council (1946-2000). A Thematic Guide.* 2001 ISBN 90 411 1722 9
51. P. Soar (ed.): *The New International Directory of Legal Aid.* 2001 ISBN 90 411 1718 0
52. C.M. Mazzoni (ed.): *Ethics and Law in Biological Research.* 2002 ISBN 90 411 1742 3
53. I. Omar: *Emergency Powers and the Courts in India and Pakistan.* 2002 ISBN 90 411 1775 X
54. M. O'Flaherty: *Human Rights and the UN: Practice Before the Treaty Bodies.* 2002 ISBN 90 411 1788 1
55. Y. Beigbeder: *Judging Criminal Leaders. The Slow Erosion of Impunity.* 2002 ISBN 90 411 1815 2
56. Marianne van Leeuwen (ed.): *Confronting Terrorism: European Experiences, Threat Perceptions, and Policies.* 2003 ISBN 90 411 1960 4
57. Ralf Bredel: *Long-term Con.ict Prevention and Industrial Development: The United Nations and its Specialized Agency, UNIDO.* 2003 ISBN 90 04 13619 3
58. Raphael Walden: *Racism and Human Rights.* 2004 ISBN 90 04 13651 7
59. Monique Leyenaar: *Political Empowerment of Women: The Netherlands and Other Countries.* 2004 ISBN 90 04 14099 9
60. Sjureur Skaale (ed.): *The Right to National Self-Determination: The Faroe Islands and Greenland.* 2004 ISBN 90 04 14207 X
61. Edward McWhinney: *The September 11 Terrorist Attacks and the Invasion of Iraq in Contemporary International Law: Opinions on the Emerging New World Order System.* 2004 ISBN 90 04 14143 X
62. B.G. Ramcharan: *The Protection Role of National Human Rights Institutions.* 2005. ISBN 90 04 14526 5
63. Chris de Cooker: *Accountability, Investigation and Due Process in International Organizations.* 2005. ISBN 90 04 14793 4
64. Peris S. Jones & Kristian Stokke: *Democratising Development: The Politics of Socio-Economic Rights in South Africa.* 2005. ISBN 90 04 14821 3
65. Roy S. Lee (ed.): *Swords Into Plowshares: Building Peace Through the United Nations.* 2005. ISBN 90 04 15001 3
66. J.A. Bovenberg: *Property Rights in Blood, Genes & Data: Naturally Yours?* 2006 ISBN 90 04 15053 6
67. Frank Hoffmeister: *Legal Aspects of the Cyprus Problem. Annan Plan and EU Accession.* ISBN 90 04 15223 7

For more titles in this series, consult our web site: http://www.brill.nl

MARTINUS NIJHOFF PUBLISHERS – LEIDEN – BOSTON